Identity and Struggle

at the Margins of the Nation-State

A book in the series

Comparative and International Working-Class History

General Editors

Andrew Gordon, Harvard University

Daniel James, Duke University

Alexander Keyssar, Duke University

IDENTITY *and* STRUGGLE *at the* MARGINS *of the* NATION-STATE

The Laboring Peoples of Central America and the Hispanic Caribbean

Aviva Chomsky & Aldo Lauria-Santiago, editors

Duke University Press Durham & London 1998

Contents

Acknowledgments

The editors would like to thank the American Historical Association, the Conference on Latin American History, the New England Historical Association, and the Latin American Studies Association for providing the opportunity and context for meeting and discussing, both formally and informally, the works that appear here. Our appreciation goes also to the *Hispanic American Historical Review* for permission to reprint Jeffrey Gould's essay in this volume. A version of it also appears in his Duke University Press book *To Die in This Way* (1998). We would also like to thank Bates College, College of the Holy Cross (Mass.), Salem State College (Mass.), and the New School for Social Research for funding to attend conferences and for technical support for every aspect of this project.

For ingenious creativity and endless patience in tracking down references, we wish to express thanks to Bates reference librarian Laura Juraska. And for those last few references that could not be found in any way except by somebody physically present in Harvard's Widener Library, we thank Mara Thomas. Our appreciation goes also to Pat Chalifoux for secretarial assistance at Holy Cross and to Sylvia Hawks at Bates.

We also would like to give special thanks to the authors and to the editors at Duke for helping us follow through and complete this project.

We dedicate this book to the peoples of Central America and the Caribbean, whose struggles are only beginning to bear fruit.

ALDO LAURIA-SANTIAGO AND AVIVA CHOMSKY

Introduction

Identity and Struggle in the History of the Hispanic Caribbean and Central America, 1850–1950

This volume brings together new research on the social history of Central America and the Spanish-speaking Caribbean in the crucial period of the late nineteenth and early twentieth centuries—a period that saw the consolidation of export economies and national states, both of which, in most cases, have left enduring legacies for our times. Traditional histories of this period have been written from the top down, and, from the international perspective, from the outside in. The contributions to this volume take the opposite approach. Drawing on recent trends in social and cultural history, the authors see the popular classes as important actors in their national histories and seek to uncover aspects of these histories that have heretofore remained submerged and silent.

The contributors to this volume define "laboring peoples" very broadly and integrate their histories into national and international contexts. Laboring peoples in Central America and the Caribbean were usually more rural than urban, and few fit the pattern of a classic proletariat. Out of this ethnically and socially diverse population of former slaves, peasants with varying relations to the land, and seasonal and permanent migrants, elites attempted to recruit or coerce a workforce for agro-export industries.

The volume's chapters examine multiple forms of worker and peasant culture, identity, consciousness, and resistance. Workers' and peasants' individual and collective struggles were centered on questions relating to community, ethnicity, land, and dignity as well as on work-related or class-based issues. Thus these essays seek to incorporate analysis of ethnicity and gender, of ideological and cultural formation, and of popular strategies of everyday resistance and accommodation. They use discourse and cultural analysis to seek a culturally sophisticated and nonreductionist class analysis. The initial assumption that underlies the contributions presented in this volume is that there are no a priori scripts in the formation of the popular sectors and the course of their struggles. Instead, the authors have painstakingly attempted to uncover the multiplicity of forces that have shaped working people's lives.

The perspectives taken here also lead inevitably to new interpretations of elite political projects. Elite-centered histories have tended to flatten complex and multilayered nonelite experiences. Elite ideologies and histories in all of these countries have served to promote distorted visions and versions of the nation that erase the experiences of popular sectors and justify their subordination. Contestation from below has been a constant concomitant to the construction of elite dominance; the character of the elites, and of the histories they have written, is very much a product of their attempts to assert their position against those who have challenged it.

Beginning at the end of the nineteenth century, national elites struggled to channel and contain social and political movements in order to promote the kind of order and progress they and foreign investors depended upon and also to construct memories, histories, and images of nations that were functional to their political and economic projects and their dreams of national power and stability. At the same time, foreign political and economic control and their own internal weaknesses and contradictions led them to seek, at least rhetorically, national unity and independence and to make strategic concessions to popular classes in an attempt to form nationalist or populist alliances. This kind of opening both influenced the ways popular struggles came to be defined and created situations in which popular forces could effectively make their voices heard in the national political arena.

The republics of Central America and the Hispanic Caribbean islands share many historical characteristics. All of these countries formed part of the Spanish colonial system for three centuries or more. Although the countries spun out of the Spanish colonial orbit at different times and in different contexts, Spanish colonialism established important elements of coherence that helped lay the foundations for the challenges of nation-state construction after independence. Furthermore, Central America and the Spanish Caribbean have shared, since the late nineteenth century, the strong political, social, and economic influence of the United States and the development of agro-export economies. Either through the direct creation of classic enclave economies (mining, sugar, timber, bananas, and so on); the development of export infrastructures; or the less visible participation in the production and marketing of other products, such as coffee, cattle, or food, foreign—especially U.S., German, and English—entrepreneurs helped connect the region firmly to the North Atlantic economy.

These factors profoundly influenced all the nations discussed in this book. However, the dilemmas of nation-state formation and the experiences of different regions show that neither the narrative of national political history nor the complex formation of diverse social sectors were driven single-handedly by the logic of the plantation and export-agriculture complexes. Incorporating the history of working peoples into the narratives of states and nation formation can illuminate the ways in which local actors and experiences differed, as well as the structural similarities among the cases.

The study of Central America since around 1980 has been influenced by key questions originating in the political and social conflicts of recent years. Among these are the tension political leaders face between preserving their own status, attracting and accommodating foreign capital, maintaining legitimacy in the eyes of their own populations, and containing challenges from below. Why were the revolutionary movements of Guatemala, El Salvador, and Nicaragua so strong? Why were some victorious and others not? Why were the states they faced so authoritarian and exclusive? Why did Costa Rica and Honduras constitute forms of exceptionalism within the larger Central American experience? From the Caribbean similar questions continue to be posed about the parallels and divergences among the islands once settled by Spain and which have followed disparate forms of development in the twentieth century.

These questions have received much attention, and they still inform the research of most historians and other scholars who work on the region. But they have often led to an impasse: they too frequently have been posed in terms of national, homogeneous, state-oriented histories that tend to obscure multiple, contradictory sources of tension and conflict—including those that had limited expression at the national or state levels. Under the influence of "new" or expansive versions of social history, the authors in this volume attempt to uncover the multiple actors in much of the history of Central America and the Caribbean, confronting the larger and often impersonal narratives of states and nations and the study of elite political projects. In doing so, they attempt to transcend the dichotomies that have too often separated the newer social and cultural historical approaches from political and economic histories and to show the ways each can illuminate the other.

The study of popular sectors in Central America has only a brief history. Although a few early accounts of the history of Central America attributed an independent role to popular sectors, most histories of the isthmus kept discussions of popular sectors subordinate to the examination of the large-scale transitions in the formation of the region's nation-states.[1] Beginning in the 1960s, under the impact of reformist, popular, and revolutionary movements and of the various calls for agrarian reform, there emerged a new but relatively small generation of studies emphasizing the history of urban and enclave workers, union history, and the role of workers in conjunctural crises, especially national political transitions. These studies tended to be urban rather than rural, and they focused especially on the challenges and obstacles facing the organization of a working-class alternative to crisis-ridden oligarchic regimes.[2] The first histories of rural Central America also appeared in the 1960s, and these were largely agricultural histories and general descriptions of social structure.[3] After the revolutionary upsurges that began in the late 1970s many writers began to examine the origins of social-revolutionary movements. As peasants and indigenous peoples participated in the upheavals of the period, scholars began to examine more deeply the rural origins of political protest, as well as giving more consideration to questions of ethnicity and racial difference. Studies that explored the comparative origins of dictatorship, democracy, and revolution in the various Central American republics tended to favor macroquestions of class structure and political process but also opened an arena for discussions of class and ethnic formation that eventually contributed to closer accounts of local history. As a result important studies published during the mid-1980s began the careful investigation of processes of agrarian class formation and ethnic relations, with the experiences of working peoples as a central focus.[4] As a result of these trends, the social history of Central America became one of the principal strands in the historical literature, but in-depth studies of local cases have remained scarce.[5]

In many respects, Costa Rican historiography has led the way in the social history of popular sectors, developing the richest literature of empirical case studies.[6] Costa Rica also has the most developed labor historiography.[7] It has also led the way in the study of rural social structures and the formation of rural economies, the peasantry, and small farmers.[8] More recently, historians of Costa Rica have extended their study to popular resistance, popular culture, and the history of indigenous and Afro Caribbean populations.[9]

The literature on other Central American countries has lagged behind, partially because of the effects of war and repression, but mostly due to the long-term effects of having weak civil societies ruled by authoritarian states. Nicaragua's historiography has recently expanded as well, with a new generation of scholars that have gone beyond the search for the origins of popular support for the Sandinista revolution.[10] In this respect the work of Jeffrey Gould has been pathbreaking and opened the door for a transition toward the microlevel study of national class- and ethnic-based processes.

The study of laboring people in Guatemala has benefited from the many ethnographic studies carried out by anthropologists since the early twentieth century.[11] More recent studies by historians extend and draw on this tradition of community-based studies, adding historical depth and the use of archival materials,[12] most often in the study of ethnic relations and the formation and history of Guatemala's Maya.[13] Guatemalan works also benefit from a more solid grounding in the colonial period beginning with such classics as Severo Martínez's La patria del criollo and continuing with the studies by Carmack and Lovell.[14]

Without a doubt, Honduras and El Salvador are the countries with the least-developed national historiographies. Studies of the popular sectors and their relation to the larger themes of national history are especially scarce. For Honduras a few studies have focused on the history of enclave workers, especially the 1954 banana workers' strike.[15] El Salvador has had a few more studies of labor history and agrarian structures.[16] Still, only recently has the country's peasantry received significant and carefully documented attention, and the histories of urban workers and other working people remain unexamined.[17]

Of the three Hispanic Caribbean countries, Puerto Rico has the most developed social history of popular sectors. Classic studies examined slavery and the impact of Spanish colonial policies upon the laboring classes.[18] During the late 1970s and early 1980s a new historiography strongly influenced by Marxist debates about the development of capitalism and its impact on class formation began to examine the origins of Puerto Rico's social classes.[19] During this period earlier studies, especially the comprehensive ethnohistorical study of the 1950s, *The People of Puerto Rico*, were rediscovered and their insights into regional class dynamics extended and linked to Puerto Rico's complex questions about nationhood.[20] An issue that framed many examinations of the history of Puerto Rico's social classes was the successes and failures of Puerto Rico's nationalist and socialist movements.[21] From the mid-1980s on, however, historians began to include the examination of women's history, while no longer subordinating the study of popular sectors to the large questions of political status and colonialism.[22] An extensive literature on the island's plantations and haciendas, the labor movement, and the formation of the peasantry has enhanced the study of the popular sectors and also contributed to the creation of a more critical, historically informed sense of national identity.[23]

The most salient studies in Cuban history written in the 1970s and 1980s focused on the transition from slave labor to free labor in Cuba's plantation economy and were led by the research of Manuel Moreno Fraginals into Cuba's plantation sector and Rebecca Scott's work on the abolition of slavery and its impact.[24] Since then, studies have addressed issues of racial and ethnic formation and identity, immigration, and social banditry, as well as the women's and labor movements.[25] Jorge Ibarra has begun a process of revision and reconsideration of the classic themes of Cuban historiography, including the island's social structure.[26]

If the historiography of Cuba's popular sectors is relatively undeveloped, that of the Dominican Republic is virtually unexplored. Few in-depth studies were published prior to the 1970s, and works since then have tended to focus on large-scale issues of capitalism, crop history, and national development. Dominican historiography, like that of El Salvador and other republics in the region, has been limited by the cultural and educational impact of authoritarian regimes. The country's poverty has also contributed to the scarcity of historical studies. Most literature is recent and strongly influenced by political debates and questions grounded in Marxist theory.[27] As with Nicaragua, popular sectors have received some attention when scholars examine the impact of and resistance to U.S. occupation.[28] In recent years regional agrarian history, including peasant politics, has come under study.[29] The contribution of local history to emigration patterns has gained interest, especially among sociologists and anthropologists.[30] Since the late 1980s the formation of the Dominican Republic's national racial identity has also been explored.[31]

The contributions in this volume carry on the project of uncovering the histories of popular sectors. They also try to take the endeavor a step further by incorporating the study of cultures and identities and by using this added dimension to show how history written from above is inevitably a distorted history: the failure to pay attention to the lives, beliefs, and actions of peasants and workers has led to assumptions about national and international developments that are at best partial and at worst erroneous. The stories the authors in this volume tell not only add to but also transform and revise previous conceptions of the region's national histories.

Cindy Forster's chapter argues that despite numerous accounts of Guatemala's 1944 to 1954 revolution, the history of the revolution from below has been virtually suppressed, although, as she argues, " 'the revolution from above' only set down roots when jealously defended, or 'tended,' by the poor." Standard accounts of the revolution have tended to focus on relations between urban revolutionary leaders, the agrarian elite, the United Fruit Company (UFC), and the United States, but Forster shows that the revolution also opened a space for campesinos and plantation workers to become critical actors on the national and even international stage and that their actions were a key factor in the direction the revolution took and in the eventual U.S. decision to overthrow it.

She shows that consciousness and ethnic identity played a major role in shaping the ways ordinary people understood and acted in the revolution. She does so by contrasting the experience of the revolution and the grassroots movements for social justice that developed in conjunction with it in two very different regions of Guatemala: the Pacific highlands coffee zone of San Marcos, with its Indian migrant labor force, and the Pacific coast banana zone, dominated by the UFC and populated by migrant Spanish-speaking ladino workers. Despite distinct social complexes in the two regions, campesinos shared a conception of social justice that Forster summarizes as a higher standard of living and dignity for the rural poor and which sharply diverged from the goals enunciated and pursued by revolutionary leaders.

Darío Euraque and Barry Carr also examine particular groups of enclave workers and their importance in national histories. Euraque focuses on the Honduran north coast banana enclave, which was the country's key economic sector during the early twentieth century but which has been viewed as peripheral to the country's social and political history. As in the Nicaraguan case examined by Jeffrey Gould, the concept of an ethnically homogeneous race emerged in Honduran elite thought, and in official documents, in the early twentieth century. In Honduras, this myth was created in direct contradiction with the existence of black populations on the Atlantic coast, rather than in the context of the social struggles in the highlands that took place in Nicaragua. As in Nicaragua, though, the myth was part of an attempt to erase the realities undergone by the workers and peasants marginalized by, or who produced for, the export sector. Euraque looks at the structuring of Honduran censuses (which after 1910 eliminated *black* and *mulato* as possible categories for Hondurans), anti-immigrant legislation, and intellectuals' discussions of the race issue to show how the myth took form.

Barry Carr's chapter challenges the standard view of the social world of the sugar plantations in early twentieth-century Cuba. Like Forster, Carr documents actions by nonelites that show the degree to which they were able to maneuver and pursue their own goals despite the concentration of economic and political power against them. By looking at labor mobility and labor shortages, which pitted employers against each other in the struggle to secure labor, he challenges the assumption that the sugar *centrales* (central factories"—modern mills that can process sugar grown by numerous small *colonos*, or tenants) and the world they created could be managed as fiefdoms. The importance of paternalism and the concession of subsistence plots are evidence that the supposed hegemony of the sugar plantation was actually more of a complex negotiation between the companies and their workers.

In her essay Eileen Findlay retraces the history of counterhegemonic working-class and feminist polemics and struggles that relate to the question of sexual practices and mores in early twentieth-century Puerto

Rico. By closely reconstructing the debates, discussions, and conflicts as they were reflected in the feminist, women's, socialist, and labor presses, Findlay reconstitutes an essential aspect of the autonomous world of alternative ideologies and practices that peppered the history of early twentieth-century working-class Puerto Rican women and men. Traditional and revisionist labor historiography have shared an emphasis on the political activities and positions of the labor movement and the working-class Left or on narrow party-based conceptions of class struggle. More recently, a new generation of feminist historians have begun to trace the specific perspectives and struggles of women within and across social classes.[32] Findlay's research aptly applies this fresh approach to the social history of gender relations and sexuality within the context of Puerto Rico during the 1910s and 1920s.

Also discussing the suppression of marginalized identities and history, Jeffrey Gould's chapter shows how the hegemony of what he calls "the myth of Nicaragua mestiza"—the belief that indigenous communities in Nicaragua had ceased to exist—developed from the struggle between indigenous communities and mestizo elites in the late nineteenth and early twentieth centuries. At the same time, he suggests that the commonsense notion that Nicaragua is an ethnically homogeneous society, which has also dominated Nicaraguan historiography, is in fact a product of the ultimate mestizo victory over Nicaragua's Indians. Yet this outcome was not a foregone conclusion, and the period he examines was one of intense struggle that both shaped and was shaped by the sense of identity of indigenous communities. The forms that resistance and identities took varied and had far-reaching implications. In some cases ethnic identities atomized, whereas in others they were transformed into a class perspective that formed part of a new culture of resistance. Gould also traces support for the Sandinistas by looking at the history of various peasant communities and how they have understood and remembered their experiences over many decades.

Coffee production in Central America has typically been portrayed as an activity dominated by oligarchies. New research, however, has begun to emphasize the participation of other social sectors in the production and marketing of this fundamental crop. Julie Charlip's essay examines important aspects of the little-studied history of small producers of coffee in southwestern Nicaragua. She finds that independent producers of varying amounts of coffee engaged in a complex set of transactions with merchants and other landowners in order to finance their activities and market their produce while holding on to their land. Her careful research is significant also in its extensive reliance on local sources, including notary files and land registers. Her methodological and conceptual innovations should open the door to closer research of Nicaragua's regions.

Like Nicaragua, El Salvador has generally been assumed to conform to the classic *latifundio-minifundio* pattern, with little if any small-holder role in the production of coffee. The development of a coffee economy has been told as the story of the displacement of subsistence-oriented Indian communities in favor of large, export-oriented planta-tions. Aldo Lauria-Santiago's chapter on El Salvador shifts the focus away from national generalizations to the regional and community levels and shows that much of El Salvador's coffee production during the nineteenth century was indeed in the hands of smallholding peasants. He studies the transformation of the ladino landholding community of Chalchuapa in the coffee zone of northwestern El Salvador from com-munally based to individually based commercial agriculture during the nineteenth century, emphasizing the strong peasant presence in com-mercial as well as subsistence production. The chapter looks not only at social and economic structures but at the cultural and ideological changes that accompanied the shift to agrarian capitalism, as peasants' communal identities were eroded in favor of defending their individual holdings. In addition to challenging the notion that commercial agri-culture was exclusively based in large plantations, Lauria-Santiago also overturns the automatic association of peasant corporate communities with Indian identities in El Salvador.

Patricia Alvarenga's contribution explores another important and understudied aspect of rural history in El Salvador. By examining judi-cial and police files, she traces the participation of peasants and workers in attempts by regional and national elites and states to carry out the daily routines of policing, coercive administration of justice, and the manipulation of class relations and conflicts. In the context of a politi-cally and militarily weak state, Salvadoran political leaders and state administrators of the 1880 to 1932 period sought the participation of local civilians in their efforts to regularize policing and mediate trans-actions among different classes. Alvarenga's chapter shows how civilians played a primary role in the Salvadoran repressive system and were incorporated into the country's state institutions by means of a network of civilian assistants, a system that contributed to the shaping of the political system. Her analysis of the collaborators' actions reveals that the Salvadoran state established its control over the countryside by converting peasants into active agents of the police and judicial system.

In recent decades a new historiography of Costa Rica has focused mostly on rural society in the central valley region. Previous studies of workers and working-class movements had usually been concerned with the better-known coastal banana enclaves and urban workers, and more marginal regions and enterprises had received less attention. Aviva Chomsky's essay examines the interaction among labor, ethnic, and peasant struggles in a region of Costa Rica usually considered marginal. Her contribution uncovers the complex struggles of mine workers and peasant squatters in legal and national ideological frameworks that were not of their making but to which they had to make strong concessions and in the context of which they framed many aspects of their identities and actions. She examines two arenas of social struggle: squatters' attempts to establish their right to cultivate land surrounding, and often claimed by, foreign-owned mining companies; and workers' protests, which focused on working conditions. The context for these struggles included a national state committed, at least on a rhetorical level, to the protection of smallholding and of national sovereignty over resources; the assertion and manipulation of competing racial and national identities, from both above and below; and Costa Rican elites' commitment to maintaining their country's "exceptionalism" in the face of foreign investment and proletarianization. Chomsky describes the ways workers and squatters responded to their situations and constructed movements, ideologies, and goals, as well as the ways their actions have been remembered and reconstructed over time.

In his research on peasant-state relations during the Dominican Republic's Trujillato, Richard Turits retraces the networks of patronage and support Trujillo's government established with peasant producers during the 1930s and 1940s. Previous historiography on the Dominican Republic has emphasized the dictatorial or autocratic character of Trujillo's regime and its connections with the earlier U.S. occupation of the country. Export-oriented plantations, foreign investment, and the development of rural society in the areas of sugar production have been the favorite themes of historians. By exposing Trujillo's policies of support for small-scale landownership Turits's chapter helps explain the longevity of this repressive regime and its ambivalent relationship with the peasant masses. But this author's contribution goes further than revealing one of the bases of support for the Trujillato. His examination of the history of land tenure systems and peasant reproduction contribute a great deal to our knowledge of these central aspects of the Dominican Republic's little-studied rural history.

Lowell Gudmundson and Francisco Scarano's concluding essay provides and in-depth discussion of the issues and questions posed by this book and those in need of further research and attention.

The risk in a collection that emphasizes the complexities, inconsistencies, and multifaceted twists and turns of history is that the reader might lose sight of the forest for the trees. However, each of the authors has carefully examined the links between the processes she/he studies and the larger trajectory of national history. Furthermore, several of the chapters suggest the need for a substantial rewriting of the larger themes of national histories—a task that should keep historians busy for many years. Together, the essays show how, to continue the metaphor, the forest itself looks very different when the individual trees are examined carefully.

Notes

Note that throughout the book Spanish quotes were translated into English by the individual chapter authors unless noted otherwise.

1. For classic political histories, see the summaries in David Bushnell and Neill Macaulay, *The Emergence of Latin America in the Nineteenth Century,* 2d ed. (New York: Oxford University Press, 1994), and James Dunkerley, *Power in the Isthmus: A Political History of Modern Central America* (London: Verso, 1988). More detailed overviews of the countries' political histories can be found in Leslie Bethell, ed., *Central America since Independence* (Cambridge: Cambridge University Press, 1991), which includes essays by Ralph Lee Woodward and Ciro Cardoso on the pre-1930 period and by Edelberto Torres Rivas, Victor Bulmer-Thomas, James Dunkerley, and Rodolfo Cerdas Cruz on the post-1930 period. For a general survey of Central American history in Spanish, see the six volumes of the *Historia general de Centroamérica,* coordinated by Edelberto Torres Rivas (San José: FLACSO, 1993). For more comprehensive general references on the region, see W. J. Griffith, "The Historiography of Central

America since 1830," *Hispanic American Historical Review,* 40, no. 4 (November 1960): 548–569; Carol Smith and Jefferson Boyer, "Central America since 1979, Part I," *Annual Review of Anthropology,* 16 (1987): 197–221; Carol Smith, Jefferson Boyer, and Martin Diskin, "Central America since 1979, Part II," *Annual Review of Anthropology,* 17 (1988): 331–364; and Ralph Lee Woodward Jr., "The Historiography of Modern Central America since 1960," *Hispanic American Historical Review,* 67, no. 3 (August 1987): 461–496.

2. Thomas Anderson's *Matanza: El Salvador's Communist Revolt of 1932* (Lincoln: University of Nebraska Press, 1971; rev. ed. Willamantic, Conn.: Curbstone, 1992) is a partial exception to this trend in its inclusion of indigenous and rural aspects of the 1932 revolt and massacre. See the chapters on Central America in Pablo González Casanova, ed., *América Latina en los años treinta* (Mexico: Siglo Veintiuno, 1970) and in Pablo González Casanova, ed., *America Latina: historia de medio siglo* (Mexico City: Siglo Veintiuno Editores, 1981), and see Rafael Guidos Vejar, *El ascenso del militarismo en El Salvador* (San Salvador: UCA Editores, 1980).

3. Among the most important contributions from this period are David Browning, *El Salvador: Landscape and Society* (Oxford, England: Clarendon, 1971); David McCreery, "Coffee and Class: The Structure of Development in Liberal Guatemala," *Hispanic American Historical Review,* 56 (1976): 438–460; Mitchell Seligson, *Peasants of Costa Rica and the Development of Agrarian Capitalism* (Madison: University of Wisconsin Press, 1980); Edelberto Torres Rivas, *Interpretación del desarrollo social centroamericano* (San José: EDUCA, 1971), recently translated by Douglass Sullivan-González as *History and Society in Central America* (Austin: University of Texas Press, 1993); Rafael Menjívar, *Acumulación originaria y desarrollo del capitalismo en El Salvador* (San José: EDUCA, 1980; rev. ed. 1995); Carolyn Hall, *El café y el desarrollo histórico-geográfico de Costa Rica* (San José: Editorial Costa Rica and Universidad Nacional, 1976); Ciro F. S. Cardoso and Héctor Pérez Brignoli, *Centroamérica y la economía occidental (1620–1930)* (San José: Editorial de la Universidad de Costa Rica, 1977); and Ciro F. S. Cardoso, "The Formation of the Coffee Estate in Nineteenth-Century Costa Rica," in *Land and Labour in Latin America,* ed. Kenneth Duncan and Ian Routledge (Cambridge: Cambridge University Press, 1977). Guatemala is an exception because of the extensive ethnographic literature on its rural indigenous communities. However, work by historians is still lacking.

4. Among the most important contributions were studies by Lowell Gudmundson, Jeffrey Gould, J. C. Cambranes, and David McCreery: Lowell Gudmundson, *Costa Rica before Coffee: Society and Economy on the Eve of the Export Boom* (Louisiana State University Press, 1986); J. C. Cambranes, *Coffee and Peasants: The Origins of the Modern Plantation Economy in Guatemala* (Stockholm: Institute of Latin American Studies, 1985); and Jeffrey L. Gould, *To*

Lead as Equals: Rural Protest and Political Consciousness in Chinandega, Nicaragua, 1912–1979 (Chapel Hill: University of North Carolina Press, 1990). See also David McCreery's "Debt Servitude in Rural Guatemala, 1876–1936," *Hispanic American Historical Review,* 63, no. 4 (1983): 735–759, and his " 'This Life of Misery and Shame': Female Prostitution in Guatemala City, 1880–1920," *Journal of Latin American Studies,* 18 (1988): 333–353; the chapters on Central America in Pablo González Casanova, ed., *Historia política de los campesinos latinoamericanos,* vol. 2 (Mexico City: Siglo Veintiuno Editores and Instituto de Investigaciones Sociales de la UNAM, 1985); Ciro F. S. Cardoso, "Historia económica del café en Centroamérica (siglo XIX)," *Estudios Sociales Centroamericanos* 4, no. 10 (1975): 3–57. For a review of the comparative agrarian and political history of Central America, see Lowell Gudmundson, "Lord and Peasant in the Making of Modern Central America," in *Agrarian Structure and Political Power: Landlord and Peasant in the Making of Latin America,* edited by Evelyne Huber and Frank Safford (Pittsburgh: University of Pittsburgh Press, 1995).

5. For a discussion of trends in the study of agrarian class formation in Latin America that has special relevance for Central America and the Caribbean, see William Roseberry, "Beyond the Agrarian Question in Latin America," in *Confronting Historical Paradigms: Peasants, Labor, and the World System in Africa and Latin America,* by Frederick Cooper et al., (Madison: University of Wisconsin Press, 1993); and William Roseberry, "*La falta de brazos:* Land and Labor in the Coffee Economies of Nineteenth-Century Latin America," *Theory and Society,* 20 (1991): 351–382, and his introduction to *Coffee, Society, and Power in Latin America,* edited by William Roseberry, Lowell Gudmundson, and Mario Samper Kutschbach (Baltimore: Johns Hopkins University Press, 1995).

6. See Elisavinda Echeverri-Gent, "Forgotten Workers: British West Indians and the Early Days of the Banana Industry in Costa Rica and Honduras," *Journal of Latin American Studies,* 24 (1992): 275–308; Philippe Bourgois, *Ethnicity at Work: Divided Labor on a Central American Banana Plantation* (Baltimore: Johns Hopkins University Press, 1989); Aviva Chomsky, *West Indian Workers and the United Fruit Company in Costa Rica, 1870–1940* (Baton Rouge: Louisiana State University Press, 1996); and Marc Edelman, *The Logic of the Latifundio: The Large Estates of Northwestern Costa Rica since the Late Nineteenth Century* (Stanford, Calif.: Stanford University Press, 1992). See also the essays in Roseberry, Gudmundson, and Samper Kutschbach, *Coffee, Society, and Power in Latin America.*

7. For recent works of synthesis, see the chapters in Victor Hugo Acuña Ortega and Iván Molina Jiménez, *Historia económica y social de Costa Rica (1750–1950)* (San José: Editorial Porvenir, 1991). See also Mario Oliva Medina, *Artesanos y obreros costaricenses, 1880–1914* (San José: Editorial Costa Rica, 1985); Carlos Luis Fallas Monge, *El movimiento obrero en Costa Rica, 1830–1902* (San

José: EUED, 1983); and Vladimir de la Cruz, *Las luchas sociales en Costa Rica* (San José: EDUCA, 1984).

8. The literature on Costa Rican agrarian formation is the most extensive of that for any country in Central America. Among the most important works on the formation of the peasantry and farmers are Gudmundson, *Costa Rica before Coffee;* Mario Samper, *Generations of Settlers: Rural Household and Markets on the Costa Rican Frontier, 1850–1935* (Boulder, Colo.: Westview, 1990); and Hall, *El café;* and Lowell Gudmundson, "Peasant, Farmer, Proletarian: Class Formation in a Smallholder Coffee Economy, 1850–1950," *Hispanic American Historical Review,* 69 (May 1989): 221–258, and his "Peasant Movements and the Transition to Agrarian Capitalism: Freeholding versus Hacienda Peasantries and Agrarian Reform in Guanacaste, Costa Rica, 1880–1935," *Peasant Studies,* 10, no. 3 (Spring 1983): 145–162. See also the *Revista de Historia* and the *Anuario de Estudios Centroamericanos,* both published in Costa Rica.

9. Iván Molina Jiménez and Steven Palmer, eds., *Héroes al gusto y libros de moda: sociedad y cambio cultural en Costa Rica (1750–1900)* (San José: Editorial Porvenir and Plumsock Mesoamerican Studies, 1992), and their *El paso del cometa: estado, política social y culturas populares en Costa Rica (1800/1950)* (San José: Editorial Porvenir and Plumsock Mesoamerican Studies, 1994). Both of these books represent innovative attempts at reconstructing the cultural and ideological history of popular sectors in Costa Rica. See Marcos Guevara Berger and Rubén Chacón Castro, *Territorios indios en Costa Rica: orígenes, situación actual y perspectivas* (San José: García Hermanos, SA, 1992), and Chomsky, *West Indian Workers.*

10. See Julie Charlip, "Cultivating Coffee: Farmers, Land and Money in Nicaragua, 1877–1930" (Ph.D. dissertation, University of California, Los Angeles, 1995); Michel Gobat, "Granada's Conservative Revolutionaries: Anti-elite Violence and the Nicaraguan Civil War of 1912," paper presented at the Third Central American Congress of History, San José, Costa Rica, July 15–18, 1996; Justin Wolfe, "Rising from the Ashes: The Formation of the Nicaraguan Nation-State, 1850–1900" (Ph.D. dissertation, UCLA, 1997), his "Becoming Mestizo: Ethnicity, Culture and Nation in Nicaragua, 1850–1900," paper presented at the Third Central American Congress of History, San José, Costa Rica, July 15–18, 1996, and his "La Riqueza de un País: Land and Community in the Creation of the Nicaraguan Nation-State, 1850–1900," paper presented at the Southwest Council of Latin American Studies, Austin, Texas, February 20–22, 1997; Michael J. Schroeder, " 'To Defend Our Nation's Honor': Toward a Social and Cultural History of the Sandino Rebellion in Nicaragua, 1927–1934" (Ph.D. dissertation, University of Michigan, 1993), his "Horse Thieves to Rebels to Dogs: Political Gang Violence and the State in the Western Segovias, Nicaragua, in the Time of Sandino, 1926–1934," *Journal of Latin*

American Studies, 28, no. 2 (May 1996): 383–434, and his "The Sandino Rebellion Revisited: Civil War, Imperialism, Popular Nationalism, and State Formation Muddied up Together in the Segovias of Nicaragua, 1926–1934," in *Close Encounters of Empire: Writing the Cultural History of U.S.–Latin American Relations*, edited by Catherine C. LeGrand, Gilbert M. Joseph, and Ricardo D. Salvatore (Durham, N.C.: Duke University Press, 1998); and Elizabeth Dore, "Coffee, Land, and Class Relations in Nicaragua, 1870–1920," *Journal of Historical Sociology*, 8, no. 3 (September 1995): 303–326, and her "Patriarchy and Private Property in Nicaragua, 1860–1920," in *Patriarchy and Economic Development*, edited by Valentine M. Moghadam (Oxford, England: Clarendon, 1996).

See also Bradford Burns's attempt at an overarching interpretation of Nicaragua's nineteenth century, E. Bradford Burns, *Patriarch and Folk: The Emergence of Nicaragua, 1798–1858* (Cambridge: Harvard University Press, 1991), and Rafael Casanova Fuertes, "¿Héroes o bandidos? Los problemas de interpretación de los conflictos políticos y sociales entre 1845 y 1849 en Nicaragua," *Revista de Historia* (Managua), 2 (1992–1993): 13–26.

11. See especially the work by Richard N. Adams, *Crucifixion by Power: Essays on Guatemalan National Social Structure, 1944–1966* (Austin: University of Texas Press, 1970), and Carol Smith's critical review of Guatemalan social history: "Ideologías de la historia social," *Mesoamerica*, 14 (1987): 355–366.

12. See Jean Piel, *Sajcabaja: muerte y resurrección de un pueblo de Guatemala, 1500–1970* (Mexico City: Centro de Estudios Mexicanos y Centroamericanos and Guatemala City: Seminario de Integración Social, 1989); David McCreery, *Rural Guatemala, 1760–1940* (Stanford, Calif.: Stanford University Press, 1994), and his "Land, Labor and Violence in Highland Guatemala: San Juan Ixcoy (Huehetenango), 1893–1945," *Americas*, 45 (October 1988): 237–249; Robert Wasserstrom, "Revolution in Guatemala: Peasants and Politics under the Arbenz Government," *Comparative Studies in Society and History*, 17, no. 4 (1975): 443–478; Ralph Lee Woodward, "Liberalism, Conservatism, and the Response of the Peasants of La Montaña to the Government of Guatemala, 1821–1850," *Plantation Society in the Americas*, 1 (1979): 109–129; and Todd Little, "Guatemala en el período liberal: patria chica, patria grande, reflexiones sobre el estado y la comunidad en transición," in *Identidades nacionales y el estado moderno en Centroamérica*, comp. Arturo Taracena Arriola and Jean Piel (San José: Editorial de la Universidad de Costa Rica, 1995).

13. The essays in Carol A. Smith, ed., *Guatemalan Indians and the State: 1540–1988* (Austin: University of Texas Press, 1990) examine aspects of popular history and class formation. Jim Handy's *Revolution in the Countryside: Rural Conflict and Agrarian Reform in Guatemala, 1944–1954* (Chapel Hill: University of North Carolina Press, 1994) dedicates significant attention to the role of ethnicity and class during Guatemala's 1944 to 1954 "revolution." See also

Deborah Levenson-Estrada, *Trade Unionists against Terror: Guatemala City, 1954–1985* (Chapel Hill: University of North Carolina Press, 1995) for a review of Guatemala's urban labor history.

14. For a pathbreaking study that integrates precolonial through modern period history while also placing local community history in a national context, see Robert M. Carmack, *Rebels of Highland Guatemala: The Quiche-Mayas of Momostenango* (Norman: University of Oklahoma Press, 1995). See also Robert M. Carmack, ed., *Harvest of Violence: The Maya Indians and the Guatemalan Crisis* (Norman: University of Oklahoma Press, 1988), and W. George Lovell, *Conquest and Survival in Colonial Guatemala: A Historical Geography of the Cuchumatán Highlands, 1500–1821* (Montreal: McGill-Queen's University Press, 1995).

15. See Robert MacCameron, *Bananas, Labor, and Politics in Honduras, 1954–1963* (Syracuse, N.Y.: Maxwell School of Citizenship and Public Affairs, 1983); Mario Posas, *Luchas del movimiento obrero hondureño* (San José: Editorial Universitaria, 1981); and Marvin A. Barahona, *El silencio quedó atrás: testimonios de la huelga bananera de 1954* (Tegucigalpa: Editorial Guaymuras, 1994). The work of Darío Euraque and a few other historians has begun to shed light on many of this country's ignored histories. See other works by Euraque and items cited by this author (this volume).

16. See Rafael Menjívar, *Formación y lucha del proletariado industrial salvadoreño* (San José: EDUCA, 1979) and *Acumulación originaria*. The classic discussion of Salvadoran agrarian history is by Browning (*El Salvador*).

17. For a groundbreaking study that examines important aspects of popular life, see Héctor Lindo Fuentes, *Weak Foundations: The Economy of El Salvador in the Nineteenth Century* (Berkeley: University of California Press, 1990). For recent studies of various aspects of peasant history, see Aldo Lauria-Santiago, "An Agrarian Republic: Production, Politics, and the Peasantry in El Salvador, 1740–1920 (Ph.D. dissertation, University of Chicago, 1992); Patricia Alvarenga, *Cultura y ética de la violencia: El Salvador, 1880–1932* (San José: EDUCA, 1996); and Héctor Pérez Brignoli, "Indians, Communists, and Peasants: The 1932 Rebellion in El Salvador," in *Coffee, Society, and Power in Latin America*, edited by Roseberry, Gudmundson, and Samper Kutschbach.

18. See Arturo Morales Carrión, *Auge y decadencia de la trata negrera en Puerto Rico (1820–1860)* (San Juan: Centro de Estudios Avanzados de Puerto Rico y El Caribe, 1978).

19. Among the most significant contributions are Francisco A. Scarano, *Sugar and Slavery: The Plantation Economy of Ponce, 1800–1850* (Madison: University of Wisconsin Press, 1984), and Laird Bergad, *Coffee and the Growth of Agrarian Capitalism in Nineteenth-Century Puerto Rico* (Princeton, N.J.: Princeton University Press, 1983). Although these works tend to rely on a structuralist view

of class formation, they consider many other aspects of peasant and slave life. The many books by Fernando Picó constitute another set of contributions to the study of Puerto Rican peasants. Among the most noteworthy are *Amargo café* (Río Piedras: Ediciones Huracán, 1981); *Libertad y servidumbre en el Puerto Rico del siglo xix* (San Juan: Ediciones Huracán, 1983); and *Los gallos peleados* (Río Piedras: Ediciones Huracán, 1983). See also Francisco Scarano, ed., *Inmigración y clases sociales en el Puerto Rico del siglo xix* (Río Piedras: Ediciones Huracán, 1982).

20. Julian Steward, et al., *The People of Puerto Rico: A Study in Social Anthropology* (Urbana: University of Illinois Press, 1956). For a critical study of this book, see Antonio Lauria-Perricelli, "A Study in Historical and Critical Anthropology: The Making of the People of Puerto Rico" (Ph.D. dissertation, New School for Social Research, 1989). For other items related to these early ethnographic studies, see the following works by Sidney W. Mintz: *Worker in the Cane: A Puerto Rican Life History* (New Haven: Yale University Press, 1960); "The Role of Forced Labour in Nineteenth-Century Puerto Rico," *Caribbean Historical Review*, 2 (1951): 134-141; "The Culture-History of a Puerto Rican Sugar-Cane Plantation, 1876-1949," *Hispanic American Historical Review*, 33, no. 2 (1953): 224-251; and "The Folk-Urban Continuum and the Rural Proletarian Community," *American Journal of Sociology*, 59, no. 2 (1953): 136-243. Other important aspects of the work on peasants and rural workers are presented in Eric R. Wolf, "Types of Latin American Peasantries," *American Anthropologist*, 57 (1953): 452-471, and his "Specific Aspects of Plantation Systems in the New World: Community Sub-cultures and Social Classes," in *Plantation Systems in the New World*, edited by Angel Palerm and Vera Rubin, Social Science Monograph no. 7 (Washington, D.C.: Pan American Union, 1959), 136-146; and Eric R. Wolf and Sidney W. Mintz, "Haciendas and Plantations in Middle America and the Antilles," *Social and Economic Studies*, 6, no. 3 (1957): 380-412.

21. See Gervasio Luis García and Angel G. Quintero Rivera, *Desafío y solidaridad: breve historia del movimiento obrero puertorriqueño* (Río Piedras: Ediciones Huracán, 1982); Angel G. Quintero Rivera, *Conflictos de clase y política en Puerto Rico*, 5th ed. (Río Piedras: Ediciones Huracán, 1986); Taller de Formación Política, *¡Huelga en la caña!* (Río Piedras: Ediciones Huracán, 1982); Gervasio Luis García, *Historia crítica, historia sin coartadas: algunos problemas de la historia de Puerto Rico* (San Juan: Ediciones Huracán, 1985); and Mariano Negrón Portilla, *Cuadrillas anexionistas y revueltas campesinas en Puerto Rico, 1898-1899* (San Juan: Centro de Investigaciones Sociales, 1987).

22. See Yamila Azize, *La mujer en la lucha* (Río Piedras: Editorial Cultural, 1985); Gervasio Luis García, "La historia de los trabajadores en la sociedad pre-industrial: el caso de Puerto Rico (1870-1900)," *Op. Cit., Boletín del Centro de Investigaciones Históricas*, 1 (1985-1986), 17-28; and Angel Quintero Rivera,

Patricios y plebeyos: burgueses, hacendados, artesanos y obreros: las relaciones de clase en el Puerto Rico de cambio de siglo (Río Piedras: Ediciones Huracán, 1988). For an important study that examines class culture and resistance, see Kelvin A. Santiago-Valles, *"Subject People" and Colonial Discourses: Economic Transformation and Social Disorder in Puerto Rico, 1898–1947* (Albany: SUNY Press, 1994).

23. See Teresita Martínez-Vergne, *Capitalism in Colonial Puerto Rico: Central San Vicente in the Late Nineteenth Century* (Gainesville: University of Florida Press, 1992); Luis Edgardo Díaz Hernández, *Castañer: una hacienda cafetalera en Puerto Rico* (Barcelona: Teorema, SA, 1982); Pedro San Miguel, *El mundo que creó el azúcar: las haciendas en Vega Baja, 1800–1873* (San Juan: Ediciones Huracán, 1989); Juan José Baldrich, *Sembraron la no siembra: los cosecheros de tabaco puertorriqueños frente a las corporaciones tabacaleras, 1920–1934* (Río Piedras: Ediciones Huracán, 1988); and Andrés Ramos Mattei, *La hacienda azucarera: su crecimiento y crisis en Puerto Rico (siglo xix)* (San Juan: CEREP, 1981). See also the many contributions in the *Anales de Investigación Histórica*, published by the History department of the University of Puerto Rico.

24. The literature on slavery, slave life, and abolition for Cuba is somewhat extensive. For the most important studies of nineteenth-century slavery, see Franklin Knight, *Slave Society in Cuba during the Nineteenth Century* (Madison: Wisconsin University Press, 1970); Manuel Moreno Fraginals, *The Sugarmill: The Socioeconomic Complex of Sugar in Cuba, 1760–1860*, trans. Cedric Belfrage (New York: Monthly Review, 1976); and Rebecca J. Scott, *Slave Emancipation in Cuba: The Transition to Free Labor, 1860–1899* (Princeton, N.J.: Princeton University Press, 1985). More recent works have focused greater attention on the regional development of sugar production. See Laird Bergad, *Cuban Rural Society in the Nineteenth Century: The Social and Economic History of Monoculture in Matanzas* (Princeton, N.J.: Princeton University Press, 1990).

25. See Aline Helg, *Our Rightful Share: The Afro-Cuban Struggle for Equality, 1886–1912* (Chapel Hill: University of North Carolina Press, 1995); Rolando Alvarez Estévez, *Azúcar e inmigración, 1900–1940* (Havana: Editorial de Ciencias Sociales, 1988); Tomás Fernández Robaina, *El negro en Cuba, 1902–1958: apuntes para la historia de la lucha contra la discriminación racial en la neocolonia* (Havana: Editorial de Ciencias Sociales, 1990); Louis A. Pérez, *Lords of the Mountain: Social Banditry and Peasant Protest in Cuba, 1878–1918* (Pittsburgh: Pittsburgh University Press, 1989); Rosalie Schwartz, *Lawless Liberators: Political Banditry and Cuban Independence* (Durham, N.C.: Duke University Press, 1989); and K. Lynn Stoner, *From the House to the Streets: The Cuban Woman's Movement for Legal Reform, 1898–1940* (Durham, N.C.: Duke University Press, 1991). A very important and often neglected study of constructions of race and gender in Cuba is Verena Martínez-Alier's *Marriage, Class and Colour in Nineteenth-Century Cuba: A Study of Racial Attitudes and Sexual Values in a*

Slave Society (Ann Arbor: University of Michigan Press, 1974; 2d ed. 1989). On enslaved women, see Hilary Beckles, "The Female Slave in Cuba during the first half of the Nineteenth Century," in *Engendering History: Caribbean Women in Historical Perspective*, ed. Verene Shepherd, Briget Brereton, and Barbara Bailey (New York: St. Martin's, 1995). See also Barry Carr, "Mill Occupations and Soviets: The Mobilisation of Sugar Workers in Cuba, 1917–1933," *Journal of Latin American Studies*, 28, no. 1 (1996): 129–158.

26. See his *Cuba, 1898–1921: Partidos políticos y clases sociales* (Havana: Editorial de Ciencias Sociales, 1992), and his *Cuba, 1898–1958: estructura y procesos sociales* (Havana: Editorial de Ciencias Sociales, 1995).

27. For an overview of labor history that combines social history with structuralist and functionalist analysis, see Roberto Cassá, *Movimiento obrero y lucha socialista en la República Dominicana (desde los orígenes hasta 1960)* (Santo Domingo: Taller, 1990).

28. See, for example, Bruce Calder, *The Impact of Intervention: The Dominican Republic during the U.S. Occupation of 1916–1924* (Austin: University of Texas Press, 1984). This book provides a groundbreaking study of the resistance of *gavilleros* (social bandits who ended up fighting against the U.S. occupation) to the United States as well as of how the U.S. occupation could not be reduced to an expression of U.S. sugar interests, as it both represented and resisted U.S. sugar interests at different points.

29. More recently, Michiel Baud and Pedro Luis San Miguel have examined the peasantry in the Cibao. Both studies emphasize peasants' relationship to the market. Michiel Baud's *Peasants and Tobacco in the Dominican Republic, 1870–1930* (Knoxville: University of Tennessee Press, 1995) studies the way peasants maintained independent and subsistence food crops during these decades even while they increasingly engaged with market forces and cash crop production. Pedro Luis San Miguel's "The Dominican Peasantry and the Market Economy: The Peasants of the Cibao, 1880–1930" (Ph.D. dissertation, Columbia University, 1987) also examines how peasants developed early into hybrid subsistence peasants and small capitalist farmers. The recent work by Julie Franks examines the formation of the gavilleros: "The Gavilleros of the East: Social Banditry as Political Practice in the Dominican Sugar Region, 1900–1924," *Journal of Historical Sociology*, 8, no. 2 (June 1995): 158–181. Also important is Catherine LeGrand's article on informal resistance on foreign-owned sugar plantations: "Informal Resistance on a Dominican Sugar Plantation During the Trujillo Dictatorship," *Hispanic American Historical Review*, 75, no. 4 (November 1995): 555–596. See also Pablo A. Mariñez, *Resistencia campesina, imperialismo y reforma agraria en República Dominicana (1899–1978)* (Santo Domingo: Ediciones CEPAE, 1984); Raymundo González, "Ideología del progreso y campesinado en el siglo diecinueve," *Ecos* (Santo Domingo), 1, no. 2 (1993): 25–43; and

Patrick E. Bryan, "The Question of Labor in the Sugar Industry of the Dominican Republic in the Late Nineteenth and Early Twentieth Centuries," in *Between Slavery and Free Labor: The Spanish-Speaking Caribbean in the Nineteenth Century,* ed. Manuel Moreno Fraginals, Frank Moya Pons, and Stanley L. Engerman (Baltimore: Johns Hopkins University Press, 1985).

30. For a recent review of these studies, see Eugenia Georges, *The Making of a Transnational Community: Migration, Development, and Cultural Change in the Dominican Republic* (New York: Columbia University Press, 1990).

31. Lauren Derby, "Haitians, Magic, and Money: *Raza* and Society in the Haitian-Dominican Borderlands, 1900–1937," *Comparative Studies in Society and History,* 36, no. 3 (July 1994): 488–526.

32. See Shepherd, Brereton, and Bailey, *Engendering History: Caribbean Women in Historical Perspective,* especially the chapters by Digna Castañeda ("The Female Slave in Cuba During the First Half of the Nineteenth Century") and Félix V. Matos-Rodríguez ("Street Vendors, Pedlars, Shop-Owners and Domestics: Some Aspects of Women's Economic Roles in Nineteenth-Century San Juan, Puerto Rico").

Central America

ALDO LAURIA-SANTIAGO

"That a Poor Man Be Industrious"

Coffee, Community, and Agrarian Capitalism in the Transformation of El Salvador's Ladino Peasantry, 1850–1900

❂

This chapter examines a series of transitions in the history of one of western El Salvador's larger municipalities, retracing the complex and contradictory ways in which a ladino peasant community was both agent and subject in the development of agrarian capitalism during the latter half of the nineteenth century.[1] By studying patterns of land use, expressions of peasant politics and identity, and commercial production in the context of local history, this essay sheds light upon a crucial period in the formation of El Salvador's peasant farmers and places it in the context of large-scale changes in the country's economy and society. In particular, this essay examines the experience of a ladino peasant community with land tenure, coffee production, and regional politics. The ladino Community of Chalchuapa and its experience with the pressures and opportunities afforded by the expanding coffee economy provide a window into the history of El Salvador's ladino peasantry and thus into a little-known and even suppressed aspect of the country's history.

The history of El Salvador during the period examined in this essay has been typically framed by two overlapping themes. The first emphasizes the development of coffee production as an activity controlled by a few oligarchic elites. Following this trend, the history of coffee production has been assumed to be a history of large, elite-owned plantations that quickly came to dominate the land and labor of western El Salvador. The second theme, closely linked to the first, is that Salvadoran elites are usually presented as fully in control of the process of privatization of land that took place during the late nineteenth century, manipulating or controlling the state to its exclusive benefit. Although both of these themes contain contributions to the historiography of the period, they also suppress and ignore a history of peasant participation in agrarian production, landholding, and politics.[2]

The lack of research into local history has allowed these assumptions to linger, and their popularity has been reinforced by their deep political roots. Both Left and Right in El Salvador have seized upon aspects of the country's history in order to draw lessons and weapons for their contemporary cultural and political battles. The image of a country ruled by despotic clans of land-grabbing coffee oligarchs who monopolized land and wealth alternates with the benign image of dynamic, progressive, and farsighted coffee entrepreneurs who provided a base for the nation's prosperity. In many ways these images are two sides of the same coin: the deeply ahistorical character of Salvadoran elite mythology. But they also contain the same silence: they ignore El Salvador's peasantry and its own autonomous participation in the emergence of agrarian capitalism and export production.

These assumptions have been reproduced in historical accounts, which rarely examine peasant participation in the export and commercial economy, emphasizing instead an absolute contradiction between small producers and export production. Thus coffee has been presented as a crop grown in large estates that were owned by a small group of landowners. As a result, historians have paid scant attention to the history of landholding peasant communities.[3] This chapter attempts to reverse this tendency and place peasants and farmers closer to the center of Salvadoran historiography.

Between the 1750s and the 1890s the agrarian landscape of Chalchuapa experienced three important transformations. Chalchuapa began as a lightly populated, Indian-dominated cattle raising, pig raising, and trading town. But by the end of the colonial period it had become more populated and ladino dominated, producing a greater variety of commercial crops. During the second transition (1850s to 1860s) Chalchuapa developed its coffee economy, leading to increased pressure on Chalchuapa's combination of community-based landholding with individually controlled commercial farming. By the 1880s Chalchuapa experienced a third transition when the country's community-owned and municipal lands were privatized and titled by individual landowners. In each of these transitions the peasants of Chalchuapa, both collectively and individually, faced conditions to which they had to respond creatively while they struggled for their subsistence and market position under conditions that were mostly outside of their control. They struggled to defend their access to land but also to sustain a larger principle: their right to help define and respond to the socioeconomic transformations they confronted.

From Indian to Ladino: Chalchuapa's Colonial Origins

The municipality of Chalchuapa is located to the northwest of San Salvador and adjacent to the western city of Santa Ana. During the late colonial period Chalchuapa became an important site for settlement and productive activities due to its strategic location between Salvadoran cities and Guatemala.[4] Chalchuapa had been a cattle-raising center throughout the colonial period. A church official who traveled to the region during the 1760s noted that Chalchuapa had twenty farms or haciendas, twelve *trapiches* (sugar mills), and many small, disperse farms and sugar mills, "which the Indians place[d] in any corner of the mountains," all controlled by Indian, ladino, and Spanish peasants and farmers.[5]

Although Chalchuapa did not become a significant producer of colonial El Salvador's principal export, indigo, it did benefit indirectly from the expansion in the production of this powdered dye,[6] and it developed important linkages with the expanding indigo economy. The expansion of indigo production raised the demand for cattle and foodstuffs throughout the provinces of San Salvador and Sonsonate. Cattle provided food for hacienda laborers, and leather was used for packaging the indigo. Relations such as this one provided a base for the strengthening of peasant communities—both Indian and ladino in the western and south-central regions of what later became El Salvador.[7]

It was also during the eighteenth century that Chalchuapa's ladino and Indian communities began to enlarge their holdings by purchasing lands from the Spanish Crown. Like most municipalities, the town of Chalchuapa had the right to a royal grant of thirty-seven *caballerías* (1,665 hectares) of *ejidos* (municipal lands) for its residents. Indian and ladino communities also had the right to obtain a title for additional lands by paying for a survey and compensating the Crown. As a result, during the 1700s the Indian and ladino communities of Chalchuapa laid claim to a significant extension of land—not because they could use it productively, but because such acquisitions strengthened their position when dealing with other communities and local hacendados.[8] In the context of the late colonial and early republican polities, controlling land meant more than owning an economic resource—it also implied political sovereignty.

By the early nineteenth century Chalchuapa was among the towns with the fastest population growth in sparsely populated El Salvador. In 1740 Chalchuapa had only about 600 people, but twenty-six years later the town had expanded to 2,200, and by 1807 to 3,000 inhabitants. By the mid nineteenth century Chalchuapa was among the most populated towns in western El Salvador, with about 4,600 people in the 1860s.[9] Although estimates of Chalchuapa's population varied after the mid-century, sources reported a population of between 5,000 and 9,000 between the 1860s and 1870s.[10] However, unlike other towns in the region where ladino and Indian populations expanded at similar rates, Chalchuapa's demographic growth since the late eighteenth century was mostly among the ladinos, which reflected both the ladino-ization of the local Indian population as well as the immigration of ladinos from other regions, including Guatemala.[11] In 1740 Chalchuapa was over 50 percent Indian, but by 1770 the Indian population had declined to about 25 percent.

Sometime during the early nineteenth century the Indian community of Chalchuapa restricted the settlement of ladinos in their town and the amount of land it would rent to these immigrants. The Indian-controlled town also did not permit the establishment of ladino households in the town center. This attitude was consistent both with colonial law and with practices of ethnic segregation, and it enhanced Indian defense of their landholdings and local municipal power. In the decades that followed, however, this restriction broke down and the ladino population increased considerably to the point where the Indian Community became a small minority. By 1864 only 6 percent of Chalchuapa's births were classified as Indian, a number significantly lower than in other nearby towns that had also begun as predominantly Indian settlements.[12]

We have few sources on the Indian Community of Chalchuapa, and it is not clear why it declined. It is possible that its decline was fueled

by the relative benefits Indian peasants could gain from physical mobility during the years of the early nineteenth century. Avoiding military conscription was a motivation for abandoning Indian identity, as
recruitment of soldiers and town militias relied heavily on the Indian
communities. The loss of lands by sale or encroachment might have
been a cause as well as an effect of the Community's decline. Eventually,
the diminished Indian Community sold part of its lands to the town's
ladino Community.[13] By 1867 ladino expansion and confidence were
such that the ladino Community members described themselves as "almost the totality and the most useful part of all this settlement."[14] The
mood reflected by this statement was based on their extensive acquisition of lands and their successful expansion of commercial agriculture.

Common Lands and Ethnic Communities around 1860

By the mid nineteenth century the municipality of Chalchuapa contained four different types of landholding: privately held haciendas, municipal ejidos, Indian-controlled communal lands, and ladino-controlled
communal and sodality lands. Private haciendas were never very prominent in Chalchuapa, precisely because of the success of peasant and
community landholding since the eighteenth century.[15] The municipal
ejidos were composed of the thirty-seven caballerías of land allotted to
the town by the Spanish Crown. After independence, republican governments continued to legitimate and support this form of land tenure
by regulating different aspects of ejido use.[16]

In Chalchuapa, the Indian Community controlled the ejidos as their
own until the Indians were displaced from municipal power by ladinos
sometime during the mid-century. By the 1860s municipal ejidos were
clearly distinguished from Community-owned lands in Chalchuapa and
throughout the country as well. The Indian Community also owned
lands outright, but the steady decline of the members of the indigenous
Community during the nineteenth century eventually led it to sell its
lands to the Ladino Community and to farmers from the nearby city of
Santa Ana.

Chalchuapa's most important landholder by far was the ladino Community. This Community made its extensive land purchases during the
late eighteenth and early nineteenth centuries. In 1755 the *común de*

ladinos purchased the fields known as San Juan, Chiquito, and Guayavos. Later, between 1809 and 1829, it added lands in the Canton Ayutepeque, and the Haciendas Santa Rosa and San José; the *sitios* (ranches) Guachipilín, Sacamíl, La Joya, and Jocotillo; and plots known as Arado, Rosario, and Dolores.[17] In addition to purchasing lands from the Spanish Crown, the local Indian Community, and other individual landowners, the ladino Chalchuapeños successfully defended the boundaries of their communal lands in a century-long conflict with the nearby municipalities of Atiquizaya and Juayua.[18] Republican laws established between the 1830s and 1860s confirmed, defined, and clarified the legal status of landholding peasant communities. By the 1860s these communities were subject to municipal supervision and had to elect officers and maintain record books. They were, in fact, together with municipal landholding, the backbone of peasant agriculture throughout the country.

By the 1870s Chalchuapa's ladino Community controlled at least eighty caballerías (3,600 hectares) of land and ranked among the largest landholding communities of El Salvador. On the basis of these lands the Community turned Chalchuapa into an attractive and successful site of peasant and farmer agriculture. Unlike Indian communities, which required members to have a long-term connection to local kin groups, ladino communities were usually more flexible in their incorporation of new members. However, they usually recognized the predominance of a core of long-term resident families as well. The ladino Community of Chalchuapa charged rent to recent settlers and outside tenants, whereas older families had the right to use plots of land without payment.[19]

The Expansion of Commercial Agriculture and the Defense of Communal Lands, 1860–1880s

In 1860 ladino officials from the department of Santa Ana complained that Chalchuapa had the most valuable communal lands in the region, "but unfortunately its residents do not take advantage of them and the municipality does not know how to increase its funds with the advantage offered by the many caballerías of lands which are envied for their fertility."[20] This observation merits attention because it marks a hiatus between Chalchuapa's earlier cattle-oriented economy and the emergence of commercial crops, especially coffee, that began around this year. It reveals clearly the circumstances the ladino Community of Chalchuapa faced during the 1860s when it began to produce coffee and confront internal and external pressures upon its ownership of extensive lands. Between 1860 and 1880 Chalchuapa experienced the development of its commercial and export agriculture at the same time as it negotiated challenges to its communal landholding practices by forces outside the community. By *both* negotiating the demands placed upon the community by farmers and investors from nearby Santa Ana—one of the nation's centers of coffee production and capitalist agriculture— and successfully developing its own form of peasant commercial entrepreneurship, Chalchuapa provides an exceptional case study of peasant and community agency in the context of rural, export-oriented capitalist development.

After 1860 Chalchuapa's ladino Community began to be pressured to provide immigrant farmers and entrepreneurs who resided in nearby towns with access to its extensive and uncultivated holdings. As part of these efforts, a group of farmers from Santa Ana city—a leading center of coffee production and the region's principal commercial center— attempted to show in court that part of the community's lands were actually owned by the state and thus subject to public use. They claimed in the Juzgado General de Hacienda that these lands held an old unpaid *capellanía* (chaplaincy) obligation, which was due to the state after the takeover of such payments by the government during the 1830s. As a result of the suit the government warned that if the lands were found to have been mortgaged, it would reserve the right to sell them back to the community in order to pay the principal and accumulated interest on the original debt of 400 pesos. This claim represented an attempt by the emerging coffee-growing elite of Santa Ana city at manipulating the legal system for their benefit. But their claim was not successful. For the ladino Community of Chalchuapa the possibility that they would have to repurchase their lands (even at *moderada composición*, "moderate payment") or that they might be sold in public auction constituted a major threat. The Community mobilized its legal representatives and local municipal authorities in defense of their lands. As part of this defense community leaders organized a response that combined legal and extralegal pressures.

The Chalchuapeño defense of their community lands could not be a straightforward legal maneuver. In order to appease the farmers who wanted to gain outright ownership of the Community's lands, the Community began to rent some of their unoccupied lands to outsiders.[21] At the same time, the municipal officials of Chalchuapa also began to publicly express devotion and acclaim for the regime of President Dueñas. But their accolades were so exaggerated that they did not entirely convince government officials of their allegiance to the current regime. As a result the governor of Santa Ana warned the minister of government that Chalchuapa's display of Dueñas's picture and coat of arms was dishonest and resulted only from their attempt to gain government support in their legal proceedings. In fact, most Chalchuapeños had supported the previous government before it was overthrown.[22] But the Chalchuapeños had had good reasons to oppose Dueñas's rule. The governor of Santa Ana—an official named by the Dueñas regime—had tried to impose a candidate in one of Chalchuapa's local elections by bringing eighty men from Santa Ana to intimidate the local people, no doubt a result of Santaneco interest in gaining control of Chalchuapa's unused lands.[23] Despite their distrust of Dueñas, the ladinos of Chalchuapa knew clearly that they had to play the game of political allegiances in their attempt to defend their lands from legal and extralegal challenges.

The community mounted a successful legal defense while also petitioning government authorities to respect long-held land rights. The commune pleaded with the government, explaining the righteousness of its claims:

Since time immemorial *que se confunde con la dominiación española* [that is confounded with the era of Spanish domination], the ladinos of this Villa associated, with fair and legitimate title, and by hereditary succession, have been possessing and still possess a portion of lands with a communal character, they administer them, work them and take advantage of them quietly and peacefully. The titles for these lands show . . . that the . . . current possessor bought them. Despite this, the community, as the sole owner of these lands has been perturbed and bothered in its quiet and peaceful possession, because the owners of adjacent lands have established legal proceedings, which while being unjust have caused them [the ladino Community] great damages for lack of a legal representative that will protect their rights. The Indian communities of Ahuachapán and the community of ladinos of the city of Santa Ana possess land in common, like Chalchuapa and other many pueblos of the Republic and . . . the community of ladinos of Chalchuapa together with the Municipal Council wants to obtain the same approval.[24]

Community leaders pleaded for their specific needs while also asking the government for its support and protection in general. As well as claiming the legality of their case they referred to the larger principle of communal landownership as practiced by many other Indian and ladino communities throughout the country. In fact, their legal defense encouraged the Dueñas regime to clarify (and extend) the legal status of community landholding throughout the Republic.

In a second letter, the Community defended itself from the attacks made against it by people from Santa Ana who sought control over Chalchuapa's unused lands because of their suitability for coffee production. In this letter, the Community not only defended the legitimacy of communal land tenure but also trumpeted the independent traditions of ethnic communities and their efforts toward subsistence and reproduction. It is ironic that they couched their defense of communal land tenure partially in the terms of the same liberalism that would be used decades later to dissolve communal and municipal land tenure:

It is known publicly that since the first ladinos, in small numbers and a century ago, their families began to increase until the state in which they find themselves today in this town; and in the same way they have been accumulating and acquiring gradually with the fruit of their industrious work the lands which they now occupy under the name of community and which they urgently need for their subsistence. . . . The lands of this community of said ladinos acquired with their own income and with the effort of their industry came to cause the envy of some badly intentioned men to the point that they denounced in the press that the possession of these lands was illegal because it was owned by the public treasury, and then the attacked parties considered that it would be sufficient to respond to them in the same newspaper and without any fear, since they rested upon the legality of their titles and in the notoriety of the events themselves. . . . What is more, the Treasury prosecutor perhaps while struggling with his kind sentiments and impulses and merely having to carry out his duty has established a claim in court requesting that the lands of the community of this town be sold in public auction in favor of the treasury.[25]

The confrontation between the Chalchuapeño peasants and their upwardly mobile neighbors from Santa Ana went beyond the legal and

TABLE I   Chalchuapa's Communal Lands, c. 1870, in Cabellerías

Locality	Extension
Ranchador	9
Rosario	8
San José	13
Ayutepeque	20
Malacara	9
Arado	13
Guachipilín	11

Source: *El Constitucional*, 2, no. 64 (January 10, 1867).

judicial channels established by the state and spilled over into the press. A public debate carried out in the official newspaper and other publications provides a useful window into the success as well as the problems associated with the expansion of coffee production in the ladino Community of Chalchuapa. The official government newspaper of January 10, 1867, published a description of the community's success in expanding its holdings. It reported that coffee was being produced by all social classes and that some community lands were rented to outsiders. The report describes the various plots held by the community, a total of eighty-three caballerías (5,312 *manzanas*, a manzana being equivalent to 1.7 acres). The community had 2,648 manzanas cultivated by local members, whereas it rented out only 583 to outsiders. Table 1 lists the various properties owned by the ladino Community.

On February 14 of the same year an extensive letter by two ladinos from Chalchuapa addressed to the National Assembly and entitled "Bienes de comunidad" (Community property) responded to an article critical of communal possession that had appeared in *Faro Salvadoreño*. In a language again reminiscent of Indian defense of community, the ladino authors cited the legitimate possession of their lands since before independence:

The Spanish government which saw us as its tenants, and as a spoils of its conquests, respected these communities: after our independence from the Federal government, the community of Chalchuapa's lands have been protected: once divided into sections the supreme magistrate of the Republic of El Salvador, has continued to protect this community, always respecting the right of property and acquisition guaranteed by all the laws, because in all the learned and civilized governments, the first duty of the supreme magistrate is to protect the person and goods of its inhabitants, do the best possible for them and avoid any damage to them.

The letter goes on to proclaim Chalchuapa's agrarian successes even before the recent expansion of coffee cultivation. It mentions the town's export of grains to nearby localities and calls for the defense of all small farmers by the government: "When agriculture is exercised in general by the rich and proletarians, why should there be no protection for the middle class in its agricultural properties?" The authors expressed their defense clearly in terms of the rights of family-based farmers: "That a poor man be industrious: that with the sweat of his brow and helped by his family, he cultivate the fields and with his manual labor he may ascend to the level of property owner; it is a virtue." The letter next celebrates the ladino Community's attitude toward agriculture and outsiders:

Chalchuapa is with its arms open for all those who want to move into its land: it esteems progress very much and it is a firm sentinel of order and law. . . . Chalchuapa loves its tenants. . . . The Indian class, has sold the most flowering part of its lands to some gentlemen from the city of Santa Ana, and these new purchasers have found in Chalchuapa, workers, security, and contributors for their agricultural enterprises. . . . Men from other towns and residents of other republics are possessing some of the communal lands, and the other communards say nothing about such purchases. Because there is no selfishness and there are no other ideas but those of progress and growth.

Finally, the authors requested that the National Assembly respect both communal property and encourage agriculture by additional means, such as the creation of a national Junta de Fomento (Economic Development Council). Later that month the mayor of Chalchuapa published a municipal decree stating that Chalchuapa would be willing to sell part of its communal lands located toward the South in Las Joyas, Guachipilín, Zacamil, and Jocotillo—more than 2,000 manzanas—to farmers from Santa Ana. The lands being offered for sale to the Santanecos were those the ladino Community had bought earlier from the Indian Community.[26]

The defense by the Community was followed by a new attack in *Faro Salvadoreño* criticizing the content and style of the Chalchuapeño article. The Santanecos brought in a new element to the conflict—the clash between peasant and elite language and discourses: "It is not our desire to establish an unequal polemic with the know-it-all writers who have read political economy, who speak of philosophy and literature, and who want to say *frijol* instead of *fréjol* which is how it appears in the Dictionary of the Language of Castille." But the Santanecos did not stop at trying to ridicule the Chalchuapeños' attempt at literacy and knowledgeable discourse for speaking of economic development and their role within it. The Santanecos who authored the attack on the community went on to claim, among other things, that the community did not have legal title and that it monopolized precious resources—"that they do not eat or let others eat," a critique that reflected the multiclass basis of the Santaneco's challenge to Chalchuapa's resources.[27]

In March, Basilio Maroquín, one of the two Chalchuapeño authors of the letter quoted earlier, published a more extensive tract in which he celebrated the rustic style of the report on Chalchuapa's agriculture published a few months earlier in the same newspaper. But he also sarcastically exposed the very same plebeian origins of one of Santa Ana's upwardly mobile challengers, who, he stated, "has not read nor does he even know the book covers of the flock of Frenchified economists, gringos, Germans and Spaniards, whose names are difficult to pronounce and hurt the ear of the poor people of Chalchuapa, but whom without doubt are sonorous to the Santanecos accustomed as they are to the foreign pronunciations which they have learned in the classrooms of Santa Lucia, the Volcán and Texistepeque."[28] Challenging the Santanecos' pretensions of higher knowledge by exposing their peasant and Indian roots (Santa Lucia, the Volcán, Texistepeque) allowed the author to reveal the basis of the Santanecos' motivations and apparent greed. Maroquín also defended the legal right of the community to own lands, stating that any attack on its rights would be promptly repulsed with violence. He also challenged the claims made by the Santanecos about Chalchuapa's tenants, stating that many of the community's tenants were from Santa Ana and that quite a few others utilized lands in Chalchuapa without paying for them.

The Chalchuapeños won their claim in court but part of the result was that they, willingly but under pressure, facilitated the rental of portions of their substantial lands to outsiders. The commune declared a more open policy of rentals in part to offset the pressure from Santaneco interests who were opposed to their control over such extensive lands but also as a means of securing greater income for the community. The Chalchuapeños explained that previously the commune did not want to lease lands for the production of coffee and other "important" crops to those who were not local residents, but that "they changed their minds, because they are fully convinced of the error in which they lived, and, although late, they want to mend it, offering their lands to all who would want to occupy them with coffee groves." In exchange for this concession, Community administrators requested the end of all legal proceedings against their community; the acknowledgment of the legality of their land titles; and the increase of local rental and tax revenues that could be used to pay for repairs to the local church, the town's school teacher, and expansion of the town's water supply system. Although the fear of their losing lands was one important reason for this reversal, the policy of more open access to untilled land extended the economic success of the Community during the next decade.[29]

Coffee and Capitalism in Chalchuapa

At the same time that the Community was debating and negotiating the terms of its existence, a boom in the local economy allowed many local ladinos to form new coffee and sugar farms. In 1867, before the further opening of their lands to Santanecos, the ladino peasants were reported to have "great coffee groves, food plantings, sugar cane fields. . . . everybody worked, and even the poorest people had their plantings of coffee." Chalchuapa, the writer of the article thought, provided the model for the country's development, a model based on government support for the efforts of poor producers to keep their lands while expanding their participation in commercial agriculture.[30]

Over the next twenty years Chalchuapa became one of the most productive and commercially successful municipalities in Santa Ana. It also became one of the largest national centers of coffee production. In 1859 Chalchuapa had only about 2 percent of all the productive coffee trees in the country and in 1862 it produced about 14 percent of the sugar in the departments of Santa Ana and Ahuachapán. By 1876, however, its production had dramatically increased to one-third of the department of Santa Ana's coffee and 28 percent of its sugar. It had also enlarged

TABLE 2   Coffee Production in the Department of Santa Ana,
1877–1881, in Quintals

Year	Production
1860	2,000
1876	31,800
1877	55,000
1878	85,000
1879	130,000
1880	145,000
1881	175,000
1915	186,000

Source: *El Constitucional*, December 31, 1876, p. 787; *Diario Oficial*,
May 11, 1882, p. 546; Gobernador de Santa Ana, "Datos para el anuario
americano," 1916, AGN-CM-MG.

its production of cattle and hogs.[31] By 1883 Chalchuapa held 44 percent
of all the coffee trees in the department of Santa Ana.[32] This required
approximately 2,500 hectares of land planted in coffee—the second-
largest extension for any municipality in the country, the largest being
the adjacent municipality of Santa Ana. (See table 2 for changes in coffee production during the period of 1877 to 1881.)

The early effects of commercial production are also reflected in the
large percentage (60 percent) of Chalchuapa's residents classified as *jornaleros* (day laborers) in 1859, the highest for the western region outside
of Santa Ana city. Nine years later this figure had increased slightly,
to 62 percent.[33] Although it is likely that, as was the case throughout
the republic, the men classified as jornaleros still had access to ejido or
community lands, their relative predominance when compared to other
municipalities is a sign of the greater development of commercial agriculture in Chalchuapa and the differentiation that began to emerge
from it. But despite this early trend toward proletarianization, the success of Chalchuapa's commercial agriculture had a mixed effect: it provided wage work for many residents, but it did not detach most from
the land, creating instead a hierarchy of producers in which only a few
were fully marginalized as full-time wageworkers.

The Privatization of Community Lands and the Peasantry

As a result of the increasing development of commercial farming in
El Salvador, the National Assembly decreed the abolition of all forms
of municipal and community lands. Beginning in 1881 all possessors
of ejido and community lands would be required to title and privatize
their plots. As a result of this legislation and its enactment by municipal governments and communal administrators during the 1880s and
1890s, most of the country's common lands passed to private hands. Although it is difficult to generalize about the effects of this complex and
extended process, it can be stated safely that it provided for the creation
of a landed peasantry as well as for the successful appropriation of lands
by investors and larger landowners.[34]

However, in the years before these national privatization decrees
Chalchuapa had taken intermediate steps in the direction of privatizing
lands. The extensive development of sugar and coffee farming there before the 1880s had led to the practice of long-term rental and possession
of plots by farmers and peasants. Rental contracts with the community
were often for ten years, and by the 1870s the sale of possession rights to
specific plots was an accepted practice.[35] Because both sugar and coffee
required long-term possession of plots (coffee because of the longevity
of the trees and their delay in producing berries, sugar because of the
need for the total clearing of plots), the tendency among Chalchuapa's
ejidal and communal tenants was to hold their plots as virtual private
property well before common forms of land tenure were broken up and
privatized by national law.[36] But during the 1870s the use and allocation
of Chalchuapa's communal lands were in a state of flux; the community
still held unused lands and was receiving many new settlers.

After the privatization decrees of the early 1880s all communities and
municipalities had to sell their lands to possessors or else in public auction. The ladino Community of Chalchuapa encountered difficulties
similar to those experienced by other nearby Indian communities in this
process of surveying and titling plots. The process in Chalchuapa and
throughout the nation spanned various presidencies, exacerbated divisions and factionalism within the communities, and involved technical
difficulties in surveying plots and solving disputes over boundaries. Although the Ministry of the Interior announced in 1883 that the Com-

munity of Chalchuapa had ceased to exist and that the possessors of communal lands had all received titles to their plots, nevertheless we find that eight years later there were many *comuneros* taking advantage of a decree that again called for distribution and privatization of communal lands that had not been processed under the 1880 law.[37]

In general the division and titling of the larger communal lands of Chalchuapa was a fragmented process in which there was no centralized communal representation. Chalchuapa's own economic success and the reliance upon intensive coffee and sugar production contributed to this trend. Most of Chalchuapa's peasants, farmers, and capitalist investors were able to privatize their holdings without major problems or controversies, at times holding out for years before even titling their lots in order not to spend money on the transaction itself. In some cases groups of peasants who had settled parts of the Community's lands encountered problems in titling their plots, which led to a plethora of petitions to local and national administrative and judicial authorities. These requests had begun in the 1880s and continued into the 1890s, when they began to obtain results. In these cases it was questions relating to the original titles and status of the communal lands that delayed the process for years.

The period of land privatization constituted another stage in the struggle among peasants, and between peasants and larger landowners, to secure access to land and effective participation in commercial production. The residents of one significant plot of land that had been part of Chalchuapa's ladino Community provide an example of the obstacles and successes that peasants encountered in their attempts to provide security for themselves. In 1892 135 comuneros who resided in El Ranchador requested individual titles to their plots from the government. Their lands had already been surveyed and divided sometime after 1889 when they were authorized to title the 403 hectares in individual plots.[38] Another petition by ninety-seven comuneros from both El Ranchador and Sitio del Niño requested titles to six caballerías. The survey of these lands had been carried out that same year by Francisco Cáceres and had received the approval of the governor of Santa Ana.[39]

But an investor from Santa Ana, Teodoro Mendoza, had denounced the Sitio del Niño lands as state-owned *baldíos* (unused lands). This dispute led the Ministry of the Interior to review the status of the lands in 1893 and issue a decree on their fate. After having the lands surveyed, the ministry acknowledged that all the lands in question had been communal but were now considered national property because the period for titling plots was long past. The ministry explained that the lands formerly belonged to the Hacienda Comecayo but had been sold in 1780 to the ladino Community of Chalchuapa. An 1824 trial had led to the transfer of the lands to the community until the hacienda's missing titles reappeared. It was determined that El Ranchador was composed of three *sitios:* La Mora, El Pinal, and Niño Dios. The lands denounced as *baldíos* were in Niño Dios.

The peasant possessors accused the governor of ordering the mayor not to title the lands within the stipulated time frame so that they could have Teodoro Mendoza denounce the lands as empty state lands and then sell them back to him. The ministry found that portions of these lands remained undivided and that they had been communal but had not been titled by their possessors. The governor of Santa Ana was then authorized to sell the already distributed parts to the possessors, while the undistributed and unused parts would be sold in public auction as a whole or in lots. The money was to be used for the construction of the new theater in Santa Ana city.[40] Peasants who were in clear possession of their lands were still able to secure title to their plots, but an important portion of lands that had been communal were lost to speculators.

In a similar 1893 conflict two large landowners from Santa Ana opposed the titling of two plots within the lands possessed and claimed by the ex-comuneros. Doña Petrona de Regalado, member of a wealthy family and wife of soon-to-be president General Regalado, opposed the titling of the fourteen-hectare lot no. 177. She claimed that it and a few other plots were part of the Hacienda Ayuta, which she owned. She called for a hearing to solve the dispute. Another wealthy landowner, Alfredo Schlesinger, opposed the titling of plot no. 167, claiming that its eighteen hectares had been his since 1882 when he titled them as ejidales. He also asked for a hearing. In this case, however, the governor ruled against both landowners and fined them fifteen pesos each for obstructing the partition process. Litigation could work in favor of peasant claims as well.

Yet the departmental governor, Preza, was not entirely sympathetic to the peasants of Chalchuapa. In 1894 twenty-one peasants filed a complaint against him. Like many others, the peasants were originally from other towns but had resided on Chalchuapa's communal lands for decades. They accused the governor of destroying an earlier petition for titles and of threatening them with imprisonment. Their previous petition originated over the fact that they had seen notices in the official newspaper for the titling of lands they considered their own, and they had wanted to register their opposition to these claims within the stipulated period of fifteen days. The owner of Ayuta, Sra. de Regalado, was also involved in this dispute. She had complained that lands from her hacienda had been appropriated in the survey and titling of plots within El Ranchador. She claimed that those who had titled these lands had not been in possession of them until after the surveyor had carried out the measure and division.[41]

Another group of peasants representing fifty families and more than 300 people presented an additional complaint in 1894. The six caballerías they possessed had come from lands owned by the Cofradía San José de Chalchuapa, which had come under the control of the ladino Community during the early nineteenth century. Their families had possessed these lands for forty years, but the lands had been recently declared state property because they had not been divided and titled in the 1880 to 1882 period. The petitioners had in fact claimed the lands and had them surveyed, and a map of the lots was prepared. But a local resident and her son attempted to take these lands, claiming that they had registered a previous request.

Yet another request in 1894 by seventy-six residents of El Ranchador explained to the Ministry of the Interior that they had already spent 12,000 pesos carrying out three surveys of their lands under three different presidential administrations but had still not obtained their titles. When they finally received their titles, they were taken for review by the governor and then finally sent to the president for approval. In their request that the titles be finally returned to them, these peasants and farmers emphasized the legitimacy of their claim by stating that they planted mostly sugar and coffee—valuable export crops promoted by the government.

There had also been an earlier attempt to attach these same lands to the nearby Hacienda Comecayo. In 1887 when Anselma Linares de Arcia—widow of a local official and landowner from Santa Ana city— and her daughters requested the "judiciary" sale of the hacienda, presumably for debts, their real goal was the attachment of the lands of the ladino Community.[42] She had also made a similar attempt in 1876.[43]

That time the original titles of the community and *cofradías* (sodalities) had been examined and the claim rejected. There had even been an earlier proposal by speculators during the 1860s to have these lands declared baldíos. Another request that these lands be declared baldíos was filed by peasant tenants of the Hacienda Comecayo, but was also rejected by the government.

At the end of this drawn-out process the ministry provided an astounding interpretation of the crisscrossing claims and complaints regarding parts of the disputed lands of El Ranchador. The 9.5 caballerías of land were within the 65 caballerías of the Hacienda Comecayo. These had been sold to a cofradía in Chalchuapa, but during the early nineteenth century a conflict emerged over four of these caballerías. Since the hacienda's titles had been lost or the claim by the new owners was spurious and thus could not be proven, the lands were left in possession of the cofradía until new evidence emerged. The ministry concluded that the lands were

not ejidal, communal or baldío, but that they originally belonged to Betancur and later the *cófrades;* that given the lack of any proof that the cofradía has sold this property neither the municipality nor the communards can be considered its owners, nor possessors but if anything its tenants. . . . That the partition of 13 July 1893 of those lands as communal is not legal for they do not belong to any community; that the transaction of 1835 is not legal because the communards were not legal participants; the lands do not belong to the nation because there is no law to declare them as such . . . since they were never communal and cannot pass now to the nation; that this property that used to belong to the cofradía is now the property of the respective Church.

Surprisingly, it was the church, which usually was not a participant in processes of this kind, that found itself favored by the government's ruling. Although we do not know what practical result this decision had for either the peasants, the church, or other claimants, it is not likely that any entrenched possessors were ever dislodged from their plots.[44]

Despite the conflicted process that involved dozens of peasant landholders, however, the bulk of the evidence on the demise of Chalchuapa's communal lands indicates that the majority of smallholders successfully titled their lands without major problems or conflicts. Most of the peasants there who were in possession of plots had been tenants or members of the ladino Community or both. Taking into account the

extension of the communal lands of Chalchuapa, the decades of possession, and the purchase of new lands, most peasants did not lose access
to their lands. After all, they had a decades-old and successful history
of land possession. But the preceding discussion shows that when legal
documentation for plots was nonexistent or ambiguous, or plots bordered haciendas, or substantial portions of lands had been rented to
"outside" farmers and peasants, the potential for conflicts and disputes
was greater and could sometimes lead to the dispossession of peasant
landholders.

It is important to remember that during the 1890s El Salvador's
agrarian frontier was not yet closed. During these years large extensions of land were being claimed and settled by people of different
classes. Even in Chalchuapa, lands that had never been claimed were
being opened up for settlement or sale, including portions reserved for
poor settlers. The government reserved thirty caballerías for use by poor
peasants in 1889.[45]

Chalchuapa Enters the Twentieth Century

By the 1890s Chalchuapa's character had changed significantly from the
1860s. In the minister of the interior's yearly report of 1893 the municipality was described in these terms:

[It] has a lot of commerce, especially with Guatemala, from where they buy
large amounts of grains and basic subsistence items especially during the coffee
harvesting season, this being the main source of wealth of all this region. . . .
[there is] an absence of the labor required to give it a greater push and to regu-
late the wages, there is a need to enforce the fulfillment of labor contracts contracted by day laborers . . . because otherwise, this state will lead to the demor-
alization of the working class and the state of agriculture will inevitably suffer.[46]

The report also pointed out the significant profits made from coffee,
tobacco, sugar, and grains, while noting a decline in the traditional activity of cattle raising. Although stock raising made a relative comeback
in the years that followed, it never became as important as it once was.[47]
But what this description exposes most strikingly is the transition from
a focus on community and land acquisition issues to questions of labor
discipline and wages.

TABLE 3   Largest Coffee Farms in Chalchuapa, 1910

Name/Owner	Trees	Production (Quintals)	Est. Cultivated Land (Hectares)
San Juan	20,000	400	14
Santa Isabel	40,000	600	28
Santa Sofía	15,000	200	11
San José	10,800	800	8
El Porvenir	30,000	200	21
I. Palacios	30,000	300	21
A. Pacas	36,000	600	25
El Ciprés	36,000	600	25
Mala Cara	30,000	500	21
El Matazano	21,000	200	15
San Jorge	36,000	400	25
San Jorge	27,000	500	19
San José	38,400	700	27
Loma Paja	45,000	400	32
F. Herrera	15,000	100	11
G. Vides	42,000	800	30
C. Lemus	75,000	3,500	53
Santa María	16,000	500	12
Santa María	15,000	300	11
Santa Teresa	27,000	400	19
La Victoria	14,000	200	10

Source: Santiago I. Barbarena, *Monografías departamentales: departamento de Santa Ana* (San Salvador: n.p., 1910), 41–42.

During this period the town's population also grew dramatically. By 1910 Chalchuapa's population had expanded to over 20,000, and in 1916 was estimated at nearly 30,000.[48] This increase took place despite the loss of various neighborhoods and haciendas that were separated into smaller municipalities during the 1880s.[49] The town's social structure also reflected the expanded role of commercial agriculture, but still in a complex manner. Although the number of jornaleros (988) had increased by 1898, so had the number of small and medium landowners (499) and artisans (230).[50] In 1910 small and medium producers still had

TABLE 4   Size Distribution of Chalchuapa's Coffee Farms, 1931

Range, in Manzanas	Number	% of Total Farms
More than 75	25	9
25 to 75	44	17
Fewer than 25	197	74

Source: "Nomina de los cafetaleros en los municipios del departamento de Santa Ana," July 1931, AGN-CM-MG.

an important role in this municipality. While still not very large, the largest farms (eight to twenty-three hectares in production) together produced around 12,200 quintals (about 20 percent) of a total of 52,450 quintals in 1910 (see table 3).[51] The remaining 40,000 quintals were produced by medium and smaller farms, *of which there were hundreds*. In the municipality of Santa Ana, by contrast, a few of the largest farms accounted *for more than half* of all production. And Chalchuapa remained a major producer of sugar and corn as well.[52] As late as 1931, two years after the beginning of El Salvador's coffee crisis, which accelerated the absorption of smaller plots by larger landowners and merchants, Chalchuapa's landowning structure still reflected the preponderance of small units of production. That year 74 percent of all the registered farms were smaller than twenty-five manzanas (see table 4).

Conclusion

The town of Chalchuapa experienced important changes in the hundred years or so between the 1770s and the 1890s. The transformation of this town from an Indian-controlled communally administered cattle-raising district to a major center of peasant and farmer coffee production on privately owned farms of various sizes was not an easy or conflict-free process. Nonetheless, although those peasants, farmers, and investors who struggled with each other or outside forces did not all compete as equals, the playing field was sufficiently complex and unpredictable that all actors sought some benefits in changes that as a whole were perhaps out of their individual control. Most of Chalchuapa's peasants and farmers did not continue to enjoy the benefits offered by a community-centered life, but most of them were able to successfully navigate the transition to private landownership and to continue the town's tradition of combining the production of sugar and coffee with food products.

Perhaps the greatest implications of these transformations were political. Chalchuapa's peasantry would no longer be able to mobilize a shared sense of identity and a series of established local resources in defense of local individual or collective interests. Ultimately, the major beneficiary of this process was the national state, which during the 1880s and 1890s had begun to centralize its power and define more clearly what it meant to be Salvadoran. It would come to benefit from the decline of the peasantry's ability to mobilize in the name of local collectivist solidarities and identities. Individual private landowners ultimately made better citizens in a liberal polity.

Notes

The research on which this essay is based was supported by a Department of Education Fulbright-Hays Dissertation Fellowship, an SSRC-ACLS Dissertation Research Fellowship, and a Ford Foundation Minority Dissertation Fellowship. Faculty Development Grants from the New School for Social Research and College of the Holy Cross also assisted the organization of research materials. My thanks go also to Avi Chomsky, Steven Topik, and Ingrid Vargas for their useful suggestions and criticisms.

1. The term *ladino* refers to Indians who had distanced themselves from their native communities and had taken on the dress and language of Spaniards and their descendants or to people who were the product of unions between Indians and other ethnic groups such as whites or Africans. Often it was used as well to refer generically to all non-Indians. See Severo Martínez Peláez, *La patria del criollo* (San José: EDUCA, 1973), 701, n. 59, and Arturo Taracena Arriola, "Contribución al estudio del vocablo 'ladino' en Guatemala (S. XVI–XIX)," in *Historia y antropología: ensayos en honor de J. Daniel Contreras*, compiled by Jorge Luján Muñoz (Guatemala: Facultad de Humanidades, USAC, 1982), 89–104.

2. For the most often cited and classic statements on the agrarian history of El Salvador, see David Browning, *El Salvador: Landscape and Society* (Oxford, England: Clarendon, 1971), and Rafael Menjívar, *Acumulación originaria y desarrollo del capitalismo en El Salvador* (San José: EDUCA, 1980; 2d ed. 1995). Héctor Lindo Fuentes initiated a critical revision of many of the accepted assumptions about the country's macroeconomic history: *Weak Foundations: The Economy of El Salvador in the Nineteenth Century* (Berkeley: University of Cali-

fornia Press, 1990). For a recent restatement that reproduces the classic view, see Robert G. Williams, *States and Social Evolution: Coffee and the Rise of National Governments in Central America* (Chapel Hill: University of North Carolina Press, 1995).

3. Perhaps the best and most significant exception is the work by David McCreery on Guatemala (*Rural Guatemala, 1760–1940* [Stanford, Calif.: Stanford University Press, 1994]). For other recent considerations of peasant and Indian landholding, see Jeffrey Gould, " '¡Vana Ilusion!' The Highlands Indians and the Myth of Nicaragua Mestiza, 1880–1925," this volume, and Elizabeth Dore, "Coffee, Land and Class Relations in Nicaragua, 1870–1920," *Journal of Historical Sociology*, 8, no. 3 (September 1995): 303–326.

4. During the nineteenth century, a few key fields in Chalchuapa became important battle sites for the cross-border and factional confrontations of the period. Among the more influential battles that took place there was the confrontation between Guatemalan troops under President Barrios and Salvadoran forces after Barrios attempted to force the political unity of the isthmus in 1885. Barrios was killed in this battle. See El Salvador, Dirección de Patrimonio Cultural, Departamento de Historia, *Chalchuapa* (San Salvador: Ministerio de Educación, 1985); Gregorio Bustamante, *Historia militar de El Salvador* (San Salvador: Talleres Gráficos Cisneros, 1935); and Pedro Zamora Castellanos, *Vida militar de Centro América,* 2 vols. (Guatemala City: Editorial del Ejército, 1966–1967).

5. See Pedro Cortés y Larraz, *Descripción geográfico-moral de la diócesis de Goathemala* (1771; reprinted Guatemala: Sociedad de Geografía e Historia de Guatemala, 1958), and the *respuestas* (priest's reports) provided to Cortés y Larraz reproduced in Santiago Montes, *Etnohistoria de El Salvador,* vol. 2 (San Salvador: n.p., n.d.).

6. For classic and recent sources on indigo production in Central America, see Robert S. Smith, "Forced Labor in the Guatemalan Indigo Works," *Hispanic American Historical Review,* 36, no. 3 (August 1956): 319–328, and his "Indigo Production and Trade in Colonial Guatemala," *Hispanic American Historical Review* 39, no. 2 (May 1959): 181–211; and José Antonio Fernández Molina, "Colouring the World in Blue: The Indigo Boom and the Central American Market, 1750–1810" (Ph.D. dissertation, University of Texas, Austin, 1992).

7. Troy S. Floyd, "Los comerciantes guatemaltecos, el gobierno y los provincianos, 1750–1800," *Cuadernos de Antropología,* 8 (1968): 33; Julio César Pinto Soria, *Raíces históricas del estado en Centroamérica* (Guatemala: Editorial Universitaria de Guatemala, 1983), 122, n. 234; Domingo Juarros, *Compendio de la historia del Reino de Guatemala, 1500–1800* (Guatemala: Editorial Piedra Santa, 1818; reprinted 1981), 21.

8. José María Ots Capdequí, *España en América: el régimen de tierras en la*

época colonial (Mexico City: Fondo de Cultura Económica, 1959); "Título ejidal de Chalchuapa," [1755] 1866; Francisco de Solano, "Tierra, comercio y
sociedad: un análisis de la estructura social agraria centroamericana durante el
siglo XVIII," *Revista de Indias,* 31 (July–December 1971): 311–365.

9. Aldo Lauria-Santiago, "An Agrarian Republic: Production, Politics, and
the Peasantry in El Salvador, 1740–1920" (Ph.D. dissertation, University of
Chicago, 1992), chap. 4.

10. Rafael Barón Castro, *La población de El Salvador* (San Salvador: UCA
Editores, 1942; rev. ed. 1978); Manuel de Gálvez, *Relación geográfica de la pro-
vincia de El Salvador (1740)* (San Salvador: Archivo General de la Nación [cited
hereafter as AGN], folleto num. 27, 1966); Cortés y Larraz, *Descripción geográfico-moral.*

11. Murdo J. Macleod, *Spanish Central America: A Socioeconomic History, 1520–
1720* (Berkeley: University of California Press, 1973).

12. "Estado que demuestra los nacidos, muertos y casamientos habidos en el
departamento de Santa Ana," January 2, 1865, AGN-CC, MI.5(865) exp. #4.

13. *El Constitucional,* January 10, 1867; Lorenzo López, *Estadística general
de la República del Salvador* (1858; reprinted San Salvador: Imprenta Nacional,
1974), 47.

14. "Solicitud de la municipalidad de Chalchuapa al Supremo Poder Ejecutivo," 1867, AGN-CDM, rollo BN-29.

15. There is little data available on the three privately owned haciendas of
Chalchuapa. One of these haciendas was separated from Chalchuapa during
the 1880s and came to form the core of the municipality of El Progreso. Santiago I. Barbarena, *Monografías departamentales: departamento de Santa Ana*
(San Salvador: n.p., 1910).

16. See Lauria-Santiago, "An Agrarian Republic," chaps. 3 and 4.

17. "Diligencias seguidas por los cofrades del Señor San José con respecto a
recuperar las tierras del cantón Ayutepeque pertenecientes al común de ladinos
del pueblo de Chalchuapa," 1809–1814, AGN.

18. "Título ejidal de Chalchuapa," typescript, 1755, renewed 1866; "Inter-
dicto de posesión de un terreno contra la municipalidad de Atiquizaya por los
Señores Aniceto Sifuentes y María Santos," AGN-CG-AH, 1864; "Juicio civil
entre el Sr. Pantaleón Rodríguez y la municipalidad de Atiquizaya por des-
pojo de un terreno," AGN-CG-AH, 1864; and "Diligencia en que consta estar
arreglada la cuestión de límites entre El Progreso y Chalchuapa," AGN-CM-
MG, 1896.

19. López, *Estadística general,* 46.

20. "Informe de la comisión del Supremo Gobierno para visitar los pueblos
de la República," *Gaceta Oficial,* 9, no. 24 (November 7, 1860): 4.

21. "Carta de los vecinos de Chalchuapa al SPE denunciando que la muni-

cipalidad pretende quitarles los terrenos de su comunidad de ladinos," July 11, 1867, AGN-CPC. The title of this document is misleading because it was not the municipality but the national government that was pursuing payment of this debt.

22. Gobernador de Santa Ana, "Carta al ministro del interior," April 26, 1867, AGN-CDM, rollo BN-28.

23. This scheme was only revealed and complained about after Dueñas was overthrown by General Santiago González. Gobernador de Santa Ana, "Carta al ministro del interior sobre elecciones en Chalchuapa," February 6, 1871, AGN-CDM, rollo BN-37.

24. "Solicitud de los ladinos de Chalchuapa al SPE," March 25, 1867, AGN-CQ.

25. "Carta de los vecinos de Chalchuapa al SPE denunciando que la municipalidad pretende quitarles los terrenos de su comunidad de ladinos," July 11, 1867, AGN-CPC.

26. *El Constitucional*, February 28, 1867, p. 1.

27. *El Constitucional*, February 14, 1867, p. 1. "That they do not eat or let others eat" derives from the saying "Como el perro del hortelano," the dog that guards the farm so well he does not eat or let others eat.

28. *El Constitucional*, March 14, 1867, p. 1.

29. "Solicitud de los ladinos de Chalchuapa al SPE," 1867, AGN-CDM, rollo BN-27.

30. *El Constitucional*, January 10, 1867.

31. López, *Estadística general*, 72–73; *Gaceta Oficial*, April 12, 1862; and *Gaceta Oficial*, December 31, 1876, p. 787.

32. Adán Mora, *Memoria del Ministerio de Gobernación y Fomento (1883)* (San Salvador: Imprenta Nacional, 1884), 58.

33. *El Constitucional*, June 6, 1867.

34. For a detailed discussion of this process see Lauria-Santiago, "An Agrarian Republic," chaps. 5 and 6.

35. *Actas municipales, 1870–1883* AMC; *Actas de la comunidad de ladinos, 1870–1883* AMC; *Libro de registros de terrenos, 1870–1884* AMC.

36. Adán Mora, *Memoria del Ministerio de Gobernación y Fomento* (1885) (San Salvador: Imprenta Nacional, 1886), 135.

37. Ibid., 41.

38. José Larreynaga, *Memoria de los actos del poder ejecutivo en el ramo de Gobernación durante el año de 1889* (San Salvador: Imprenta Nacional, 1890), 133.

39. "Copia de los expedientes de titulación de los terrenos comunales Ranchador y Sitio del Niño en Chalchuapa," 1894, AGN-CM-MG.

40. "Libro de acuerdos del Ministerio de Gobernación," 1893, AGN-CM-MG.

41. "Copia de los expedientes de titulación de los terrenos comunales Ranchador y Sitio del Niño en Chalchuapa," 1892, AGN-CM-MG.

42. Her husband had been killed in the 1871 land-related revolt of the Volcán de Santa Ana ladino peasant community. See Lauria-Santiago, "An Agrarian Republic," chap. 8.

43. "Incidente de apelación del juicio ejecutivo promovido por doña Anselma Linares de Arcia contra la comunidad de ladinos de Chalchuapa, para que se le entreguen unos terrenos," 1876, AGN-CT, sección/caja 3.

44. "Copia de los expedientes de titulación de los terrenos comunales Ranchador y Sitio del Niño en Chalchuapa," 1894, AGN-CM-MG.

45. "Tránsito Lagúan de Chalchuapa pide terrenos para avecindarse en La Soledad," AGN-CG-AH, 1889.

46. El Salvador, *Memoria presentada por el ministro de gobernación, guerra y marina doctor Domingo Jiménez a la Asamblea Nacional (1892)* (San Salvador: Imprenta Nacional, 1893), 85.

47. Miguel Escamilla, *Geografía económica de la República de El Salvador* (San Salvador: Imprenta Meléndez, 1908); Juan Francisco Castro, *Geografía elemental Salvador* (San Salvador: Tipografía La Union, 1905).

48. Gobernador de Santa Ana, "Datos para el anuario americano," December 2, 1916, AGN-CM-MG; and Barbarena, *Monografías . . . Santa Ana.*

49. In 1886 one large hacienda was made into its own municipality (San Sebastián) and eventually turned into smaller farms owned by Santa Ana investors. Another town, El Porvenir, was established in 1883 from cantones that had belonged to Chalchuapa and two other *cantones* (neighborhoods) were incorporated into the city of Santa Ana itself. In all likelihood, these included the lands that were rented and then privatized by investors from Santa Ana.

50. These numbers are taken from a local tax list in which small landholders benefited from declaring themselves jornaleros in order to pay a lower tax. "Lista de impuestos," AGS, 1898–1903.

51. Barbarena, *Monografías . . . Santa Ana,* 43.

52. L. A. Ward, ed. and comp., *Libro azul de El Salvador* (San Salvador: Bureau de Publicidad de la América Latina, 1916).

JEFFREY L. GOULD

"¡Vana Ilusión!"

The Highlands Indians and the Myth of

Nicaragua Mestiza, 1880–1925

❂

In 1908 Walter Lehmann, a German linguist, initiated fieldwork in Sutiava, Nicaragua, as part of his research project on the Indian languages
of Central America. For days he wandered through the village searching
unsuccessfully for a native speaker of the Sutiavan language. He eventually met an elderly lady, Victoria Carrillo, who offered her collaboration
in recording a vocabulary. Carrillo informed Lehmann that the other
elderly Indians had feigned ignorance because they were "ashamed of
their language."[1] A few years later, another Indian lamented that Sutiava was "without life, without character, and without a future."[2]

This image of the Sutiavan Indians on the brink of extinction as an
ethnic group captures an important aspect of a contradictory process
that affected one-half of the populations of El Salvador, Honduras,
and Nicaragua. In those Central American countries, between 1880 and
1950 the Indian populations suffered dramatic losses of land, language,
and identity. Those losses were codified in census returns that reported
the virtual disappearance of the Indians into the ladino populations.[3]
So powerful was the dominant discourse that hundreds of thousands
of Central American Indians, like the Sutiavas, became "ashamed" of
their ethnic markers, as the word *Indian* became a synonym of "ignorant" or "savage."

This article challenges Jaime Wheelock's widely accepted explanation
for the demise of the indigenous population. The pioneering social scientist underscored the loss of land and consequent proletarianization as
the principal cause of ladinoization. For Wheelock the decisive moment
in this process came in 1881, following the repression of the Matagalpan

Indian rebellion, when "the oligarchic avalanche swallowed up morsels of thousands of hectares a piece. The rupture of the communities produced the separation of the Indian from his communal parcel and threw him onto the labor market . . . converting him into a rural worker."[4] Similarly, the authors of the otherwise excellent agrarian history *Por eso defendemos la frontera* support this perspective, stating that "the indigenous communities near Jinotega and Matagalpa were destroyed . . . before the turn of the century."[5]

Despite different explanatory frameworks, Wheelock shares with traditional elite intellectuals the notion that Indians had ceased to exist in any meaningful sense by the dawn of the twentieth century.[6] Census reports have played an important role in justifying both perspectives. The 1920 Nicaraguan census, for example, showed that the indigenous population had dropped precipitously from 30 percent to under 4 percent between 1906 and 1920.[7] These statistics, however, are profoundly misleading. For the census recorded no Indians (listed as *cobrizos*, or "copper colored") in the semiurban communities of Sutiava and Masaya, which had highly visible indigenous populations. The miscount did not stop there, however; the census listed not a single cobrizo in eleven out of the remaining thirteen *Comunidades Indígenas* (communal indigenous organizations). Finally, by omission, the census assumed that some 30,000 to 40,000 *indios bravos* (wild Indians) had become ladinoized overnight.

Although the census's phenotypical category *cobrizo* included most people defined as "indígenas," biological mestizaje did not automatically affect ethnic definitions. A review of birth and other records in Boaco at the turn of the century shows that people listed as *indígenas* were often described as *trigueño* (wheat colored). If color did not define the indigenous, what did? By 1920 no Indians outside of the Atlantic coast region still spoke a native language, and few wore native dress. In order to analyze this problem, it is useful to appropriate Richard Adams's working definition for an ethnic group: "a self-reproducing collectivity identified by myths of a common provenance and by identifying markers. . . . The sociological salience of an ethnic group emerges most importantly when it is both self-identified and externally identified."[8] Our assumption is that the internal and external definitions of an Indian involved a sense of belonging to a Comunidad Indígena, institutions that have been sites of cultural, political, and economic battle throughout this century. In effect, the Comunidad evolved into the last ethnic "marker" for many Indians. Membership in a Nicaraguan Comunidad during the early decades of this century entailed notions of common provenance, land rights, religious and political autonomy, and a bitter history of conflict with ladino neighbors.[9] An approximation of the size of the indigenous population in 1920 can be obtained through a study of the same census (and election returns) for the villages that belonged to the Comunidades. Through this exercise we have arrived at an estimate of the membership of the Comunidades: between 90,000 and 125,000 people, or between 15 and 20 percent of the country's population.[10]

The Comunidad has played a defensive role similar to that of the *municipio* (municipality) and the *cofradía* (lay fraternities) in the other Central American republics. In El Salvador, in 1881, the government effectively abolished the Comunidades Indígenas and their communal land. In Nicaragua, on the contrary, the threats and realities of indigenous resistance in the context of a deeply divided political elite thwarted eight governmental attempts to abolish the Comunidades between 1877 and 1923.[11] This remarkable record of survival certainly is worthy of more than the blank page in the extant historiography.

The suppression of the ethnic dimension of contemporary Nicaraguan history reveals the power of the myth of Nicaragua mestiza. That myth emerged with the defeat of the Indian rebellion of 1881, when elites trumpeted the victory of "civilization" over indigenous "barbarism." This article analyzes how that discourse undermined highlands Indians' identity and examines their response to the undeclared war on their communal resources.[12]

The Nicaraguan elites have been criticized for their failure to construct hegemonic forms of domination. Indeed, the very disunity that allowed ethnic forms of community to develop surely blunted the elites' capacity to achieve anything approximating representative government. However, this essay does suggest that despite the elites' failure to unite, they did construct an important hegemonic form, a mirror of Nicaraguan society that reflected only the faces of mestizos.[13]

The construction of this hegemonic form involved the appropriation of racial categories that scholars have come to take for granted. Before the 1930s, all sectors of society employed the term *ladino* to refer to non-Indians or to "whites." During the same period the term *mestizo* meant the offspring of unions between Indians and whites (broadly defined). By 1950, however, *mestizo* not only had supplanted *ladino* but had become a self-description for the whole of society. This linguistic transformation symbolized the triumph of the myth of Nicaragua mestiza. Although it reflected a growing trend toward biological mestizaje, the myth also rendered spurious all claims to indigenous identity and rights. A critical understanding of its development requires a narrative history of ethnic relations, the myth's substratum. The following narrative reconstructs Matagalpan Indian-ladino relations between 1880 and 1925, the formative years of the myth of Nicaragua mestiza.

The Formation of the Matagalpan Indians

Migrations and ethnic fusions over the preceding hundred years created the Matagalpan Indians, who went on to rebel in 1881. During the early eighteenth century three *parcialidades* (lineage groups) — residents of the pueblos of Matagalpa, Molagüina, and Solingalpa — united for the purposes of purchasing a large tract of communal land. Between 1750 and 1820 these lineage-based villages apparently disbanded, and their residents moved into the nearby mountains. Although no documents specifically refer to these migrations, there is no doubt that by the 1840s the Matagalpas resided in the mountain valleys.[14] Excessive colonial tribute demands and ladino migration contributed to this apparently slow disintegration of the pueblos. In the mountains, the three parcialidades (also called barrios) formed villages or joined preexisting ones.

The Matagalpan Indians also experienced the birth of a new barrio, Laborío, composed of converted and resettled "Caribes" (probably Sumo) Indians. These Caribes also migrated into the surrounding mountains, usually into villages inhabited by the other Matagalpas. By 1816, Laborío, augmented by a flow of "reduced" Caribes, formed the largest parcialidad among the Matagalpan Indians.[15] Moreover, the barrio continued to grow at a faster rate than the other groups over the next decades; by 1841, Laborío accounted for 43 percent of all Indian births in Matagalpa.[16] The rapid growth of Laborío suggests a continuous process of integration of Caribes and a quite fluid boundary between the "civilized" and the "wild" Indians.

Throughout the nineteenth century, the four parcialidades continued to maintain a vital existence, though their members no longer inhabited specific geographical areas. Two neighbors of the *cañada* (dispersed settlement of Indians) of Samulalí, for example, might belong to the same local political structure led by a *capitán de cañada* but belong to different civil-religious hierarchies corresponding to their respective parcialidades. The religious function of the lineage groups united barrio members in different villages and thus perpetuated a basic unit of ethnic identity despite the scattering of the original populations. The elders of each lineage group appointed helpers, *regidores, priostes,* and *mayordomos* for each of seven saints. The *alcalde de vara* was at the apex of the parcialidad's religious organization; the four alcaldes also comprised the political directorate of the entire Comunidad.

The slow growth of the ladino population in the city of Matagalpa also had a significant impact on the economy of the highlands Indians well before the introduction of coffee. One writer, recalling a visit in the mid-1850s, described the Indians' economy as "impressive" and "abundant."[17] Market relations, however, between the Indians and ladinos were not harmonious. Indicative of the strained ethnic relations, during the 1860s townsfolk would travel several miles to meet Indian traders. At one point the Indians, in effect, went "on strike," refusing to sell any produce to the ladinos, "being dissatisfied with the shabby way in which the townspeople had behaved."[18] A reinforced military garrison eventually persuaded the Matagalpas to resume trade.

The missionary work of the Jesuits from 1871 to 1881 also played a major role in stimulating the ethnic pride and unity of those Indians who rebelled in 1881. The Jesuits' willingness to accept the Indians on their own terms and in their own villages contrasted notably with the practices of other ladino political and ecclesiastical authorities.[19] And the Jesuits' alliance with the Chamorrista faction of the Conservative Party in the context of the government's hostility to the order (and to the Chamorristas) added a volatile ingredient to the Indians' view of ladino authority. Moreover, the Jesuits' antidemocratic conviction—a disdain for the progressive Conservative government and for parliamentary democracy—in no way impeded their evangelical efforts among society's most marginalized groups. Indeed they had a special commitment to indigenous groups in Nicaragua. Whatever their intentions, the Jesuits contributed to the ethnic unity of the Matagalpas.

The Rebellion of the Matagalpan Indians

On March 30, 1881, some 1,000 Indians attacked the town of Matagalpa in protest against many abuses by the local authorities, in particular compulsory and underpaid labor during the building of the telegraph from Managua. The rebellion was not, as Wheelock and others have argued, directly related to coffee cultivation. In 1880, there were only 18,000 coffee trees in production.[20] Agrarian capitalism contributed to the rebellion chiefly in the form of a rumor that circulated through the Indian villages: "the government wanted to sell their children to the yanquis and take 500 women to Managua to make them pick coffee for nothing."[21]

The Jesuits' account, supported by other observers, cited in addition to conscripted labor other grievances: census taking for tax and military purposes and a prohibition against making *chicha* (a corn- and sugar-based alcoholic drink).[22] A letter to the Jesuit priest Cáceres underscored the Indians' resentment against the labor drafts: "Since these señores see that we are Indians, they want to hold us with a yoke. But today we cannot stand it any more because we are not Thieves to be carried off, tied up."[23] Following the attack on March 30, a one-day armed protest against forced labor and racism, the rebels withdrew into the mountains but did not disarm. In late May, the government, bowing to long-time pressures from Guatemala, expelled the Jesuits and blamed them for involvement in the March rebellion.[24] Provoked by the expulsion, in July 1881 some 5,000 Indians initiated a guerrilla war against the government troops. On August 9, the rebels again attacked the town of Matagalpa. After a day of fighting, government reinforcements drove them back toward the mountains, where the Indians continued to engage in armed resistance until November.

During the second phase, the rebels began to broaden their language of protest to include notions of ethnic solidarity and of an Indian "nation." Thus, one leader wrote to a sympathizer: "We consider and feel you to be at the side of your Indian Nation."[25] An Indian captain also used the term *nation* to describe the indigenous forces, in a note ordering a rancher to sell steers to his troops, "so that the nation can wage war against the enemy."[26]

General Elizondo, in charge of antirebel operations, formulated a program that would meet the threat of indigenous political autonomy by establishing "a [political] regime . . . as that of other villages." A second stage would involve a modern version of the colonial *reducción* policy: "bring [the Indians] into civilian life, making them live in towns."[27]

The general's strategy was congruent with the official view of military repression as "a struggle of civilization against barbarism, of darkness against light, of idleness against labor."[28] Similarly, government officials justified executions of Indians as part of the struggle of "civilization versus barbarism."[29] This victory of "civilization" over the Indians gave birth to the myth of Nicaragua mestiza.[30]

The defeat of the insurrection caused death, destruction, and disunity to the Comunidad. Indeed, what had been in part an expression of ethnic affirmation ended in division. The military defeat exacerbated old and created new divisions. The government reported that toward the end of the rebellion many Indians turned on their leaders. Similarly, some capitanes de cañada and their followers joined the government troops.[31] Finally, in Managua "an escort of Indians loyal to the government, armed with arrows, [brought] into custody prisoners of their caste."[32]

Nevertheless, it would be a mistake to conceive the defeat as the last battle cry of a dying way of life. On the contrary, the movement's protonationalistic rhetoric expressed a strong, if implicit, demand for autonomy. Military defeat did not eradicate those feelings nor those demands. In 1884 Indian rebels joined an antigovernment conspiratorial movement. The movement, although a failure, underscored a fact that the local ladinos understood well: many Indians had not accepted their defeat as final.[33]

The Highlands Indians under the Zelaya Regime, 1893–1909

Nicaraguan historiography portrays the Zelaya regime as one that modernized the country, effectively mobilizing resources for the agro-export sector. Scholars disagree about whether such economic growth was "capitalistic" or not, given the extensive use of extraeconomic labor coercion.[34] There is, however, no doubt that the regime did foster land expropriation and the coercion of Indian labor, although in this regard

Zelaya did little more than intensify the policies of his Conservative predecessors. What the historiography has overlooked is the flexibility the regime displayed when confronted with diverse forms of indigenous resistance. Beyond compelling the state to devise methods to contain their military potential, the Indian rebellion of 1881 also delayed the development of the coffee industry by a decade.[35] In 1890, however, Americans, Germans, and Nicaraguans acquired more than 13,000 acres of government-owned land that they soon planted with more than 1.2 million coffee bushes. The *cafetaleros* attempted to create a permanent labor force of Indian *colonos* (resident laborers) to clear, plant, tend, and harvest their plantations. The Indians, however, were fairly successful in resisting the imposition of this new labor regime through escape and occasional violence. In 1895, for example, of 196 workers obliged to pay off debts or finish contracts with nine planters, 92 had escaped.[36]

The Matagalpan Indians also directly resisted church efforts to transform their religious practices. In 1891, for example, the Indian alcaldes wrote to the church authorities asking for the replacement of the local priest. They argued that he had hidden two of their sacred images and stated that "the virgin is a mask of an old face." Underscoring their own cultural difference, they charged that the priest was "very tyrannical with our way of being."[37] The ecclesiastical authorities did respond to the alcaldes' petition by removing the priest from Matagalpa.

Toward the end of the nineteenth century the church policy shifted away from its tolerance of indigenous control over sacred images; in the 1890s, it launched an attack against Indian religious practices.[38] Conjunctural factors influenced the church's change from its protective role to its participation in the global effort to undermine ethnic culture. Faced with an economic retrenchment under Zelaya, it needed to collect the fees charged for the masses and processions associated with the images. Moreover, triumphant Liberalism probably provoked the church into tightening its ideological control over its flock; the clergy needed to mobilize its forces for the struggle against the Zelaya regime.

In 1893, immediately following the triumph of the Liberal revolution, the new priest of Matagalpa, Alfonso Martínez, ordered the Matagalpan cofradía to deliver four steers to finance the anti-Zelayista organization, La Unión Católica. Despite the priest's threats, the Indians remained intransigent. The priest lamented that "they still think that they run the cofradías. You know how the Indians are incapable of deliberating in anything but small matters."[39] Indigenous cultural resistance evidently wore some holes in the church's traditional habit of paternalism.

The Indians' rupture with the church reached dramatic proportions on August 1, 1895, when the government newspaper reported the following: "A few days ago the Indians who live in the cañadas . . . created a movement due to the most absurd spells cast by a few fanatics; recently they have risen in rebellion in several places near the departmental capital."[40] The following day, after announcing the end of the movement, the paper published the letter the Indians had written to the church preceding the brief rebellion. They recounted twelve apparitions since April 1895 and claimed that the authorities did not understand these miracles and were "threatening to burn us because they say that we have become witches . . . [the apostles appeared] because we had abandoned the Devotions to the Sacred Heart. God has wished to use his forgiveness by having the apostles come down to this earth to give us the Examples and show us that if we do not mend our ways we will be punished with Divine justice. . . . they are trying to intimidate us. . . . they locked up the Indian Alcaldes."[41] The Indians also asked the church to send a priest whom they knew and trusted and "any Jesuit" to aid them. The text suggests that the apostles appeared in the villages to purify the Indians. This movement, akin to the Ghost Dance movement of the Sioux in 1890, should be understood in the context of five years of violent changes in the Indians' lives: loss of thousands of acres of communal land, forced labor, internal economic and political divisions, and a conflict with the church over ownership of their cofradías and possession of images that included representations of the "apostles." The movement responded to and fomented ethnic strife: the apostles appeared so that the Indians would rectify their own ways. But the ladino authorities were aborting this purification process, violently disobeying the message of the apostles.

The re-creation of the religious symbols—especially the inclusion of women among the twelve apostles—also suggests the existence of a religious belief system analogous in its distinctiveness, if not its complexity, to that of the Mayan Indians. The ladino authorities did not, of course, view the apparitions with much ethnographic curiosity. For the regime, the movement revealed "a social sore that it is necessary to heal as soon as possible . . . an evil to be eradicated at its roots."[42]

Although the Zelaya regime made some attempts to heal the social "sore" through education, its principal cure involved strong doses of repression.[43] General Reuling, the *jefe político* (departmental governor) of Matagalpa from 1897 to 1898, not only used ample coercion to compel Indians to labor on plantations but also collected tribute in the form of "food contributions."[44] In carrying out these policies, Reuling relied on the army and on the capitanes de cañada. A treaty (perhaps informal) between the victorious government and the Indian leaders who survived the rebellion of 1881 aided Reuling's efforts to manipulate the capitanes. A key proviso established that although the capitanes would be elected by the Indians and would be responsible for the defense of their communities, the state reserved the power to ratify their election and to exert authority over them.[45] More prosaically, Reuling jailed those capitanes who disobeyed his commands, often burning their huts for emphasis.

Although Reuling had the support of the military, it is not clear to what extent Zelaya approved of his activities. For example, the regime did not respond to Reuling's call (a request that echoed General Elizondo's 1881 proposal) for the resettlement of the Indians near the coffee plantations.[46] The central government, however, was surely aware of Reuling's colonial-style policies and his military pressure on the villagers. Indeed, it was the threat of another Indian rebellion that forced Zelaya to remove Reuling from his post.

The Matagalpan Indians did resist Reuling, even though they had to confront their own capitanes. *El Comercio* reported in March 1898 that the jefe político "had given such scandalous orders to the capitanes that every day a murder took place in the cañadas."[47] Several days later *El Comercio* reported that the townsfolk feared for their lives: "the Indians conspire and are planning to attack the city." The attack never materialized, but the Indians achieved their objective: the replacement of Reuling as jefe político and the end of "the forced contributions of goods."[48]

But Reuling left his stamp on the political culture of the highlands. Before his removal, Reuling had wreaked havoc in the cañadas, sowing bitter divisions between those who obeyed and those who resisted his brutal reign. Moreover, despite the key role played by indigenous resistance in toppling Reuling, their reliance upon Zelaya brought legitimacy to the regime's power over the comunidades.[49]

The regime formalized its control in 1904, when it approved the statutes of the Comunidad Indígena of Matagalpa. It was surely no coincidence that Zelaya chose to legitimize the Comunidad in 1904, the same time at which he sanctioned a survey of communal lands (demanded by the Indians). When the alcaldes bitterly protested the surveyor's methods, the official response was to approve the statutes that eliminated the alcaldes' temporal authority.[50] Before 1904, the four alcaldes, elected by La Reforma (the Council of Elders), had formed the political directorate of the Comunidad Indígena. The statutes, however, mandated the election of a directorate that had no connection either to the communal religious structure or to the parcialidades. Although the alcaldes continued to exercise a religious role and informal political authority, their removal from the state-legitimized political leadership eventually led to the secularization of communal authority.

Although the Zelaya era was trying for the Matagalpan Indians, at times the Liberal government responded favorably to indigenous pressure, as it had in the Reuling case. Similarly, the government chose to loosen its repressive grip on rural labor. In 1903, part of the indigenous population of Chontales backed an abortive Conservative rebellion. During the rebellion, the government sought to appease the Indians by abolishing forced labor in that area. During the same year, at least partially in response to petitions from highlands Indians, the Congress voted 26 to 1 to abolish the *boleta de ocupación*, a work pass that all adults with a capital of under 500 pesos had to carry. The boleta system, in effect, obliged the majority of rural inhabitants including smallholders to work for an employer.[51] The legislators defied Zelaya by overriding his veto, thus revealing serious cracks in the Liberal Party. Many of the congressmen seemed to have grown tired of seeing their region's workers shipped off to work for the Managua cafetaleros, and others probably chafed at seeing artisans treated like peons. Their formal opposition to the boleta, however, was based on the principles of the Liberal revolution of 1893. One congressman stated that "the system kept the worker tied to the boss's hitching post."[52]

Compromise legislation approved the following year did promote coercive labor relations by outlawing vagrancy, by obliging workers to maintain a passbook, and by sentencing workers to fifteen days of public works for breaking a contract. Nevertheless, the new labor code was less coercive than earlier ones, and it prohibited *mandamiento* (labor draft) style practices. In addition, the 1905 Constitution outlawed imprisonment for debts. This loosening of the system stimulated, it seems, high levels of labor disobedience, despite a police presence on the haciendas and in the cañadas.[53] In 1908, the Matagalpan coffee planters' organization complained to Zelaya that the 1904 legislation had "led to immorality and disorder. . . . Today the workers, whether they owe or not, do not want to go to work, not even those who have debts."[54]

The government also responded positively to Indian demands when it halted land evictions in Boaco and Jinotega. In 1893, the Indians of Boaco had played an important role in the revolutionary events and had seized on the political conflict to militarily confront the local ladino population.[55] In 1904, following political unrest, the government sent a commissioner to resolve land conflicts between the Indians and the ladino-controlled municipal government. The commissioner urged the regime to block evictions caused by the municipal government's rental of formerly indigenous lands: "after thinking about the Indians' inveterate desire to be *comuneros* . . . and their lack of intellectual capacity [and] since our enemies would find a favorable political conjuncture and stir up a rebellion . . . we should distribute the land free to the Indian families immediately . . . [that] would end the ancient system of communal land and the natural negligence of our primitive race that are . . . obstacles to progress.[56] The commissioner's reasoning revealed the racism that flowed through progressive discourse. Especially irksome was the Indians' "inveterate desire" to be members of a Comunidad, an institution that both reflected and perpetuated their intellectual inferiority, blocking the nation's progress. But the official's racism did not blind him to the political ramifications of the region's ethnic divisions. The split between Indian and ladino in Boaco, as elsewhere, seemed to derive directly from the existence of the Comunidad and its lands.

In 1906, after two years of relative political tranquility, the Zelaya regime fulfilled a decade-old promise by decreeing the abolition of the Comunidades Indígenas. Following a venerable Latin American Liberal formula, the law called for the distribution of one-half of the communal land to individual Indian families and the sale of the remainder to ladinos, with the profit used for indigenous education. Despite indigenous resistance, the surveyors began their work in 1908, and as a consequence the highlands Indians lost additional land to ladinos.[57]

The abolition of the Comunidades culminated the prolonged attack on the highlands Indians that had followed the defeat of the rebellion of 1881 and had gathered strength with the development of the coffee industry in the 1890s. This said, the common assumption that coffee growers expropriated most of the communal lands in the highlands is simply not borne out by an examination of available data. Coffee growers did appropriate some 50,000 acres of Indian territory in Matagalpa from 1890 to 1910.[58] Indeed, some of the area's leading coffee plantations sit upon former communal plots sold as national land during the Zelaya era. Yet when Zelaya fell in 1909, the Comunidad of Matagalpa was still functioning, with 5,000 to 7,000 families possessing more than 135,000 acres of land.[59]

The coffee industry eventually stratified more than it proletarianized Indian society. The Matagalpan Indians controlled a large proportion of coffee land at least until the 1930s. Since the dawn of the industry, kin groups had planted coffee as a cash crop on their communal land. Although the elites insisted that they needed to privatize the Comunidades to foment export agriculture, often they expropriated not subsistence farmers but small coffee producers. It should also be stressed that some of the expropriators were themselves Indians. The coffee industry and the Liberal revolution did not destroy the Comunidad Indígena, but they did weaken its economic base and divide indigenous society in ways it possessed no cures for.

The Comunidades of Matagalpa and Boaco in the end did find the opportunity for revenge against the regime, by forming an essential component of the anti-Zelayista military forces. Conservative politicians mobilized indigenous support by conjuring up the rumors of 1881 and the nightmare of 1898 in appeals like the following: "they [the Zelaya regime] treated you like beasts of burden. . . . they took away your wives and daughters and forced them to go to the haciendas of the sierra of Managua. . . . they sacked the cofradías."[60]

The Indian-Conservative Alliance, 1911–1924

Zelaya's policies toward the Indians aimed to put into practice what his Conservative predecessors had already codified in laws. From 1880 to 1910, bipartisan elite policy had favored the formula: privatization of communal lands plus education equals civilization. The post-Zelaya Conservative regime, however, questioned and modified that program. The most significant change came in 1914, when the Congress overturned the Zelaya abolition of the Comunidades Indígenas: the legalization of the communal lands and organizations proved vital to the survival of many Indian groups.[61]

The policy shift probably had less to do with ideological differences between Liberal and Conservative elites than with a pragmatic recognition by the U.S.-supported regime that it needed indigenous support. The importance of their support had already manifested itself in the anti-Zelayista revolution. Similarly, the caudillo Emiliano Chamorro — and in this he sharply delineated himself from the Liberals and indeed most Conservatives — had cultivated long-standing political and family ties with the Matagalpan and Boaqueño Indians. The indigenous population of the highlands represented up to 15,000 votes (some 15 percent of the electorate). Chamorro's political skills and the legalization of the Comunidades solidified indigenous support for the Conservatives. Finally, the Conservatives used the legislation as a political entrée into Comunidades in historically Liberal areas such as León and Jinotega.

The policy shift had immediate consequences in Matagalpa. Although the alcaldes had lost their legal status under Zelaya, they had continued to play an important political role. Nevertheless, their undefined status had become a source of internal conflict and outside political manipulation. In March 1912, La Reforma withdrew recognition from the alcaldes and staged new elections, arguing that, "without carrying out a legal election these people appear as . . . alcaldes . . . since the Jefe Politíco installed them in office without knowing by whose authority."[62] The elders suggested that the jefe político, through ignorance or design, intervened in Comunidad affairs by arbitrarily naming three of the alcaldes. Moreover, according to the elders, he had refused to recognize the authority of the capitanes de cañada. Whatever the jefe político's motives — and Conservative factionalism was surely one — the problem was exacerbated when the three ousted alcaldes refused to recognize the winners of the new elections, thereby throwing the Comunidad into turmoil.

In May 1912, as the Liberals unleashed a revolutionary insurrection in León, the government sent a commissioner, J. Bárcenas Meneses, to resolve the problems of the Comunidad. Following his visit to Matagalpa, Bárcenas wrote a report urging the government to call new elections, which he was sure would result in a Conservative victory (he believed that the three alcaldes that had been appointed by the jefe político were allied with the Liberals). More significant, he argued for a reformulation of the Comunidad statutes that would legitimate the alcaldes, the *capitán-general* (chief indigenous official in charge of the whole department), and other traditional authorities. He stated: "[they] play such an important role that I believe it to be extremely useful, indeed, indispensable, to include them in the statutes."[63]

The captains, perhaps for military reasons, did receive government recognition, but the alcaldes never did regain the political and cultural prominence the position had commanded before 1904. As a direct consequence, the "barrio" began to lose its importance: over the next forty years, as the alcaldes were reduced to ceremonial roles, the barrios lost their function as endogamous kinship units and as the principal site of religious practice.

Bárcenas, a Conservative who shared with Emiliano Chamorro an understanding of the importance of the Indians for their party, sought to protect not only the role of the alcaldes but also the land of the Comunidad. He attacked the usurpers, pointing an angry finger at one Antonio Belli, whose "atrocious survey" in 1904 had purposefully left out the communal lands to the north of the city. Using the commissioner's report and the land title, we can estimate that Belli's survey had converted some 17,000 of 100,000 manzanas (1 manzana equals 1.7 acres) of communal into national land, which was then sold to coffee growers. In response Bárcenas urged measures that would impede ladino settlement on communal lands.[64]

That the commissioner's recommendations were never fully enacted reveals the limits of the government's Indian policy. The Conservatives never posed a direct challenge to ladino domination over indigenous land and labor precisely because they formed the party of the landed oligarchy, which included many coffee planters. Nevertheless, Emiliano Chamorro's faction did carve out a semi-independent political position through support for Indian rights at a time when other elite factions desired their disappearance.

In 1917, President Chamorro explained his support for the Matagalpan Indians' land claims in the following terms: "Knowing your [the Indians'] feelings . . . the Comunidades Indígenas that were victims of outrages in past administrations and moreover have been the most loyal . . . when they were called upon to sacrifice for the prestige of the party [deserve retribution]."[65] Chamorro's support for the Indians yielded political dividends. Although migration from Conservative Granada had somewhat changed the political complexion of the elite, Chamorro could still play upon the highlands Indians' identification of ladinos with Liberalism. Both Chamorro and the local caudillo, Bartolomé Martínez, courted Indian support through patronage and through positive responses to Indian petitions. In particular, in 1924, Martínez, as president of the republic, distributed 3,600 manzanas of land to the Comunidad Indígena.[66]

Indians not only supplied crucial political support for Conservatives but moreover created a space, however reduced, in which they defended their Comunidades and defined their identity in a hostile ladino world. In 1919, the Matagalpan Indians spurred the distribution process through land occupations. Similarly, indigenous mobilizations in Boaco, Jinotega, and Sutiava received Conservative backing.[67]

Let us focus on the case of the highlands Comunidad Indígena of Jinotega. Since 1895, some 2,000 Indian families who inhabited small villages near the town of Jinotega had struggled in defense of their 35,000 manzanas of communal land against ladino ranchers and coffee growers. On May 29, 1915, the Indian-ladino conflict entered a violent phase. That morning Macedonio Aguilar, capitán-general of the Comunidad, led 100 Indians in cutting down the barbed-wire fences of a Sr. López Guerra, who had built his cattle ranch on communal land. Several months later the police captured twenty of the Indians including Aguilar and his sons. Two rebels, Benigno Granados and Abraham González, escaped the roundup. But some time later the authorities killed González.[68]

With the tacit backing of the Chamorristas, the Indians continued to engage in direct action in defense of their land. In 1918, *El Correo* reported that they had "repeatedly engaged in destroying all the ladinos' properties on these lands, thus deepening caste hatred."[69] In early 1919, when the court in Matagalpa sentenced twelve Indians to eight months in jail, Jinotegano rebels cut the barbed wire on many ladino properties. The local Chamorrista police chief phrased the problem in the following terms: "our strength has been with the Comunidad and now its chiefs are on trial for destruction of property. The Liberals have done this to prevent the leaders from helping us; those that are being tried were the true friends of General Chamorro, and they will continue to be so if they are set free."[70] The Chamorrista support of the Jinotegano Indians led to the release of the prisoners and to a halt in further ladino

encroachment on their lands. Moreover, the pro-Indian policy created
a firm base of support for Chamorrismo where none had existed before
1914. In Jinotega, the Liberal allegiance of the ladinos created such a
transparent political landscape that by the late 1920s an allegiance to
Chamorrismo often informed indigenous identity. Thus, for example,
a U.S. Marine Corps officer, stationed in Jinotega, wrote: "We have
found that the Indians around here, those who are Conservative, wor-
ship only one GOD, and that one is Chamorro. Some of them have
letters that they treasure as one would an earned medal of honor."[71]

The political identification, of course, was neither as immutable or
as irrational as the analysis suggested. Less than two decades earlier it
was nonexistent, and within a year a large number of those same Chamorrista Indians would become Sandinistas. What remained constant
in the politics of the Jinotegano Indians was the Liberalism of their
ladino opponents and their own understanding that cross-ethnic alliances were necessary for the defense of their lands and community.

Varieties of Ladino Discourse

Despite their decisive support and sympathy for the highlands Indians,
neither Bartolomé Martínez nor Chamorro ever mounted an ideological challenge to the dominant discourse of ladinoization. Both politicians demonstrated ambivalent attitudes toward the Comunidades
Indígenas.[72] In part the ambivalence of these two Conservative caudillos
toward the Comunidades reflected their need to maintain legitimacy
among the national elites. They shared, as well, the positivistic view
that Indians must become ladinoized or perish as obstacles to progress.
Nevertheless, although they took abolition arguments seriously, neither
of the two presidents ever mounted a push to eliminate the Comunidades Indígenas.

Notwithstanding their ambivalence, Chamorro and Martínez stood
alone among Nicaragua's political elite as pro-Indian sympathizers.
Their support for Indians, traceable in part to individual psychology,
had a specifically regional focus and was heavily biased in favor of the
indigenous elite. Let us examine the biography of Bartolomé Martínez:
the illegitimate son of a planter and a Jinotegano Indian woman, he
was nicknamed "El Indio." Late in life he married the daughter of a

mozo (farmhand) on his coffee plantation (following the birth of several children) in the indigenous area of Muy Muy. Perhaps not surprisingly, then, as jefe político in Matagalpa he developed an easy rapport with the highlands Indians, a sympathy he did not demonstrate in regard to other indigenous groups.

Despite Martínez's unusual background, he worked with his clients as would any other politician. To cite a typical example, he bought an accordion as a birthday present for the son of the capitán-general of the Comunidad of Jinotega. His relationship with the capitán-general of Matagalpa, Ceferino Aguilar, however, does stand out from the rest for its duration and moreover because it often resembled a friendship between equals. Aguilar received numerous favors from Martínez, ranging from scholarships for his children to his release from prison for political and less noble offenses. In turn, Aguilar offered Martínez incisive political analysis from the grass roots and made consistent efforts to maintain political support that aided Martínez politically and economically. And Aguilar pushed his friend's programs, in particular education. The friendship with Ceferino Aguilar was strong and fruitful enough that Martínez was usually aware how policies would play among the highlands Indians. Although Martínez never embraced an Indian communitarian political perspective, his friendship with Aguilar allowed him to appreciate the political value of Indian leadership, a value that would erode if the Comunidad were abolished or disintegrated.[73]

Martínez juggled his political needs; his sympathies; and his search for a method to "civilize" his indigenous friends, workers, and neighbors. During his thirteen-month term as president of Nicaragua, in addition to returning the land to the Comunidad of Matagalpa, he founded a teacher-training school for Indians.[74] If not for Martínez, then for other members of the elite, education posed thorny definitional problems. Ladinos often distorted the characteristics of "educated." Although El Indio understood that the relatively educated Aguilar was an Indian, most ladinos relegated the category of Indian to distant "primitives." Consider the view of the León municipal government on the neighboring Sutiavas, who were fighting for official recognition as a Comunidad Indígena with territorial rights: "The castes live in complete separation and never mix. . . . in the Matagalpan cañadas they live in ignorance of the laws of the state. . . . [the Sutiavas] are quite advanced intellectually . . . and cannot be confused with the Indian castes . . . who live in . . . areas inhabited by uncivilized Indians."[75] Congruent with the discourse of Nicaragua mestiza, the Indian here is defined as noncivilized, as barbarous. Thus the Sutiavas, culturally more advanced and more urbanized than the Matagalpas, no longer qualified as Indians. True Indians were pitiful, static, locked in the past, and incapable of progressing on their own. Education, therefore, would wrench the Indians out of the past and convert them into civilized ladinos, with the same rights as other citizens, but with no special rights to the land. At the same time elite discourse framed the Comunidad Indígena of Sutiava as a farcical ruse for holding onto territory better suited to elite needs.

The question raised by the Leonese elite is worth pondering further. What distinguished the Indian from the ladino, at a time when pressures were brought to bear on the former to change ethnic identities? Few, if any, Indians outside of the Atlantic coast still spoke a native language in 1920. Whether in urban Sutiava or rural Matagalpa, the lives of Indians had changed dramatically with respect to the language, dress, religion, labor relations, and communal organization of their parents' generation. Indigenous ethnicity had become tightly interwoven with the Comunidad Indígena and with those political alliances necessary for its defense. Similarly, ethnicity provided the only language of rural class protest that some elites could understand. They could, for example, understand the claims of a Comunidad, but a rural labor union was an alien concept.

The highlands ladinos helped shape national opinion about the Comunidades. For instance, one Matagalpan lawyer who for ten years had engineered land grabs headed a national commission to study "the Indian Problem." Another highlands ladino involved in a land conflict claimed that the Comunidades perpetuated the Indians' "stubborn way of life, refractory to all progress"[76] A Managua newspaper supported a petition of the Jinotegano ladinos in similar terms: "We judge that the comunidades retard national progress. . . . [The Indians] live hermetically. . . . certainly they conserve their racial tradition . . . and the stamp of primitive sovereignty . . . but at the center everything stagnates and petrifies."[77]

Although partisan Liberals (out of power) draped themselves in the same banner of progress, they blamed the Indian problem on Conservative slavedrivers who manipulated their votes. Juan Mendoza, a Liberal, added a twist on ethnic relations when he wrote in 1920: "For them [the Conservative oligarchs] the ladino was the quintessence of perfection. . . . The mixing of blood with the Indian was unacceptable. . . . The ladinos failed to understand what has been resolved by the most advanced sociologists . . . and confirmed by those elements, the product of miscegenation, who today forge ahead with the dynamic force of capital united with expert . . . and progressive leadership."[78] Mendoza's view of ethnic relations is important because he enunciated the "mestizo" variant of the ladino myth (to be later radicalized by Sandino and then appropriated by Somoza). In so doing, he underscored the limits of Conservative *indigenismo,* in particular the deep-seated racism of its "white" leadership (curiously both Chamorro and Martínez were mestizo exceptions). But at the same time Mendoza's construction of an ideal mestizaje that would guide Nicaragua to capitalistic progress depended upon a dehumanized vision of the Indian: "Thus we see the Indian move in herds, like beasts, half-naked, like a primitive. . . . And the *patrono* looks at him with disdain; . . . the governments indifferent, with eternal neglect."[79] The Indian as an autonomous subject simply did not exist in ladino discourse during this era. When Indians achieved education but still desired an indigenous identity, lands, and organization, they were dubbed ersatz, artificial creations, as in Sutiava. When they rebelled, as in Sutiava or Jinotega, landowners and editorialists depicted them as primitive savages and stooges of unscrupulous politicians. Moreover, the class position (as cafetaleros) of a Chamorro or a Martínez blinded them from seeing any alternative to a ladino road of progress. By 1950, after the ladino state had crippled the institutions that defined indigenous ethnicity, it took but a short leap of faith to declare that the Indians were dead upon the arrival of the twentieth century.

Nevertheless, in 1919 the ladino imagery was still blurry: Indians slothfully vegetated in the past but stirred up ethnic hatred. Although petrified they become animated long enough to cut the barbed wire of ladino planters. Ladinos viewed Indians as objects of pity, a degraded race moving in "herds," but redeemable through education. These conflicting images of goodness-bestiality and passivity-violence related, it seems, to conflicting ladino needs and to the bitter quality of ethnic relations in the highlands. For the highlands elite wished to convert Indians into laborers and their land into plantations. But at the same time they needed to justify coerced labor on their plantation in ethnic terms. The violence that surrounded labor relations merely confirmed ladino notions about Indians as a degraded race.

Labor, Authority, and Violence in Matagalpa

The Matagalpan cafetaleros viewed the "degraded race" as inherently slothful and thus had difficulty envisioning a free labor force on their plantations. Despite the abolition of forced labor in the 1905 and 1911 constitutions, an informal debt peonage system continued to be a key feature of the coffee industry in the central highlands until the 1930s. As scholar-diplomat Dana Munro explained in 1918, "the cafetaleros, incapable of enforcing their contracts with the Indians, often have difficulty with their harvest. The fact is that the local authorities, in many cases, illegally have enforced the old laws."[80] Moreover, they lobbied Congress unsuccessfully to pass debt enforcement legislation in the 1910 to 1911 session, but won approval in 1919. Finally, the Matagalpan cafetaleros, alone, lobbied in 1923 against a law that once again abolished all forms of debt bondage and forced labor.[81]

The highlands cafetaleros obtained significant benefits from the system. They used advance payments not only to attract local labor but also to maintain subsistence-level wages despite rapidly rising productivity. Between 1919 and 1925, for example, coffee production in Matagalpa doubled without any corresponding increase in wages or in the labor supply.[82] Thus the cafetaleros' argument that they needed to pay subsistence-level wages due to the high cost of transportation seems weak. Similarly unconvincing is the argument that Indians would not have responded to wage incentives because of the conflicting demands of their own family economy. On the contrary, as we shall see, workers did respond to wage incentives and often moved from hacienda to hacienda in search of advances rather than return to their milpas.

A more adequate understanding of highlands labor relations might be obtained if we situate them within Alan Knight's innovative typology of debt labor. He distinguished among situations where debt was "an inducement" in the creation of voluntary labor force (type 1); where debts were a "customary" part of the negotiation between the landlord and resident labor (type 2); and where debts were a central feature of a coercive system of recruitment and retention of labor (type 3).[83]

Matagalpan labor relations, however, seem to spill over into all three categories. Although the Indians themselves demanded advances (type 2) they did not resemble a resident labor force (or use hacienda land as did the Peruvian sheepherders). Unlike the Guatemalan case (type 3), the Matagalpan planters did not face an absolute shortage of pickers in the coffee region. In 1925 U.S. consul Harold Playter wrote: "Labor is more plentiful in the Matagalpa region, hence cheaper, but the Indian of that section, 60 percent of the population, although a good worker cannot be counted on to report when needed."[84] Finally, despite a degree of labor mobility, the highlands labor relations did not resemble those of coastal Peru or Soconusco (type 1), because coercion in Matagalpa was used to retain laborers well after their initial recruitment.

Although Matagalpan labor relations seem anomalous, the array of forces that shaped them was not unique. The highlands laboring class came into existence as the state and the cafetaleros expropriated nearly 30 percent of indigenous land. The loss of land contributed to the availability of indigenous labor, but the nature of that expropriation—by the very cafetaleros who sought their labor—decisively influenced the quality of social productive relations. Moreover, as we have seen, ladino authorities often treated the Matagalpas as a conquered people. The question of whether labor was free or unfree thus can be grasped only in the context of a highly unequal ethnic power struggle: the coffee laborers were at the same time an ethnic group who worked for those who recently had taken their land and imposed political authority upon them.

If these interconnections of land, power, and ethnicity are not taken into account, the highlands labor relations appear, to a large degree, voluntary. For Indians and planters did share a mutual dependency on the *adelanto* system. By demanding advances worth several weeks' wages at the start of a harvest, the indigenous workers seem to have acted in conformity with the revisionist view of Arnold Bauer and others who argue for a predominantly noncoercive role of debt in rural labor relations.[85] But the planters did use force against those who, like their contemporaries in Guatemala and El Salvador, treated their cash advances as earned wages and sought work on other plantations. According to the cafetalero, Alberto Vogl, "With time all the Indians became legally obligated to work with the *finqueros* [planters]. Then they would leave to go work in Managua or Jinotega where they worked as *ganadores* [nondebtors] and not as *desquitadores* [debtors]. The Indian authorities did not carry out the orders . . . because it would be like capturing their own fathers or brothers. . . . in reality it bled the cafetaleros dry and provided an easy source of income for the Indians."[86] This cafetalero's recollection coincides with documentary sources in one important respect: the Matagalpan Indians usually did not desert the plantation to go back to their milpas but rather to work on other coffee plantations. Indeed they played one cafetalero against another. Thus, for example, in 1913 Bartolomé Martínez, then jefe político and owner of a coffee plantation, received a telegram from his foreman: "There are mozos registered to you working in the hacienda of Federico Fley."[87] That this indigenous labor resistance involved moving from cafetal to cafetal suggests that the planters' problem with the "reliability" of labor had little to do with the Indians' degree of commitment to seasonal wage labor. In fact, female workers, in particular, responded to piecework incentives, often earning enough to pay off their debts.[88]

The perpetuation of this system into the 1920s, then, seems to have derived from the conflict between the cafetaleros' desire to maintain subsistence-level wages and the Indians' defense of "customary" rights to a cash advance that reflected their own concept of a just wage. Notwithstanding Vogl's idyllic vision of the advances as a form of welfare, the cafetaleros' reaction to labor resistance brought out the brutality of the adelanto system and corroded the bonds of the Comunidad Indígena.[89] The elite's unwillingness to accept a voluntary labor system derived, in large part, from its racist view of indigenous labor. The system legitimized a repressive apparatus that turned foremen and indigenous authorities into police agents. Indeed, this police presence on the plantation makes the problem of free labor more complex. For when foremen jailed laborers for failing to show up for work they put severe limitations on the workers' freedom even when the laborer might have arrived at the plantation voluntarily. Moreover, racism — a conception of Indians as primitive, ignorant, superstitious, and servile — also informed the framing of those productive relations just as did indigenous resentment against the land expropriations of the cafetaleros.[90] The ladino elite could neither see the Indians as worth the higher wages that might end their desire for advances nor could they conceive of the Indians' working in a system that did not depend ultimately upon coercion. The labor system, itself, generated evidence for this picture of the Indian as a creature submerged in a world of violence.

Local indigenous authorities often captured fellow Indians. Servando Ochao, for example, complained to the jefe político that indigenous authorities had jailed his sons for not possessing a work pass. Similarly an American cafetalero, in 1921, complained to then vice-president Martínez, that the "capitán de cañada was capturing people . . . who owe no money to anybody."[91] The gradual conversion of Indian village authorities into government authorities provided the political underpinning for the labor system. Once the indigenous authorities ceased to derive their legitimacy from the Comunidad, the incidence of violent abuses increased dramatically. In an earlier case of indigenous authorities capturing Indians in 1910, Jorge Pérez, a captain, received an order to take Ciriaco Obregón prisoner and deliver him to a coffee plantation as a "labor deserter." After Obregón had been delivered and the foreman had cut his hands loose, Obregón turned to Pérez and said, "sooner or later you're going to pay for this." Two years later Obregón, then an Indian village authority himself, captured Pérez and nearly killed him.[92] This case and others mentioned previously suggest that in the highlands the terms *free* or *servile labor* only have meaning when analyzed in the context of the surrounding web of contradictory social relations mediated by ladino authority and power.

Authoritarian violence also erupted over land disputes. Ladino efforts to expropriate property turned indigenous authorities against their own people. Thus, in 1913 Ceferino Aguilar protested to Martínez about the complicity of Indian leaders in the loss of communal territory. Aguilar accused the president of the Comunidad of forcibly evicting Indians in order to rent lands to ladinos: "On March 17 in Matazano, Bacilio Figueroa, accompanied by 20 people arrived to look over some land . . . that a non-comunero wanted to fence. . . . since the land belonged to us comuneros we decided to fence it off. . . . when we finished the president came back and had six [Indians] tied up."[93] This incident underscores the violent, disruptive consequences of the loss of communal land. For despite his brutal tactics, the president of the Comunidad believed that he was acting on behalf of his people. As we saw, between 1904 and 1913 the Matagalpas had lost thousands of acres of land to "defense" lawyers and surveyors who charged exorbitant rates to the community, thus forcing land sales as payment. The president in 1913 wished to rent this land to head off yet another forced sale.

The growing commodification of the products and structures of the communal land — the crops, fences, buildings, and corrals — also gnawed away at indigenous ties. By the second decade of this century dozens of Indian kinship groups were planting coffee for sale on the market. Their *mejoras,* improvements such as fences and trees, could be legally seized for nonpayment of debts. Although the land itself could not be expropriated (after the 1914 law), Indians could lose their mejoras as a result of debts to other Indians or to ladinos. Indeed the majority of the land conflicts during the period of 1916 to 1924 pitted Indians allied with ladinos against other Indians.

The ladino elite's manipulation of Indian authorities turned labor recruitment and land into highly divisive issues among the Matagalpan Indians, impeding the kind of unified resistance that took place to the north in Jinotega. Although earlier we saw how Chamorrista politics often aided the indigenous communities, politics simultaneously weakened communal solidarity. During the election campaign of 1916, for example, the government and Chamorrista factions of the Conservative Party competed for Indian votes. The government's method of "campaigning" consisted of the forcible recruitment of Chamorrista Indians into the military; the jefe político replaced forty of the forty-five capitanes with anti-Chamorristas.[94] Ceferino Aguilar recounted to Bartolomé Martínez the actions of one Indian authority: "The captain, Félix Pérez . . . recruited a great many people. . . . many were tied up. . . . those citizens sadly await with the hope that he will be removed from that post. . . . Pérez caused much disorder. . . . with the prisoners bound, dying of hunger, why should we Indians have to die in this way?"[95] Thus the Indian authorities, following ladino orders, unleashed a campaign to terrorize the Chamorristas into submission. Once again we can glimpse the epoch's image of repressed indigenous life: the *amarrados,* a long file of Indians with their hands tied behind their backs pulled by their ethnic brethren on horseback toward an army encampment or to the peons' quarters of the plantation.

The Matagalpan Indians clearly did not wish "to die in this way." In their own defense, they pursued three types of strategies to cope with the reign of violence that afflicted their communities. Migration was the response that probably had the greatest long-term consequences for the Comunidades. For the coercive quality of politics and labor drove many people east into the sparsely inhabited mountains. One capitán wrote to Bartolomé Martínez in 1921: "The Indians have been very exploited and have come to these mountains fleeing from the communities."[96] Although it is impossible as yet to quantify the emigration from the Indian villages, oral testimony suggests that many villages lost more than one-half of their inhabitants to *la montaña* (the mountain jungle) during this period. Perhaps 25 percent of the total Matagalpan Indian population of some 30,000 to 35,000 at the turn of the century fled the area between 1910 and 1950.[97] Moreover, those who established small farms in the mountains lost contact with the rest of the Indian population. Commenting about a similar migratory process fifty miles to the south that took place during the 1940s, Emilio Sobalvarro wrote: "As the ladinos acquired more and more lands, the Indian withdrew far away. The law always went against them. . . . the immigration was constant and by the hundreds. Towards the east where the millenarian trees had never been touched by a hatchet. . . . To these mountains . . . they fled."[98]

Self-imposed withdrawal from contact with ladino society was another strategic response. Using the epithet *ladinazo* which originated during this epoch of violence, one elderly Indian summarized the perspective of those who remained in their villages: "When we saw the Indians tied up and dragged off to a hacienda . . . we learned that we had to stay out of debt to the ladinazos. And the only way to do that was to have nothing to do with them. For a long time you never saw a ladinazo around here. We'd go to Matagalpa to sell our coffee and oranges, but we'd stay in the *común* [the Indian center] and never mix with anybody."[99]

Despite their relative isolation, during the 1940s the Matagalpan Indians suffered new and powerful blows. In 1942, malicious departmental authorities interpreted a wartime agreement with the United States restricting cotton output to include *algodón silvestre* (nonindustrial cotton bushes). The National Guard then uprooted the cotton bushes, from which the Indians wove their clothes.[100] Understood as a ban against the manufacture of their clothing, the Indians ceased to wear distinctive dress (in fact, they were the last indigenous group to do so). The second blow occurred during the late 1940s, when the church, under the early influence of Acción Católica ("Catholic Action"; a group founded in Nicaragua in the early 1940s to purify religious practice and also engage in works of Christian charity), removed all of the sacred images that belonged to the four parcialidades and placed them in chapels. These two actions had a severely demoralizing effect on the communities but did little to break down their isolation or overcome their distrust of ladinos.[101]

Los Mozos de Vita: Land Expropriation and Ladinoization

The third and least typical strategic response began with direct resistance to ladino aggression but eventually gave way to a degree of relative submission. Although in 1881 Yúcul had been the bastion of the rebellion, between 1911 and 1916 José Vita (the second-largest cafetalero in Matagalpa) conquered the village and its lands. Vita accomplished what most of his elite compañeros had only dreamed about: the abolition of communal land and the conversion of Indians into peons.

In 1910 Vita paid $1,000 (between 1912 and 1940 one peso was equal to one dollar) for 1,000 *manzanas* of Yúcul land at an auction. The Comunidad had to sell the land because it owed money to Eudoro Baca, a lawyer who had purchased the debt from Antonio Belli (the brother-in-law of Emiliano Chamorro), whose survey, as mentioned before, had lopped off 17,000 manzanas of communal land. Vita manipulated the title to include an extra 1,500 manzanas bordering his coffee plantation La Laguna. Claiming the village of Yúcul as his own, Vita ordered the thirty-five extended families who cultivated cash crops and basic grains on some 2,000 manzanas either to leave or to work on his plantation.

By 1913, Vita had persuaded ten extended families who cultivated approximately 500 manzanas to accept his deal: "those who have cultivated lots can keep them if they agree to clean one *cafetal* (3,000 *cafetos* [coffee bushes]) three times a year; the owner will pay them what the labor is worth, and those who do not fulfill their obligation will have to leave." [102] In this brief accord, we can see the process of primitive accumulation at work; in Yúcul, as elsewhere, the process was not peaceful.

Bibiano Díaz, a leader of the Comunidad of Matagalpa, argued that Vita "has used his superiority and influence to do what he wishes with the Indians of Yúcul. . . . he founded his *vinculación* through terror." [103] Bibiano Díaz inverted the elite referent of *vinculación* (entailment), a word that had been used to question the legality of the Comunidades. Similarly, Díaz adeptly attacked Vita in ways that would appeal to the ladino elite: he accused him of being "un extranjero pernicioso" (pernicious foreigner) and of reestablishing "slavery in the twentieth century." [104] No ladinos, however, were listening.

Díaz organized more than verbal resistance against Vita; for three years the majority of Indian families remained on their land while refusing to fulfill their labor obligation to Vita. But the Italian cafetalero was not easily intimidated. Throughout the year he scored important triumphs, including the eviction of four families. According to one account, "because they could no longer endure Vita's hostilities against the Indians . . . [sixteen families] . . . abandoned their fincas."[105] By the end of 1913 only five families continued to resist.

Despite Bibiano Díaz's prominence in the Comunidad, his group fought alone. As we have seen, the internal divisions in the Comunidad were deep and Díaz suggested that its president had aided Vita. Nor was Martínez available in this battle; he had a long-standing friendship with Vita, his next-door neighbor in Matagalpa.

While Díaz argued in the courtroom, Vita ordered his mozos to tear down Díaz's fences and destroy his crops. Moreover, as Díaz testified, "Many times he has slandered me and even whipped me for no motive, only because he has grown accustomed to doing that to *la servidumbre* [hired help] that he has established." Díaz's travails in the courtroom taught him bitter lessons about power and justice: "At the beginning of the trial, out of love for the land I innocently believed in the equality of rights. *¡Vana ilusión!*"[106] Vita's henchmen terrorized the Indian witnesses, and the presiding judge sent them to jail before they could testify. Díaz and the other four families held out until 1916. Rather than become part of Vita's "servidumbre" Bibiano Díaz left behind his fifty-manzana farm and went to live on a relative's land in another village.

The other four extended families joined la servidumbre. Soon the victorious Vita confiscated their fincas, leaving them with but one manzana per male adult. In return for that parcel, all family members were obliged to pick his coffee and weed 8,000 coffee trees a year, at far less than the going wage. Between 1916 and 1963 if a Yuculeño did not show up to work on a given day, Vita (and in later years, his son) sent his own "civilian police" to drag the recalcitrant worker off to the plantation jail.[107]

Vita's proletarianization of the Yuculeños was accompanied by a process of ladinoization so thoroughgoing that the grandchildren of Bibiano Díaz do not recall that he was an Indian, much less a leader of the Comunidad Indígena. From 1916 to 1950 the Yuculeños lost contact with the Indian villages but ten miles away. Gradually they began to look upon the Indian women who came to pick Vita's coffee in the 1930s and 1940s as people of a different ethnic group. The Yuculeños called them the *mantiadas*, on account of their dress, and those of *lenguaje enredado* (tangled language) for their Spanish-based dialect.[108] Thus, in one generation the Indians of Yúcul had lost their own ethnic identity.

The Yúcul experience seems to support the perspective that links proletarianization and ladinoization. However, Yúcul is not an open-and-shut case. For the Yuculeños did maintain a separate identity and a sense of their own history, a reflection on their daily, practical experience. They recognized, for example, that although they made up a small minority of Vita's workforce, they were highly overrepresented in his jail. Moreover, in 1963 the grandchildren of Bibiano Díaz organized a union that broke the *colonato* system and by 1965 had won back 300 manzanas of their land. A dim memory of their past informed that labor and subsequent struggles. Although they did not consider themselves to be indios, they did believe that "before Vita took it, the land was free."[109]

For decades after Vita's takeover, the local folk referred to outsiders as "ladinos" and to themselves as either "indígenas" or simply "Yuculeños," and they ascribed a particular set of character traits to each group.[110] Moreover, they continued to practice aspects of Matagalpan Indian traditions that helped to maintain a degree of communal unity. For example, a local Reforma played a prominent role in religious practices in Yúcul. Furthermore, they were proud of their pre-Columbian ancestry and their forebears' role in the rebellion of 1881. Although the Yuculeños internalized the dominant discourse and so regarded "indios" as uncivilized, their contradictory consciousness suggests a more complex relation between proletarianization and ladinoization than a forced detour onto a one-way street.

John Comaroff ended an article on ethnicity with the following challenge: "Much more vexing . . . is the question of when and why ethnic ideologies break down and class consciousness rises to replace it [the ideologies]—if indeed this ever happens in straightforward terms."[111] The Yúcul case suggests that the agrarian elite's conquest of indigenous villages may create conditions for such an ethnic ideological breakdown and its replacement by something resembling a rural proletarian consciousness. But as we have seen, withdrawal into closed communities and migration were far more common indigenous responses to elite aggression against their land and labor. The retreat to marginal communities perhaps did sustain a form of ethnic consciousness. Family migrations, however, led to the breakup of communities from Boaco to

Honduras and to the erosion of their ethnic identity without a corresponding emergence of class consciousness.

Comaroff's challenge remains unanswered, but the descendants of the highlands Indians have provided some clues for further research. Ethnic identities that died out under decades of ideological, political, and economic harassment generally became atomized into kin-based identities. In Yúcul, on the contrary, the violent takeover of the Indian village eradicated its ties to the Comunidad Indígena and dissipated its sense of ethnic identity. But in response to a knowable and visible history of oppression the villagers developed a class perspective that hinged to a large extent on an "indigenous" sense of identity.[112] Here, a precondition for rural proletarian consciousness was an autochthonous identity, however muted and removed from "Indianness."

Conclusion

The ladinoization of the Yuculeños and the high level of Indian emigration provide evidence for the view that the highlands communities were, if not dead, at least severely wounded early in this century. One reading of this essay might reasonably be, then, that it essentially involves a scholarly dispute about chronology with Wheelock and other social scientists. But our differences are more substantial. Wheelock, for example, posits the demise of the Nicaraguan Indians (outside of the Atlantic coast) before 1900, whereas my research suggests that many indigenous groups survived as ethnic communities well into this century—indeed, many of their descendants today consider themselves to be "indígenas."[113] Moreover, I argue that the highlands Indians played such a vital economic and political role from 1880 to 1925 that their absence from the standard historical portrait leaves a seriously distorted image of Nicaragua's social and political development. Without understanding this prolonged, multifront assault against the Comunidades Indígenas, it would be impossible to recognize a submerged cornerstone of elite hegemony. Such recognition is important because many interpretations of modern Nicaraguan history have hinged upon its bourgeoisie's putative incapacity to construct hegemonic forms of domination. My previous work *To Lead as Equals* questioned that view through a study of labor and peasant movements; this essay extends that challenge by examining one of the elite's most enduring hegemonic achievement, the commonsense notion that Nicaragua is an ethnically homogenous society.[114]

In concluding this essay, I would like to reflect on why this elite achievement and the ethnic conflicts that produced it have slipped into the crevasses of history. The answer, I believe, may be derived from an analysis of the construction of ladino discourse. From 1880 to 1920 elites projected images of Indians as marginal primitives who blocked progress because of their ignorance and wasteful practices on their communal property. These images at once rationalized and reflected policies that led to the expropriation of the Indians' land and the crude exploitation of their labor. The images of abject misery or of an Indian amarrado both justified "civilizing" practices while reflecting the Indians' changing social reality of land loss, forced labor, and military recruitment. Indigenous resistance merely confirmed the ladino discourse. Evading debt obligations in order to earn a just wage demonstrated the Indians' supposed deviousness and their childish irresponsibility. Likewise, the religious-based protests of 1895 in Matagalpa or the agrarian battles in Jinotega from 1915 to 1920 reiterated the need to educate the primitives and to abolish the Comunidades.

During this epoch, then, ladino discourse exhibited a remarkable, totalizing capacity as it parried then assimilated every indigenous effort at autonomous expression. And when Indians did receive an education they ceased to be "real" Indians, and their demands became false by definition. But the question remains, How and when was this discourse transformed from an ideological weapon in the hands of the ladino elite into a form of hegemony? As Jean and John Comaroff suggest, "Hegemony . . . exists in reciprocal interdependence with ideology; it is that part of a dominant world-view which has been naturalized and, having hidden itself in orthodoxy, no more appears as ideology at all."[115]

In the Nicaraguan highlands, the transformation of elite ideology into a hegemonic form was symbolized, I suggest, by the actions of the putative experts and defenders of the Indians. Let us consider briefly four cases. First, the lawyer-poet, Samuel Meza, appropriated 1,500 hectares of communal lands from the Indians of Sébaco, while writing articles in his capacity as Indian expert and benefactor. For example, Meza argued that the abolition of the Comunidades would be "an extremely noble, great act that would save this *raza desgraciada* [disgraced race] from the clutches of ignorance and superstition." Similarly, Modesto Armijo, though perhaps less enriched in the process, aided in the expropriation of Matagalpan lands and then in 1919 headed a national commission that studied the Indian question (later he served as rector of the national university and as minister of education). Let us next consider Eudoro Baca, the lawyer who, in 1910, delivered Yúcul to José Vita. In 1923, Baca became the defense attorney of the Comunidad Indígena of Matagalpa. And finally let us recall the kindly cafetalero who told us that the Indians bled his class dry. It should be stressed that not one ironic smile shines through this historical record. These people apparently believed in their own expertise and goodwill, and moreover their testimony was credible to the bureaucrats and intellectuals in Managua.

How did these moments of personal triumph symbolize and contribute to the transformation of elite ideology into a hegemonic form? It is not just that these local "lies" became national "facts," but rather that the creation of these "experts" involved the passive participation of the Indians. In other words, they were compelled to remain silent about the radical distortions of recent history that those careers signified. Perhaps the Indians' desperate circumstances led them to passively accept these "defenders," who offered "solutions"—usually a kinder version of the venerable privatization plus education equals citizen formula—at precisely the moment when the disintegrating Comunidad was under attack from all sides. Compared to some of the thugs dragging people through the mountains, Armijo, Baca, and Meza might have seemed friendly faces indeed. Whatever the cause, these lawyers, poets, and cafetaleros could take advantage of the indigenous silence and invent a version of social history that notwithstanding a blatant disregard for local facts rapidly became a canon: despite the noble efforts of their enlightened defenders, a primitive race tragically died off, victims of their inability to modernize and of unscrupulous outsiders who took advantage of their simplicity.

Comparative research might help us to understand if the personification of these inversions of history ultimately made the victors' accounts more affective and meaningful or whether such careers merely added a bitter, ironic flavor to the narrative. Notwithstanding our ambivalence on this issue, there is little doubt that the history of such experts signaled a moment when ideology assumed a hegemonic form.

The ladinos' creation of a mythical history that suppressed the existence of Indians in the twentieth century has produced devastating effects on those highlands communities that managed to survive this epoch of violence. Since 1950, the indigenous groups have distinguished themselves from the ladino rural poor through a collective sense of history. Yet as they lost the land, dress, religious symbols, and institutions that allowed people to understand their identity, there remained little that made indigenous history real to the new generations. As one highlands Indian lamented, "The youth do not care about our history."[116]

That lament reveals the depth of the ladino victories scored throughout this century. But this essay has also shown how the indigenous peoples of the highlands resisted on many fronts: from the 1870s until the 1940s they blocked church efforts to control their religious practices, they waged an often successful struggle against servile labor relations, and they thwarted elite efforts to abolish their Comunidades Indígenas. Indeed, a century after their communities' scheduled disappearance thousands of highlands folk still identify with their Comunidades, which survive in the shadows of official history.

Notes

1. Walter Lehmann, *Zentral America*, 2 vols. (Berlin: D. Reimer, 1920), 2:907.

2. *El Heraldo (Managua)*, March 21, 1918.

3. For a discussion of the manner in which the Sutiavan Indians dealt with biological mestizaje, see my "'La raza rebelde': las luchas de la comunidad indígena de Subtiava, Nicaragua (1900–1960)," *Revista de Historia* (Costa Rica), nos. 21–22 (1990): 100.

4. Jaime Wheelock, *Raíces indígenas de las luchas anticolonialistas* (Managua: Editorial Nueva Nicaragua, 1981), 117.

5. CIERA-MIDINRA, *Por eso defendemos la frontera: historia agraria de las Segovias Occidentales* (Managua: MIDINRA, 1984), 107.

6. For the perspective of Nicaragua's cultural elite, see José Coronel Urtecho, *Reflexiones sobre la historia de Nicaragua*, 2 vols. (León: Instituto Histórica Centroamericano, 1962), 1:125; Jorge Eduardo Arellano, *El güegüence o macho ratón* (Managua, 1984), 36; and Pablo Antonio Cuadra, *La aventura literaria del mestizaje* (San José: Libro Libre, 1988), 38.

7. The U.S. State Department estimated on the basis of the 1906 census that there were 170,000 Nicaraguan Indians out of a total population of 520,000 (27 percent—both figures including 20,000 *indios bravos*). Wands to Secre-

tary of State, May 3, 1911, U.S. National Archives (hereafter cited as USNA), RG 59, 817.51/31, p. 52; see also Gustavo Niederlein, *The State of Nicaragua in the Greater Republic of Central America* (Philadelphia: Philadelphia Commercial Museum, 1898), 45. Using vital statistics from the mid-1890s, he cites Indian births as slightly over 30 percent and Indian deaths as 35 percent of the total (not including Atlantic coast and indios bravos). The 1920 census, Oficina Central del Censo, *Censo general de la república, 1920* (Managua: Tipografía y Encuadernacion Nacional, 1920) reports under 4 percent *cobrizos* ("copper colored") in the country and 2 percent excluding the Atlantic coast.

8. See Richard N. Adams, "Ethnic Images and Strategies in 1944," in *Guatemalan Indians and the State,* edited by Carol A. Smith (Austin: University of Texas Press, 1990), 152.

9. Fourteen communities were still functioning in 1942. See the report by Leonardo Argüello, *ministro de gobernación* (minister of the interior), in *Memorias del Ministerio de Gobernación* (Managua: n.p., 1943), 90.

10. Similarly, the cobrizos in the departments of Chontales and Matagalpa accounted for only 15 instead of 60 percent of the population. If we include the Atlantic coast, and the unrecorded estimates of indios bravos in the central highlands, the indigenous proportion of the total Nicaraguan population was between 20 and 25 percent. For a more detailed explanation of my estimates for 1920 and 1950, see Jeffrey Gould, "Y el buitre respondió, Aquí no hay indios: la política y la etnicidad en Nicaragua Occidental," appendices one and two, in *Las etnias en Nicaragua,* edited by Marcos Membreño (Managua: Editorial de la Universidad Centroamericana, forthcoming).

11. The government decreed the abolition of the Comunidades in 1877, 1881, 1895, 1906, and 1918. See *Nicaragua Indígena,* 1, nos. 4–6 (April–December 1947): 3–20. In 1919 and 1923 abolition legislation was blocked.

12. On myths in history, see Emilia Viotti da Costa, *The Brazilian Empire: Myths and Histories* (Chicago: University of Chicago Press, 1985).

13. On hegemony and ethnicity, see Brackette F. Williams, *Stains on My Name, War in My Veins: Guyana and the Politics of Cultural Struggle* (Durham, N.C.: Duke University Press, 1991), 27–32; on hegemony see Jean and John Comaroff, *Of Revelation and Revolution: Christianity, Colonialism, and Consciousness in South Africa* (Chicago: University of Chicago Press, 1991), 19–27.

14. See, for example, Francisco Ortega Arancibia, *Cuarenta años de historia de Nicaragua, 1838–1878* (Managua: Banco de América, 1975), 108–109; Bedford Pim, *Dottings on the Roadside in Panama, Nicaragua, and Mosquito* (London: Chapman and Hall, 1869), 78; Carl Scherzer, *Travels in the Free States of Central America,* 2 vols. (London: Longman, Brown, Green, Longmans, and Roberts, 1857), 159–183.

15. See Julián Guerrero, *Monografía de Matagalpa* (Managua, 1967), 67. Cit-

ing a *tabla de tributaciones*, he lists Laborío with 447 tribute payers, Pueblo Grande (formerly Matagalpa) 379, Molagüina 343, and Solingalpa 323.

16. Based on a study of baptismal records in the Casa Cural of Matagalpa for the years 1817, 1841, and 1865. For the latter date, births were no longer recorded by parcialidad, but rather divided into indígena or ladino.

17. Ortega Arancibia, *Cuarenta años*, 108–109.

18. Pim, *Dottings on the Roadside*, 78.

19. In one village, a Jesuit reported hearing confession from nearly 700 Indians, with only three refusing to confess. Rafael Pérez, S.J., *La Compañía de Jesús en Colombia y Centroamérica*, 4 vols. (Valladolid, Spain: Imprenta Castellana, 1898), 3:432–433.

20. *La Gaceta* (Managua), May 5, 1881. A total of 500,000 coffee trees in roughly 500 acres had been planted before the rebellion. The only coffee grower of any importance, a German, repaired the muskets of the Indian rebels. See G. Von Houwold, *Los alemanes en Nicaragua* (Managua: Banco de América, 1975), 270. It is unclear whether the German performed this service out of fear for his life or out of sympathy for the rebels.

21. Padre P. M. Valenzuela, S.J., quoted in the pamphlet by Padre F. M. Crispolti S.J., *El mensaje del 24 de febrero y el dictamen del 21 de febrero en el Congreso de Nicaragua en 1882* (New York: n.p., 1882), 64.

22. Pérez, *La Compañía de Jesús*, 3:491–492. The Jesuit Cáceres also alluded to the effects of a decree that aimed to abolish the Comunidad Indígena and sell its land (approved March 1881). It is certainly possible that the Indians heard of the decree issued the same month as the rebellion, but it is extremely doubtful that the decree was put into effect.

23. Letter to Alejandro Cáceres, S.J., dated April 6, 1881, signed "todos en jeneral la gente," reproduced in ibid., 3:500–501.

24. On the government's view of Jesuit involvement, see *El Porvenir* (Managua), June 11, 1881. For a more thorough treatment, see Franco Cerutti, *Los jesuitas en Nicaragua en el siglo XIX* (San José: Libro Libre, 1984); on the insurrections, see Julián Guerrero and Lola Soriano de Guerrero, *Caciques heróicos de Centroamérica: rebelión indígena en 1881 y expulsión de los jesuitas* (Masaya, Nicaragua: Sold by Librería Loaisiga, 1982), and Enrique Miranda Casij, "La guerra olvidada," *Revista Conservadora de Pensamiento Centroamericano*, no. 142:75–82.

25. Teniente Coronel José Lorenzo Pérez to a ladino ally, Pedro Garquín, August 20, 1881, published in *El Porvenir*, September 24, 1881.

26. Máximo Moreno to Sr. Don Isaac Sobalbarro, August 14, 1881, published in ibid.

27. *La Gaceta*, June 6, 1881.

28. Ibid., September 20, 1881.

29. Arancibia, *Cuarenta años*, 501.

30. For an excellent discussion of foreign views of the Indian as a progressive figure during the middle of the nineteenth century, see E. Bradford Burns, *Patriarch and Folk: The Emergence of Nicaragua, 1798–1858* (Cambridge: Harvard University Press, 1991), 143–145. In this sense, the defeat of the rebellion marked a downgrading of the Indians' status to that of "semisavage."

31. *La Gaceta*, October 29, 1881. One official report on a battle at Yúcul on September 24 listed ten Indian rebels dead and two dead and two wounded on the government side, "tres de estos individuos de la casta indígena y recién aliados a las fuerzas nacionales."

32. Ibid.

33. On the conspiracy of 1884, see "Informe del prefecto de Matagalpa," November 30, 1884, in *Memorias del Ministerio de Gobernación, 1884* (Managua: n.p., 1885), and *La Gaceta*, November 11, 1884. As late as 1910, former rebels fondly reminisced about the insurrection. See Alberto Vogl Baldizón, *Nicaragua: con amor y humor* (Managua: Editorial Garco, 1977), 131.

34. On the debate, see Oscar-René Vargas, *La revolución que inició el progreso: Nicaragua, 1893–1909* (Managua: Ecotextura, 1991), 25–37, and Amaru Barahona, "El gobierno de José Santos Zelaya," *Revista de Historia*, 1, no. 1 (January–June 1990): 90–91. Also see Charles Stansifer, "José Santos Zelaya: A New Look at Nicaragua's Liberal Dictator," *Revista Interamericana*, 7 (1977). Benjamin Teplitz, in "Political Foundations of Modernization in Nicaragua: The Administration of José Santos Zelaya, 1893–1909" (Ph.D. dissertation, Howard University, 1974), points out that Zelaya tried to persuade Sioux Indians to migrate to Nicaragua as farmers, suggesting a nonracist dimension to his indigenous policies.

35. The 1881 movement had coincided with other Indian-led rebellions in León and Masaya, raising the specter of a caste war. See, for example, *El Porvenir*, June 11, 1881, August 27, 1881, and September 24, 1881.

36. See W. C. Newell, *The Handbook of Nicaragua* (Washington: Bureau of the American Republics, 1892), 31. The data on land is confirmed by the *Indice del Archivo Nacional*, Sección de Tierras (Managua: n.p., 1916). On resistance, see *Diario Oficial*, June 8, 1895. The leading German planter, Wilhelm Jericho, was assassinated in 1893. Von Houwold, *Los alemanes*, 271.

37. Indian alcaldes to the *vicario general*, Matagalpa, April 20, 1891, Archivo de la Diócesis de León (hereafter cited as ADL), León, Nicaragua, sección de correspondencia, box 389/1.

38. Letters to the vicario general in Sección de Correspondencia, ADL, Rivas, November 26, 1893, box 386/1. El Viejo, September 7, 1896, box 220/3; and Sutiava, September 24, 1894, box 220/3.

39. Alfonso Martínez to the secretary of Bishop, Matagalpa, August 25, 1893, and September 25, 1893, ibid., box 389/1.

40. *El Diario de Nicaragua* (Managua), August 1, 1895.

41. Ibid., August 2, 1895.

42. Ibid.

43. Ibid., September 17, 1895. The Zelaya government proposed the establishment of an Indian normal school. Although the idea never got off the drawing board, the government did found at least a dozen schools in Indian villages.

44. The labor system in the early 1900s functioned better in Matagalpa (where, for example, only 18 percent of the workers deserted in 1900) than elsewhere. Benjamin Teplitz, in "Political Foundations of Modernization in Nicaragua," suggests that Indian passivity—their compliance with labor laws—derived from their loss of land in the 1890s.

45. For examples of naming capitanes de cañada in Matagalpa, see *Diario Oficial*, March 12, March 15, and September 9, 1898. For references to the treaty and to the role of the capitanes, see Beaulac to the secretary of state, March 18, 1932, USNA, U.S. State Department, RG 57, 817.00/7373, and J. A. Willey to Allen Dawson, October 18, 1934, ibid., 817.00/8160.

46. On the relocation decree, whose efficacy is unknown, see "Informe del jefe político de Matagalpa al ministro de Gobernación," July 15, 1897, Matagalpa, in *Memorias del Ministerio de Gobernación* (Managua 1898).

47. *El Comercio*, March 11, 1898.

48. *El Comercio* (Managua), March 11 and April 15, 1898.

49. In 1899, the regime exercised that authority with little apparent resistance: the Indians' nightmare of 1881 became a reality as they were forced to pick coffee in the Sierras. See Emiliano Chamorro, *El último caudillo: autobiografía* (Managua: Editorial Unión, 1983), 28, 145.

50. On the numerous protests of the alcaldes, see the testimony included in the land title of the comunidad reprinted in *Nicaragua Indígena*, 2, nos. 7–10 (January–December 1948): 98–246.

51. On the vote, see *Diario Oficial*, October 25, 1903. On January 10, 1901, for example, the Indian-led municipal government of Boaco sent a protest letter to Zelaya asking him to rescind orders that sent local laborers to the Sierra coffee plantations; he responded positively to the petition. *Libro de actas y acuerdos de la acaldía de Boaco de 1901*, January 10, 1901.

52. *Diario Oficial*, January 11, 1903.

53. See, for example, the Matagalpan weekly *El Noticiero*, January 12, 1908: "Eight roving police agents will visit the coffee plantation so that there will be no difficulties during the coffee harvest." The same paper suggested on November 7, 1907, that all workers without a passbook would be imprisoned or sent to the plantations "so that the harvest does not suffer." This seems to be an example of coffee region exceptionalism insofar as the labor law was concerned.

54. *El Diario de Granada* (Granada), September 20, 1908. The Matagalpan

demand for the reimplantation of forced labor should be taken as evidence for the relative success of the abolition of the 1901 labor legislation.

55. On Jinotega, see testimony in the land title of the comunidad indígena of Jinotega, published in *Nicaragua Indígena* 1, nos. 4–6 (April–December 1947): 13–14 and 60–81. On the 1893 conflict, see Julián Guerrero, *Boaco* (Managua: Tipografía Alemán, 1957), 195–198.

56. See "Informe del comisionado del gobierno," sent to resolve the dispute between the comunidad indígena of Boaco and the municipality of Boaco in *Memorias del Ministerio de Gobernación, 1904–1905* (Managua: Compañía Tipográfica Internacional, 1905).

57. On the decree, see *Nicaragua Indígena*, 1, nos. 4–6 (1947): 81, and *Memorias del Ministro de Gobernación, 1905* (Managua: Compañía Tipográfica Internacional, 1906).

58. See Jeffrey Gould, "El café, el trabajo y la Comunidad Indígena de Matagalpa," in *El café en la historia centroamericana*, edited by Héctor Pérez-Brignoli and Mario Samper (San José: FLACSO, 1994). Also see the title of the Comunidad Indígena of Matagalpa, surveyed in 1904 and published in *Nicaragua Indígena*, 1, nos. 4–6 (1948), and see *Memorias del Ministerio de Gobernación, 1911–12* (Managua: n.p., 1913).

59. Harold Playter, in 1925, noted that the Indians comprised 60 percent of Matagalpa's population (or 46,800), USNA, U.S. State Department, RG 59, 817.61333/1, p. 34. It is probable that such an estimate reflects the Comunidad population of Matagalpa, Muy Muy, and Sébaco.

60. "A nuestros coreligionarios indígenas de Boaco, Jinotega, Matagalpa y Subtiava," handbill produced by the Comité Conservador Indígena, 1920, Archivo del Instituto Histórico Nicaragüense, Universidad Centroamericana, leg. 573. On the military role of Indians in counterrevolution, see *La Regeneración*, September 30, 1910.

61. *Nicaragua Indígena* (1947): 45.

62. *Libro de actas de la Comunidad Indígena de Matagalpa*, fragments, 1911–1913, in private archives of Aurora Martínez (daughter of Bartolomé Martínez), Matagalpa, hereafter cited as PAAM.

63. "Informe al Ministerio de Gobernación, J. Bárcenas," June 4, 1912, in *Memorias del Ministerio de Gobernación, 1911–1912* (Managua: n.p., 1913), 199–200.

64. *Memorias del Ministerio de Gobernación, 1911–1912*, 204. He also noted that fifteen properties within their territory had also been sold to ladinos. Belli, an Italian architect by profession, was the brother-in-law of Emiliano Chamorro.

65. Speech printed in *Memorias del Ministerio de Gobernación, 1917* (Managua: Tipografía y Encuadernación Nacional, 1918), 302.

66. *La Gaceta*, May 14, 1924. The 3,600 manzanas represented the fifteen

properties inside the revised Comunidad boundaries cited in Bárcenas's report and not the lost 17,000 manzanas (100 square kilometers). On Martínez's relations with the Indians, see Gould, "El trabjo forzoso."

67. On the land occupation, see Luis Arrieta (jefe político) to Bartolomé Martínez, Matagalpa, June 8, 1919, PAAM. On Camoapa, see *Libro de actas y acuerdos, 1920–1923* in the municipality of Camoapa. On Sutiava, see Jeffrey Gould, "La raza rebelde," 85–98.

68. Based on an examination of court documents without titles in the Juzgado Civil (civil court), Matagalpa, March 1–25, 1919, and on M. Borgen to Bartolomé Martínez, July 18, 1918, PAAM.

69. *El Correo* (Granada), March 22, 1918. See also, *Memorias del Ministerio de Gobernación y anexos, 1918* (Managua: Tipografía Nacional, 1919), 342.

70. Lisandro Moreira to B. Martínez, Jinotega, March 6, 1919. PAAM. An internal party report underscored the recent origin of that base: "The Conservative party barely had five members before the campaign [of 1916]." Borgen to Martínez, Granada, July 22, 1918, PAAM.

71. Julian Frisbie to Major H. Schmidt, Jinotega, Nicaragua, July 13, 1928, USNA, U.S. Marine Corps section, RA 127, E220, box 11. A copy was kindly provided by Michael Schroeder, University of Michigan.

72. In 1919, the Chamorro administration called for a public discussion on the (re)abolition of the Comunidades. *La Tribuna* (Managua), March 11, 1919. New Conservative abolition legislation was introduced in 1923, but shelved by Martínez in 1924, notwithstanding his public appeal for abolition in 1918. See *Memorias del Ministerio de Gobernación, 1918* (Managua: Tipografía Nacional, 1919), 312.

73. The preceding paragraph is based on ten letters from Aguilar to Martínez between 1911 and 1925, PAAM.

74. On the normal school, see Josefa T. de Aguerri, *Puntos críticos sobre la enseñanza nicargüense* (Managua: Imprenta Nacional, 1933), 327–329. On the contradictions of government education policy, see *Memorias del Ministerio de Instrucción Pública, 1919* (Managua: Tipografía y Encuadernación Nacional, 1920), 156–157.

75. *El Cronista* (León), July 18, 1919.

76. *El Correo*, March 22, 1918; Modesto Armijo, a progressive Liberal lawyer who had aided land grabs in Matagalpa, headed the commission. See *La Evolución* (Managua), February 20, 1919.

77. *El Comercio* (Managua), February 18, 1919.

78. Juan Mendoza, *Historia de Diriamba* (Guatemala: Staebler, 1920), 78–81.

79. Ibid., 4.

80. Dana Munro, *The Five Republics of Central America: Their Political Development and Their Relations with the United States* (New York: Russell and Russell, 1967), 94.

81. See report by Admiral Kimball, March 12, 1910, USNA, U.S. State Department, RG 59, #6369/811. On Matagalpan opposition to abolition, see *La Gaceta*, May 11, 1923. The Managüense cafetaleros, in contrast, favored the abolition because they realized that forced labor hurt productivity and that many workers were fleeing to Costa Rica.

82. Playter, "Report on Coffee in Nicaragua," USNA, U.S. State Department, RG 59, 817.00/6133/1.

83. Alan Knight, "Debt Bondage in Latin America," in *Slavery and Other Forms of Unfree Labor*, edited by Leonie J. Archer (London and New York: Routledge, 1988), 106–107.

84. Harold Playter, "Report on Coffee in Nicaragua."

85. See, especially, Arnold Bauer, "Rural Workers in Spanish America: Problems of Peonage and Oppression," *Hispanic American Historical Review*, 59, no. 1, (1979): 34–63, and Peter Blanchard, *The Origins of the Peruvian Labor Movement* (Pittsburgh: University of Pittsburgh, 1982). For a critical review of the literature, see Tom Brass, "The Latin American Enganche System: Some Revisionist Interpretations Revisited," *Slavery and Abolition*, 11, no. 1 (May 1990): 74–101. Knight's "Debt Bondage in Latin America," 116, does point out in a footnote the existence of "additional factors" within a mode of exploitation that induce workers to yield a surplus. He would undoubtedly recognize land expropriation by employers as one of those factors.

86. Vogl Baldizón, *Nicaragua: con amor y humor*, 129.

87. Telegram from J. L. Fernández to B. Martínez, Muy Muy, Matagalpa, January 13, 1913. PAAM. In another case located in the Juzgado Civil, Matagalpa, dated March 24, 1913, *Jacinta Hernández v. Florentino Pérez*, a worker deserted three different local cafetaleros in two years, running up debts for the equivalent of $75.00, which yet another cafetalero paid off.

88. Based on data from the *corte* (court) log books from Bartolomé Martínez's coffee plantation El Bosque. In 1918, when he paid less than ten cents a *medio* (40 medios of picked berries produced 100 pounds of beans), women averaged 24.3 medios a week while men averaged 15.8.

89. Despite Vogl's lament, on the average coffee planters earned annual profits of 35 percent on the sales price and 10 to 15 percent on the investment after five to ten years. See Harold Playter, *Nicaragua: A Commercial and Economic Survey* (Washington: U.S. Government Printing Office, 1927), 30.

90. For an example of benevolent elite racism, consider Samuel Meza, a poet, landowner, and reputed defender of the Indians: "from the clutches of ignorance and superstition. . . . this disgraced race will never emerge from its abject misery without schooling." *El Noticiero* (Matagalpa), March 2, 1919.

91. Servando Ochoa to B. Martínez, San Dionisio, Matagalpa, January 14, 1913, and Eric Smith to B. Martínez, El Gorrión, Matagalpa, November 28, 1921, PAAM. Even Ceferino Aguilar probably used his authority to recruit

mozos for Martínez: in 1919, when his hacienda was short of labor, Martínez received the following telegram from the jefe político, L. Arrieta: "Capitán-general, Ceferino Aguilar, tiene gente lista para trabajar en su hacienda," October 24, 1919, PAAM.

92. "Jorge Pérez demanda a Ciriaco Obregón, por lesiones," May 9, 1912, document located in the Juzgado Civil, Matagalpa.

93. Ceferino Aguilar to B. Martínez, Susulí, Matagalpa, June 10, 1913, PAAM.

94. Report sent to B. Martínez, August 1916, PAAM.

95. C. Aguilar to B. Martínez, Susulí, September 8, 1916, PAAM. Four letters from other Indians asked Martínez for protection from the indigenous authorities Bibiano Herrera and Félix Pérez.

96. Capitán de cañada to B. Martínez, Guasaca, Matagalpa, December 21, 1921, PAAM.

97. Census returns are not adequate enough for quantifying intramunicipal migration. Given the vast eastern regions of the Indian municipalities, migration estimates are also impossible. However, the census does show that the Indian cañada population did not grow at the same rate as did the national population. See my article "Y el buitre respondió." My estimate is based on interviews with members of La Reforma of the Comunidad, including Gregorio Aráuz, Francisco Arceda, Pablo García, Patrocinio López, Valerio Mercado, and Santos Pérez, Matagalpa, January 1992.

98. *La Flecha*, June 17, 1950.

99. Interview with Patricinio López, El Chile, Matagalpa, April 1990.

100. *La Gaceta*, August 19, 1942. Interviews with La Reforma, Matagalpa, January 1992.

101. Interviews with La Reforma, Matagalpa, January 1992. The precise date of the church action is unclear, but numerous testimonies agree on the removal of the images.

102. The data on Yúcul derives from a series of court cases found in the Juzgado Civil, Matagalpa. Vita's takeover of the Yúcul land is revealed in "Ejecutoria a favor de Eudoro Baca contra los indígenas de esta ciudad," 1909–1910. The quote comes from "Recurso de apelación de Bibiano Díaz et al.," July 21, 1913, ibid.

103. "Recurso de apelación de Bibiano Díaz et al.," September 2, 1913.

104. Ibid.

105. Ibid. In "Recurso de apelación," July 21, 1913, one witness on Díaz's behalf claimed that Vita "shot an Indian for shouting near the casa hacienda."

106. "Recurso de apelación de Bibiano Díaz et al.," September 2, 1913.

107. Interviews with Delfina Díaz (1990), Blas García (January 1992), Macaria Hernández (1990–1992), Juan Polanco (1990), Urbano Pérez (1990), and Eusebio Urbina (1990, 1992), Yúcul, Matagalpa.

108. Ibid.

109. Interview with Delfina Díaz, Yúcul, March 1990.

110. Interviews with Blas García and Eusebio Urbina, Yúcul, Matagalpa, January 1992. These informants stated that they believed that ladinos were always *altivos* (haughty) and the indígenas were *humildes* (humble) and *respetuosos* (respectful).

111. John Comaroff, "Of Totemism and Ethnicity," *Ethnos*, 52, nos. 3–4 (1987): 319.

112. In the 1990 elections, for example, the Sandinistas won over 60 percent of the vote in the Yúcul area while losing in the areas of the comunidad indígenas of Matagalpa and Jinotega by margins of 4 to 1 and 5 to 1.

113. On indigenous organizing, see *La Prensa* (Managua), January 27, 1992.

114. Jeffrey L. Gould, *To Lead as Equals: Rural Protest and Political Consciousness in Chinandega, Nicaragua, 1912–1979* (Chapel Hill: University of North Carolina Press, 1990).

115. Jean and John Comaroff, *Of Revelation and Revolution*, 25.

116. Interview with Mercedes López, Camoapa, Boaco, January 1992.

JULIE A. CHARLIP

At Their Own Risk

Coffee Farmers and Debt in Nicaragua,

1870–1930

❂

In the late nineteenth and early twentieth centuries, the majority of the laboring people of Nicaragua were not landless workers. Instead, they were small farmers, struggling to succeed in the same milieu as their richer counterparts. Contrary to common conceptions of Nicaraguan agrarian history as the story of peasant displacement and proletarianization, the rise of the coffee economy was characterized by the widespread participation of small farmers. In the department of Carazo from 1877 to 1909, small and medium farmers accounted for more than 90 percent of the coffee farms, comprising more than half the area planted in coffee.

However, the survival and even vitality of the smaller sectors do not negate the fact that the smaller grower faced exploitation. The small grower was not an equal player in the coffee market, since s/he relied on larger growers for financing to harvest the crop, as well as for the purchase of the crops for processing and export.

In 1908, an anonymous editorial writer, urging the formation of a farmers' association and bank, complained in the Carazo newspaper *Pabellón Nacional:* "Currently the farmers are no more than agents—*ad honorem*—of merchants, who extort the farmer after years of spending his life, supreme forces, and large sums of painfully acquired money to plant coffee—then the merchant acquires it for the price he wants as though he were doing the poor worker a favor."[1] The use of the term *worker* in reference to the farmer emphasizes the small farmer's position: though not a landless proletarian, neither was s/he a privileged bourgeois producer immune from other forms of exploitation.

Coffee growers tended to borrow money every year to pay for the harvesting of their crops or to meet other expenses. Robert G. Williams suggests that up to 5,000 trees (5 *manzanas* [8.7 acres], fully planted) could be harvested and maintained by a family, and up to 20,000 trees could be maintained, with extra labor needed for the harvest. Cash advances were needed to pay for the outside workforce. But even the smaller growers, who theoretically could handle all of the work with family labor, at times needed extra cash. "If a family ran out of corn and beans or needed cash for an emergency, it could get an advance on the coffee crop instead of having to sign a labor contract," Williams writes, "though implicit interest rates on such advances were typically high." [2]

Financing coffee crops was a profitable business: lenders allowed loans to lapse for years, while they collected interest. If the borrower defaulted, the lender usually chose to sell the land to another small or medium grower, starting anew the profitable cycle of debt. The debtors' maxim may well be drawn from the mortgage documents themselves, which often stipulated that loans were to be repaid in coffee, delivered to the lender's processing plant or the local railroad station, at the debtor's own cost and risk.

Coffee and Nicaraguan Development

Scholars agree that coffee production in Nicaragua, which began in the department of Carazo in the 1840s, brought Nicaragua into the modern world economy and laid the groundwork for twentieth-century social and economic conditions. They disagree, however, on the form these developments took, particularly in the evolution of land tenure and class structure. This debate was particularly significant during the Sandinista agrarian reform program dispute over private versus collectivized property. Both those who studied the reform process and those who made policy were divided into two camps, which have been described by David Kaimowitz as the capitalist agro-export model and the peasant capitalism model.

The capitalist agro-export model, which has become predominant, has been expounded by Jaime Wheelock and Jaime Biderman. This approach maintains that with the introduction of coffee in the nineteenth century, the peasants of Nicaragua lost their land and gradually became an agricultural proletariat, with the chief conflict in society between landowners, who made use of extraeconomic measures to obtain their land, and their workers. The peasant capitalism model, presented by Eduardo Baumeister, rejects the capitalist-proletarian bifurcation set out in the former model and stresses the importance of rising middle sectors.[3] Until now, neither model has been tested historically.

This essay focuses on Nicaragua's first coffee-producing province, Carazo. At 950 square kilometers, Carazo is one of the smallest and most densely populated departments in the country. It rests on a high plateau, bordered by the department of Masaya to the North, the Pacific Ocean to the South, and the departments of Managua to the west and Granada and Rivas to the East. Originally a subprefecture of the department of Granada, Carazo was given departmental status in 1891. Before the introduction of coffee, Carazo was primarily a sugar-producing region.

Carazo's development bears out Baumeister's theory of peasant capitalism. Records of property transactions in the *Registro de propiedad* show that *minifundios,* small farms, and medium farms accounted for 97 percent of the number of farms and 64 percent of the area cultivated from 1877 to 1903.[4] A national coffee census conducted in 1909 shows that these three categories still accounted for 94 percent of the farms and 55 percent of the area. Thus the rise of the coffee economy did not create a large landed class that precluded others from becoming producers. On the contrary, the organization of the economy encouraged the small producer, although his enterprise could be risky.

The world of coffee producers was a fluid one: from 1878 to 1904, while 175 people apparently sold the only coffee-producing property they owned, another 102 people with no record of owning other coffee property were buying such land for the first time. Furthermore, the farms sold rarely contributed to the construction of latifundios. When property was merged into larger units, 72 percent went into the minifundio, small, and medium sectors, with the small-farm sector claiming the largest share: 43 percent. Even by the 1909 census, we find that the area of large farms and latifundios grew by only 9 percent. The year 1909 is a telling one because it coincides with the end of rule by José Santos Zelaya, the Liberal credited with facilitating the coffee boom.[5]

Just as the *minifundistas* and small farmers held the bulk of the property, they also constituted the majority of the people who borrowed money. They faced terms that were more onerous than those incurred by the larger farmers, especially higher interest rates. Minifundistas repaying their loans in coffee were more likely to have a price specified in advance than were larger growers, and only minifundistas agreed, though rarely, to the option of paying their debts in labor.

Yet minifundistas were not the most likely to default on their loans. It was the large farmers and latifundistas who failed completely to redeem their property sold in resale agreements known as *pactos de retroventa;* and medium-sized farmers, represented out of proportion to their numbers were most likely to default on a *hipoteca,* or mortgage. Another surprising finding is that there were 202 lenders, presenting borrowers with multiple options. Further, most of these lenders were locally based, not absentee landlords or out-of-town merchants.[6]

The image we end up with, then, is not of the landless worker nor the witless and exploited "peasant," both the targets of rapacious, expanding latifundistas. Instead, we see a complex strata of minifundistas and small and medium farmers, operating alongside their larger counterparts, with some succeeding and others failing. The larger growers were diversified businessmen who saw profits to be made in lending as well as in growing, processing, and exporting coffee. Although they exploited smaller growers, they also facilitated the continued existence of the smaller coffee sectors.

The Pacto de Retroventa

The earliest form of moneylending to appear in property records was the pacto de retroventa, in which the borrower sold his property to the lender, while retaining usufruct, with the agreement that he would repurchase the property by a certain date. Although most common before the turn of the century, the pacto de retroventa continued at least through 1930.

This form of borrowing was most beneficial to the lender because the property was registered to him. If the borrower did not repay his loan as stipulated, the lender did not need to seek legal recourse to obtain title to the land. Moreover, it took the filing of a new deed to return the property to the seller-borrower. One Jinotepino coffee grower said it was not uncommon for lenders to be "unavailable" when borrowers came to repay their loans; the due date would come and go, and the lender-buyer now had full title to the property. The new owner most commonly would then resell the property to another small grower, making a profit on the sale, and then finance the new owner, starting anew the cycle of debt.

The large growers as well as the small used this system to borrow money, and in all size categories there were losers and winners, those who could repay their debts, conserving their property, and those who could not.

There were eighty-seven cases involving pactos de retroventa recorded in the *Registro de propiedad* between 1879 and 1903. In 63 percent of the cases, the original owners were unable to rebuy their property; in another ten cases, they rebought the property only to subsequently lose it in another pacto de retroventa. In other words, in the long run, 75 percent of these owners lost the property. However, most of them also owned other property and did not join the ranks of the landless.

Loan Terms

The terms of the sales and loans varied widely in every respect, including the method of repayment, interest rates, and duration of the loan. Most commonly these were short-term loans for the upcoming harvest and were to be repaid in coffee from that harvest, valued at a predetermined price that implicitly included interest because the price was set below the market value.

In twenty of the thirty cases that were to be repaid with coffee, reimbursement was stipulated in pesos per *fanega* (125 pounds) or *quintal* (100 pounds), or the agreement specified the volume of coffee required to repay the loan. From 1879 to 1889, the price per unit remained fairly uniform, averaging 5.17 *pesos fuertes* per fanega,[7] while ranging from 4 to 8.20 pesos fuertes, with a median price of 4.80. This can be compared to Paul Levy's estimate of the price for coffee of 6.40 pesos fuertes per quintal circa 1870, showing that pactos were repaid with coffee valued at 19 to 25 percent below the market price.[8]

From 1890 to 1902, there was much more variation in the price paid for the coffee, and higher prices prevailed. Prices ranged from 4.80 to 17.50, with a median of 9 and an average of 10.15 pesos fuertes. However, these figures are skewed by three unusually high reimbursement prices of 16 and 17.50 pesos fuertes. When the three outliers are dropped, the average price drops to 8.15 pesos fuertes, still some 7 percent *above* the market price, using U.S. consul Harold Playter's average of $7.59 from 1906 to 1926.[9] Interestingly, the highest prices during the 1890 to 1902 period—16 and 17.50 pesos fuertes—were paid by the richest and most prominent coffee growers in the region: José Esteban González, José María Siero Gutiérrez, and Enrique Baltodano, none of whom fit the stereotype of the greedy latifundista.

In a few cases, the borrower/seller was required to repay the loan with more goods than just coffee, testimony to the continued value of other crops. For example, in 1897, Diriamba (a town in Carazo) farmer Lorenzo Días was required to repay Salomé Barbosa, a Diriamba housewife, five fanegas of coffee and eleven *cargas* (a carga equals 200 pounds) of sugar to repay a debt of eighty pesos sencillos.[10] In 1891, Barbosa wanted Laureano Ortiz, another Diriamba farmer, to repay a debt of 100 pesos sencillos with fifty-seven fanegas of corn, in addition to eight fanegas of coffee.[11]

Several lenders stipulated that they would pay a higher price the first year of the loan than in subsequent years, essentially giving a premium to those who repaid rapidly. In an 1887 pacto, Cleto Asenjo would pay 10 pesos fuertes the first year and 6.40 the next; in 1892 Anastasio Somoza would pay 8 pesos fuertes the first year and only 4.80 the next.[12]

Small farmers could use their labor as well as their goods to repay loans, but such agreements were rare and did not constitute another means of trying to acquire a workforce in a labor-poor country. In only two cases were loans to be repaid entirely through labor: Felipe Ramos of Diriamba promised to repay his 1897 debt of 200 pesos fuertes to Enrique Baltodano through the labor of José Hernández.[13] (The property registry does not indicate why Ramos, identified as a day laborer, had the right to promise Hernández's labor rather than his own.) San Marcos farmer Lázaro Chagón agreed to provide his labor to lender José Herrera, also a San Marcos farmer, to repay his 1899 debt of 126 pesos fuertes. Herrera stipulated that Chagón would be paid forty centavos per day or task, and if he missed even one day, he would lose the property.[14] One pacto called for a combination of goods and labor: San Marcos farmer Ponciano Hernandes was to repay 117 pesos borrowed from Ygnacio Martínez in 1889 with coffee at six pesos sencillos per fanega, three cargas of sugar, and labor valued at 70 pesos per *jornal* (work period) on the hacienda of Francisco Castro, perhaps in turn repaying a debt or fulfilling a contract that Martínez owed Castro.[15]

Other debts were to be repaid in a combination of coffee and cash, with only two cases specifying that the loan was to be repaid exclusively in money, and one loan that was to be repaid in commercial drafts. Because the vast majority of the pactos were to be repaid with coffee, they appear to be essentially advance sale agreements that served the purpose of providing larger growers with more coffee to process and sell.

Usually, no explicit interest was called for when loans were repaid with coffee. But in four cases, the lenders demanded interest: Alejo Mendieta in 1893 and José Valerio in two 1897 pactos wanted to be paid interest of 1 percent per month.[16] In a much more complex agreement, more typical of mortgages than of pactos de retroventa, Daniel Lacayo, a Granada hacendado, was to pay Wilhelm Georg Oetling an annual interest rate of 6 percent, plus 20 percent on both capital and interest, and a commission of 2.5 percent, to be paid in coffee or in letters of exchange drawn on European houses on his 1898 loan of 1,041 German marks.[17]

Oddly, only 23 percent of the cases not paid in coffee specified that interest would be paid. In 46 percent of the cases requiring interest, the interest rate was 1.5 percent a month. In 27 of all the loan cases examined, the agreement stated that the property would be resold for the same price, and only seven of those agreements indicated that interest would be paid. The obvious question is why lenders would provide money at no interest, expecting to get back the same amount. The most obvious answer seems to be that they expected the borrower to default and that they would acquire the property, make a profit by reselling it, and renew the debt cycle.

Indeed, as mentioned earlier, in 75 percent of the cases the original owners were unable to rebuy their property, or rebought it only to subsequently lose it in another pacto de retroventa. However, losing property did not mean falling into the ranks of landless proletarians. In all but seventeen cases, the owners had other property as well, that is, 74 percent of those who lost the encumbered property also owned other land.

Property Size and Loss

Of the eighty-seven pactos, sixty provide information on the size of the landholding. With the exception of large *fincas* (farms), the weight of each size category in the pactos de retroventa conforms closely to their prevalence in the property transactions recorded from 1877 to 1903.

Minifundio constituted 55 percent of the property and 58 percent of the pactos. Small property constituted 31 percent of the property transacted and 28 percent of the property sold in pactos. Medium property was 8 percent of the property traded and 10 percent of the property sold in pactos. Latifundio represented 1 percent of the property and 2 percent of the pactos. But large property, which constituted 1 percent of the property transacted, made up 5 percent of the pactos de retroventa.

Surprisingly, the owners of smaller properties show a better track record for reclaiming property: 21 percent of the minifundios, 18 percent of the small farms, and 33 percent of the medium farms were repurchased, whereas none of the large farms and latifundios was reclaimed. Further transactions were recorded for only 26 percent of the sixty-five cases of lost property. It appears, then, that in the majority of cases in which property was lost via the pacto de retroventa, the new owner did not merge the new property with existing holdings to create larger properties or use the property as collateral for his own loans. It is possible, in fact, that the previous owner-borrower may have kept the usufruct of the property, even after formal title passed to the lender-purchaser.

This possibility is suggested by the cases in which property was sold while a pacto de retroventa remained in effect. For example, on May 3, 1902, San Marcos housewife Petrona Aguirre sold her three-manzana farm for 200 pesos fuertes to Benjamín Zapata, a San Marcos amanuensis, in a pacto de retroventa, to be repurchased by March 1903 for twenty-nine fanegas of coffee.[18] On May 18, 1902, Zapata sold the property, with the pacto still in effect, to Camilo Zúniga, a Jinotepe doctor, for 200 pesos fuertes.[19] Zúniga, in turn, sold the property to Antonio Salinas, a Jinotepino farmer, for 200 pesos on June 21, 1902.[20] On May 9, 1903, Vicente Salinas Leiva, apparently Antonio Salinas's heir, resold the property to Petrona Aguirre for 750 pesos.[21] The same day, Aguirre resold the property in another pacto de retroventa to Jinotepino farmer Ezequiel Sotelo Navarro for 1,195 pesos.[22] There is no record of the resale; however, the next transaction shows the farm back in Aguirre's hands, as she obtained a formal loan of 163.20 pesos fuertes, rather than a pacto de retroventa, in May 1906.[23] Aguirre managed to repay the debt in early November 1907, only to enter into another pacto de retroventa later that month with Pablo Emilio Chamorro for 280 pesos. She never repaid the amount and lost the property to Chamorro in 1909.[24] While awaiting Aguirre's repayment, Chamorro promised to sell the farm to Liberato Valerio Ramos, a Granada farmer, for forty fanegas of coffee. The agreement noted that Valerio received immediate possession of the property.[25]

Despite the many transactions and changes of ownership that took place, the property remained in the hands of the original owner-borrower, Aguirre, until it was passed to Valerio. The intermediate buyers never took possession of the farm themselves, but they were able to buy and sell it, using it as an asset. Clearly what we are seeing is an active market in property and loans; the profitability is indicated by the preference for sales and loans rather than accumulation of land and expansion of production.

Who were the people who sold property in pactos de retroventa? There were seventy-six people, sixty-nine of them men. The vast majority, fifty-eight, identified themselves as farmers. There were also six housewives, six day laborers, two merchants, and one each identified as an hacendado, a musician, a businessman, and a pyrotechnist.

There were five farmers who each sold two properties, and their success or failure in repurchasing was not uniform. Juan Ortiz of Diriamba and Venancio García of San Marcos lost both; Fulgencio Muñoz of San Marcos and Carmen Cordero of Jinotepe lost one and rebought the other; Juan Rojas Román of Diriamba repurchased both of his properties, only to lose them in subsequent pactos de retroventa. All five also owned other property. Only one person, Salvador Castro, a Diriamba farmer, appeared more frequently in the records: he sold four properties, losing all but one; however, he also owned many other properties.

The list of buyer-lenders, however, is much shorter, with only fifty-seven buyers in eighty-seven pactos de retroventa. The percentage of farmers among lender-buyers was a bit lower than among the borrower-sellers—66 percent of the lenders, compared to 76 percent of the borrowers. Merchants were more heavily represented, at 20 percent, than among borrowers, where they only constituted 2 percent. There were also five housewives, one amanuensis, and one medical doctor.

The lion's share of purchases-loans was made by Enrique Baltodano, an illiterate former day laborer who built a fortune, starting with some uncultivated land given to him by his father-in-law. Enrique's brother, Ireneo, and sons, Ignacio, Román, and Moisés, were among the wealthiest and most powerful leaders of Diriamba. Enrique Baltodano purchased nine properties on the list of pactos, and only three of them were resold to the original owner. Fourteen other lender-buyers bought more than one property, among them Anastasio Somoza—father of Anastasio Somoza García, the founder of the Somoza dynasty—a San Marcos farmer who bought three properties, one of which was reclaimed.

These properties may have added in a small way to the holdings of such larger growers, but they certainly do not appear to be the basis of their landed wealth. However, they do represent a significant way of making money through lending and a highly precarious source of funding for the borrowers, given that 75 percent defaulted. Few people who availed themselves of pactos de retroventa appear in the records of the hipotecas, where the default rate was much lower.

The Hipoteca

The second form of lending, which appears throughout the period 1877 to 1930, is the hipoteca, a mortgage on the farm or on another property, to guarantee the loan that is used as *habilitación*, financing specifically for coffee production. In all but a few cases they were issued by individuals rather than by institutions.

Williams's contention that "the most regular source of finance followed the colonial pattern of short-term loans, using future crops, not improved land, as security," proves wrong in the Carazo hipotecas.[26] Although most loans were to be repaid with coffee, the collateral for the loan was indeed the property on which the coffee was grown. The exceptions were for those borrowers who had usufruct of ejidal land, who then could mortgage only the crop. Others chose to mortgage a different piece of property, often a plot of urban land, rather than risk the coffee farm itself.

Like the pactos de retroventa, these were generally short-term loans for the current or upcoming harvest, to be repaid with coffee from that harvest, either at a price agreed upon in advance or at the market price at the time the coffee was delivered. Few loans stipulated that the coffee would be purchased at below-market price, though that may have been the effect with prearranged prices and market fluctuations.

In Carazo, the lender was more likely to be a larger local grower than an out-of-town merchant. The moneylender with the highest volume of loans in Carazo, José Esteban González, also owned the largest *beneficio*, (coffee-processing plant) and served as a principal exporter.

Of the 372 hipotecas recorded between 1877 and 1902, 157 list both size and usable loan amount information. The loans for all years averaged 2,981.52 pesos fuertes, with a median of 1,180, and an average farm size of 44.68 manzanas, but a median of 11.

More meaningful is the examination by size category: minifundios accounted for the greatest share of the hipotecas, with 43 percent of the total. Small farms held 29 percent of the total, medium farms 25 percent, and large farms 3 percent. There were no hipotecas on properties categorized as latifundios. However, owners of latifundios did borrow money on properties in other size categories. In comparison to the weight of each size category in pactos de retroventa, we find that the share of minifundios decreased, dropping 10 percent. Small farms stayed relatively uniform, representing 29 percent of hipotecas and 28 percent of pactos. The share of medium-sized farms rose sharply, from 10 percent of pactos to 25 percent of hipotecas. Large farms constituted a more modest 3 percent of hipotecas, compared to 5 percent of pactos. But latifundios dropped from the picture completely.[27]

Minifundios

It might be expected that the minifundio would be the smallest category for loans because they could most likely be run with family labor alone. Yet, minifundio loans were the greatest in number. For the sixty-seven minifundio loans, the average farm size was 4.83 manzanas, with a median of 5. Loan amounts ranged from 36 to 3,000 pesos fuertes, with an average of 857.06 and a median of 500. The amount of the loans seems out of proportion to the size of the holdings, but the majority of borrowers—59 percent—were indeed minifundistas, not larger growers using their smallest parcels for collateral. Another 36 percent were smallholders, and only three borrowers were medium-sized farmers.

In thirty of the forty-one loans with known results, the loan was repaid and the owner kept possession of the property (at least during this period—eight of them went on to lose their property in subsequent loan agreements). In other words, in 71 percent of the minifundio hipotecas for which we have an outcome, the owner was able to repay the loan, and only twelve, or 29 percent, lost their property. Of those twelve, eleven were sold to the lender, who resold the property. In one case, the property was sold to another party in order to pay the loan. In none of the cases was the property taken over by the lender.

There is virtually no difference between the average amounts of the loans and size of the property that was lost and that which was retained. The average size was 5.07 manzanas for the property that was kept and 5.18 manzanas for the lost property. The average loan defaulted on was 923.16 pesos fuertes, whereas the average loan repaid was slightly higher, at 986.03. The median amount of the defaulted loans was 660 pesos fuertes, compared to the slightly lower median of 633.50 pesos fuertes for the loans repaid.

The one factor that differentiates those who could repay their loans from those who could not was the possession of other properties. Thirty-six percent of those who lost their property did not own any other land recorded in the registry. And most of those who owned more land did not own enough to provide sufficient resources—55 percent of those who lost their land were minifundistas, that is, their total landholdings did not reach ten manzanas; the remainder were small farmers.

Of those who repaid their loans, only 11.5 percent did not own any other land. For example, Francisco Jiménez Vargas used a seven-manzana farm as collateral for a 1,400-pesos-fuertes mortgage in 1899. But he also owned several other properties, totaling roughly 128 manzanas. Minifundistas constituted 38 percent of this group, while 54 percent were small farmers. Two borrowers had holdings that categorized them as medium-sized farmers. However, the amount of the loan was not limited by the size of the property. The largest loan secured by minifundio, 3,063.13 pesos fuertes, was borrowed by minifundista Juan Manuel Villavicencio. His collateral consisted of shares of various properties he owned with others, including one-fourth of a six-manzana farm fully planted in coffee; one-fourth of a three-manzana *huerta* (plot) with a banana grove, and one-fourth of a .25-manzana lot with a house. His May 31, 1897, loan was due in February 1898; on June 14, 1899, Villavicencio sold the property for 3,000 pesos to José Félix Gutiérrez, a Granada farmer, in order to pay the amount owed to the lender, Masaya farmer José Manuel Gutierres.[28]

Villavicencio's case indicates how much could be done with little property and that it was not just the wealthy growers who could secure sizable loans. Also, rather than losing the property to legal action or confiscation by the lender, Villavicencio headed off disaster by selling the property for enough to pay the loan. There is no indication, however, that Villavicencio ever acquired more coffee property.

Small Farms

The small-farm loan category shows some sharp differences from that of the minifundistas. First, a greater percentage of the farms mortgaged were actually owned by people of this category, that is, 75 percent were owned by small farmers, compared to 59 percent of the minifundistas with minifundio loans owning their farms. Perhaps because of that difference, we also find that the ability to repay was contingent less on the amount of other property owned and more on whether the property in question was mortgaged beyond what it could produce.

The average-sized farm mortgaged in the small-farm category was 20.8 manzanas, with an average loan of 2,139.71 pesos fuertes, or a median of 16 manzanas and 800 pesos fuertes. We know the fate of thirty-seven of the forty-five hipotecas recorded: eleven defaults and twenty-six repayments. Therefore, 70 percent of those in the smallholder category repaid their loans (compared to 71 percent for the minifundio).

Unlike the minifundio hipotecas, the smallholder category showed a sharp difference in average costs between the repayment and default categories. Whereas the average small hipoteca was 2,139.71, the average for those who defaulted was 3,393.70, and the average for those who repaid was only 1,651.39. The median hipoteca was 800, while the median for those who defaulted was 1,503.70 and the median for those who repaid was 500 pesos fuertes. There was only a slight difference in the size of the property, with the average small hipoteca on a 20.8-manzana farm, the average farm defaulted on at 25.09, and the average size for repayment at 18.19.

One of the big losers in the small-farm category, Abraham Mejía, carried inexplicably heavy loans for the size of his landholdings. On August 10, 1897, Mejía, a San Marcos farmer, borrowed 4,203.25 pesos fuertes from San Marcos farmer Lázaro García at 2 percent monthly interest to be repaid in three years with the entire product of his coffee fincas.[29] On September 20, 1900, García and Mejía renegotiated the debt, which now amounted to 7,814 pesos fuertes, including principal, interest, and the cost of legal action that García had taken against Mejía. García now wanted to be paid in money, in installments of 1,000 pesos a year. Since the loan was contracted, Mejía had sold off twelve manzanas of the farm to Diriamba attorney Fernando Montiel, and Montiel now agreed to be a party to the loan. Meanwhile, Mejía borrowed another 2,500 pesos fuertes, using the same property for collateral, on June 7, 1902. The loan, owed to Jesús Lejarza Jr., a Granada farmer, was to be repaid with coffee, which was already committed to García.[30]

In 1904, lawsuits resulted in both Montiel and Mejía losing their properties. On April 27, Judge Fernando Cornejo adjudicated Mejía's property to Juan Pío Medal, a Jinotepino farmer who took the loan over from García. The debt at this point amounted to 5,333.35 pesos fuertes.[31] No further reference was made to Jesús Lejarza, who presumably lost his money.

The other heavy debt was owed by Masaya farmer Fernando Nuñes to his own mother. On October 5, 1897, Nuñes borrowed 11,800 pesos fuertes from Emilia de Nuñes at 10 percent annual interest, with the principal and interest to be paid in legally recognized minted silver, paying the interest every May and, in case of default, paying damages to the lender. For collateral, he mortgaged his San Marcos farm, Las Guavas.[32] On August 24, 1899, he gave the farm to the lender, here identified as Emilia Danson v. (short for viuda, "widow") de Nuñes, in payment for the loan, which now amounted to 13,930.45 pesos fuertes.[33] In 1908, Danson sold the farm back to Nuñes, who now described himself as a businessman, for 12,000 pesos, and he sold it almost immediately to San Marcos farmer Manuel Alfonso Urbina for 20,000 pesos, to be paid in coffee. Urbina succeeded in repaying the loan by May 6, 1914.[34]

Two questions cannot be answered with the information provided in the mortgages. Why did Mejía and Nuñes need to borrow so much more than the average? It was not to finance more coffee production on other land: Mejía's total properties only amounted to thirty-seven manzanas, and Nuñes only owned the one twenty-eight-manzana farm. And why would lenders continue to provide money knowing that Mejía still had outstanding debts? At least one lender simply lost his money in this process. Nuñes's case is interesting because of the familial relationship between lender and borrower, which did not seem to ameliorate the terms of the loan, such as the 10 percent interest rate. However, the worth of this farm clearly was higher than the loan amount. After settling the debt with his mother for 12,000 pesos fuertes, he sold the farm for 20,000 pesos, payable in coffee. Presumably the now landless

Nuñes, who had changed his occupation from farmer to businessman, sold the coffee to a processor-exporter for shipment abroad.

Medium Farms

As occurred in the small-farm category, the medium-farm loans pivoted on the size of the loan rather than the resources of the borrower. Whereas the average hipoteca in the medium-farm category was 9,294.48 pesos fuertes, the average for those that defaulted was 8,796.46, and the average for those that repaid was 4,445.18. The median for the category was 4,705.88 pesos fuertes, while for those that defaulted it was 5,519 and for those that paid it was 4,000.

The medium-farm borrowers fell between the minifundistas and small farmers in terms of outside holdings: 67 percent of the borrowers were actually medium-sized farmers. Approximately the same proportion of those who defaulted and those who repaid were medium farmers — six of the eight people who defaulted and seven of the eleven people who paid their debts, or 63 and 64 percent. There were also a large farmer and a latifundista who defaulted, and three large farmers and one latifundista who paid. There was little difference in size between those that were defaulted — 103 manzanas — and those that were kept — 117 manzanas.

The medium-sized farmers tended to borrow more frequently than the farmers in the smaller categories: there were forty hipotecas and only eighteen borrowers. Six hipotecas were taken out by Carlos Emilio Gonssen, a Granadino merchant, all for his farm La Amistad, a 100-manzana San Marcos hacienda. The property was first acquired by Hilario and Carlos Emilio Gonssen through legal action that had resulted in a judgment against Ygnacio Padilla, and the property was auctioned to Gonssen for 6,519.60 pesos fuertes. In the title of November 9, 1887, La Amistad is described as having a house with a tile roof supported by wooden columns, a patio to dry coffee, and 20,000 coffee trees under the shade of black wood and bananas, with 741 fruit trees that served as shelter for the coffee trees. Carlos Emilio Gonssen inherited the property, along with his siblings Hilario Alejandro, Leonor, Rosa, Adelaida, and Emilia, in 1890, when the property was valued at 7,747.50 pesos fuertes.[35]

On May 11, 1897, Gonssen borrowed 7,000 pesos fuertes from Granadino merchant Fernando Chamorro at 2 percent monthly interest, with the loan due October 31, 1897 and to be paid in silver without any paper money. The hipoteca also mentions that there were two previous mortgages but gives no details about them. On June 11, 1897, Gonssen borrowed another 8,200.46 pesos fuertes, this time from Pedro Joaquín Chamorro, again to be paid in silver, with 2 percent monthly interest charged after the missed due date of November 30. The agreement notes that there were three existing hipotecas on La Amistad, which bordered El Dionicio, the hacienda owned by the Chamorros (though later lost to debt).[36]

On October 28, 1897, Gonssen took on yet more debt, this time from Granadino merchant Alejandro Jorge Fretropp. Fretropp agreed to give Gonssen 2,000 pesos fuertes in installments of 100 to 200 pesos each week at 1.5 percent monthly interest; once that amount was repaid, Gonssen would get another 2,000 in installments of 500, this time without interest. In return, Gonssen promised to give Fretropp all the coffee that La Amistad produced in the next harvest, which was not to be less than 500 quintals; the coffee was to be delivered on Gonssen's account and at his risk to the railroad station in Masaya, with the deliveries to begin at the end of December and to conclude by February 1898. Once he received the coffee, Fretropp would send it to Hamburg at Gonssen's expense and risk, and from the liquidation of the coffee he would take the amount Gonssen owed.[37]

Gonssen began a new series of debts the next year: On April 20, 1898, he took on a loan of 11,456.66 pesos fuertes, again from Pedro Joaquín Chamorro, at 1.5 percent monthly interest, to be repaid within six months. This loan notes that the first hipoteca on the property was for 8,000 pesos to César Costigliolo, who passed the loan on to Fernando Lacayo. On August 21, 1899, Gonssen reached another agreement with Fretropp, this time for 5,000 pesos fuertes, again to be delivered in installments. Then on May 15, 1901, he borrowed 10,000 pesos fuertes at 1.5 percent monthly interest from his sisters Rosa Gonssen v. Chavarría, Leonor de la Encarnación, and Adelaida Gonssen. In return, they demanded the entire 1901 to 1902 harvest, no less than 1,200 quintals of coffee, to be shipped to Europe.[38]

With all of this debt burdening him, Gonssen ended up in court. First, a lower court ordered an auction of the property based on a claim by his own sister Rosa, at which the highest bidder was his sister Adelaida, in what may have been an attempt to keep the farm in the family. At that point, Fernando Chamorro took his unpaid debt to a higher court, and a new auction was ordered on September 6, 1902, by the senior judge for the civil district of Granada, Juan Vado. The farm was valued at 90,000 pesos silver, and the best bid was made by Jinotepino merchant Alberto Chamorro for 70,000 pesos. The proceeds would go to paying the debts, and Gonssen never appeared in the Carazo property records again.[39]

Another frequent debtor apparently ended in happier circumstances, although not without difficulty: Gerónimo Ramírez, a Managüense doctor and farmer, contracted ten hipotecas totaling 52,396.75 pesos fuertes in debt between 1896 and 1901, from lenders as diverse as Casa Federico Gerlach of Hamburg, prominent Managüense merchant Teodoro Tefel, and the unidentified Manuela Cardenal, who never appears as a lender again. All did not go smoothly: On December 9, 1898, he gave his hacienda, La Reforma, along with other properties, to Masaya merchant Abraham Cardoze, to whom he owed 4,000 pesos fuertes. The properties were worth 25,000 pesos, and with title to them, Cardoze agreed to pay the 49,346 German marks (11,610.82 pesos fuertes) that Ramírez owed Tefel, who had filed suit in district court in Managua. Although Cardoze held the title, Ramírez kept possession of the property and used the coffee proceeds to settle his debts. By 1909, he had regained title to the property; he appears in the 1909 census as the owner of La Reforma, described as 140 manzanas with 80,000 trees, producing 600 quintals of coffee and worth 264,000 pesos in national bills.

The difference between Gonssen and Ramírez may be that Gonssen only planted 20,000 trees on his 100 manzanas, whereas Ramírez planted 80,000 trees on his 140-manzana parcel. In effect, Gonssen had the equivalent of a small-farm planting on his medium-sized parcel, and he borrowed at a rate that required the return from medium-sized plantings.

Although one might expect medium farms to be able to handle heavier encumbrances than smaller farms, loans in this category were actually more likely to end up in default: 42.5 percent of the medium loans were defaulted, compared to 29 percent of the minifundio and 30 percent of the small-farm loans. Because medium-sized farms are disproportionately represented among the hipotecas and more likely to default, it appears that the medium-sized farm was in the most precarious position of all the size categories. The medium-sized holding would clearly be dependent on outside labor but would lack the greater resources available on larger holdings. It is also important to note that the typical farm in this category covered more than 100 manzanas. Williams, in his categorization of farm sizes, would consider these to be large capitalist enterprises. But the weakness of this farm size's position, shown in mortgage defaults, is markedly different from the strength shown of the larger holdings starting at 200 manzanas and would seem to further legitimate the categorization used in this study.

Large Farms

There were only five hipotecas in the large-farm category, of which one defaulted, three were repaid, and one had an unknown fate. The overall average amount for the five loans was 5,801.36, with a median of 6,000 pesos fuertes, and the loan defaulted was for 6,000. In fact, the three loans that were repaid averaged a higher amount—7,041.49 pesos fuertes, with a median of 7,973.87.

All of the companies and individuals involved in these loans were latifundistas: Pedro Joaquín Chamorro e hijos of Granada, the commerce house with diversified holdings owned by one of Nicaragua's oldest and most powerful families; Casa de Comercio Gabriel Lacayo e hijo, also of Granada, and frequently intermarried with the Chamorros; José Esteban González, one of Diriamba's most prominent coffee growers, processors, and lenders; and Desiderio Román, who listed himself as a Jinotepino farmer.

The default was by Pedro Joaquín Chamorro e hijos, showing that even the most wealthy and powerful sometimes could not or did not repay their loans. On December 15, 1897, the company borrowed $6,000 (*oro americano*, "American gold") from Gustavo Amsinck and Co. of New York, at 6 percent interest per year, to pay for the harvesting of coffee on the San Dionisio finca; the harvest would be used for repayment of the loan.[40] Sales records, however, show that the Chamorros sold the farm on July 27, 1897 (although the document was not filed until January 29, 1898), in a pacto de retroventa to Francisco Alfredo Pellas, an Italian national and Granadino merchant, for £7,000. San Dionisio was described as a 200-manzana hacienda equipped with a coffee-processing plant and accessories.[41]

In two September 27, 1897, documents, also filed on January 29, 1898, Pellas transferred his rights in the farm to Juan Schuback and Gustavo Amsinck of the commercial houses Juan Schuback and Sons of Hamburg and Gustavo Amsinck of New York for £7,000.[42]

On August 2, 1902, Pellas, representing Schuback and Amsinck, sold San Dionisio to Adolfo Benard, Granadino merchant and farmer, for 5,000 pesos, to be paid in three installments at 6 percent interest per year, an agreement that was not filed until August 1904.[43] When Pellas died in 1912, Benard filed documents indicating that San Dionisio and many other properties were actually jointly owned with Pellas, who contributed half the money to purchase the properties but allowed them to be registered to Benard, probably because of Pellas's role as representative for Schuback and Amsinck. According to the documents, Benard wanted to be sure that Pellas's widow, Rosa Vivas v. de Pellas, would receive her rightful inheritance, so he titled half-interest in the properties to her.[44]

Clearly, large farms were in the strongest position of all the size categories. These farms were the least likely to even need loans and the least likely to default. The amount of the average large loan was far smaller than medium loans (5,801.36 versus 9,294.48 pesos fuertes). None of the large farms was actually mortgaged by large farmers, that is, those who owned between 200 and 499 manzanas, further testimony to the strength of that size landholding. All of the borrowers in this category were latifundistas, who clearly were using just one of their many holdings for collateral on a loan that most likely also paid for larger operations.

Loan Terms

The key difference between loan terms for hipotecas and pactos de retroventa was the charging of interest: only 20 percent of pactos charged interest at all, whereas 68 percent of hipotecas specified interest rates. The lack of interest charges undoubtedly made the pacto an appealing alternative, although as has been shown it was a far more dangerous option. Hipoteca lenders were less likely to end up with title to the property, which may be the reason for charging interest.

The interest rate charged on hipotecas differed by size of landholding

—the smaller the property, the higher the interest. Of the 157 hipotecas for which we have both size and usable loan figures, 106 specified that interest would be paid. The most common interest rate, cited in 44 hipotecas, was 2 percent per month. The majority of minifundio loans, 64 percent, were charged at this rate. Jumping up one size category made a difference; although 2 percent was the most common rate for smallholders, only 38 percent of the loans were charged at this rate.

The interest rates improved dramatically in the larger categories. For medium farms, only 16 percent of the hipotecas carried interest rates of 2 percent. The most common rate in this category was 1.5 percent a month, the rate charged on 50 percent of the loans. The rate was even better for large farms: none was charged 2 percent; two of the three loans that indicated interest rates for large farms were at 6 percent a year, that is, .5 percent a month.

Higher interest rates typically were charged as a penalty for late or missed payments, which may explain why lenders tended to allow loans to stay active well past their due dates. Final payments ranged from two months to ten years past the due date in eighteen cases. Another frequent penalty was to require payment in money rather than in coffee, indicating the scarcity of cash in the economy and the preference for paying in coffee, especially when the loan was being made by a larger grower who needed the coffee to market or to repay his own loans.[45]

The vast majority of the loans—59 percent—called for repayment in coffee. Only 22 percent of the loans asked for repayment in money, although another 5 percent provided the option of coffee or cash. The loans to be repaid in money were often specific about the type of currency: most were to be repaid in silver, with only a few in *moneda corriente* (paper money). One even specified silver or bills issued by the Nicaragua branch of the London Bank of Central America Ltd. Two loans were to be repaid by labor on the lender's coffee harvest, and one loan offered the option of being repaid in coffee or labor on the harvest, indicating the options open to minifundistas.

Examining the terms by size category, we find that 70 percent of minifundio loans were to be repaid in coffee, compared to 54 percent of small-farm loans, 52 percent of the medium farms, and 40 percent of the large-farm loans. The use of bank drafts or commercial paper first appeared in the medium-farm category, with 16 percent of the loans.

In the hipotecas, prices were less likely to be quoted for the coffee used for repayment than in the pactos de retroventa, and specific prices were most often quoted in loans on smaller property. In twenty-nine of the fifty-two hipotecas specifying coffee prices, it was to be paid at the current price at the time of delivery. Only eight cases specified prices, and six of them were for minifundio loans.

A few loans specified that they would be paid at the price set by area processors such as José Esteban González or that the loans would be reimbursed at the coffee price paid by two undesignated merchants at the time of delivery. Only three loans specifically stated that they would reimburse at one or two pesos below the market price at the time of delivery.

In other terms, such as length of time to repayment, the hipotecas differed little from the pactos. Most of the loans were to be repaid within a year, indicating that they served as short-term financing for the current harvest. In that respect, no size category had an advantage.

Lenders and Lending Institutions

There were 202 lenders on record from 1877 to 1903, including a few who worked both alone and as partners in companies. Most of these individuals only lent money on one occasion. The exceptions are notable: José Esteban González made twenty-five loans; his brother, Diriamba coffee grower and medical doctor José Ignacio González, made ten loans. Jinotepino hacendado Agustín Sanches made twelve loans. Seven loans each were recorded by wealthy Diriamba coffee farmer Enrique Baltodano and Jinotepino farmer José León Román Reyes.

Most of the lenders—67 percent—lived in the department of Carazo. Another eleven lenders, or 6 percent, were from towns in the neighboring department of Masaya, including Masaya, Nandaime, and Masatepe. Though stereotypically the economy was dominated by the merchants of Granada, they represented only 13 percent of the lenders here (twenty-four), with another three lenders from León and seven from Managua. Eight more lenders were from other Nicaragua towns. Foreign lenders only numbered eight (4 percent), with three from Germany, one from France, three from England, and one from New York.

Most of the lenders identified themselves as farmers (52 percent), while 22 percent were merchants and 9 percent were businessmen. Six percent were housewives, and another 6 percent were professionals (six doctors, three attorneys, and two engineers). There were also four priests; two tailors; and a teacher, mechanic, sea captain, and general.

That so many people were involved in lending indicates several phenomena: lending was lucrative, and everyone with a little extra capital wanted to take advantage of the opportunity. Although lending was dominated by several large coffee growers and merchants, it was also wide open to anyone with capital, and borrowers had a wide array of possible lenders to choose from. And stereotypical visions of domination by foreigners and larger cities are not reflected here.

There were few businesses or corporations involved in lending and only one bank, the London Bank of Central America Ltd., which made only two loans in Carazo during the main period of this study, 1877 to 1903. In 1901, Managüense farmer Vicente Rodríguez borrowed 150 pesos fuertes from the bank for the harvest on his Diriamba farm, Santa Cecilia, and in 1903 the Nicaragua Co. Ltd. of Managua borrowed 2,000 pesos fuertes for the harvest on the several properties the company owned, including the eighty-manzana Santa Elvira in Diriamba.[46]

The London Bank of Central America was one of several names used by the first bank to function in Nicaragua, which was financed by British capital. Formally established as the Banco de Nicaragua in 1888, the bank was actually a subsidiary of the Bank of London and South America Limited. During the ensuing years, the bank operated under a variety of names, including the Bank of Nicaragua Ltd. (1894), London Bank of Central America (1896), Cortez Commercial and Banking Co. Ltd. (1905), Commercial Bank of Spanish America Ltd., and the Anglo–South America Bank Ltd. (1925), and finally in 1936 it fused all operations under the title Bank of London and South America Ltd.[47]

The 1882 law that allowed banks to emit currency remained in force until 1911, when the Banco Nacional de Nicaragua was incorporated in Hartford, Connecticut. The formation of the bank was the result of an agreement between the government of Nicaragua and the New York bankers Brown Brothers and Co. and J&W Seligman. The main objective of the bank was to facilitate conversion of the Nicaraguan currency from the peso to the cordoba, a monetary reform negotiated with the United States as part of the economic changes imposed by the U.S. government after the overthrow of the Zelaya government.[48] The bank remained headquartered in Connecticut until 1940. It became the most important bank lender in Carazo, eclipsing the British banks.

Such banking institutions had little impact in Carazo, however, where most of the lending continued to be done by individuals. The *Registro de propiedad* shows a total of 160 bank loans recorded beginning with a 1913 loan from the Anglo–South American Bank Ltd. and ending in 1930.[49] However, during the same period of time, José Esteban González, and his heirs after his death in 1922, issued 195 loans. González was just the most prolific of the many private lenders, who far outnumbered the banks. Whereas González and other private lenders provided funding in amounts as small as ten cordobas, the smallest bank loan was for $100. Typical bank loans were larger than private loans, with five-figure amounts not uncommon for the banks and rare for González.

Conclusion

Credit was made widely available to the smallholder in Carazo, but on different terms and with different results from those loans offered the larger borrower. Those who undertook pactos de retroventa were likely to be those who had little opportunity to get a mortgage: only 27 percent of those who sold property in pactos were also hipoteca holders. The terms appear to be better than in hipotecas—most often no interest was charged, and when it was, the interest rate tended to be lower than in hipotecas. But the stakes were higher—pactos were more likely to result in default. However, the lender-buyer did not keep the property to add to his holdings. Instead, the property was resold, or perhaps used as an asset while the previous owner remained as a tenant, maintaining the property and producing the coffee.

In the hipotecas, smallholders were more likely to be charged higher interest rates and to be paid less for the coffee they used to pay back their loans. While 64 percent of minifundio loans were at 2 percent, only 38 percent of small loans, 16 percent of medium-farm loans, and none of the large farms were charged at that rate. Work as an option for repayment was rare and used only in minifundio loans, and repayment in bank drafts or commercial paper only occurred in the medium- and large-farm categories. Most loans were repaid in coffee at the market rate at the time of delivery; but those who were most likely to be assigned a price in advance were the minifundios, and the only agreements to specify below-market prices were for minifundio and small property.

Minifundio loans were most likely defaulted by those who owned no other property, but small and medium loans were most likely defaulted because of higher-than-average debt burdens. Surprisingly, medium farms were overrepresented in the hipotecas and more likely to default than any other size category, showing the vulnerability of the sector that depended heavily on outside labor but that lacked the extensive resources of the larger grower, processor, and exporter.

Yet we also find that with little property, people could borrow a great deal of money and manage to pay it back. Large and small growers defaulted, although the latifundistas probably let go of a losing proposition while holding on to more lucrative haciendas. There were also many more lenders than has been assumed, giving the smaller grower more options in the market. The small grower clearly operated at a disadvantage compared to the larger grower, but was not kept out of the market.

The image presented here differs from that offered by such scholars as Oscar-René Vargas, who contended that "Another of the elements that would limit the broad reproduction of social capital was the lack of bank credit to small and medium production. This lack of bank credit limited the possibilities for widening the scale of small and medium capital, because these sectors couldn't reinvest their surpluses because they were appropriated by the usurer, who hoarded it, transferred it abroad or spent it on sumptuous and unproductive goods."[50]

Mendoza also complained about the greed of the usurers in his 1920 profile of his hometown, *Historia de Diriamba*. "The *puchiteros* [worthless leftovers] that dedicate themselves to this cultivation are going to die in the clutches of the half dozen impresarios who have no competitors and invade and dominate everything with their multiple, monopolizing octopus tentacles. Among them, some are more sly than others, but there is no lack among them of those who speculate without causing greater extortion nor the total collapse of small property."[51] Mendoza left Diriamba—some say he was driven out—for Guatemala, where his book was published, much to the chagrin of many of Diriamba's mighty. But one of the few leaders who comes out well in the account is José Esteban González, to whom, Mendoza said, Diriamba was indebted for causing the disappearance of monopolies that were on the point of forming and strangling the small proprietor. According to Mendoza, González saved the poor by paying a good price for coffee and striking a terrible blow to the trusts.[52]

"The Gonzálezes dabble in stocks and face the consequences to gain greater profits," Mendoza wrote. "They export more coffee than they harvest, because they invest great sums in buying from the second- and third-order producers. Without fear of price fluctuations, they speculate with the ups and downs of the European and North American markets, through their agents. Through this system they obtain the best chance of hitting: their safes are fuller each year and widen the currents that nourish the main fountain of their credits."[53]

The truth lies somewhere between Vargas's claims of usury and Mendoza's view of the benevolent lender. Clearly, differentiation among the coffee growers created a hierarchy based on wealth and power. The larger grower, in his roles as lender, coffee buyer, processor, and exporter, grew wealthy at the expense of the small grower, who kept him supplied with the coffee to market. Data indicates that another 30 percent profit was earned by processing and exporting coffee, on top of profits ranging from 30 to 50 percent at the production level.

Coffee, often seen as the great democratic crop, did indeed offer opportunity. As French engineer Paul Levy observed circa 1870, "[Coffee's] advantages are: it produces after little time and one can create an average cafetal with little capital. In spite of that, many cultivators don't have this modest capital, and to get it, they sell their harvests in advance at scandalous prices. In coffee, as in all products, the businessman/buyer earns more than the producer."[54]

Notes

1. *Pabellón Nacional*, 1, no. 11 (February 9, 1908): 2.

2. Robert G. Williams, *States and Social Evolution: Coffee and the Rise of National Governments in Central America* (Chapel Hill: University of North Carolina Press, 1994), 148.

3. See Jaime Biderman, *The Development of Capitalism in Nicaragua: Economic Growth, Class Relations and Uneven Development* (Stanford, Calif.: Stanford-Berkeley Joint Center for Latin American Studies, 1982); Eduardo Baumeister, "Agrarian Reform," in *Revolution and Counterrevolution in Nicaragua*, edited by Thomas W. Walker (Boulder, Colo.: Westview, 1991); David Kaimowitz, *Agrarian Structure in Nicaragua and Its Implications for Policies towards the Rural Poor* (Ph.D. dissertation, University of Wisconsin, Madison, 1987); Joseph R. Thome and David Kaimowitz, "Agrarian Reform," in *Nicaragua: The First Five Years,* edited by Thomas W. Walker (New York: Praeger, 1985); and

Jaime Wheelock, *Imperialismo y dictadura* (Managua: Editorial Nueva Nicaragua, 1985).

4. Size categories used in this study are minifundios, under 10 manzanas; small farms, 10 to 49 manzanas; medium farms, 50 to 199 manzanas; large farms, 200 to 499 manzanas; and latifundios, 500 and more manzanas. The manzana, Nicaragua's unit of land measure, is equivalent to 1.74 acres or .69 hectare. This categorization differs from the conventional classification of property sizes for Central America: under 10 manzanas, 10 to 49, 50 to 499, and 500. See Centro de Investigación y Estudios de la Reforma Agraria, *La Reforma agraria en Nicaragua, 1979–1989* (Managua: CIERA, 1989). It also differs from the model proposed by Williams, who focuses on the hiring of labor as more meaningful than property size. Williams suggests that farms of fewer than 5,000 trees, "peasant farms," could be maintained and harvested by family labor alone, and farms of up to 20,000 trees, "family-sized farms," could be maintained by family but require extra labor at harvest. Any larger farm he terms "capitalist farms," because they would need hired labor for both maintenance and the harvest. He further divides the capitalist farms, "somewhat arbitrarily," into small capitalist farms of 20,000 to 49,000 trees, medium-sized capitalist farms of 50,000 to 99,000, and large capitalist farms of more than 100,000 trees.

5. For more on property in Carazo, see Julie A. Charlip, "Cultivating Coffee: Farmers, Land and Money in Nicaragua, 1877–1930" (Ph.D. dissertation, University of California, Los Angeles, 1995).

6. This contrasts with William Roseberry's study of Boconó, Venezuela, a smallholding community with many similarities to Carazo. Roseberry found that lending there, however, was dominated by out-of-town merchants. See *Coffee and Capitalism in the Venezuelan Andes* (Austin: University of Texas Press, 1983).

7. Prices are in *pesos sencillos,* equivalent to .8 peso fuerte, and in pesos fuertes, equivalent to one dollar.

8. Paul Levy, *Notas geográficas y económicas sobre la República de Nicaragua* (Paris: Librería Española de E. Denné Schmitz, 1873).

9. Harold Playter, *The Coffee Industry in Nicaragua* (Corinto, Nicaragua: American Consulate, 1926).

10. *Libro de propiedad,* Granada, August 17, 1887, no. 401, f226–227.

11. Ibid., Granada, August 2, 1891, no. 576, f278–9.

12. Ibid., Granada, August 4, 1887, no. 357, f203; *Registro de propiedad,* Jinotepe, June 22, 1892, no. 285, f304–305.

13. *Registro de propiedad,* Jinotepe, July 29, 1897, no. 221, f170–171.

14. *Registro de inmuebles,* Jinotepe, December 6, 1899, no. 319, f234.

15. *Libro de propiedad,* Granada, December 21, 1889, no. 673, f412.

16. *Registro de propiedad,* Jinotepe, May 2, 1894, no. 117, f430–431; March 1, 1897, no. 49, f40; and June 3, 1897, no. 156, f121–122.

17. Ibid., Jinotepe, December 6, 1898, no. 263, f104d–105d.

18. *Registro de la propiedad y derechos reales,* Jinotepe, May 11, 1902, no. 179, f110.

19. Ibid., Jinotepe, May 20, 1902, no. 211, f130–131.

20. Ibid., Jinotepe, October 16, 1902, no. 511, f307.

21. Ibid., Jinotepe, May 28, 1903, no. 210, f117–118.

22. Ibid., Jinotepe, May 28, 1903, no. 211, f147–148.

23. *Libro de propiedad,* Jinotepe, May 22, 1906, t11, f80–81.

24. Ibid., Jinotepe, November 23, 1907, t11, f81–82; and April 9, 1909, t11, f82, and t22, f302.

25. Ibid., Jinotepe, May 12, 1908, t22, f302–303.

26. Williams, *States and Social Evolution,* 154.

27. Record keeping was less than optimal during this time period, and for many loan agreements, there was no notation made as to whether the debt was paid. The question was answerable for those properties that left a paper trail of further transactions. For minifundios, we know the outcome for 63 percent of the hipotecas; for small farms, the outcome was recorded for 82 percent. All of the medium-farm hipotecas are accounted for, as are all but one of the five large-farm hipotecas.

28. *Registro de propiedad,* Jinotepe, July 30, 1897, no. 61, f444–445; *Libro de hipoteca y gravámenes,* Jinotepe, November 12, 1900, no. 397, f320–321.

29. *Libro de hipoteca y gravámenes,* Jinotepe, August 12, 1897, no. 65, f447–448.

30. *Registro de la propiedad y derechos reales,* Jinotepe, June 7, 1902, no. 243, f150–151.

31. *Libro de propiedad,* Jinotepe, December 27, 1904, t2, f84–85.

32. *Libro de hipoteca y gravámenes,* Jinotepe, October 6, 1897, no. 77, f459–460.

33. *Registro de inmuebles,* Jinotepe, August 27, 1899, no. 204, f140–141.

34. *Libro de propiedad,* Jinotepe, January 20, 1908, t21, f260–261; and February 5, 1908, t21, f261–262.

35. *Libro de propiedad,* Granada, November 14, 1887, no. 587, f340–341; and June 3, 1891, no. 382, f188–190.

36. *Libro de hipoteca y gravámenes,* Jinotepe, May 17, 1897, no. 13, f413; and June 3, 1897, no. 19, f422–423.

37. *Libro de hipoteca y gravámenes,* Jinotepe, November 8, 1897, no. 84, f465–467.

38. Ibid., Jinotepe, April 21, 1897, no. 7, f407–408. *Registro de inmuebles,* Jinotepe, August 25, 1899, no. 203, f139–140; and May 15, 1901, no. 154, f122–123.

39. *Libro de hipoteca y gravámenes,* Jinotepe, February 12, 1903, no. 54, f37–39.

40. Ibid., Jinotepe, December 28, 1897, no. 89, f473–474.

41. *Registro de propiedad,* Jinotepe, January 29, 1898, no. 2, f1H–2D.

42. Ibid., Jinotepe, January 29, 1898, no. 3, f2D–3D; and January 28, 1898, no. 4, f3D–3H.

43. *Libro de propiedad,* Jinotepe, August 8, 1904, t1, f147–149.

44. Ibid., Jinotepe, May 21, 1915, t56, f128–133.

45. While José Esteban González was the leading lender of Carazo, he was also borrowing money for his own properties. For example, on April 14, 1898, using his hacienda La Palmera as collateral, he borrowed 34,640 German marks from Managüense merchant Teodoro Tefel. The loan, which was to be repaid in commercial drafts and with 1,200 quintals of coffee, was repaid in two years, though it was due in one *Registro de Hipotecas y Gravámenes,* Jinotepe, April 16, 1898, no. 10, f205h–206d. Similar loans followed in subsequent years.

46. *Registro de inmuebles,* Jinotepe, February 16, 1901, no. 42, f38, and October 13, 1896, no. 328, f172–173; *Libro de hipoteca y gravámenes,* Jinotepe, July 16, 1903, no. 45, f33–34; *Registro de inmuebles,* Jinotepe, October 30, 1900, no. 388, f313–314.

47. "Reseña historia de las instituciones bancarias que funcionan en Nicaragua," *Economía y Finanzas,* no. 4 (August 1944): 6–9.

48. Ibid.

49. The loans made by each bank were by Banco de Nicaragua, 107; Commercial Bank of Spanish-America Ltd., 12; Anglo Central-American Commercial Bank Ltd., 33; Banco Commercial de Nicaragua Ltd., 4; and Anglo–South America Bank Ltd., 4.

50. Oscar-René Vargas, "Acumulación, mercado interno y el desarrollo del capitalismo en Nicaragua: 1893–1909" (unpublished manuscript, Managua, n.d. 76–77.

51. Juan M. Mendoza, *Historia de Diriamba* (Guatemala City: Imprenta Electra, 1920), 145.

52. Ibid., 230.

53. Ibid., 239–240.

54. Levy, *Notas geográficas,* 461–462.

PATRICIA ALVARENGA

Auxiliary Forces in the
Shaping of the Repressive System

El Salvador, 1880–1930

❖

This article analyzes a subject that, until now, had not been taken into account in the historical studies of El Salvador: civilian collaboration in repression. When I began this research, I suspected that civilians had played an important role in the repressive system. However, I believed that their participation had been informal, that is, at the margin of the institutional system. In the course of my investigation I discovered that this mechanism of social control was much more generalized than I had originally believed and, furthermore, that the builders of the Salvadoran state incorporated this system into the institutions of the country. I also discovered that only by recognizing the nature of civilians' incorporation into the repressive system was it possible to explain the character of domination and the subordinated groups' construction of strategies of resistance. The research process also made evident that the relationship between state formation and the character of the repressive system is a rich and unexplored field for study. The central hypothesis of this chapter is that the incorporation of peasants into the repressive system made a major contribution to domination. By using peasants as *auxiliares*, national authorities could erode community links and, to some extent, prevent peasant communities from shaping strategies of organized resistance to domination.

The term *auxiliares* encompasses a range of people, from those who acted under intense coercion, to those who acted more or less voluntarily. Moreover, I later refer specifically to auxiliares through use of the term *collaborator*.[1] My analysis of the civilian auxiliares establishes the ways in which the Salvadoran state shaped its control in the countryside by converting peasants and farmers into active agents of the network of domination. I will examine the effects this expansion of the repressive system had inside the peasant communities and also how this mechanism of domination contributed to shaping and curbing peasant resistance.[2]

My analysis begins with the 1880s, as that decade marked a period of noteworthy changes in Salvadoran history: the oligarchy's power in the context of the growth of coffee production grew steadily. Although a significant group of peasants could adapt to the commercial specialization and survive as proprietors,[3] there was a process of concentration of the means of production. The privatization of land that took place at the beginning of the 1880s greatly transformed the distribution of this resource. This agrarian reform affected thousands of families throughout the coffee region, and as a consequence a significant number of peasants lost access to land. During the following decades, control of the credit system in the hands of the richest members of the oligarchy contributed to the expulsion of peasants from the land. Peasants were forced to mortgage their lands in order to receive financing; when they could not pay, the financier confiscated their lands. This process of commercialization of the economy was accompanied by the creation of a repressive infrastructure to legitimize and put into action a system of forced labor: debt peonage. Consequently, during the expansion of the commercial economy the conditions of land privatization and the forced character of new production relations characterized the general framework in which class struggle developed.[4]

During this period the state was the oligarchy's most powerful instrument of domination. The state implemented policies in favor of oligarchic interests, as was the case of the auxiliary forces, born in the colonial period and re-created by the oligarchical state as a tool in the hands of the mayors (the main local authorities), whose primary task was the defense of oligarchic interests. The relationship between state and landowners was so close that the state even allowed landowners to create auxiliary forces to maintain order in their haciendas.

This essay is inspired by Michel Foucault, especially his book *Discipline and Punish: The Birth of the Prison*.[5] Foucault analyzes how the system of surveillance in modern European societies permeates the whole social fabric. At different moments in life, individuals participate as objects and subjects of surveillance. Thus the "victims" of a system of control, of the subtle violence of discipline, are at once conspirators. This perspective allows us to decipher how the complex network of domination is woven, as well as to discover the contradictory relationships hidden behind the immense power machine. Although according to Foucault resistance does not exist, his analysis gives insight into new expressions of power, and using elements of his analytic method in fact allows us to unveil unexplored areas where resistance to domination operated.[6]

In the following pages I will examine the relationship between peasants and auxiliares in repression in western El Salvador, where Indian and mestizo communities coexisted. This analysis centers on the mestizo communities. Most of the information available corresponds to the department of Santa Ana, located in the heart of the coffee region. Western El Salvador was characterized by smallholder peasant communities, which to a great extent were based on shared communal lands.[7] The impact of the state's reshaping of power relations in these communities is the subject of this essay.

The History of Auxiliary Forces

Until well into the twentieth century the Salvadoran police did not have an effective presence in the countryside—not even in the region of greatest economic importance: Santa Ana. Although there was a police force charged with maintaining order in the countryside, this institution did not play an effective role in controlling rural spaces. The rural police existed until the creation of the National Guard in 1913. Before then, only a few dozen men were responsible for patrolling the entire coffee area. The army also had repressive functions in the countryside, but it was more concerned with the pursuit of professional criminals. Consequently, keeping peasants under control, to a great extent, fell within the duties of the *auxiliares civiles* (civilian auxiliaries).[8]

What, then, were the origins of this system? Although there are no studies about the repressive apparatus in El Salvador, it is clear that as early as the 1870s, and perhaps before, members of the Salvadoran state intended to provide for a civilian role in the repressive system.[9] The commissioners were the mayor's civilian helpers in the pursuit of transgressors. The *alcaldes auxiliares,* also called *alguaciles,* were civilian members of the patrol commanded by commissioners or mayors and were dedicated to repression in the villages. In general terms, the members of the patrol under the commissioner's command were dubbed auxiliares civiles.

The builders of the state assigned an important role to the auxiliares civiles in controlling the rural population. In the 1880s they delegated two sensitive functions to the auxiliares: the arrest of labor deserters (*jornaleros* who, having received money in advance from a landowner that compelled them to stay on the hacienda, left their place of work without having liquidated the debt) and the expulsion of peasants from the land. Because of the minimal presence of the police, the civilian assistants usually carried out such repressive tasks, a duty they fulfilled until approximately the late 1910s. A decree of the municipal mayor Domingo Salguero declared that "the alcaldes auxiliares will patrol every day in their respective neighborhoods capturing and detaining any who they find drunk, creating a scandal, fighting, or committing any other offenses."[10] The Police Law of 1882 assigned a key role to civilian assistants in peasant repression, particularly with respect to the persecution of labor deserters. According to Article 1142, "inspectors, the rural judges, the assistants or commissioners of valleys and villages, and mayors of the towns, are *obligated* to persecute and arrest all jornaleros who do not satisfy on time the work debts they have acquired, and also those who abandon their jobs."[11] Article 213 of the Agrarian Law of 1904 established that "the authority in charge of order and effecting the evictions will be the municipal mayor from the place the land was located. The mayor will always have this mission whatever the status or condition of the tenant."[12]

The public forces under command of the municipalities at the time were the auxiliary forces and the police. Given that the police were in charge of keeping order in the town rather than in the countryside, the eviction of peasants fell to the civil patrols, who operated under the authority of the mayors. In 1909 the Assembly revised the Agrarian Law of 1904, declaring that the auxiliares civiles were watchmen or guardians of property. The legislators established that the alcaldes auxiliares and the *comisionados de cantón* (cantonal commissioners) were required to "seize . . . anyone stealing wood for construction or firewood, uprooting trees in the forest or down the mountains, without the respective license of the owner. These authorities had to place the guilty party at the disposition of the municipal mayor within twenty-four hours."[13]

Unfortunately there is no research about the number of peasants ejected from lands through the use of force. However, the data does allow us to analyze how important or frequent the labor deserters' activities were in relation to other crimes committed. According to the statistics of the Ministry of the Interior, in 1883 there were 782 arrests in the department of Santa Ana alone, of which 296 were for drunkenness, and 186 (24 percent) were for breaking labor contracts.[14] During 1889 the largest number of arrests recorded in the country corresponded to the category "scandal and peaceful drunkenness." These amounted to 3,655 offenders, of whom 3,518 were men and 137 women. The second item in importance with respect to the number of arrests in 1889 was "labor deserters." In that year 1,107 persons—907 men and 200 women—were arrested for this offense. As might be expected, most of the arrests took place in the coffee region: San Salvador, Santa Tecla, Santa Ana, Ahuachapán, Sonsonate, Chalchuapa, and Izalco. In contrast, in the eastern part of the country only seventeen were arrested as labor deserters, or only 1.53 percent of the country's total arrests.[15] The exact number of labor deserters arrested by the auxiliary forces is not clear; however, the presence of the latter in all the criminal records concerning labor contract breaches demonstrates that the state had assigned the task of confronting one of the strongest labor conflicts to the mayor, the commissioners, and their assistants (alguaciles).

How many peasants were integrated into the repressive system? It is impossible to calculate exactly, but it is known that in every *cantón* (neighborhood) there was supposed to be at least one commissioner and his assistants totaled between five and eleven men. It is possible that in the small cantones, this system did not work. Nevertheless, the system of civil patrols permitted the recruitment and integration of an impressive number of people into the repression—without the need for the state to make expenditures or any effort to support them as population, investment, and peasant resistance grew.

The substitution of the civil patrols with the National Guard in the task of repression is evident in that by the beginning of the 1930s most of the tasks of the auxiliares civiles consisted of patrolling the countryside and carrying out office tasks. They were charged with policing the use of fire, gathering economic data, vaccinating pigs, and overseeing the construction of roads.[16] But the most important mission assigned to the auxiliary forces in the early 1930s was collecting information for the census that the government would publish in 1932. The mayor of Sonsonate, Benigno Rodríguez, explained in a letter to the chief of the Agrarian Section that he had serious problems in advancing the agrarian census because he had commissioners only in Las Salinas, La Ensenada, and El Cacao—that is, in three of the sixteen cantones of the central district of Sonsonate. This report clearly indicates the decline of such rural figures.[17] Possibly because of the lack of civil assistants, the state also ordered the *comandancias cantonales* (military assistants), a group created to supplement the auxiliares, to participate in the census.[18]

The obligatory and unpaid service persisted even though it had been outlawed in 1912. In 1920 an inhabitant of the town of Armenia sent a letter to the *Diario Latino* asking the minister of the interior to intercede to free him of the obligation of serving as alguacil. He stated that despite the illegality of this activity, the mayor required him to provide the service in the neighborhood of San Juan. When the minister questioned the mayor of Armenia, the latter justified his proceedings, saying that "in this city there is neither a military detachment nor a *policía de línea* [urban police force]. Consequently, we have no other recourse than to use the residents in this service *as has always been the custom.*"[19] We can draw two conclusions from the words of the mayor: first, in 1920, even in Armenia (one of the oldest and most important coffee regions of the country) the lack of an official repressive force obligated the local authorities to depend on the auxiliares civiles; and second, the law that proscribed such services was systematically violated.[20] In his study of the Indian population of Panchimalco, Alejandro Dagoberto Marroquín attests that the service of *mayordomos* (Indian authorities) in some areas and of the neighborhood alguaciles in others persisted into the 1940s.[21] It is interesting to note that the system of domination incorporated traditional Indian authorities into the repressive apparatus, giving them functions similar to those of commissioners.

The state, however, did not begin consistent expansion of the National Guard until the 1920s. Nonetheless, even with the increase of the repressive force during the 1920s (for the most part directly financed by the landowners), the local authorities continued depending on auxiliary forces. In addition to the civil patrols composed of commissioners and alguaciles, the state created the comandancias cantonales, an auxiliary force just as useful as its former system but very much dependent on the army. These individuals responded to the orders of a commander and collaborated with the army on a regular basis. The detachments were constituted by people considered to be "honest and good workers." The earliest document providing information about this new service is from 1901, when the military authorities of Cojutepeque informed the president that "local commanders had been placed in all towns of the department and others in each of the valleys or cantones. . . . their principal obligations are to keep the order in their respective regions and to pursue and arrest deserters or those absent from Sunday training."[22] In 1922 there were local commanders "in many towns in the country" in charge of training reserve forces.[23] These forces were composed of peasants who were not integrated in the army as regular forces but who had to be prepared to participate as soldiers in case of war. One of the main functions of the local commanders was to oblige members of the reserve forces to train once a week. In 1924, a regiment of the reserve forces of the army detailed the functions of the military assistants. They were in charge of keeping *milicianos* (members of the reserve militia) under strict control. The local assistants would record detailed information in notebooks about every miliciano under their jurisdiction.[24] In 1928 President Romero Bosque stated that the members of the assistant patrols worked *ad honorem* and played an important role in organizing the country's militia,[25] "compelling the milicianos to participate in Sunday training; actively pursuing army deserters and criminals; and confiscating national arms . . . keeping under active surveillance suspect individuals; taking care of railways and telegraph lines; practicing night patrols; pursuing every kind of smuggling activity; supporting civilian authorities and making effective any measures dictated by the superior authorities in case of earthquake and other civil disasters."[26] According to Manuel and Raúl Andino in their propagandistic book on the Meléndez Quiñónez dynasty, those assistants who commanded the local headquarters received "several and determined privileges" as the only payment for commanding the labors of the militia and the reserves.[27]

Therefore the military assistants were specifically in charge of the milicianos, although the milicianos could act as authorities according to the law at any moment as demanded by circumstances. The military assistants acted fundamentally as a branch of the army. They primarily helped in the organization of the reserve militia. According to Manuel and Raúl Andino, in 1924 this service was voluntary.[28] Nevertheless, in the context of the construction of relations of domination in El Salvador, it is difficult to believe that a system of auxiliary forces could be completely voluntary. During the 1930s, recruitment for these army patrols was coercive. The recruitment process was performed by reserve forces and soldiers, and both mayors and local commanders were in charge of organizing the patrols.[29]

In summary, besides the traditional functions of the civilian auxiliaries, the state imposed new and no-less conflictive ones for the domain of the military assistants. Sunday training sessions and forced recruitment produced constant conflicts between peasants and the army.[30] Assigning military assistants to intervene in this kind of conflict contributed to a deepening social polarization expressed not only in terms of class but also in the degree of power within groups of individuals sharing similar conditions of existence. Although it is difficult to determine the exact time at which the state created such a mechanism of civilian incorporation into repression, by 1932 the system embraced the entire national territory. According to the War and Navy Ministry "in all the population groups of the nation the services of neighborhood and cantón commanders are organized with their respective patrols."[31]

Although the sources suggest that the military assistants acquired special importance, whereas their civilian counterparts had been officially proscribed for years, the latter continued to have an effective presence in the country.[32] In 1930 Jacinto Pérez, the mayor of Cuisnahuat in Sonsonate, protested against the town's military assistants, revealing a common frustration of the mayors during this period: the loss of their power to the recently created position of military assistant. Further insult stemmed from the fact that the new position had been implemented at a time when the policía de línea and the National Guard were both undergoing expansion.[33]

Revealing to the governor of Sonsonate that drunken men armed with pistols and machetes roamed the town streets, the mayor affirmed that what made this conduct even more problematic was that many of these men were military assistants under the orders of a negligent commander. The mayor, however, had not lost complete control over his particular role within the local repressive system. Although he noted that "because there were not enough auxiliares civiles, they laugh at my orders," it is clear that even in 1930 he had a group of armed civilians under his orders.[34]

In the same year Rodrigo Guerra of Sacacoyo, from the department of La Libertad, asked the governor "to order the mayor of that town . . . not to obligate him to render unpaid service as alguacil."[35] He based his petition on Article 15 of the Constitution, which established that no one could be obliged to provide personal services or to work without fair remuneration and without consent except for motives of public utility established by law.[36] The governor, for his part, claimed that the service Rodrigo Guerra was obligated to provide was in fact "motivated by necessity and public utility."[37] Thus, by finding a loophole in the legislation, the governor showed that Article 15 was less than reliable as a defense for petitioners.

In summary, the auxiliary forces were vital in the process of shaping the Salvadoran state. It was not until the 1910s that policymakers attempted to modernize the repressive system. At that time they tried to abolish the use of auxiliares civiles, most of which consisted of untrained and undisciplined men, closer to a gang of bandits than a police institution. Nevertheless because of the high degree of conflict that existed in the country, the difficulties of forming a police institution to control the whole national territory, and the contribution these assistants made in reproducing relations of domination, the state continued its dependence on them. Although Araujo had made them illegal since 1912, the assistants continued to multiply in the Salvadoran countryside. They persisted either as civilian patrols (the commissioners and his auxiliares) under control of the mayor or landowners, or in the new category of military assistants, under control of the army. They intervened not only in conflicts between workers and employers, but also in those between civilians and the army. Both kinds of conflicts frequently exploded into violence, although this was not articulated in a political project. The discussion that follows centers exclusively on the civil patrols, for the sources indicate that these constituted the most powerful instrument used by the state, landowners, and local authorities to impose order in the countryside.

Confronting the Collaborators:
The Experience of Inés Perdido and Her Family

In 1885 criminal proceedings were opened against Inés Perdido, her husband, Bartolo Hernández, her son-in-law Bríjido López, and her two daughters, Luz and Jesús Perdido. They were taken to trial because Julián Argueta, the commissioner of Cantón Limo-Zapote, had denounced them. Inés and her husband had a small plot of land and described themselves as farmers. The land they owned, however, was not enough to support the family, and as a result they had to supplement their agricultural work with wage labor. Bartolo was a jornalero, Inés worked as a clothes washer, and her son-in-law declared in the interrogation that he was also a jornalero. Bartolo did not comply with his obligations as a jornalero, for though a landowner had advanced him money, he left the hacienda without completing the work for which he was responsible. This was precisely the incident that touched off the events leading to the trial, an occasion that was hardly new for Bartolo, who at one point in the proceedings declared that "he had previously been in jail, [but] only for problems of debt."[38]

The problem between the commissioner and this peasant family may have originated in the nonfulfillment of Bartolo's labor obligations, but Bartolo was not the central character of this story. According to the witnesses who testified on behalf of the commissioner—the ten members of the official's civilian patrol—the main character in the events that motivated the denunciation was Inés, Bartolo's wife. The witnesses' story goes as follows: obeying the orders of the district's mayor, the commissioner and his assistants had gone to capture Bartolo for his failure to fulfill his labor obligations. They found him in his small cornfield near his house and proceeded to tie him up. At that moment Inés appeared, and according to the commissioner's declarations, which were supported by his assistants, "without motive she came to where we were capturing the convict, and used a lot of outrageous and disobedient expressions with me. For example she said to me 'you are not more than a gossip monger, shameless thug, shit-eater, my ass has more shame than you, you are no authority because you are not a good man and you are no more than a shit-eater,' and other obscene insults." But the rudeness of Inés's expressions did not surprise the commissioner because prior to the arrest one of his assistants had told him that if they arrived at Bartolo's house, "he [the commissioner] would see what kind of reprimand Bartolo's wife would give him . . . because she had said that she was going to do that if he went there because he was no authority in their eyes."

Immediately after the civilian authorities arrested Bartolo, they walked with the convict to his house to look for his clothes. Then, according to the commissioner it was not enough for Inés to repeat the previous insults, for she added new ones, including the remark that "the speaker is a son of a bitch and he was made commissioner for being a *sacón* [gossip monger] and that she was going to repeat all these insults in front of the judge." According to one of the assistants, the commissioner demanded that Bartolo exert his patriarchal authority and order his wife to remain silent. To this Bartolo answered that "she was completely free to say whatever she wants," and, without suspecting the price both of them would pay for such daring, he seconded the insults his wife had directed at Julián Argueta. The peasant then shouted that "he [the commissioner] was no more than a shameless sacón, that he was no commissioner to him, and that neither the jail nor any son of a bitch would destroy him."

At that moment the daughters of the arrested man, Luz and Jesús Perdido, followed the example of their rebellious parents by adding their own insults as the commissioner led their father away. "There goes that shameless man with my father as prisoner," was one of their alleged comments. The commissioner also explained that when he had entered the house, Bríjido López, a twenty-five-year-old day laborer and son-in-law of the convict, "drew his dagger and prepared to attack the declarant in a threatening way." Argueta ordered him to sheath his weapon, to which Bríjido responded, "not even ten like you could make me sheathe it." When the commissioner and his assistants approached him to tie him up, however, the young man obeyed and sheathed his dagger.

Bríjido offered a different narration of the events, stating that he threatened the commissioner only after he "tried to slash his mother-in-law with a machete." Inés Perdido, for her part, denied that she had insulted the commissioner, stating that she had only told him that "she did not approve that he arrived at her house because of a previous offense which she had already denounced, as appears in the records from this office." "She was offended," the sources say, "because he [the commissioner] had raped her daughter, and that if he had any shame he would have entrusted his post to another commissioner instead of presenting himself in her house." Meanwhile the daughters declared that they were ignorant of all that had happened with regard to the family's conduct during the arrest. In addition, Bartolo stated that he did not know who insulted the commissioner and affirmed that the commissioner must have been lying because of the old animosity that had existed between himself and the family.

The jury absolved Luz and Jesús Perdido, but to gain their freedom they had to post bail of thirty pesos each and, worse, they had had to spend six months in prison before the court declared the final verdict. Bartolo Hernández, Inés Perdido, and Bríjido López were condemned "to *arresto mayor* [major arrest] in its maximum degree of guilt." Furthermore, López had to pay a ten-peso fine for carrying a forbidden weapon, Inés had to pay twenty-eight pesos, and the guilty three had to assume the expenses of the trial. It fell to the justice of the peace of Metapán to order the seizure of Bartolo and Inés's belongings, in the amount of eighty pesos, a task he entrusted to another commissioner from Limo-Zapote, Santos Umaña. The assessment determined that absolutely all the couple's belongings—"two houses, a small bread oven . . . , one plot with sugar cane [and] coffee, and a wood cane mill, a little spoiled, [and] one plot with corn surrounded by wood and cane"—equaled the value of the fine determined by the court. All these goods were sold at auction. When Inés and Bartolo left prison, then, they had to confront a new reality: they had lost all their belongings. Because they did not answer a court citation, the judge ordered an investigation of their whereabouts. As a result of these events, they were forced to move into an hacienda, presumably as laborers.

This case is exceptional because the dialogue was given greater importance than the action. Criminal records almost always privileged the detailed establishment of all the facts of the case. The richness of this case derives from the fact that much of the juridical inquiry was centered on the verbal resistance of Inés Perdido. In contrast, her son-in-law's armed resistance occupied a secondary role in the construction of the events that culminated in the conviction of the family. Consequently the document offers an excellent opportunity for analyzing how popular culture constructed a key actor in the genesis of the repressive Salvadoran system: the commissioner.

What was Inés's intent in staging a verbal attack on the commissioner? Throughout her audacious performance this peasant woman manifested anger and bitterness born of the vexations that the local authority had caused her family. But her offensive words also demonstrated a daily form of resistance that included such devices as disapproval and

intimidation. In other words Inés was prepared to utilize moral sanction to shame and threaten the commissioner in order to deter him
from arresting her husband.[39] Initially she had sent a verbal message to
the authority through one of his assistants, a message whose aggressive
tone was meant to alarm and shame him from going to her house. The
assistant had told the commissioner, as mentioned earlier, that "if he arrived at Bartolo's house he'd see what kind of reprimand his wife would
give him . . . because she had said she was going to do it." Inés, it is important to observe, intended to frighten the commissioner from going
to her house not only through threatening verbal aggression but also
through her message that the family refused to recognize his authority.

Her first attempt at intimidation did not succeed, however, and Inés
had to directly attack the commissioner. One of the valiant peasant's
most frequently used adjectives expressed not only the target of her discourse of resistance but also the peculiar construction of the relations of
power woven among the civilian auxiliares and the peasantry. I refer to
the popular Salvadoran word *sacón*, which has two meanings: the first
is "informer," or "gossip monger," and the second, "flatterer."[40] When
Inés shouted to Argueta that he had been made commissioner because
he was a sacón, she implied that the authorities of Limo-Zapote had
discovered that he was disposed to betray his own community in order
to obtain the crumbs of power that accrued from this behavior and that
because of this attribute he had been assigned the task of "facing" the
peasants when class conflict reached a critical point. The same feeling
of betrayal was expressed by the labor deserters Margarito and Mauri-
cio Alvarado, when in 1892 the commissioner from Metapán, Lorenzo
Cisneros, tried to capture them. On that occasion, while the two Al-
varados threatened him and his assistants with their weapons, they also
insulted them, shouting: "Son of pigs, *sacones.*"[41]

The commissioners Argueta from Metapán and Cisneros from Limo-
Zapote defined themselves as farmers when they signed their declarations. Nevertheless, it was very common that commissioners declared
themselves to local authorities to be jornaleros so they would not have
to sign up as commissioners. In other words, the auxiliares civiles were
peasants chosen by mayors and landowners to carry out the tasks of repression in the countryside.[42]

For the peasants the rural policeman who patrolled the countryside
was an unknown person commanding fear and respect; he also be-

came an object of the peasants' aggression, but only when they held the upper hand.[43] The civil patrol may have had institutional support, but it was difficult for a peasant to accept the authority of a neighbor, an equal, with whom he or she shared a common history. Because of this, Inés Perdido gave herself the pleasure of telling the commissioner from Limo-Zapote that she did not recognize him as an authority.

Another example of peasant disaffection with the authority of the commissioner was the 1913 case of two peasants caught fighting with machetes in the road from San Juan Opico to Santa Tecla. When a local commissioner, Alfonso Merino, intervened in the fight, one of the fighters, Valentín Rivera, wounded him when he did not heed his warning "[i]f you interfere, you have to pay the consequences."[44] At that moment Rivera did not see the commissioner as a figure of authority but simply as a neighbor intruding in his business.[45]

The Collaborators Pass the Bill to the Peasants

In the last decades of the nineteenth century, the process of land privatization was accompanied by peasants' being evicted from their land. In 1892 the alcalde auxiliar from the cantón of Portezuela, accompanied by the civil patrol, arrived at the homes of Feliciano Molina and Luis Martínez, where he intended to evict both of them. In turn Molina and Martínez presented a complaint to the criminal tribunal of Santa Ana stating that their properties were properly registered. In their declarations they placed special emphasis on the abuses committed by the mayor, Raymundo Dueñas, and the members of the civil patrol. They alleged that five brothers from the Rodríguez family, members of the commission in charge of the eviction, not only threw aside some of furniture they found in the house, but also wounded Molina and Martínez with machetes, and stole "four wooden beds, three grinding stones, one cedar chest, three *tercios* of tobacco, two *arrobas* of rope, ten *fanegas* of corn, ten dozen hens, a yucca plot measuring two *tareas* or eight *áreas*, sixteen áreas of beans, and two tiled huts."[46]

These accusations led the judge to order the arrest of the Rodríguez brothers, which the mounted police then carried out. The brothers denied stealing from and attacking the complainants, affirming that they carried out the eviction accompanied by a mayor and under the orders of a *juez ejecutor* (executive judge). The mayor's version was slightly different: he said that he had accompanied the Rodríguez brothers to carry out the eviction "by petition of Guillermo Rodríguez, who told him that he was going with a *juez ejecutor* to dispossess Luis Martínez and Pablo Colocho, Feliciano Molina's son, and that his presence as mayor was necessary."[47] The mayor explained that "Rodríguez was accompanied by a man *acting* as judge, giving or communicating orders."[48] The trial showed that, in effect, the mayor and the Rodríguez brothers acted under the orders of the *juez segundo de paz* (assistant justice of the peace). This was enough to rule that the case should not continue because, according to the judge in charge of the case, "no proof exists of the crime committed by the accused."[49] Consequently there was no reason to continue the investigation.

The procedure against the mayor and the civil patrol evidences the gross irregularities in which members of the judicial system frequently engaged. The case was stopped without any investigation into the accusations of physical aggression and robbery; nor was legal cognizance taken of the victim's claims that they had documents to prove they were the legitimate owners of the properties. For the bureaucrats of the Juzgado Criminal (criminal court) of Santa Ana it was enough that a juez ejecutor had given the eviction order to deny these peasants the opportunity to fight for the land through legal channels. The mayor revealed his irresponsibility when he declared to the jury that he went to evict the peasants obeying the orders of Guillermo Rodríguez, without even inquiring into the name of the supposed juez ejecutor or even asking him to prove that he was the proper authority to carry out the eviction.

Who were the Rodríguez brothers? From where did they derive their authority and power? Although the five brothers defined themselves as farmers, none of them could sign his name, which clearly indicates that they did not belong to the most powerful sectors of society. The judicial report clarifies that their capacity to accumulate lands at the expense of other peasants came from their collaboration with the repressive system.[50] Consequently this kind of collaboration had a double function in the process of reproduction of the dominant system. While it provided the state with enough people to impose authority in the countryside, it also contributed to domination in an indirect but no less effective way through its ability to disintegrate communal cohesion. Thanks to the power the state gave them, the men involved in this system had an open door through which to enrich themselves by abusing the rest of the peasants.[51] This was the only payment they could aspire to for performing a service that in fact had no official remuneration. Thus some of the assistants took charge of finding their own payment for the services they gave to the state and the landowners. This was the case of the Rodríguez brothers, portrayed in the criminal records as taking their neighbors' land, and this was also the case for commissioner Argueta, who presented a bill for his services in giving himself the right to demand "sexual favors" from Inés Perdido's young daughter.[52]

The case of the Rodríguez brothers was exceptional because the commissioners tended to partake in evictions to defend not their own interests but those of the landowners. Nevertheless it was inevitable that the conflict turned against the auxiliares. In the case of the eviction of the tenant farmers Dionisia Menjívar, a widow, and her two sons from don Luciano's property, a commissioner, a mayor, a lieutenant from the *resguardo*, (garrison) two witnesses, and the secretary of the *alcaldía* (municipality) handled the direct confrontation. Of all these figures the commissioner had most of the responsibility for confronting peasants. The mayor, for example, had ordered that while the eviction was taking place, the Menjívars "were to be under the surveillance of the commissioner, Mr. Burgos."[53] The authorities were afraid that the tenant farmers would resist the eviction, but the Menjívars obeyed the mayor's order submissively, possibly because of the impressive force that arrived to effect it. When the commissioner ordered them to leave the house empty, they proceeded to "take their pots out. . . . Then they took out a little of the corn they had in land belonging to the same plot as the house."[54] Immediately the authorities proceeded to destroy the huts in which the family lived "because don Luciano had ordered it."[55] According to don Luciano, because the Menjívars had not made any improvements and did not have crops and, finally, because the wood they used to build their huts belonged to the hacienda, they only had the right to carry with them the few things they had at home.[56]

Undoubtedly, the constant intervention of armed neighbors in disputes between peasants and landowners in favor of the latter contributed to the disintegration of communal links. Consequently, the oligarchy benefited from the civil patrols in two different ways: on the one hand, they contributed to resolving the problem of lack of repressive force in the countryside, and, on the other, they contributed to weakening the

ability of peasant communities to resist land privatization and the op-
pressive labor relations imposed by the oligarchy. Through the system
of dividing the peasantry, their sense of solidarity was disintegrated.

The role that the system of domination gave the civil patrols (confronting peasants as agents of the dominant class in the conflictive
process of capitalist accumulation), accompanied by that implicit right
to abuse other community members, quickly turned their neighbors
against them. Nevertheless, the existence of these civilians incorporated into the repressive system made it particularly difficult for the
community to respond collectively to the system of domination. The
disintegrating effect on communal links wrought by the auxiliares did
not necessarily derive from their numbers but from their impact on
daily and routine community relations. An auxiliary or some neighbor
disposed to utilize gossip to gain the trust of the hacendado or of the
local authorities could easily gain access to conversation in the haciendas, bars, roads, and street corners.

The surveillance service that civil patrols provided was very useful not
only because the auxiliares moved in the same spaces as the community
but also because they knew almost everyone. They possessed knowledge about the population: where they lived, their habits, how dangerous they might be, and the cultural values they could use to cement
collective responses to domination. In this way, surveillance, as a kind
of violence intended to shape human behavior through intimidation,
not through direct physical aggression, was supported and promoted by
those charged with the responsibility of "arbitrating" in social conflict.

Challenging the Auxiliares

All systems of domination generate resistance. Peasant resistance to
civil auxiliares exploded frequently in violent confrontations between
the two. But resistance came not only from peasants subjected to the
control of the auxiliares civiles but also from the auxiliares themselves.
Such authorities were not always integrated into the civil patrols voluntarily. Furthermore, they were in a very complex situation. On one
hand, they tried to please the mayors and landowners, but, on the other
hand, they lived as neighbors with the rest of the peasants. As I show
in this section, these were contradictory positions.

Peasants frequently confronted and challenged these authorities. In 1912 a journalist complained about those he referred to as *autoridades en pequeño*—that is, commanders and commissioners. He emphasized that because of fear of peasant revenge, petty authorities often refrained from arresting criminals and that they would even protect criminals when the police then tried to capture them, advising the offenders of their pursuers' route. Comandantes and commissioners even hid criminals in their houses.[57] It is difficult to know if those responsible for the civil patrols acted out of conviction or out of fear, but the frequent retaliations suffered by the civil auxiliares at the hands of outraged peasants indicate that fear of peasant revenge was absolutely justified. We find a typical example of intimidation in a scene from 1885, in which Ignacio Ticas was the protagonist. In this case a commissioner, Pedro Duarte, complained to the Juzgado Segundo de Paz of Metapán that Ticas entered his house riding a mule and "threatened him with an unsheathed dagger, and told him that he was going to wound him with the dagger and that he was not going to leave until he had killed him."[58] But the commissioner escaped, went to call his auxiliares civiles, and captured the offender. On the way to jail Ticas again assailed commissioner Duarte, telling him that "some day he was going to be out of jail and then he was going to kill him."[59] Ticas, in fact, would not spend much time in jail: the jury declared him innocent.[60] In another case from 1882, the commissioner from San Miguel de Metapán, Clemente Hernández, accused Francisco Menjívar of attacking him. According to the commissioner, the reason for the attack was that he had recently arrested Menjívar for refusing to assist in public works projects. In this case the court declared Menjívar not guilty.[61]

The auxiliares civiles frequently refused to apprehend peasants not only out of fear of dying at the hands of some community member, but also because powerful people were not likely to intervene in their favor during the trials that often ensued. For these auxiliares, falling into the snares of justice could be very risky. After all, they were usually poor peasants themselves; and even if they acted in self-defense, they had to confront a randomly chosen jury that might or might not be inclined to hear their side of the story. In 1912, for example, Gabriel Deodones, a forty-two-year-old jornalero and resident of Panchimalco, was condemned to six years in prison for killing Dolores Miranda. Deodones declared that he had killed Miranda in self-defense because when he was drinking in a bar, Miranda arrived and attacked him with a knife. When the authorities asked Deodones if there had been previous incidents between him and the victim, he said that there was only one. He referred to, "an occasion in which he sent Miranda to do public works by order of the mayor from Panchimalco, at which he took offense because he said he had not been paid for his work."[62] Deodones appealed the verdict to the Cámara de Tercera Instancia (Appeals Court), but because of the witnesses' contradictory declarations, the magistrates did not declare him innocent. With respect to the witnesses from Panchimalco: "some said that José Dolores Miranda attacked Gabriel Deodones without any motive and wounded him with a knife. . . . others said that after that, Miranda left running, and Deodones went after him; and others [said] that Miranda was the one who went after Deodones with a knife in his hands telling him 'stop, son of a bitch.'"[63] Although Deodones placed his case in the hands of the most influential juridical authorities in the country, he only succeeded in having his sentence reduced by two years. Thus, though it may seem contradictory, the system repaid his services as participant in the repression with four years of jail.

The role of witnesses was crucial in determining the fate of the commissioner who attacked a peasant (or vice versa). As in the case of Deodones, another community proved itself unwilling to collaborate with a commissioner from Las Flores, Feliciano Alvarez, when in 1874 he denounced Mardoqueo Durán for attacking him. By 1885 the case was still unresolved in court. When Durán supposedly attacked the commissioner, the latter was accompanied by only one of his assistants, who himself backed the commissioner's version of the events. But the judge asked the commissioner to present other witnesses, and he chose four of his neighbors. All of them refused to corroborate his story, saying that they did not know anything about the events. In 1885 the court declared the case closed.[64]

The frequent killings of auxiliares by peasants indicate that members of the civil patrol had good reason to be afraid for their lives and to protect themselves. Members of the civil patrols did not receive any self-defense training and they were not even armed with guns. Peasants, and especially professional criminals, had more possibilities for successfully confronting civil patrols than confronting army battalions or the rural police. Auxiliares became easy targets for resentful peasants or for others who had opted for criminality as a way of life. As a 1901 editorial of the *Revista Judical* points out, while the collaborators were armed with *corvos* (knives or sickles) and machetes, "the criminals who they were going to capture perhaps banded together to confront the authority and were armed with shotguns and other firearms. In this way the criminals resisted, wounded, and even made the alguaciles and the other individuals who are members of the patrol flee."[65]

In the year 1912 alone the *Revista Judical* registered four trials for attacks on commissioners.[66] But these cases did not represent the number of commissioners that became victims, for this publication described only those cases of technical interest to the intellectuals of the legal system. Consequently it is possible that the number of attacks significantly surpassed the cases presented in this journal. For example, in the same year, the *Diario del Salvador* referred to two attacks on civilian auxiliares that were not mentioned in the *Revista Judical*. One of them took place in Ahuachapán, when the commissioner from the cantón of Cuyananzul and his patrol confronted a group of cattle thieves. During this incident one alguacil died and another was wounded.[67]

In Santa Ana, during 1883 alone there were eight trials of peasants accused of wounding or killing commissioners.[68] In the cases presented in this essay, the 1880s were years of sharp conflict between the peasantry and the low-level authorities, who, at the behest of the state, had recently multiplied throughout the countryside to discipline the rural working classes. This was precisely the time in which Inés Perdido lived.

The members of the civil patrols were regarded by the mayors and especially by landowners as servants. In the eyes of peasants, members of the civil patrols were only poor community members who did not deserve to have power over the rest of the peasantry. Peasants frequently repudiated the mounted police and especially members of the National Guard, but they were afraid of them and they respected them. Peasants would attack guards, but they would do so in secret.

Although the commissioners attacked, stole from, and raped peasants, the peasants also confronted and challenged them in an open way. In the descriptions of confrontations between commissioners and peasants, there are feelings of revenge and anger on both sides. As events unfolded, either side could lose control and violently attack the other. But the arrogance that characterized the behavior of the National Guard was not found in these records. The commissioner imposed himself by brute force, but he did not have the training of the national guardsman, who conceived of himself as different and superior to other peasants and as someone who had to remind the peasantry, even when they were not challenging him, that he wielded power.[69]

The rural policeman was a product of an institutional framework that generated a specific kind of behavior in its members. By contrast, the commissioner could be an abusive man, but he struggled daily to obtain the obedience and respect of his peers—either by trying to convince them that they owed him this or by attacking them. Though the civil patrol had the advantage in numbers, it still had to confront and accept the constant peasant challenge. At the moment of confrontation, peasants on one side, and commissioners on the other, measured their forces. By comparison, the rural policeman (and especially the guardsman) acted before being challenged, and at every challenge he went beyond simply trying to curb the rebellious peasants, evidencing the role that arrogance and power played in shaping this figure. He would show peasants that he could crush them at any moment and, what is more, do whatever he wanted to with their bodies including subjecting them to torture.[70] The policemen did not commit such acts out of anger or fear, but as authorities who had been trained to do so.

Through this system of social manipulation the state was able to control the countryside and therefore to impose a model of social relations of production. What is most important, however, is that this system encouraged a great deal of conflict within the peasant communities. Through the use of mayors and commissioners as mediators between the peasants and the dominant classes, the oligarchy was also able to convert these figures into easy targets of peasant resentment toward the system. In this way most of the resistance exploded at the community level. Because of the broad web of surveillance the state established through these collaborators, it was difficult for the community to articulate collective resistance to the system of domination.

Thus, through this system the state sought to break the effectiveness of community representatives, closing the roads to discourses of resistance through the absorption of the mediators between the community and the state. As soon as the auxiliares obtained posts in the local institutions, the machinery of power compelled them to confront peasants in the most conflictive situations, thereby converting them into targets of the resentful peasant.

Public authorities, however, were ready to confront the challenges posed by peasants who tried to create a discourse of resistance against the community brokers. Inés and her husband were condemned to such an especially harsh punishment because their challenge expressed much more than an attack on a specific authority. They were participants in the reshaping of popular culture in order to articulate a discourse of resistance in which the right to govern is given by the subordinates. This was clear when Inés told the commissioner that he was no authority because she did not recognize him as such. Because the commissioner was a figure that the state constructed to dominate particularly through force and not through consensus, Inés's words had the potential to offer more of a challenge to this repressive system than did the constant armed peasant attacks on its representatives. If Inés's words spread through the countryside, they could help cement links within the peasant community and create a collective strategy for confronting authority. The community could join together to reject the orders of a commissioner, and it could practice mechanisms of social exclusion that could isolate collaborators, however temporarily. In this way the community would impose sanctions against civil auxiliares in order to try to obligate them to renounce the role the oligarchy and the state had assigned them. The state, however, had created mechanisms for neutralizing such strategies of communal action. One of these was the attraction of power. Another was based on the coercion the state exerted to compromise individuals into collaboration. The following section discusses the second of these measures.

The Interplay of Force and Consensus in the Shaping of the Collaborators

The system of auxiliares civiles had never functioned without the predominance of voluntary collaboration. In order to operate a repressive system such as this—one that was not centralized and that was based on personal relations—the acquiescence of members was a basic requirement. If the authorities had had to resort systematically to coercion to form the civilian collaborators, they never would have accomplished the task the state had assigned them. Nevertheless, the civil service was not conceived of as voluntary, and when commissioners and alguaciles resisted collaboration, force was used to bend their rebellious attitudes to the state's will.

In 1885, for example, Rito Mancía accused Tomás Cerritos of having caused him serious injuries. Mancía, as commissioner of Coatepeque, tried to tie Cerritos up in order to obligate him to participate in the civil patrol. Cerritos resisted by attacking Mancía with his machete.[71] As late as 1930 civilians continued complaining to the superior authorities that the mayors obligated them to serve in the patrols.

The role of coercion in the shaping of collaboration is clear in the case of labor deserters. The law contained an effective mechanism for forcing the commissioners to accomplish the task the state assigned them: the Agrarian Law of 1882 established that if they did not arrest the deserters, the landowners would denounce them to the mayors, who would in turn punish them with the requirement that they themselves pay the breaker's debt.[72] If a mayor committed a transgression of this law, the landowner had to complain to the governor, who would punish the mayor with the deserter's debt payment and also with the cost of the trial.[73] The Agrarian Law of 1904 systematized the punishment for both authorities. If they did not accomplish the task of arresting offending workers, they would be fined five pesos.[74] In 1909, through an amendment to the Agrarian Law of 1904, the auxiliary mayors, commissioners, and rural policemen who did not arrest those who stole wood or firewood and destroyed forests without permission from the landowner would be punished by the mayor with a ten-peso fine.[75] Thus small-time collaborators were placed between a rock and a hard place. They could not deny collaboration because the state obligated them to comply with the demands of landowners. Thus their capacity to co-opt people under their control weakened, and violence exploded in the daily relations between them and the peasantry.

Do the developments discussed imply that the patrols were formed exclusively through coercion? If not, when did people start acting through consent instead of through fear of repression? How do we establish the moment at which, through daily practice, the system of domination was internalized? How do we know when the rebel collaborator overcame the disgust that caused him to face his neighbors in the name of the powerful, and when he started enjoying the feeling of superiority that power gave him? Possibly a sense of consent and of coercion coexisted in contradiction inside these peasants, who, feeling unable to change the relations of power, decided to play both sides. They supported the powerful because they did not have any other option but also because knowing how to take advantage of collaboration could give them personal benefits. On the other hand, they allied themselves with peasants because they feared losing the solidarity of those who, after all, were their people, and because history had repeatedly showed them that peasant revenge was something to fear.

Conclusion

The creation of an extensive network of civil patrols was one of the key policies that permitted the state to keep the countryside under control. This particular repressive mechanism contributed to domination in two important ways. First, it permitted the state to create quickly and without expenditures, an impressive repressive force that covered the entire country. These collaborators might have been far from efficient and disciplined policemen, but at least they permitted local authorities and landowners to incorporate as many people into the system of repression as they thought they needed.

Second, this setup contributed to the erosion of communal unity not only because it co-opted those individuals more disposed to collaborate, but also because the state had mechanisms to obtain the collaboration of those not convinced that they wanted to. The state found a way of creating a network that made resisting collaboration very difficult. Local authorities were integrated in collaboration by consensus or force. In doing this the state was prepared to destroy the legitimacy of the people who could bring together the community to confront the state and dominant classes.

By placing those reluctant to collaborate in a difficult situation, and by integrating into collaboration those who wanted to enjoy power within the community, the state found an effective mechanism for forging a complex network of participants in the service of the oligarchy's interests. This system of domination, which permitted the state to create an efficient group of collaborators who would act to deter the individual and collective protests of the peasants, did not experience significant challenges from the subordinated classes until the 1920s. This approach led to increased violence inside peasant communities. The sharpest class conflicts frequently erupted between people who shared similar living conditions. Peasants assigned responsibility for the system of domination to other peasants with power over them.

These collaborators contributed to the erosion of communal cohesion by trying to reap compensation for their service at the expense of their weaker peers. Yet they also positioned themselves between two contradictory currents. On the one hand, compliance with dominant elements gave them power over the community, but on the other, the exercise of this power demanded some degree of legitimacy. Often, legitimacy and obedience to the oligarchy and to the state were contradictory goals. The efforts of the civil assistants to create consensual spaces in their relations with the rest of the peasantry could not alter the triumph of the oligarchical project: disintegration of peasant communities brought about by the collaboration of some of their members in the repressive system.

Notes

1. For a discussion of similar themes, see Robert Carmack, ed., *Guatemala: cosecha de violencias* (San José: Facultad Latinoamericana de Ciencias Sociales, 1991).

2. The basic sources are the criminal records. I reviewed the criminal section of Santa Ana's public records for the years 1883, 1885, 1890, 1892, 1910, and 1920. In addition, I read all the issues of the *Revista Judicial* from 1900 to 1932. Whereas the criminal records from Santa Ana facilitate an in-depth analysis of a specific region, the cases analyzed in the *Revista Judicial* make it possible to link the experience of the department of Santa Ana with that of the rest of the country. The Colección Gobernación of the National Archive of El Salvador contains materials helpful for study of the history of auxiliares civiles in relation to other instances of local and state power. Finally, the documentation from the 1920s and early 1930s in the Alcaldía de Sonsonate (Sonsonate mayoral office) reveal the changes that occurred to the system of auxiliary forces with the expansion of the National Guard in the whole coffee region.

3. Aldo Lauria-Santiago, "An Agrarian Republic: Production, Politics, and the Peasantry in El Salvador: 1740-1920" (Ph.D. dissertation, University of Chicago, 1992), chap. 7.

4. See, for example, Rafael Menjívar, *Acumulación originaria y desarrollo del capitalismo en El Salvador* (San José: EDUCA, 1980; 2d ed. 1995).

5. Michel Foucault, *Discipline and Punish: The Birth of the Prison* (New York: Vintage, 1979), 137.

6. Carla Pasquinelli, "Poder sin estado," *Poder y control: revista hispanoamericana de disciplinas sobre control social,* 1 (1987): 56.

7. Lauria-Santiago, "An Agrarian Republic."

8. See Patricia Alvarenga, *Cultura y ética de la violencia: El Salvador, 1880–1932* (San José: EDUCA, 1996), chap. 3.

9. For example, in 1874 Nicanor Fonseca, commander of the department of Sonsonate, ordered that "all the municipalidades, mayors, and commisioners obey and make the people obey police laws." "Colección de bandos del corriente año," 1874, Archivo General de la Nación (hereafter cited as AGN), Sección Alcaldía, Sonsonate, N.2.

10. Ibid.

11. "Leyes de agricultura," *Boletín de Agricultura*, February 15, 1882, p. 60; emphasis added. See also "Ley de policía de la codificación de leyes patrias de 1879," in *Recopilación de leyes administrativas,* edited by Miguel Barraza (San Salvador: Imprenta Nacional, 1917), 136.

12. "Ley agraria de la República de El Salvador," *Revista Judicial,* 10, no. 15 (January 1905): 350–351. See also Article 213.

13. "Poder legislativo," *Revista Judicial,* 14, nos. 15-16 (August 1909): 337.

14. *Memoria de Gobernación y Fomento de 1883* (San Salvador: Imprenta Nacional, 1884), 56.

15. *Memoria de Gobernación y Fomento* (San Salvador: Imprenta Nacional, 1890), 40.

16. "Incendio de un potrero del señor Durán," *Diario de Occidente,* April 4, 1933; "Copias de diciembre," December 3, 1932; "Copias de abril," April 3, 1933, f.1; and "Copias de junio," June 3, 1933, all in Alcaldía de Sonsonate, uncatalogued.

17. "Copias de setiembre," September 1, 1933, ibid.

18. "Copias de mayo," May 1, 1933, ibid.

19. February 5, 1920, f.iv, AGN, Sección Gobernación, uncatalogued; emphasis added.

20. On the continuation of this service without remuneration, see "Carta al Dr. Quiñónez," *Diario del Salvador,* January 27, 1919, p. 4; and "Dificultades para el pago de alguaciles," *Diario la Prensa,* September 2, 1926, p. 7.

21. See Alejandro Dagoberto Marroquín, *Panchimalco: investigación sociológica* (San Salvador: Ministerio de Educación, 1974), 49.

22. "Informe de autoridades militares de Cojutepeque al presidente," June 1901, f.23, AGN, Sección Guerra y Marina, uncatalogued.

23. *Memoria del Ministerio de Guerra de 1922* (San Salvador: Imprenta Nacional, 1923), 39.

24. See Rafael Barraza R., *Segundo apéndice de la nueva recopilación de leyes administrativas* (San Salvador: Imprenta Nacional, 1925), 251–253.

25. *Recopilación de leyes militares* (San Salvador: Imprenta Nacional, 1929), 332.

26. Manuel and Raúl Andino, *La obra del gobierno del Dr. Quiñónez* (San Salvador: Imprenta Nacional, 1925), 306.

27. Ibid.

28. Ibid.

29. "Notas de noviembre," November 16, 1933, Alcaldía de Sonsonate, un-catalogued.

30. See Alvarenga, *Cultura y ética*, chap. 3.

31. "La municipalidad de Ayuxtepeque solicita se apruebe el restablecimiento del servicio gratuito de patrullas," March 1932, f.2, AGN, Sección Gobernación, uncatalogued.

32. See "Se solicita nombramiento de comisionado en el caserío El Chapernal," 1930, f.1, ibid.

33. "Notas de gobernaciones políticas del mes de mayo," May 28, 1930, f.1, ibid.

34. Ibid.

35. "Rodrigo Guerra pide ordenar al alcalde de La Libertad no lo obligue a prestar servicio gratuito como alguacil," 1930, f.1, AGN, Sección Gobernación, uncatalogued.

36. Rafael Barraza S., *Nueva recopilación de leyes administrativas* (San Salvador: Centro Editorial Elios, 1928), 1:6.

37. Ibid.

38. This case is based on "Criminal contra Bartolo Hernández, Bríjido López, Inés, Luz y Jesús Perdido por desacato a la autoridad," 1885, AGN, Sección Jurídica, Criminales de Santa Ana, B15, N.20. The quotes through to next note also came from this source.

39. For an analysis of moral sanction as a mechanism of resistance in peasant communities, see James Scott, *Weapons of the Weak: Everyday Forms of Peasant Resistance* (New Haven, Conn., and London: Yale University Press, 1985).

40. See Real Academia Española, *Diccionario manual e ilustrado de la lengua española* (Madrid: Espasa Calpe, S.A., 1989).

41. AGN, Sección Jurídica, Criminales de Santa Ana, B22-2, N.15, 1892, f.2v.

42. Don Pedro Flores, who requested the capture of the labor deserter Casiano Solórzano, assisted in his capture as a member of the civil patrol. This case, however, is exceptional. See "Criminal contra Casiano y Valentín Solórzano por atentado a la autoridad de las Negritas," 1910, fs.6-6v, AGN, Sección Jurídica, Criminales de Santa Ana, B20-2, N.2.

43. See Alvarenga, *Cultura y ética*, chap. 3.

44. "[Q]ue si él se metía él se la llevaba." See *Revista Judicial*, 18, nos. 15–16 (August 1913): 376.

45. Similar disrespect for the authority of the commissioner was expressed in 1877 by Fernando Granadino of San Lorenzo. The commissioner knew that Fernando produced illegal alcoholic drinks at his house and went to arrest him. But when the commissioner arrived there and ordered Granadino to open the

door of his house Granadino refused, telling him "Usted no me amuela a mi," a very pejorative way of saying "do not bother me." "Criminal contra Fernando Granadino y Luciano Segobia," 1877, f.iv, AGN, Sección Jurídica, Criminales de Santa Ana, B7-4, N.167.

46. AGN, Sección Jurídica, Criminales de Santa Ana, B22, N.4, 1892, f.1.

47. Ibid., f.19; emphasis added.

48. Ibid.; emphasis added.

49. Ibid., f.37v.

50. In 1890 Cupertino Escobar of cantón Primavera killed the commissioner Reyes Rodríguez when, according to Escobar, the commissioner badly wounded him while on his farm. The commissioner had gone there to demand that Cupertino give him three pesos. When the latter refused, the commissioner attacked him. "Criminal contra Reyes Rodríguez por homicidio y atentado a mano armada contra el comisionado," 1890, AGN, Sección Jurídica, Criminales de Santa Ana, B20-22, N.45.

51. See ibid., C10-16, N.86, 1910.

52. According to a journalist of the *Diario del Salvador* in 1912 in San Pedro Masahuat, four alguaciles who believed their posts gave them immunity from the law raped and killed a woman. "Horripilante crimen," *Diario del Salvador,* August 9, 1912, p. 1. In another case the mayor from Tapalhuaca (town in the department of La Paz) and his civil patrol entered by force the home of Francisca de Paz with the excuse of investigating illegal alcohol production. They stole 300 pesos from the woman. It is likely that the reason the newspaper registered this abuse of power by the civil patrol is because the victim was not a poor peasant. "Sucesos diversos," *Diario del Salvador,* November 10, 1920, p. 2.

53. "Juicio de lanzamiento seguido por don Luciano Eufemía contra Dionisia, viuda de Menjívar," 1915, f.10, AGN, Sección Alcaldía, Sonsonate, N.2.

54. Ibid., f.16v.

55. Ibid.

56. See also "Exhibición decretada en favor de Andrés Pérez," 1910, AGN, Sección Jurídica, Criminales de Santa Ana, C10-13, N.205.

57. *Diario del Salvador,* November 18, 1912, p. 1. See also "Información salvadoreña," ibid., November 29, 1912, p. 4.

58. AGN, Sección Jurídica, Criminales de Santa Ana, B15, N.14, 1885, f.2.

59. Ibid.

60. Ibid., f.62v.

61. "Criminal contra Francisco Menjívar por atentado a la autoridad," 1892, AGN, Sección Jurídica, Criminales de Santa Ana, B22-4, N.38.

62. "Incidente de apelación ante la Cámara de Tercera Instancia," *Revista Judicial,* 21-22 (November 1912): 499.

63. Ibid.

64. "Incidente de consulta contra Madoqueo Durán por atentado a la autoridad," 1885, AGN, Sección Jurídica, Criminales de Santa Ana, B15, N.15.

65. "Consideraciones sobre la criminalidad en El Salvador," *Revista Judicial* 4 (February 1901): 100.

66. See the *Revista Judicial*, 1–2 (January 1912): 34; 7–8 (April 1912): 166; 19–20 (October 1912): 443; and 21–22 (November 1912): 497–501.

67. "Pequeños telegramas," *Diario del Salvador*, March 22, 1912, p. 1. See also "Notas Rojas", ibid., May 30, 1912, p. 1.

68. See AGN, Sección Jurídica, Criminales de Santa Ana, B12-1, N.150, 1883; ibid., B13-1, D3, N.76, N.82, N.100, N.188, N.182, and N.189; and B13-2, D3, N.142.

69. See Alvarenga, *Cultura y ética*, chap. 6.

70. See ibid., chap. 2.

71. AGN, Sección Jurídica, Criminales de Santa Ana, B20-1, N.16, 1885, fs.1–3.

72. Article 1143 in "Leyes de agricultura," *Boletín de Agricultura*, February 15, 1882, p. 61.

73. Ibid.

74. See Article 78, "Ley Agraria de la República de El Salvador, " *Revista Judicial* (December 1904): 305.

75. "Poder legislativo," *Revista Judicial*, nos. 15–16 (August 1909): 337–338. See also *Memoria de Gobernación y Fomento de 1891* (San Salvador: Imprenta Nacional, 1892).

DARÍO A. EURAQUE

The Banana Enclave, Nationalism, and
Mestizaje in Honduras, 1910s–1930s

❂

All the banana plantations grouped men of different categories and places, with diverse degrees of culture, of heterogeneous qualities, but whom, when living together were known as *campeños*. They included whites, Indians, mestizos, blacks, and even some yellows. RAMÓN AMAYA AMADOR, *Prisión verde*

Caribbean jungles have been converted into modern communities, unified economically by the banana industry. But these banana communities do not possess cultural unity. In place of the jungle there appears a social jungle in which widely divergent nationalities, races, social classes and economic interests are intertwined as confusedly as were trees, underbrush and parasitical vines before the coming of man. CHARLES D. KEPNER JR., *Social Aspects of the Banana Industry*

Traditional Honduran historiography has emphasized the lack of economic linkages between Honduras's banana exporting north coast and its interior development. In addition, William S. Stokes, who when writing in the mid-1980s accepted as a given that "Honduras is not hampered in its organization of government by a political aristocracy of Spaniards, or retarded by a racially inferior Indian or negro proletariat." Stokes also argued other critical points: "the average Honduran admits being a *mestizo* with no loss to his dignity"; "with few exceptions, the Indian is accepted by the Honduran as a Honduran, and as a racial equal"; and "the negroes have not only been accepted into the political pattern on a basis of equality, but in actuality have been represented in Congress and in the executive branch in numbers far out of proportion to their population."[1] This essay aims to change that version of Honduran history by offering a new interpretation of the relationship between a regional banana enclave economy and national history, in particular by providing an alternative reading of the race question as it relates to the banana plantations. It argues that the triumph of a mestizo Honduras by the 1930s was the ideological result of a process of social and economic change that had brought foreign capital and foreign immigrants to Honduras's north coast and had threatened, on many levels, elites' domination of their country. Elites and the Honduran state were too weak politically and economically to challenge or reject foreign capital; thus they attempted to reassert their dominance, at least in the ideological sphere, by asserting a national unity based on a homogeneous Honduran mestizo race and excluding, in particular, the West Indian immigrants brought in by the banana companies but also the indigenous north coast Garifuna populations.[2]

In Honduras, this process reached its culmination in the immigration laws of 1929 and 1934. According to the 1929 legislation, immigrant *árabes, turcos, sirios, armenios, negros,* and "coolies" were required to deposit $2,500 when entering the country. Local relatives from these "races" could secure temporary permits for immigration of their kin, though these did not lead to waiving of the deposit. The Immigration Law of 1934 restated many elements of the 1929 legislation. Article 14 of the law simply stated that "the entry of Negroes, coolies, gypsies and Chinese into the territory of the Republic is prohibited."[3]

This essay argues that the anti-immigrant legislation was connected to the emergence of a vision of Honduras as a homogeneous, mestizo country and that this vision's construction was connected to the rise of the foreign-owned banana industry on the north coast. The anti-immigration legislation of 1929 and 1934, as well as antiblack labor legislation introduced into Congress between 1923 and 1925, must be seen in the context of changes in the way the government counted and classified the population—eliminating entire categories of people and reducing Honduran ethnicities to an all-encompassing mestizo—and in the context of intellectuals' and politicians' attempts to define the nation for themselves and for the population in a way that reaffirmed Honduran identity in a society and economy increasingly dominated by foreigners. The legislation established the racial and ethnic parameters for the acceptable homogeneous, mestizo Honduras, thus also flattening a more complicated narrative of twentieth-century Honduran history.

Counting the Population

A good place to begin exploring different hypotheses on these issues is the Honduran census of 1910. The published results from the 1910 census "are limited to total number of inhabitants in comparison with 1905, number of houses, and number of inhabitants per house," despite that the questionnaires also included total population, age, sex, marital status, citizenship, literacy, race, language, number of children with elementary education, number of professionals, property ownership, and vaccination history.[4]

It is not clear why the results of the 1910 census, published in 1911, exclude all the other valuable information, but other contemporary sources that enjoyed access to the unpublished 1910 data do report statistics on the critical questions of race and ethnicity.[5] The information reported in those documents is startling not only with respect to the numbers but also regarding the racial and ethnic classifications employed in the questionnaire. Included are distinctions not reported in the 1930 census and its published results, nor in others published thereafter, namely, distinctions between ladinos and mestizos and even distinctions between negros and mulatos.

The racial classifications contained in the 1910 census questionnaire represent a distinct complexity not present in the 1887 census; the 1910 data seems to have recuperated the broad heterogeneous racial and ethnic Honduras of the colonial period (see table 1). The 1887 census data, on the other hand, as published in the *Anuario estadístico* of 1893, is limited to the racial classifications of *ladinos* and *indígenas*.[6] *Negros* and *mulatos* are not categorized, even though the *Anuario estadístico* mentions the existence of *blancos* (whites) and *morenos*.[7] Various efforts to take censuses between the 1890s and 1910 did not produce national estimates and were very poor.[8]

Other material from the first decade of the century confirms that officially Hondurans remained divided between *ladinos* and *indios*. One *Guía de Honduras*, probably published in 1905, recounts the following data: "Births by races" for 1903 and 1904. As in the 1887 census, but unlike in its 1910 counterpart, the racial classification was again limited to ladinos and indios.[9] Therefore, the multiethnic categorization offered in the 1910 census sharply departed from previous practices. Moreover,

TABLE I   Racial Distribution of the Honduran Population, 1910

Group	Number	%
Ladinos	341,653	61.1
Indios	90,469	16.2
Blancos	27,980	5.0
Negros	19,176	3.4
Amarillos (Yellows)	7,416	1.3
Mulatos	18,274	3.3
Mestizos	53,889	9.6

Source: "Raza de los habitantes de la República de Honduras en el año de 1910," in *Noticia geográfica y estadística de la República de Honduras, Centro América,* edited by Antonio A. Ramírez F. Fontecha (Washington: U.S. Government Printing Office, 1917), 56.

given the post-1930 census-based racial distinctions, it appears that officially between the 1910s and the 1920s ladino and mulato Hondurans disappeared.[10]

In other words, after the 1930s a new official discourse was reflected in the censuses, and this discourse has been faithfully echoed by subsequent historians. There were several assumptions that guided discussions of race in Honduras. First was the assumption that by the first decades of this century most Hondurans were probably mestizos and very few Indians remained in the territory. The second was that an even smaller percentage of negros or morenos lived on the north coast and that Honduran and Salvadoran mestizos were Central American Hispanics and essentially identical in racial composition. This generalization about mestizos was held despite the fact that the 1910 census made distinctions between ladinos and mestizos (see table 1).

The distinction between ladino and mestizo is important for a number of reasons. During the colonial period *ladino* implied a heterogeneity, inherited from the first years of the conquest, that included a range of mestizos, that is, racially mixed peoples. This was the case because initially, *ladino* was a term used by the Spanish Crown to label subjects of the empire who "spoke the rudiments of the official languages [Castilian Spanish or Vulgar Latin]."[11] The term disregarded race, creed, and national and civil status, but in the Americas, in the context of conquest and the deployment of African slaves, it most often came to mean nonwhite and non-Indian Spanish speakers, including possibilities like negro ladino, mulato ladino, and other mestizos.[12]

By the early twentieth century, however, *mestizo* slowly came to represent a particular kind of "mixed" person, that is, a person of "Indian" and "Spanish" miscegenation and hence different from the broader range of miscegenation suggested by *ladino*. The prominence of the ladino category in the 1910 census shows the process was then in its infancy. However, by the 1920s various processes, particularly those occurring on the north coast around the conflicts between labor and capital, proved to be the critical factor for the prominence attributed to the more narrow mestizo category after 1930. Thus the emergence of a mestizo Honduras in official census data reflects a transformation that took place in the imagination of the country's official elites, a transformation that tied to social, political, and economic events on Honduras's north coast.

Banana Plantation Labor and Elite Racism

Between the 1870s and the 1930s, the territories of the Honduran north coast experienced the greatest population growth since the arrival of the Spaniards in the 1520s. By the 1930s, the population of the north coast departments represented about 20 percent of the country's 900,000 inhabitants, compared to less than 5 percent during the nineteenth century. This broad structural demographic shift within Honduras was especially due to large migrations from the country's interior, generally after the 1920s.[13]

The new population of the north coast included recent arrivals of races and nationalities previously unseen in the area. Visitors and residents of the Honduran north coast in the 1920s and 1930s were keenly aware of the presence in that region of *negros, amarillos, morenos, ingleses* (English), *turcos,* and others. During the 1920s, this diversity was the topic of vigorous debate among Honduran elites. However, after the 1930s, during the dictatorship of General Tiburcio Carías (1933–1949), commentators on the issue, such as William Stokes, lost sight of the earlier and much-debated "race" and "immigration" questions. The complexity of the north coast's ethnic tapestry, as well as its political implications, disappeared as an issue of public debate.

The first stable black population employed by the banana companies were the Honduran Garifuna. These were black Caribs who had occupied the Honduran Atlantic littoral since the late eighteenth century. About 2,000 black Caribs were deported from Saint Vincent to Honduras by the British. The black Caribs' tradition of struggle can be traced back to their ancestors, enslaved West Africans. During transport to the New World in the 1600s they survived a shipwreck and intermarried with local Carib Indians in Saint Vincent. By the late eighteenth century, biological and cultural miscegenation produced a people whom the British called black Caribs.

The British originally left the black Caribs on the Honduran Bay Islands, presumably to help them defend the islands against the Spanish. From there the black Caribs moved to the Honduran mainland, near Trujillo, a town that in the 1910s became a major United Fruit Company center of operations. Although not warmly received by the Spanish military outpost there, the black Caribs soon dedicated themselves to cultivating rice, manioc, sugarcane, cotton, plantains, and squash. They not only supplied their own demands, but also sold surpluses to the town of Trujillo.

At different times, the black Caribs migrated east and west on the Honduran north coast, toward Guatemala and toward Nicaragua. Nancie González, the most prominent ethnographer of the Garifuna, has identified three periods in what she calls the evolution of the Garifuna's "work identity" aspect of their "ethnogenesis" between the 1790s and the 1930s. From the 1790s to the 1820s, the black Caribs served as traders and even raiders of settlements all the way to Belize. Between Honduran independence in the 1820s and the 1870s, they also became smugglers, temporary soldiers of fortune in the country's civil wars, and also temporary wage workers in the lumber operations established in the river valleys of the coast. Their employment in lumber operations continued into the 1880s. Finally, between the 1890s and the 1930s, black Caribs participated in wage work in the banana economy, both before the establishment of foreign-owned plantations and railroads and after.[14]

González and others familiar with the Garifuna have recognized the importation of West Indian laborers, and the ensuing competition for work between them and the black Caribs, Hispanic, and indio Honduran migrants to the area.[15] However, González argues that the black Caribs abandoned the plantation work, returned to "the coast-line itself," their traditional homes, and apparently left the plantation work to the indios and the newly recruited West Indians. In González's view, "perhaps because dock work was less regular, and also because it was on the seashore where Caribs were at home and could easily travel, they came to predominate in the labor gangs of ports such as Barrios, [Puerto] Cortés, Tela, and La Ceiba."[16]

González does not offer a more precise periodization of this process. However, the Garifuna were soon joined by black West Indian mi-grants at the banana plantations. The 1912 railroad concessions granted to the United Fruit Company allowed for the importation of workers, but excluded Asians, coolies, and blacks.[17] However, it also allowed the company to import West Indian blacks in specific cases if granted gov-ernment permission. The company did make use of this provision. Thus even in 1914, when the foreign companies employed only about 4,000 workers, it is clear that the workers formed a more complex ethnic tap-estry than is usually acknowledged.

Immigration Laws and the Hegemony of Mestizaje

Early in 1923, Liberal Party deputies associated with the Federación Obrera Hondureña (Federation of Honduran Workers; FOH), estab-lished in 1921 by Tegucigalpense artisans, introduced legislation that sought to prohibit "the importation into the territory of the Republic of Negroes of the African race and coolies." The bill also called for the banana companies to deport, within a year, "the Negroes and coolies that they have brought into the country." Finally, the deputies sought a census of all negros and coolies and the issuance of identification cards.[18] The left-wing Federación Socialista Hondureña (Honduran Socialist Federation; FSH), established in opposition to the FOH in 1929, declared its support for the racist 1929 immigration legislation but also called for a campaign to get the "black element into the organization in order to discipline him and conduct him in the struggle for his emancipation."[19] Clearly, Honduran elites preferred to direct the FSH in the direction of the disciplining campaign rather than the conducting one.

The banana companies, the British Embassy, and the U.S. Embassy united to oppose the 1923 bill, as well as similar bills introduced into

Congress in 1924 and 1925, and the bills failed.[20] Nonetheless, these efforts converged with the elite racism espoused by politicians and intellectuals regarding the ethnic diversity of the north coast, and they show the relationships the elites perceived between race, immigration, and nationality. Members of the elite preached a nationalism based on racial exclusiveness, which could appeal to a cross-class alliance of Hondurans and undermine the FSH's attempts to unite with black workers. After 1924, powerful caudillos and various future presidents not only condoned this racism but also wrote publicly about it. For example, in 1924 provisional president General Vicente Tosta rejected black immigration.[21]

During the 1925 presidential campaign, General Tiburcio Carías Andino, who would serve as president between 1933 and 1949 through the Nationalist Party, pledged to oppose immigration of black workers to the north coast.[22] The Nationalist Party victor in the 1925 elections, Dr. Miguel Paz Barahona (1925–1928), claimed that Honduras needed "serene races" which "are essential for peace and necessary for the permanence of democracy. Blood is a commodity of utmost necessity. We must import it."[23] A year later, a future Honduran president denounced the "black race" on the north coast and argued that "the compensation received from black labor could not be compared to the incalculable damage done to our species."[24]

The elite Nationalists of the 1920s did not have a monopoly on racism or on the effort to make official what the Honduran "species" or "race" could not be—black or mulato. The 1929 Immigration Law that finally institutionalized antiblack racism, as well as other forms, was signed by Liberal Party president Vicente Mejía Colindres, closely supported by Froilán Turcios (1875–1843), one of the most prominent intellectuals of the period. Indeed, in 1930 the Liberals finally established the Immigration Office that had been called for in the Agrarian Reform Law of 1924, enacted during the provisional presidency of General Vicente Tosta. The Liberals complemented that strategy by contracting J. H. Komor, a British subject, to promote "white immigration."[25]

In 1930, top-ranking officials in the Mejía Colindres administration produced a volume detailing their views on race, immigration, and Honduran nationality. Rafael Díaz Chávez, the country's vice-president, proclaimed the necessity of importing "vigorous races" as in Argentina.[26] Salvador Zelaya, the governor of Tegucigalpa and president of the Office of Immigration, called for assiduously prohibiting entrance of undesirable races. President Mejía Colindres's private secretary, Coronado García, professed a national need for a "healthy and competent immigration that might inject us with vital blood."[27]

The race and nationality question was put somewhat prosaically by Julián López Pineda, in 1930 a Left-leaning Liberal but later an ideologue of the Carías dictatorship. In 1930, he saw the new Office of Immigration as a sign that "our statesmen are beginning to understand the need to begin with the principle of nationality's architecture."[28] In López Pineda's view, the nation's racial architecture excluded blacks and, by extension, mulatos. He condemned "the preferential employment of individuals of the Negro race in agricultural and railroad work, to the detriment of the national peons and laborers, white or *mestizo*."[29] It is no surprise, then, that late in 1930 López Pineda's newspaper *El Sol* nonchalantly reported the establishment of a Ku Klux Klan chapter in San Pedro Sula, the north coast's most industrially productive city.[30]

Finally, Manuel M. Calderón, a main supporter of the Mejía Colindres administration and publisher of what was then Tegucigalpa's most important daily, *El Cronista*, linked this kind of immigration to more than economic needs. In 1930, Calderón explicitly connected white immigration to the black threat against the nation. Calderón wished that the new immigration might contribute, in time, to a needed "racial homogeneity," as in Argentina.[31] Given the convergence of official views after 1929, and especially the racist immigration promulgated in that year, it is no wonder that the 1930 census neutralized the racial heterogeneity reported in the 1910 census.

The 1929 and 1934 racist immigration legislation no doubt institutionalized a discourse with colonial and even nineteenth-century roots and with parallels throughout the continent. Ramón Rosa, the country's most important intellectual of the late nineteenth century explicitly privileged immigration from Europe and the United States as the means for rejuvenating the country.[32] Nonetheless, the institutionalization of this discourse in the late 1920s must be understood in the context of the conflictive and, to elites, threatening racial and ethnic realities of the banana plantations of the north coast. Comparison between the 1906 Immigration Law and its 1929 substitute, especially in the context of the 1910 census, indicates that in the first decade of the twentieth century an "official" Honduran ethnic identity had yet to be created. The

1906 Immigration Law prohibited only the immigration of people sixty years or older and of "individuals lacking good health and morality."[33]

The 1906 law more summarily repeated prohibitions stated in the 1895 Foreigners Law. According to the 1895 law, Honduran authorities could deny admission or expel immigrants if they suffered contagious diseases, if they had committed felonies before immigrating, if they conspired against the public order, or if they conducted "themselves viciously or knowingly endanger[ed] the public tranquility."[34] The 1906 Ley de Extranjería that replaced its 1895 counterpart simply summarized these prohibitions into an article that granted authorities the right to expel immigrants for "reasons of public order or social morality."[35] The racial, ethnic, and national prohibitions remained absent from this legislation.

In the 1910s, Honduran elite antagonism against blacks, which reflected Tegucigalpa elites' concerns about the kind of economic development taking place on the north coast as well as their attempt to portray themselves as the natural leaders of their nation, began to explicitly officialize the racism eventually detailed in the 1929 and 1934 laws.

Intellectuals and Racism

The anti-immigration legislation of 1929, as well as its antecedents in the concessionary contracts signed with the United Fruit Company between 1912 and 1914, represented Honduran elite and nonelite racial and ethnic anxieties over control of the only economic region producing substantial revenues for the weak state. This explains the widespread racist convergence in the 1920s among many sectors of Honduran society in preventing black immigration, fomenting European immigration, and simultaneously assigning everyone official status as mestizos. A broad range of Honduran intellectuals contributed to this process.

An early assault on black immigration and, by extension, on a "black or mulato Honduras" originated with Froilán Turcios, one of the most important literary intellectuals of the first three decades of this century. Turcios's anti-imperialist alliance with Augusto César Sandino between 1926 and late 1928 has been often and rightfully celebrated. By the 1920s he had apparently abandoned traditionalist politics and the sinecures he enjoyed form cabinet-level positions in the dictatorial governments of General Terencio Sierra (1899 to 1903) and Manuel Bonilla (1904 to 1906) and especially in Francisco Bertrand's administration (1912 to

1919).[36] During these earlier years, Turcios published in Tegucigalpa one of the country's most important newspapers, *El Nuevo Tiempo*. This newspaper's articles clearly delineated the relationships between race, immigration, and nationalism.

Beginning in 1912 Turcios's *El Nuevo Tiempo* publicized many of the pro-European and U.S. immigration projects of the Central American International Office (CAIO). This organization was established early in 1912 in a conference attended by representatives from the region's five countries. The CAIO devoted much energy to publicizing the wealth of Central America in Europe and the United States in order to attract foreign investment. It was also authorized to establish offices in these countries to attract white immigrants.[37]

Few European immigrants came to Honduras, however. As the 1929 and 1934 immigration legislation suggested, the new groups that did arrive included mostly people from Lebanon, Palestine, and Syria.[38] By the late 1910s, they became the dominant commercial elite on the North Coast.[39] This process, combined with the increasingly monopolistic presence of the banana companies, emerged as the broader backdrop for reevaluating the relations between race and nationality in Honduras. An eventual outcome included the neutralizing of colonial and nineteenth-century discourses on the racial heterogeneity of the population. It also meant the sanitizing of the 1910 census.

In April 1916 Macedonio Laínez, active in the reconceptualization process, analyzed Honduras's "economic deficiencies" and prefaced his discussion by noting "our slow progress when compared to the other countries of Latin America." Laínez did not focus on technical economic problems but on how the slow progress seemed tied to the "displacement, by foreigners, of our control over resources." Laínez also claimed that foreigners controlled at least 50 percent of all modern communications. More important, he also decried how Hondurans' "national sentiment" had progressively declined. "We have almost given away all our national resources to the foreigners, fatally, to such an extent that our personality as a people and even as a race is now dangerously threatened."[40] But the intellectuals' attempt to recover national sovereignty was reduced to a battle around which they believed Hondurans could unite without threatening fundamental social criticism, without even, in the end, threatening the position of foreign investors: the battle against immigrant workers.

In July 1916, Turcios published in his *El Nuevo Tiempo* three long editorials on "Unnecessary Immigrants." Turcios admitted that he lacked "exact statistics" on the issue, but he nonetheless unleashed a tirade against black immigrants, who, he argued, were causing all kinds of debauchery on the north coast. He decried government policy, surely the Immigration Law of 1906, that obstructed the government from expelling members of a race made arrogant by their "nationality"—that is, West Indian subjects of the British Empire. He also condemned the possibility that this "inferior race" might mix with the "Indian element." This, in other words, meant the "danger" presented by *zambos* (in Honduras, the result of a black and Indian mixture).[41]

A few months later, Paulino Valladarés (1880 to 1926), another major Honduran intellectual, a friend of Turcios, and later a cofounder of the Nationalist Party, seconded Turcios's views and called for new legislation, stating that "we" did not want "retarded ethnic elements, like the Caribs imported by the concessionary companies."[42] In 1919, Valladares's National Democratic Party, the predecessor of today's Nationalist Party, was the first political party to call for a study of the "immigration problem."[43]

Turcios's and Valladares's racism was expounded in the absence of any actual data on north coast labor. They were aware that some banana companies were importing West Indian labor but possessed no knowledge of the numbers. They, as surely most elites residing in Tegucigalpa, knew almost nothing about the Garifuna, and apparently they lacked information about the extent to which that group labored on the banana plantations. Thus their statements reflect their fears about their own loss of position in a nation dominated by foreign concerns as much as a response to immigration per se.

A month after his reflections on "retarded ethnic elements," Valladares more clearly articulated the issues at stake. He prefaced his discussion by noting that now "any citizen or president . . . affirms as categorical that our progress is evident because today we register more import revenues, we export more, and we live among greater luxury and comforts like electric lights, theaters and automobiles." However, Valladares also noted that Honduran laws preferred export crops and neglected the subsistence economies from which most Hondurans obtained their sustenance. On the north coast, the paradoxes seemed more contradictory because there, in the midst of the most evident "progress," merchants imported the needed flour from San Francisco, and other Central American countries supplied most of the local demand for sugar.

Like Laínez, Valladares related these difficulties to their implications about what Laínez had called "our personality as a people." The major problems with the new modernity and its nexus to the world economy lay not with its "economic deficiencies," not with continuous budget deficits nor with unstable monetary policies, nor even with the unpaid foreign debt. The major issue involved the very viability of local state order and a Honduran "nation" in the world community. The ultimate danger, claimed Valladares, was the viability of a Honduras "with defined characteristics, with uniform aspirations, and with a name within the world community."[44] In other words, economic development had escaped the control of local elites, and they sought, in attacks on immigrants and assertion of the racial unity of Hondurans, to reaffirm a nation that seemed to be moving more and more under foreign control.

Conclusion

By the late 1930s the debates of the 1920s and early 1930s seemed to have vanished or, more correctly, were in the process of being neutralized. A key text of this transitional moment is Augusto C. Coello's *La epopeya del campeño,* published in 1938. This short text offers the travel ruminations penned by the son of the author of Honduras's national anthem, Augusto C. Coello, Sr. In this book, Coello Jr. travels among various towns in the interstices of the banana plantations. He takes note of the region's racial composition, so different from the country's interior, but simultaneously neutralizes yesteryear's conflicts. In Coello's words, "racial differences are not relevant in our country, but blond hair and white skin always provoke a sensation of conquest among the black workers disseminated on the north coast."[45]

This evidence challenges the hegemony held by William Stokes's views and those of others regarding the "racial factor" in Honduran politics prior to the 1940s. Only a few Honduran monographs written in the 1980s have challenged Stokes's overall scholarly authority on the contours of Honduran social and political history before World War II. As we have pointed out elsewhere, a close perusal of Stokes's *Honduras: An Area Study in Government* will not yield detailed analyses of the ties between Honduran political history and its social and economic development.[46] In Stokes's book the rise of the banana economy after the 1910s, its consolidation in the 1920s, and its collapse in the 1930s is generally excluded from the analytical picture. The role of the banana industry, which had been surveyed in various books readily available then, including the often cited Charles Kepner and Jay Soothill's *The Banana Empire* (1935), are omitted from discussions of Honduran political and economic history.

In the late 1940s, various publications offered an entirely different picture from that available in Stokes's work. First, in 1949 Kepner and Soothill's *The Banana Empire* was translated into Spanish as *El imperio bananero: las compañías bananeras contra la soberanía de las naciones del caribe*. Various editions appeared in the 1950s and 1960s. Second, also in 1949 William Krehm's *Democracia y tiranías en el Caribe* supplied the first sustained Spanish narrative that placed Honduran political history in the context of banana imperialism. Nonetheless, the race and immigration debates once associated with banana company activities remained silent, even in the work of Medardo Mejía (1907 to 1981), Honduras's most prominent leftist historian of the twentieth century.[47]

Since the 1980s, Hondurans like Mario Posas, Víctor Meza, and Mario Argueta, to mention the most prominent, have begun to fill in perhaps one of the most glaring faults in Honduran historiography: the absence of working-class history, and especially the history of the working peoples of the north coast. These newer accounts not only narrate working-class history, they link it to broader narratives of the country's political system. Even so, major issues remain unresolved, and some important questions have yet to be addressed.[48] In Mario Argueta's view, the following questions merit research: "To what extent did the black West Indian workers incorporate themselves into the national culture and labor unions? Did they identify more with the corporation that contracted them and transferred them to Honduras, or with their class? Did they transcend the barriers of race, language and customs of Hondurans? Did they become Hondurans in a cultural sense? How many remained and how many returned to their places of origin or even to a third country?"[49]

Although our essay only tentatively addresses Argueta's questions, we hope that our contribution here provokes a new era in north coast working-class history and its relationship to the construction of Honduran national identity and national political narratives.

Notes

This chapter is a revision of "Labor Recruitment and Class Formation on the Banana Plantations of the United Fruit Co. and the Standard Fruit Co. in Honduras: 1910s-1930s," paper presented at the Annual Conference of the American Historical Association, San Francisco, California, January 6-9, 1994.

1. William S. Stokes, "The Racial Factor in Honduran Politics," *Modern Language Forum,* 29 (1944): 25-30, quote is on p. 25.

2. This process has important parallels throughout Latin America, where this period saw a wave of scientific racism and immigration laws intended to whiten the population. The most interesting comparisons are with Nicaragua—with regard to which Jeffrey Gould has argued that in the early twentieth century indigenous communities were devastated by "real" violence at the same time as they were erased from Nicaraguan history by "symbolic" violence ("¡Vana Ilusión! The Highlands Indians and the Myth of Nicaragua Mestiza, 1880-1925," *Hispanic American Historical Review,* 73, no. 3 [August 1993]: 429)—and with Costa Rica, about which Avi Chomsky has argued that during this period elite nationalists tried to bring workers into a nationalist alliance based on attacking immigrant West Indian workers, while Costa Rican radicals attempted (in the end without success) to ally with immigrant workers in a more radical version of anti-imperialism that challenged the United Fruit Company as well as Costa Rican elites. Avi Chomsky, "West Indian Workers in Costa Rican Radical and Nationalist Ideology, 1900-1950," *Americas: A Quarterly Review of Inter-American Cultural History,* 51, no. 1 (July 1994): 13.

3. The 1934 Immigration Law is available in the U.S. National Archives (Hereafter cited as USNA), RG 84 (Washington: *Confidential U.S. Diplomatic Post Records, Honduras: 1930-45,* 1985), microfilm reel 9, frames 148-156.

4. Doreen S. Goyer and Eliane Domschke, *The Handbook of National Population Censuses: Latin America and the Caribbean, North America, and Oceania* (Westport, Conn.: Greenwood Press, 1983), 216.

5. "Raza de los habitantes de la República de Honduras en el año de 1910," in *Noticia geográfica y estadística de la República de Honduras, Centro América,* edited by Antonio A. Ramírez F. Fontecha (Washington: U.S. Government Printing Office, 1917), 56.

6. República de Honduras, *Primer anuario estadístico, correspondiente al año 1889* (Tegucigalpa: Tipografía Nacional, 1893), 151.

7. Ibid., 96-97.

8. U.S. Bureau of the Census, *Honduras: Summary of Biostatistics* (Washington: U.S. Government Printing Office, 1944), 5.

9. This rare *Guía de Honduras* is located at the Biblioteca Gallardo in Santa Tecla, El Salvador. Unfortunately, it does not have a date of publication or authorship. See pp. 315, 339.

10. The Honduran census of 1930 was the first to use the mestizo classification. Stokes used the 1940 census.

11. José Piedra, "Literary Whiteness and the Afro-Hispanic Difference," in *The Bounds of Race: Perspectives on Hegemony and Resistance*, edited by Dominick LaCapra (Ithaca: Cornell University Press, 1991), 293.

12. Jack Forbes, *Africans and Native Americans: The Language of Race and Evolution of Red-Black Peoples*, 2d ed. (Urbana: University of Illinois Press, 1993), 76, 176.

13. Rafael del Cid, "Populating a Green Desert: Population Policy and Development, Their Effect on Population Distribution. Honduras, 1860–1980" (Ph.D. dissertation, University of Texas, 1988), 120–151.

14. Nancie L. Solien González, *Sojourners of the Caribbean: Ethnogenesis and Ethnohistory of the Garifuna* (Urbana: University of Illinois Press, 1988), 125–143; Ruy Galvão de Andrade Coelho, *Los negros caribes de Honduras* (Tegucigalpa: Editorial Guaymuras, 1981), 40.

15. Galvão de Andrade Coelho, *Los negros caribes*, 43.

16. González, *Sojourners of the Caribbean*, 136.

17. Mario Argueta, *Historia de los sin historia* (Tegucigalpa, Editorial Guaymuras, 1992), 58.

18. Despatch 274, Franklin E. Morales, U.S. minister in Tegucigalpa, to secretary of state, February 5, 1923. USNA, RG 59, 815.55/1. See also Mario Posas, *Luchas del movimiento obrero hondureño* (San José: Editorial Universitaria, 1981), 85.

19. Rina Villars, *Porque quiero seguir viviendo . . . habla Graciela García* (Tegucigalpa: Editorial Guaymuras, 1991), 85.

20. Despatch 579, Franklin E. Morales, U.S. minister in Tegucigalpa, to secretary of state, January 12, 1924, USNA, RG 59, 815.55/2; Despatch 821, Lawrence E. Dennis, chargé d'affaires, to secretary of state, July 30, 1925, USNA, RG 59, 815.55/3.

21. Despatch 641, Morales to secretary of state, July 23, 1924, USNA, RG 59, 815.5045/51.

22. Despatch 52, Willard L. Beaulac, U.S. vice-consul in Trujillo, to secretary of state, July 16, 1924, USNA, RG 59, 815.5045/46.

23. República de Honduras, *Manifiesto del Dr. Miguel Paz Barahona al Pueblo Hondureño* (Tegucigalpa: Tipografía Nacional, 1925), 7–8.

24. Ramón E. Cruz, "La ley de inmigración y el problema de la raza negra en la costa norte," *Revista Ariel*, 35 (November 15, 1926): 700. Cruz was president from 1971 to 1972.

25. David J. D. Myers, U.S. consul in Tegucigalpa, "Memorandum for Mr.

Summerlin, U.S. Minister in Tegucigalpa," November 11, 1929. USNA, RG 59, 815.5571/1.

26. Rafael Díaz Chávez, "Gobernar es poblar," in Hugo F. Komor, *Apuntes de un viaje por los departamentos de El Paraíso, Olancho y Yoro* (Tegucigalpa, Tipo-Litográficos Aristón 1948), unpaginated.

27. Coronado García, "Inmigración y colonización," in ibid.

28. Ibid.

29. Interview in Charles D. Kepner Jr., *Social Aspects of the Banana Industry* (New York: AMS Press, 1967), 173.

30. Mario Posas, *Imaginación: revista de narrativa hondureña*, 12 (March–April 1992): 4–5.

31. Manuel M. Calderón, "Corrientes que se desvían," in Komor, *Apuntes de un viaje.*

32. Rafael Heliodoro Valle, comp., *Oro de Honduras: antología de Ramón Rosa*, 2d ed. (Tegucigalpa: Editorial Universitaria, 1993), xi–xii.

33. "Ley de Inmigración, 1906," Decreto no. 76, February 8, 1906, *La Gaceta*, no. 2685.

34. Alfred K. Moe, *Honduras: Geographical Sketch, Natural Resources, Laws, Economic Conditions, Actual Development, Prospects of Future Growth* (Washington, D.C.: Government Printing Office, 1904), 172–180, quote is on p. 180.

35. Decreto no. 8, February 8, 1906, *La Gaceta*, no. 2682.

36. Medardo Mejía, *Froylan Turcios en los campos de la estética y el civismo* (Tegucigalpa: Universidad Nacional Autonoma de Honduras, 1980), 21–26.

37. Marvin A. Barahona, *La hegemonía de los Estados Unidos en Honduras (1907–1932)* (Tegucigalpa: Centro de Documentación de Honduras, 1989), 48–50.

38. Nancie L. González, *Dollar, Dove, and Eagle: One Hundred Years of Palestinian Migration to Honduras* (Ann Arbor: University of Michigan Press, 1992). See also Darío Euraque, "Formación nacional, mestizaje y la inmigración árabe palestina a Honduras, 1880–1930," *Estudios Migratorios Latinamericanos*, 9, no. 26 (April 1994): 47–66.

39. Darío A. Euraque, "Estructura económica, formación de capital industrial, relaciones familiares y poder político en San Pedro Sula, 1870s–1958," *Revista Polémica* (Costa Rica), 18 (September–December 1992): 31–50.

40. Macedonio Laínez, "Deficiencias económicas centroamericanas," *Revista Económica*, 10 (April 1916): 609.

41. Froilán Turcios, "Inmigrantes innecesarios," *El Nuevo Tiempo* (Tegucigalpa), July 7, 15, and 18, 1916.

42. Paulino Valladares, "Leyes sobre inmigración," *Foro Hondureño*, 1–2 (September 1916): 5.

43. Rafael Bardales Bueso, *Historia del Partido Nacional* (Tegucigalpa: Servicopiax Editores, 1980), 7.

44. Paulino Valladares, "Paradojas del progreso industrial," *Foro Hondureño,* 3 (October 1916): 80–81.

45. Augustino C. Coello, *La epopeya del campeño,* 2d ed. (San Pedro Sula: Editorial Coello, 1988), 136–137.

46. Darío A. Euraque, "The Social, Economic and Political Aspects of the Carías Dictatorship in Honduras: The Historiography," *Latin American Research Review,* 29, no. 1 (1994): 240.

47. Medardo Mejía, "Nace en Honduras una clase social: el proletariado," in *Historia de Honduras,* vol. 6 (Tegucigalpa: Universidad Nacional Autónoma de Honduras, 1990), 323–334.

48. A critical contribution is the work of Elisavinda Echeverri-Gent, particularly her "Labor, Class and Political Representation: A Comparative Analysis of Honduras and Costa Rica" (Ph.D. dissertation, University of Chicago, 1988). Echeverri-Gent explores some of the same issues explored here in "Forgotten Workers: British West Indians and the Early Days of the Banana Industry in Costa Rica and Honduras," *Journal of Latin American Studies,* 24 (1992): 275–308.

49. Argueta, *Historia de los sin historia,* 66.

AVIVA CHOMSKY

Laborers and Smallholders in Costa Rica's Mining Communities, 1900–1940

⚬

Traditional historiography has portrayed Costa Rica as an exception to the Central American pattern of large plantations and exploited workers, as a rural democracy based on coffee and small landholding.[1] Compared to other countries in Central America, Costa Rica indeed appears exceptional. But the tendency to approach Costa Rica's history by comparing it to its neighbors has obscured as much as it has illuminated about Costa Rica itself. It has meant that historical phenomena that do not corroborate the picture of Costa Rica as a rural democracy have been bypassed in favor of those that more directly seem to "explain" why peace and democracy have been less elusive in Costa Rica than in the rest of the isthmus. But foreign-owned plantations and mines, though often assumed to be more characteristic of other Central American countries, were in fact an important aspect of Costa Rica's history as well, and studying them can shed light on new aspects of Costa Rica's supposed exceptionalism.[2]

This essay looks at the lives of people who do not fit the standard image of Costa Rica's history and who cannot be used to explain Costa Rica's "exceptionalism": the workers and peasants who migrated to work for or near foreign-owned mines outside of the central valley. These significant participants in Costa Rica's history can tell us a great deal about the character of state and society there in the early twentieth century. Their lives were shaped by Costa Rica's third-major twentieth-century export product, after coffee and bananas: precious metals. Unlike coffee plantations, the mines were established by foreign corporations and outside of the heavily populated Meseta Central (Central Plateau). Thus they created new communities of migrants from other parts of Costa Rica and from elsewhere in Central America and the Caribbean. Some were workers, some were squatters on company or state lands, and some were tenants or small farmers who contracted with the foreign companies, but none were precisely the yeoman farmer that other studies have assumed characterize Costa Rica's population.[3]

The goals, hopes, and consciousness of these migrants were far from uniform. Some hoped to save money working for the foreign companies; some hoped to return home to purchase a plot of land; some hoped to obtain land in their new communities. The migrants were divided by ethnic, racial, and national identities as well as by their particular relations with the companies. But on several occasions, migrants organized collectively to challenge the social organization imposed by the companies, which apparently maintained almost unchallenged power in these enclaves distant from the centers of state power. Workers protested, rebelled, and engaged in various forms of everyday resistance; squatters took over land and successfully appealed to national authorities to protect their interests.

This study will examine how race, class, ethnic, and national identities interacted in the formation of these movements, and in the state's reactions. I begin by describing the social make-up of the migrant communities and then focus on two types of social movements in the mining district. The contrast between the ways in which mine workers, on one hand, and peasant farmers, on the other, formulated their goals and acted collectively to achieve them, was striking. In addition to a socioeconomic basis for this distinction, a major factor was the difference between the two groups' access to state power and different elements in the government and police's willingness or ability to support workers and peasants in their challenges to company domination.

Migrants in the Mining Region

Costa Rica's gold mines, in highland Guanacaste and Alajuela provinces to the west of the coffee-growing central valley and the east of the cattle-ranching (and later cotton-producing) Pacific lowlands, were owned by sister companies to the United Fruit Company (which controlled Costa Rica's banana production) and employed over 3,000 workers at their height in the 1910s and 1920s. The first of the Abangares gold mines was discovered in 1884, and it and others in the range quickly passed into the hands of United Fruit Company (UFC) affiliates such as Minor Keith and his business partners.[4] Although mining in Costa Rica never achieved the stature it did in neighboring Nicaragua and Honduras, and mineral exports never approached in value those of Costa Rica's principal exports, coffee and bananas, minerals were the third-highest revenue-generating product exported until 1920, when gold was overtaken by cacao.[5] Gold exports passed the $500,000 a year mark in 1906 and remained that high (with one exception, in 1921 to 1922) until 1926, passing the $1 million mark twice (1911 and 1916).[6]

Despite mine workers' traditional militancy in other regions, there were two types of factors that led to a situation of apparent labor discipline and peace in Costa Rica's mines. First, certain structural factors inhibited worker protest and organization. The mines were located in isolated areas, where American-owned mining companies had an almost complete monopoly on force. State authority was weak or nonexistent, so workers were completely subject to company domination. However, this is not enough to explain workers' apparent docility: very similar structural factors existed in the banana districts, yet workers there did protest and organize. And peasants and squatters in the mining districts were subject to the same structural impediments as the miners but proved to be formidable challengers to company power.

The other type of factor was ideological. For a variety of reasons, and in a variety of ways, the company was able to legitimize its social order and to deflect worker discontent into arenas other than organization or protest. Worker discontent certainly existed, and virtually every worker testimony from the time is filled with protest and resentment against the American companies. Yet there is no recorded case of organized protest comparable to either worker protest in the banana regions or squatter protest in the mining regions. Worker protest in the mining region took the form of "everyday resistance" rather than organized movements. The one major uprising recorded among mine workers was quickly deflected into taking the form of—and remembered later as—an attack by Hispanic miners on West Indians.

Squatters in the mining districts had a very different social, cultural, and political profile. The mines were established on the agricultural frontier, as pressure on the land caused by the spread of coffee in the central valley encouraged peasants to move west and establish communities in areas with similar climate to the central valley.[7] These peasants were organized and militant, and they presented a long-standing challenge to the mining companies' control of the land they claimed, using means ranging from nonviolent resistance and land invasion to often successful appeals to state intervention, to armed defense of their lands.[8]

Resistance and Accommodation among Mine Workers

The combination of physically intense and dangerous work in the mines with an all-male, mostly migrant labor force led to a cultural-social complex similar to that of other enclaves: long work hours punctuated with sporadic binges of drinking, gambling, fighting, and time with prostitutes at each monthly payday.[9] Official reports describe how towns came to life on payday, as prostitutes, alcohol, and gambling attracted workers as they emerged from days or even weeks underground.

For all its official disapproval, the company tacitly accepted and perhaps even encouraged this kind of behavior. At least during some periods, the company actually closed operations for three days after each payday, to allow spirits to cool before the men returned to work.[10] Machismo, based in defiance of death, and hard drinking, gambling, and womanizing could contribute to the company's ability to control labor. Payday pleasures could divert miners from pondering seriously and collectively on their condition; as one ex-miner put it, the miners "went down to the town to drown their sufferings from the life in the mines in *guaro* [cheap, distilled rum],"[11] and the company certainly recognized that it was in their interest that the workers "drown their sufferings" this way.

Fights could release aggressions "safely" without turning them against the company, and alcohol tended to lead to this type of response. Payday "always ended in fist- and knife-fights. The Company decided to buy large quantities of pine boards to make coffins and bury the dead after each payday. The number of injured was never less than five."[12] Certainly the company did not call upon the resources they certainly could have mustered had they wished to control the payday excesses: "Even though the Company had its rules, the *machos* [i.e., North Americans; *macho* is Costa Rican slang for a person of fair coloring] never intervened to put a stop to the craziness. On the other hand, they were secure, well-guarded in their houses, and never, that I recall, did any North American die violently."[13]

It is interesting to note that worker machismo contributed to workers' quickly spending whatever money they had earned the previous month. Whether in alchol, gambling, or women, a worker usually ended his payday spree penniless. This too certainly served the company's purposes. As long as workers had no savings, they would be forced to remain in the mine, working. One ex-miner's account describes over and over again how miners went to the mine hoping to save money and return home, but hardly ever fulfilled this dream.

Company officials rarely voiced concern about labor control. This lack of complaint is in striking contrast to their repeated appeals and protests to both the Costa Rican government and their home offices in the United States against local peasants and squatters on lands the company claimed. Thus they seem to have been successful to a great extent in containing worker discontent or directing it into nonthreatening spheres.

Despite company physical, economic, and ideological control of its workforce, protests and in particular "everyday resistance" did take place. The most common form of worker resistance to the mining companies' social control was simply to take control of the means of production quietly and work outside of company control, extracting and selling gold on their own. Many supported themselves both while officially employed and while unemployed by working as *colligalleros,* or independent miners. Others hid bits of gold from the mines on their bodies—in their shoes, in their hair, inserted in the rectum, or even swallowed—before exiting the mine. Workers' testimonies show that they did not accept the company's claim to its exclusive right to the gold. In the wryly uttered words of one ex-miner, "Of course the Company considered this work to be theft."[14] But the miners concurred with nationalist Costa Ricans and squatters on mineral lands in questioning the rights by which the American companies claimed sovereignty over everything in the mineral districts. "But it was not that they stole, no," continued the ex-miner, "the miner who saw gold leave for the United States in bars of one hundred or two hundred kilos did not consider it a theft to take a *una pelotita* [tiny bit] of gold that weighed five grams, for *la tenía ganada en gran mérito* [he had more than earned it]. In those days the worker could be fired at any time, for he was almost always so ill that he could no longer produce."[15]

In 1911, the company attempted to crush this form of "everyday resistance" with the ingenious ploy of recruiting a group of Jamaicans to serve as a guard or police force specifically to track down gold "thieves." The company brought these English-speaking, black workers numbering somewhere between 50 and 100 to the various mines of the Abangares district sometime in 1910 or 1911. Language, race, and cultural differences separated the Jamaicans from the Hispanic workers,[16] and the company clearly took advantage of this fact in bringing in the Jamaicans for policing purposes. A Hispanic worker's testimony shows how he perceived the new arrivals: "In the evenings, the blacks danced in the *galerón* [shed] of their house beating hollow tree trunks which they covered at one end with a snake skin. And they danced, with a *taca bamba-taca bamba*, for up to three hours dripping sweat from all parts of their bodies."[17] Clearly deep social prejudices divided Hispanic and black workers.

By bringing in a racially and culturally distinct group of people to enforce company discipline, company officials hoped to deflect workers' attention away from the company itself and onto the Jamaicans, who were actually victims of company power as much as—if not more than—Hispanic miners. To a certain extent they succeeded, for though miners' resentment against the company is clear in many of the documents, it never approaches the fever pitch of hatred that workers evidenced toward the Jamaican guards.

The Hispanic workers in Abangares saw the blacks as allies of the company. "Any order that they gave in English, the blacks would understand. That accounts, surely, for their preference for the Jamaicans,"[18] explained one ex-miner. The miners perceived that blacks monopolized police and guard functions, although this was not actually the case.[19]

The company agreed with the workers' assessments about the blacks' social identification, if not about their occupational place. The mine's manager told the British consul that, unlike Hispanic workers, "the majority of the Jamaicans were hard working, sober and faithful, and they did not steal ore."[20] In contrast to management's benign attitude toward the black workers, the mine superintendent referred to Hispanic workers as "dagoos" (*sic.*)[21] However, despite Jamaicans' perceived identification with management, the manager himself felt little obligation to protect them when Hispanic workers turned on them; he told the consul that he was "sorry for the Jamaicans, many of whom were excellent men, but [since] there was no force to protect them here, . . . [he] could only advise those who were in distant places [working in isolated areas away from company headquarters] . . . to leave."[22]

Mine officials used the Jamaicans to attack illicit gold extraction on two fronts: uncovering and destroying hidden hand mills, and frisking workers as they left the mine.[23] The Jamaicans were stationed at the mine entrances and charged with searching each worker as he exited the mine. Body searches meant that workers were forced to undress; after company officials caught on to the miners' trick of inserting ore in the rectum, the searches included a rectal examination as well.[24] Clearly the humiliation, as much as the rage at being robbed of what miners believed to be a just return for their labor, created a strong hatred between the two groups. One ex-miner recalled that blacks "occupied the best positions and they treated those of us from Costa Rica and other foreigners who weren't black *a pura patada* [like dirt]."[25]

The 1911 riot, uprising, or massacre—depending upon whose account you read—took place after an altercation between a black Honduran guard and a Hispanic worker. On December 20, the miners rioted and took over the mine, attacking black workers and killing at least four.[26] Unfortunately we have no accounts written by eyewitnesses at the time of the events. The British consul and a Costa Rican journalist visited the area immediately afterward and wrote accounts, and several ex-miners published their accounts—based on their own memories of the events or on versions they heard from other miners—in the 1960s and 1970s. I shall begin by examining the miners' recollections, because my conclusions about worker identities and consciousness are based as much on analysis of the way that they remember the event as on a reconstruction of the details of the event itself.

Although the details of the uprising vary slightly in the three ex-miners' accounts, they share certain important features. All begin with a black (Honduran or Jamaican) guard attempting to carry out a body search on a Hispanic Costa Rican miner, the miner resisting, and the guard shooting him. All depict the smoldering, long-term resentments of Hispanic miners bursting forth with something close to glee in brutal and violent collective attacks against blacks: "The news spread like wildfire; more miners arrived and shouting '*¡A matar negros!*' [kill the blacks]; they got shotguns and machetes from their houses. . . . The group surrounded the hotel. They dragged out the black man and they finished him off with machete blows. . . . They pursued the other black guards, firing on them as they ran terrified towards the hillside."[27] Another account describes the ostentatious dress of one black victim and recounts how Hispanic workers tied him to a bridge with a carton of dynamite: "From a distance, the miners hurled insults at the black who, injured, bleeding and *fiero* [ferocious] watched without even stopping to think about the fuse that was burning."[28]

Interestingly, Salguero's informants, Gamboa, and León Sánchez all describe the prominent participation of a woman contraband liquor seller in the uprising. According to León Sánchez, the prelude to the uprising was the fact that Jamaican employees had captured and condemned to the *cepo*, or stocks, a Costa Rican man and woman accused of selling contraband liquor in the mines. This couple was quickly freed by the miners, and "they devoted themselves to hunting blacks" and were among the few jailed by the authorities after the rebellion was subdued. According to Gamboa, a woman named Mercedes Panza took the lead in inciting miners to go after the blacks, waving a flag made of a handkerchief on a stick and shouting "¡come on, come on, *muchachos,* let's kill those *negros desgraciados* [wretched blacks]![29] In Gamboa's account Panza led the attack on one of the few blacks who tried to defend himself.[30] She also egged the miners on by distributing liquor and shouting encouragement to the miners to kill both blacks and machos, or North Americans.[31] One of Salguero's informants characterized her as a *mujerona* [huge woman] and said that she "seemed to be the leader of the group" that attacked the black policeman in the bodega. "Machete in hand, she shouted and said that we had to finish off all the blacks."[32]

Another account describes how a black man was thrown in a stream behind the butchers' and slaughtered among the carrion.[33] The British consul recounted that the wife of the Jamaican who was killed and mutilated tried to approach the corpse "and was frightened away by threats of death by the men" who were robbing it. She was so terrorized that she could not even later identify the men who had threatened her.[34]

Although the details of the uprising vary slightly among the three accounts and can probably never be determined with certainty, the accounts shed light on beliefs, ideologies, and social relations at work both during the time of the event, and subsequently, as the stories became embellished and altered in ways that reveal the worldview of the miners. The Hispanic miners' rage and hatred against the Jamaicans found vent in these brutal attacks. Surely the satisfaction with which they recount the murder on the bridge, whether or not the details reflect what really happened, reflects the Hispanic workers' resentments and desire for revenge. The mutilation of corpses, the racist war-cries, and the terror experienced by the black workers also show the degree of hatred among the miners.

The emotions that ex-workers reported decades after the riots were surely real. However, reports from the time suggest that despite their unanimity, workers' recollections tell only part of the story. The one journalist present in the days following the attacks provided numerous details that were left out of workers' later descriptions. On December 20, he reported that workers "broke into and sacked the commissary."[35] The following day he added that "among the *estragos* [outrages] of the *alzados* [rebels], was the dynamiting of the La Sierra jail, the telegraph station, and several other buildings."[36] Some 500 miners participated in what was really an armed uprising.[37] The miners were briefly "owners of the mine,"[38] but police reinforcements quickly arrived and occupied the mine for a month and a half.

Clearly what this journalist saw was not a race riot, but a veritable rebellion, targeted not against blacks but against mining company and governmental installations. Why did workers leave this aspect entirely out of their later testimonies? Perhaps this phenomenon had to do with their subsequent continued dependence on the company for work and for state and mine officials' willingness to overlook and even accept the attacks on blacks, while smothering with severe measures the attacks on the Company itself.[39]

The attitude of the state in this situation was ambiguous. At the same time as state authorities defended the foreign company's property, they tacitly acknowledged the right of miners to attack foreign workers. The British consul reported that the government was not eager to prosecute anybody or even investigate the murders, except under pressure by the British authorities.[40] When some Jamaicans made their way to San José and approached the British consul and Costa Rican president Jiménez for redress, Jiménez reportedly answered that "the fault lay not with the country but with the foreigners and their mistreatment."[41] Once again, mine owners—and the state that supported them—were reluctant to take any action that might make the true power structure behind the mines explicit. As long as Hispanic workers turned their resentment against black workers, who of course were brought in for that very purpose, the power holders could remain behind the scenes. A journalist reporting on the situation wrote, "all of the authorities were here when [one of the murders] occurred and nobody went after the criminal. There have been no prisoners taken as a result of the *motines* [uprising] and I don't believe that there will be any. It seems that they want to calm things down by leaving everybody free." [42] Thus the attitude and actions of state authorities contributed to the rewriting of the history of the events in nationalist and racist terms.

The legends, and the importance that the *matanza* [massacre] holds in testimonies given years after the fact, confirm its place in the consciousness of the workers. It was one of the only—if not the only—time miners actually acted collectively in protest, yet it was a collective action that by its nature and particularly by its consequences showed the degree of the company's ideological control. Although workers demonstrated by their actions that they were capable of taking over the mine facilities, they did not use this power to make any demands at all regarding social or economic issues. Their testimonies present the uprising as an attack on blacks, not an attack on the mines as a social institution and not on their North American owners.

Thus workers did resist, in many different ways, their condition. Yet they generally chose a means of resistance that would not overtly threaten the social order. And the company permitted and even encouraged certain forms of resistance that deflected miners' anger away from the company itself.

Peasants, Squatters, and Thieves in the Aguacate Mines

If workers did not frequently directly challenge the mining companies, local peasants and squatters did. Peasants burned forest, cut trees, fenced in properties, and planted on land the company claimed as its own, and they fiercely resisted any challenge to their rights to do so. [43] The miners, when faced with this challenge to company power, laid their bets with the company and even took up arms to "defend" the company's property rights.

As opposed to other Central American landowners, who wanted to enclose the land they owned—or claimed to own—for cultivation or pasture, the mining companies were interested in the land primarily for timber.[44] In fact, the company's sole legal claim to the land was, as company officials acknowledged, the right to timber.[45] Thus there is no parallel in the mining districts with what happened later in the cotton-growing areas, where landowners tolerated peasants' clearing and planting land because they could then expel them and take advantage of the work they had done preparing the land for cultivation.[46]

Documentation of the long-standing conflict between the Aguacate Mining Company (based in New York) and residents of the mining district runs from 1911 through the 1930s, with no clear resolution except perhaps the exhaustion of the contested timberlands and the collapse of the mining industry during the depression. A group of extended families maintained what was practically an independent polity in the isolated mining district over the course of two decades. They armed and organized themselves to repel any challenge to their claimed right to fence and farm their land and to maintain access to timber from the surrounding forest. They clearly rejected both mining company *and* *state* jurisdiction over the land, expelling police and military officials on several occasions. Yet they did not hesitate to appeal to state authorities to uphold their claims.

State authorities negotiated a conflicting set of goals and ideals. On one hand, they sought to attract and then protect foreign investment as a source of national progress. On the other, they believed that agriculture was the source of national wealth and development and had a clear goal of colonizing frontier areas and bringing them into productive use. The Aguacate settlers repeatedly challenged the state to protect their rights on these grounds. At the same time, however, officials vacillated between wanting to assert state authority and wanting to avoid devoting resources to a battle they had little chance of winning. Thus the company and the squatters both attempted to mobilize state power on their behalf, and they also organized independent power bases in the region.

Squatters were occupying and planting on land in the mining district as early as 1911, and the question of ownership was and remained murky. The company asked for government intervention in that year, to remove squatters from the land, and the government arranged a compromise allowing the occupants to reap their harvest and continue planting for three more years, but not to cut any more of the valuable (to the mines) timber.[47]

Government investigators in 1911 found that there were numerous settlers in the mineral district, some of whom had managed to obtain titles and some of whom had not, despite having been there for a year or more. They noted that local authorities had not interfered with squatters, saying that "they have not been able to find out about the infractions . . . because the injured party [the mining company] itself has not complained about these acts, except very recently since they have recommenced work in the mines."[48]

Many of the squatters probably established themselves during the period prior to 1911 when the mines were closed; some may even have been former workers. The company's objections to squatters clearly began when their work resumed in 1911. Despite the 1911 agreement, a special investigator wrote in 1929, "the Aguacate Mines was not freed of squatters on its lands, nor has it been freed in the following sixteen years."[49]

The chief of police of the Aguacate mineral district from 1913 to 1919 testified later to the weakness of state authority in the area, which gave squatters space to enforce their own authority over the land. He reported that despite his "zeal" in opposing them,

it was not possible for him to avoid the introduction of these people who with complete violence took over the lands and cut the forests. . . . Time after time, he had to repel attacks from these squatters, who, armed with rifles, shotguns and other arms attacked him as Police Agent and his subordinates for opposing the felling of trees. . . . He became convinced that against these people it was completely impossible to try to avoid their destructive impulses and their determination to take possession of the land unless the government had decided to send a respectable number of *gendarmes* and with orders to kill the rebels.[50]

Thus squatters in the mineral district went beyond quietly occupying and planting the land (perhaps assuming it to be *baldío* [untitled public land]) to overtly challenging company rights and state authority there, and the state did not take a strong stand against them. From 1919 to 1920 Isidro Rodríguez occupied and fenced a pasture then in use by the company, and only 100 meters from the company's main office. When the company removed the fencing, Rodríguez sued it for damages![51] The following year Pedro Sánchez attacked a police agent who was trying to remove a fence he had put up around another field claimed by the company, and he succeeded in maintaining his possession of the land, to the company's dismay.[52]

Among the boldest of the squatters was the extended Pérez family. Early in 1921 Lisandro Azofeifa, the police chief, informed company administrator Juchem that "yesterday we found out that the Perezes and Compañeros *voltaban montana* [*sic.*] [were felling trees] belonging to the mineral district close by. Today we caught them in flagrante delicto; they fled shooting at us [. . .] later entrenched they continued opposing us with firearms. They say that they will not leave until they are killed."[53] The "we" he referred to were miners who worked for the company. When Juchem passed on the information later to the company's president in New York, he explained that

members of the Pérez family, squatters on mineral land, were cutting down timber near the river. They were reported to be in the number of about seven or eight. The chief of police with five miners duly deputized were sent to stop the felling and to arrest the men and bring them in. . . . [They] were met by a fusillade of shot from rifles and shot-guns. Without returning the fire, they went ahead to try to make the capture of the men who retired firing and then took to the bush and escaped.[54]

Although the company could exert economic and ideological control over its workers, local squatters and peasants perceived their interests to be firmly in opposition to the company's.

The company was not amused. "Apparently squatters getting together," a local mine official wrote to Juchem. "Reports of large bunch [near] Ojochal."[55] Another official wrote, "I have news that they are continuing to cut down forest near La Sierra. Calixto Pérez with others tore down some new fences. Isidro Rodríguez did the same. Enemies of the Company are trying to poison *agua cañería* [water supply] and are also damaging La Sierra *tubería* [pipes]."[56] Company officials were particularly worried because the rebellious squatters seemed unified, well-organized, well-armed, and apparently emboldened by liquor: "I received the report later in the day that the squatters had congregated to the numbers of some seventy or eighty and were raising a row, having gotten drunk on contraband liquor. They were reported to be fully armed with rifles, shot-guns, and the long knives of the country."[57]

The government sent four police agents, who, a mine official wrote, were "completely useless for capturing the *revoltosos* [rebels] who appear to be more than seventy. Azofeifa says that to shoot them or drive them away, he can do it, but to capture them, impossible, and it does not seem advisable to enter the forest."[58] So Juchem reached out to higher quarters, and the conflict escalated:

I immediately asked for help from the Department of War. The department asked for details and confirmation of the firing on the police. . . . I then went to the ministry personally, and, finding the minister absent, then to the President. The latter . . . agreed to take the necessary steps to quell the rebellion against authority and so ordered the Minister of War. Nevertheless I went [the] next day to Alajuela to push the minister and got him to send out twenty uniformed and disciplined policemen from the San José police force. The men left for the mine and, having been placed under the orders of the Jefe Político [appointed local political representative responsible to the governor of the province], went into the mineral district and attempted to arrest the rebels. These uniformed men were met with fire also and returned it. No one was hit. The Jefe Político's extremities began to feel the chill [i.e., he got nervous] and he called off the battle. The department then sent out a colonel who took command. The following day the detail went into the hills and brought back a total of twenty-one men, but only one old shot-gun, the rest of the arms having been hidden. Seven of the prisoners were freed and the rest sent to San Mateo and thence to Alajuela.[59]

Those who were jailed were freed several weeks after, with charges of resistance to authority, damage to the mineral district, and stealing company timber pending against them.[60] However, this incident did not deter the squatters, for "they returned to the mines where they continued their *fechorías* [evil deeds], cutting trees and terrorizing everybody even more than before."[61]

Realizing the tenuousness of his position, Juchem also asked the governor of the province "to see if the thing could not be patched up peaceably between the government and the squatters." Some of the squatters were willing to arrive at a settlement by which they would acknowledge company ownership and agree to pay rent in return for permission to continue cultivating the land. Juchem even offered to provide space and use part of the rental income to start a school for squatters' children.

Not all of the squatters, however, were willing to concede company ownership of the land, even with the sweetening of the deal with the school. As Juchem explained, "later the men came to me here and declared the agreement off because some of the squatters would not agree. As soon as possible I will continue action against them. There is no choice if we are to continue operating."

When the squatters rejected the agreement, officials' fears increased:

The mine is an armed camp. We have seven government rifles and ammunition for them. . . . Nobody leaves camp alone. The danger is a matter of getting shot in the back or of having to shoot someone without witnesses. The difficulty in handling the situation consists in the main of keeping anyone from getting shot or cut up. If they attack one of the miners it will be impossible to keep the miners from killing them all off, now that there is bad blood. And if one of them is killed it would likely turn public opinion against the company and the miners. Mr. Sanford and I wear guns for the first time since we have been in Costa Rica.[62]

Later in March two representatives of the squatters, Salvador Pérez and Francisco Araya, met with the minister of war. Araya apparently "came back very happy because the minister asked them only that they not confront [mine officials] under any circumstances, to avoid difficulties with the 'machos,' but that not only could they continue occupying their "*derechos* [rights] that they actually have in Mining Company lands, but that they have a perfect right to expand their cultivations planting on any Company lands which are not forested, because only the latter must be respected."[63] In the Pérez brothers' dealings with the government—which was clearly sympathetic to their claims—they presented themselves as farmers, who wanted only the right to "cultivate the land that they possess this year, harvesting its products."[64]

In the face of government refusal to protect its claims to the property, the company itself financed the San Ramón *resguardo* [police or military detachment, sent in reinforcement] for several weeks to remain in the district, after a mine official informed Juchem that "there are persistent rumours here of a proposed raid on the mine by the . . . squatters. [An ex-police agent] is supposed to be one of the chief agitators."[65] In fact, the company believed that the same individuals arrested in 1921 were simply emboldened by their apparent immunity to the law, "reaching the extreme in 1922 of threatening to blow up the mines with dynamite, and it was necessary again to send an armed police squad."[66]

In February 1926 another mine official wrote plaintively to the jefe político of San Mateo, complaining that the same people (the Pérez

clan and Francisco Araya) "are occupying Mine lands without any right
and they are the ones who are bothering us, especially the former who
respect[s] nothing and nobody. Anything that you could do to impose
order on these people would be much appreciated."[67] Despite the company's payments to the police, and the Ministry of the Interior's professed support for the company, the situation continued. A mine official
complained that "none of the squatters has paid attention to anything,
especially the Perezes who boast of their disobedience to the Authorities, setting a bad example for the good *terratenientes* [landowners] who
now respect nothing and nobody." He noted that two formerly docile
tenants who had contracts with the mine for the land they occupied
had been emboldened to extend their occupancy. Ismael Mayorga "with
no right and knowingly has occupied and is preparing to sow and *hacer
una habitación* [build a home] in a part of the Mine's pasture," while
Lisimaco Ledezma "is going to begin building a house in a plot that
he knows we are going to need. Beyond that I can tell you that we
have ordered both to be told that they should not carry out this work,
but they pay no attention." In addition, "right after [somebody] burned
down . . . the 'big house' in San Juan which is at the entrance of the
mules' pasture (closed) one of the Perezes has installed himself and is
preparing to sow." He ended with a plea: "Since all of these labors are
just either being prepared or beginning, I believe that this is the moment for you to take the necessary steps to stop them, thus avoiding
future problems."[68]

When the district authorities attempted to enforce the company's
jurisdiction over the land in question, the Pérezes pursued another ingenious plan. They developed contacts with the authorities of the neighboring municipality of San Ramón and demanded that the contested
property be shifted from San Mateo's to San Ramón's jurisdiction. In
fact "important residents" of San Ramón supported the plan—perhaps
out of their own interest in increasing the size of their municipality. In
any case, those officials agreed that if granted authority over the land
in question, they would "obtain property titles from the Government
for all those who claim lands belonging to the Aguacate Mines." If
this plan failed, however, the squatters would continue to defend their
occupancy themselves. A government investigator concluded that in
the event that the contested property not be shifted to San Ramón's
jurisdiction, "the Pérez Vargases are not prepared to cede and they have
armed themselves with machetes and revolvers."[69]

In the face of this opposition, the company attempted a strategy of ceding plots of land to residents in exchange for loyalty against the Pérez clan. They used these loyal residents both as a physical barrier to the hostile squatters and as a symbol to the government of their beneficence, in hopes that the government would support the rights of these tenants that conveniently dovetailed with company interests. In retaliation in early 1929, a group of six of the Pérezes attacked the home of a widow who was a company ally, allegedly raping a young girl and burning their hut.

The jefe político of San Mateo wrote an angry letter to the police chief of the mining district in February, when the chief declared himself unable to arrest the six Pérez brothers: "If you can't capture them because you don't dare . . . the response that I should obtain from you is your resignation from you post," he wrote.[70] Meanwhile, several of the Pérezes openly occupied and fenced part of the land the company had granted to the widow and continued to flaunt the constituted authorities, including an incident in which they riddled the house of Ismael Herrera, the justice of the peace, with bullets.[71]

It is not clear whether the incident that led to the gravest crisis between state forces and the Pérezes was related to the accusations of rape. During the months following the accusations, state authorities attempted with increasing force to arrest a man named Juan Herrera Campos, an ally of the Pérezes. Apparently the Mayor of San Mateo ordered the jefe político to arrest Herrera, and the jefe político so ordered the police chief. The police chief carried out "several expeditions" but failed to capture Herrera and finally commissioned a group of local residents to arrest him. "The residents succeeded in capturing him but as soon as the Pérezes found out about it, they attacked the residents and freed Herrera, cutting several of the guards in the process."[72]

The Jefe Político then gave the order to the police chief of the mineral district, who was attacked by a gang of about twelve of the Pérezes as he waited on a road hoping to intercept Herrera. He was not injured in this attack.[73] It was clear, a government investigator reported, that the squatters "would not listen to any order coming from the San Mateo authorities."[74]

Finally, on July 20, the same police chief with some aides returned to the area to call some of the Pérez clan as witnesses in Herrera's case. This time, he was assassinated, "in the most atrocious manner" by a gang who shot him in the back, mutilated his body with machete blows, and then threw it off a cliff, at the same time wounding one of his assistants.[75] In apparent understatement, government investigators concluded that "this is the result of the discontent which has reigned here for such a long time."[76]

After this murder, the government assigned a special investigator to prosecute the case, and Pedro Pérez Cortés and Alberto, Fernando, and Venancio Pérez Vargas were jailed in Alajuela, while Silverio and Miguel Vásquez Mora and Santiago Pérez Torres were incarcerated in a lower-security jail in San Mateo. Two others, Filadelfo Alvarado Alvarado and Julián Vásquez Mora, were arrested then freed without charge.[77] All the accused apparently submitted to arrest without resisting, "but they tried to use their vestment of authority to avoid apprehension. They turned in only two revolvers which they said was the extent of their arms, in spite of how well-supplied they were for their shoot-out on July 20."[78]

The Pérezes' power did not end, however, with their arrest. Local residents united loyally behind them, making the case exceedingly difficult to prosecute. Mine administrator Juchem complained that "many of the witnesses have testified—or have declined to testify—coloring their testimony—or what they have failed to testify—because of their relationship to the Pérezes, or others . . . because of their fear; others who could testify *no se han presentado como uno que cita el perjudicado* [have not spoken as witnesses for the injured party]. It's enough to say that the residents closest to the place where the crime was committed did not see anything or hear anything."[79]

Juchem also believed that authorities were not diligent in prosecuting the case. He wrote that he personally knew of witnesses who could testify that the Pérezes had threatened " 'to kill the first authority of San Mateo who came, be that whom it may,' preferably the Mayor," that the day after the crime the Pérezes were congratulating each other on it, and that an uncle of theirs was boasting that he had hidden their arms." In addition, Juchem quoted Filadelfo Alvarado (who had been freed for lack of evidence) as saying that "we warned Luis [Campos— police chief] beforehand not to *trepar el alto* [show his face here]. Juchem complained that it was not known whether these witnesses had been called to testify but that he did know that the police aide who witnessed the crime was not called.[80]

According to Juchem, the Pérez allies were "saying publicly and repeatedly that when the Pérezes who are now in prison come back that together they are going to kill Afortunado Madrigal, Teodoro Carvajal, honorable residents who have not joined the Pérezes, the Mayor of San Mateo, who captured them himself with the resguardo of Esparta, Mr. Sanford, and your humble servant who is writing these lines, in inverse chronological order from the way they are listed."[81] Attacks against mine property did not end with the arrests either, Juchem continued: "Silverio Vásquez and one or two others have cut trees on the banks of the Quebrada Honda River and by the emergency exits of the mine's underground galleries thus obstructing the exits. . . . This means that now it isn't only on the surface that they want to destroy everything but underground also; it means that they do not care about the lives of the miners."[82] Juchem feared that emboldened by their success in evading punishment for Campos's murder, the Pérezes would "burn buildings, demolish tunnels (which they have already started to do), kill us and thus finish off the mining industry in Costa Rica."[83]

Juchem's litany of the mines' suffering at the hands of the Pérez clan warrants extensive quoting:

The major destroyers of Mineral woods have been the Pérez Cortez family and their numerous descendants. This family has directly destroyed at least ninety-five percent of the forests belonging to the Minerals. Through the years the Pérezes have gone on felling forest, burning the cut trees, to cultivate on their own only once, and then sell the cleared area to people less daring but no less clever in taking over what is not theirs, to go on to fell other parcels in growing number with their constantly growing number of sons and grandsons, sons-in-law and other in-laws until they destroyed the last three manzanas of virgin forest in 1925. Ever since they began this task, deadly for mining, there have been difficulties with them on the part of the Mining Enterprise. Seeing the tolerance and even the complicity of the constituted authorities, sometimes veiled but other times open and frank . . . the Pérezes and their followers have come to believe that they are above the law, as in effect they are. Audacious and ferocious to an extreme, they have been emboldened and have created an atmosphere of fear among the inhabitants of these regions such that their word has come to be law in the mineral areas. . . . nobody dares to contradict them.

The destruction of the last piece of forest in the mineral district [took place] in 1925 . . . if there have been no difficulties with the Pérezes on the part of the Company since then it is because there has been no forest left to cut. But, emboldened and in possession of the countryside . . . they have taken to ignoring the constituted authorities of San Mateo.[84]

Another official noted, "This horrifying crime has still not put an end to the reign of terror afflicting the Company, for even now the threats and material damage continue, obstructing the work of the mines."[85] Clearly these were no meek squatters trying only to gain access to enough land to grow corn and beans. Another flurry of correspondence from late 1931 shows continuing attacks, this time more on property than on timber—perhaps because Juchem was correct that the timber in the area had been exhausted. Residents smashed and broke pipes that carried ore from the mill to the cyanide plant, paralyzing all work in the mine.[86]

Interestingly, despite the violence, an unsuccessful congressional proposal in 1933 to resolve the conflict by expropriating company lands emphasized the inhabitants' peaceful nature. "The squatters in the Aguacate Mineral District are hard-working people who have cultivated their plots for many years and live in them with their families quietly and peacefully, without any disturbances save the incessant claims by the mining company," wrote congressional representative Ismael Murillo. The 225 inhabitants "have fenced farms, with stable cultivations, with their houses where they live permanently dedicated mostly to agriculture and others to mining."[87] Although the proposal was rejected, it sheds an interesting light on possible changes that had occurred in the squatter communities and their relationship to the mines. It may be that with contracting markets in the 1930s, mining company pressures on squatters, and thus squatter violence, declined, paving the way for these squatters to be absorbed into Costa Rica's "rural democratic myth."[88]

The government finally carried out a census of inhabitants in 1932, showing 173 farms within the Aguacate mines land and 21 in the neighboring Sacra Familia mines. Most of the company's old antagonists were still there and were revealed to be small farmers with permanent cultivations, just like their neighbors. Manuel Vásquez Mora, for example, occupied two fenced plots: one of seven manzanas planted with coffee, corn, and beans, and the other with three manzanas of corn. Francisco Araya occupied two five-manzana plots, both fenced and planted with corn; Silverio Vásquez Mora planted a one-and-a-half-manzana plot with coffee and sugarcane and had another, fenced, eight-manzana plot devoted mostly to pasture. Pedro Pérez Cortés kept four manzanas for pasture and eleven for planting in his fenced fifteen-manzana plot, while Calixto Pérez had two plots, of nine and three manzanas, divided among sugar, bananas, corn, beans, and pasture. There were many other Pérezes, but the Pérez Vargases seem to have either left or registered their plots under the names of other relatives. The history of violence, conflict, and resistance behind these peaceful small farmers was on its way to being obliterated.

Conclusion

The forms resistance took were influenced by a myriad of factors, not the least of which were workers' and peasants' conceptions of the art of the possible. Costa Rican workers and peasants negotiated for areas of weakness in the structures of power—or areas in which they could take advantage of official policy or rhetoric to press their case with the constituted authorities. The state too negotiated a complex series of sometimes conflicting goals and policies. On one hand it was committed to a model of economic development through foreign investment; on the other, in line with an official ideology of Costa Rica as a land of white smallholders, it pursued a populist strategy of advocating defense of national sovereignty in the face of foreign takeover of the economy and of the racial "threat" imposed by foreign companies importing black workers.[89] If national identity was embodied in whiteness and smallholding, this necessarily mediated governmental allegiance to foreign capital.

Workers and peasants proved adept at framing their protest in ways that corresponded to official ideology on these issues. It is difficult to determine the precise relationship between official ideologies and the nature of protest from below. To what extent did official rhetoric capture or formalize popular beliefs and to what extent did popular forces adopt ideologies imposed from above? To what extent did popular forces use official ideologies purely instrumentally, to gain what support they could from above? Peasants clearly believed—correctly—that they could expect official support in their claims contesting the mining company's right to land; company workers hoped only that state officials would look the other way when they rose to challenge the company.

Looking closely at moments of popular organizing reveals aspects of popular consciousness and the myriad of factors that can shape consciousness as well as the ways that ideologies travel up and down the power spectrum and influence popular expectations and state responses to popular mobilization. In the Costa Rican mining district, both workers and peasants proved adept at discovering the weak points in the alliance between foreign capital and the national government and pressing their claims as far as they could without overstepping the limits of official tolerance. Because of the specific factors in the relationship between the foreign company, the state, and the Costa Rican population, company workers found that they had little room for maneuvering, while smallholders in the mining area were able to practically create a liberated zone under their own armed control and still be treated as loyal citizens.

Notes

I thank Víctor Acuña, Fabrice Lehoucq, and Victor Silverman for their assistance in obtaining archival material from the Archivo Nacional in Costa Rica and the Public Record Office in London, and Cindy Forster and Aldo Lauria-Santiago for their comments on earlier versions of this essay.

1. Most general histories of Central America still promote this view of Costa Rica. James Dunkerley, *Power in the Isthmus: A Political History of Modern Central America* (London: Verso, 1988), 20–21; John A. Booth and Thomas W. Walker, *Understanding Central America,* 2d ed. (Boulder, Colo.: Westview, 1993, 29, 30; first published 1989); Edelberto Torres Rivas, *History and Society in Central America,* translated by Douglass Sullivan-González (Austin: University of Texas Press, 1993), 18.

2. On Costa Rica's banana plantation complex, controlled by the United Fruit Company, see Aviva Chomsky, *West Indian Workers and the United Fruit Company in Costa Rica* (Baton Rouge: Louisiana State University Press, 1996).

3. Costa Rica's Atlantic coast banana plantations were similar to the mines in these respects, and like the mines they have received relatively little attention from historians until recently. Studies of Costa Rica's central valley have shown that "rural democracy" was more of a myth than a reality there too. See Lowell Gudmundson, *Costa Rica before Coffee: Society and Economy on the Eve of the Export Boom* (Baton Rouge: Louisiana State University Press, 1986), and Mario Samper, *Generations of Settlers: Rural Household and Markets on the Costa Rican Frontier, 1850–1935* (Boulder, Colo.: Westview, 1990).

4. See Ricardo Jinesta, *El oro en Costa Rica* (San José: Imprenta Falco Hermanos & Cia, 1938), for a history of the discovery and beginnings of exploitation of Costa Rica's various mines. For the Aguacate range, see pp. 18–21, for Abangares, 21–23, for Líbano, 23. See also Costa Rica Secretaría de Gobernación, *Guanacaste: libro conmemorativo del centenario de la incorporación del partido de Nicoya a Costa Rica* (San José: Imprenta María V. de Lines 1924), 131–161.

5. See Carlos Araya Pochet, "El enclave minero en Centroamérica, 1880–1945: un estudio de los casos de Honduras, Nicaragua y Costa Rica," *Revista de Ciencias Sociales*, 17–18 (1979): 49.

6. Ibid., 48.

7. Lowell Gudmundson and Mitchell Seligson have debated the causes and meaning of these late nineteenth- and early twentieth-century migrations. See Lowell Gudmundson, *Costa Rica before Coffee*, 130, 131, his "Las luchas agrarias del Guanacaste, 1900–1935," *Estudios Sociales Centroamericanos*, 11, no. 32 (May–August 1982): 75–95, and his "Peasant Movements and the Transition to Agrarian Capitalism: Freeholding versus Hacienda Peasantries and Agrarian Reform in Guanacaste, Costa Rica, 1880–1935," *Peasant Studies* 10, no. 3 (Spring 1983): 145–162; and Marc Edelman, *The Logic of the Latifundio: The Large Estates of Northwestern Costa Rica since the late Nineteenth Century* (Stanford, Calif.: Stanford University Press, 1992). See also Samper, *Generations of Settlers*.

8. In this respect mining district inhabitants contradicted conventional wisdom that assumes that peasant farmers are generally conservative or reformist, whereas workers—especially for foreign-owned corporations—tend to become organized and militant. Much of Costa Rican historiography has been informed to a certain extent by that conventional notion.

9. Both José León Sánchez and José Gamboa A. describe not only prostitution but also intense competition over scarce local women among the miners. José León Sánchez, *La colina del buey* (Naucalpán de Juárez, Mexico: Organización Editorial Novara, 1972), passim, and José Gamboa, *El hilo de oro* (San José: Imprenta Trejos Hermanos, 1971), 116–117. Salguero's informants described paydays when "hundreds of miners, buried during the month in the tunnels, arrived [in the towns] with thirst to drink, to play [gamble], and to be with a woman. Then the peaceful town would turn into a gigantic human *molote* (uproar), with no God or law." Miguel Salguero, "Quimeras y sepulturas," *La Nación*, May 3, 1972, p. 8.

10. Salguero, *La Nación*, May 7, 1972, p. 8.

11. Quoted in Salguero, *La Nación*, May 5, 1972, p. 8.

12. León Sánchez, *La colina del buey*, 82–83.

13. Ex-miner, quoted in Salguero, *La Nación*, May 6, 1972, p. 8.

14. León Sánchez, *La colina del buey*, 147–148.

15. Ibid., 83.

16. The Costa Rican accounts refer to the guards as "Jamaicans" or "blacks"

and the nonblack Central Americans (and other Latin Americans) simply as "miners." Salguero's informants refer to themselves as "whites." At least one of the black company police agents who was killed was Honduran, not Jamaican. For clarity, I've used the term *Hispanic* for the original miners, by analogy from the banana districts, where workers clearly identified themselves (and each other) as either black or Hispanic.

17. León Sánchez, *La colina del buey*, 112.

18. Ex-miner quoted in Salguero, *La Nación*, May 7, 1972, p. 8.

19. The British consul who investigated the 1911 events at the Tres Hermanos Mine (three miles from Las Juntas and fifteen miles from Las Cañas) quoted the mine's manager as saying that "only two out of eight shift bosses were Jamaicans, of whom one, Sinclair, was a skilled miner, and had been [t]here almost since the mine started." F. Nutter Cox, British consul in San José, "Narrative Account of the Riot of 20th December 1911, at Tres Hermanos Mine, Guanacaste, Costa Rica," January 20, 1911, British Foreign Office (BFO) 288/139, p. 27. One ex-miner recalled that Jamaicans also worked as miners, but insists that they were paid more than Hispanic workers. Quoted in Salguero, *La Nación*, May 7, 1972, p. 8.

20. Cox to Mallet, January 20, 1912, BFO 288/139, p. 27.

21. Ibid., p. 28.

22. Quoted in Cox, "Narrative Account," ibid.

23. The British consul wrote that in the months preceding the uprising at the end of 1911, officials had destroyed over seventy "illicit hand mills." Ibid.

24. León Sánchez, *La colina del buey*, 111.

25. Testimony quoted in Salguero, *La Nación*, May 7, 1972, p. 8.

26. British consul F. Nutter Cox to Claude C. Mallet, British minister in Panama, January 20, 1912, BFO 288/139, p. 30. Cox insisted that no more than three Jamaicans and one black Honduran were killed, as well as two Hispanic miners. Guillermo García M. put the number at "around fourteen" (Guillermo García Murillo, *Las minas de Abangares: historia de una doble explotación* [San José: Editorial Universidad de Costa Rica, 1984], 59) and Francisco Gamboa G. claims that forty were killed (*Costa Rica: ensayo histórico* [San José: Imprenta Trejos Hermanos, 1974], 73.

27. Gamboa, *Costa Rica*, 160–163.

28. León Sánchez, *La colina del buey*, 112–113.

29. Ibid., 111–113; Gamboa, *Costa Rica*, 160.

30. Gamboa, *Costa Rica*, 163.

31. Ibid., 164.

32. Quoted in Salguero, *La Nación*, May 7, 1972, p. 8.

33. Ibid.

34. BFO 288/139, pp. 28, 30.

35. *La Información*, December 20, 1911, quoted in Salguero, *La Nación*, May 7, 1972, p. 8.

36. Quoted in Salguero, *La Nación*, May 8, 1972, p. 8.

37. "I found an uprising of 500 men, which turned [the district] into a *campo de Agramante* [battlefield]. All the miners are armed to the teeth. You can hear shots everywhere, even from [Las Juntas]." *La Información*, December 21, 1911, quoted in Salguero, *La Nación*, May 8, 1972, p. 8.

38. Gamboa, *Costa Rica*, 163.

39. Jeffrey L. Gould has suggested a similar reluctance to remember failure at benefiting from a strike, on the part of Nicaraguan workers. *To Lead as Equals: Rural Protest and Political Consciousness in Chinandega, Nicaragua, 1912–1979* (Chapel Hill: University of North Carolina Press, 1990), 43-44.

40. F. Nutter Cox, "Report on the Letter of Edward Reid Dorman, relative to the Outrages on Jamaicans at Tres Hermanos Mine, December 1911," March 28, 1912, BFO 288/139, p. 31.

41. Gamboa, cited in García, *Minas de Abangares*, 61.

42. Quoted from *La Información* (December 22 or 23, 1911) in Salguero, *La Nación*, May 8, 1972, p. 8.

43. In addition to the case discussed here, see Edelman's description of squatter resistance at the El Líbano mine in *Logic of the Latifundio*, 146-250.

44. The company estimated that it spent 94,000 *colones* ($32,476.19) on lumber between 1914 and 1930. A *manzana* (1.7 acres) of land could produce 823.20 colones worth of wood, so 4,000 manzanas should have produced 3,292.80 colones' worth, but officials estimated in 1932 that "vandals . . . cut down and sold-burned etc. I imagine at least @ 50% to 60% of the timber on the Mineral Zone." Unsigned memoranda, "Cálculo mínimo de madera en una manzana en el Aguacate" and "Memorandum Regarding Timber," June 1932, Archivo Nacional de Costa Rica (hereafter cited as ANCR), Serie Congreso, 16360.

45. The timber rights were based in an 1855 law granting each mine the exclusive use of timber in *tierras baldías* (untitled public lands) in a one-league radius around each mining district. Decree 3, December 16, 1855, art. 6, reproduced in a 1931 memorial from Keith to the president, ANCR, Serie Congreso, 16360.

46. See Robert G. Williams, *Export Agriculture and the Crisis in Central America* (Chapel Hill: University of North Carolina Press, 1986).

47. Acuerdo no. 60 of March 31, 1911, instructed the political authorities in San Mateo and Atenas to forbid any further occupation of the land around the mines and to eventually expel the current occupants. Reprinted in Costa Rica Ministerio de Fomento, *Memoria* (1911), 11-12. Also cited in Keith to president of the republic, November 26, 1931, ANCR. The agreement is also cited extensively in the "Special Investigator's Report to the Promotor Fiscal," August 3, 1929, ANCR, Serie Congreso, 16360.

48. Acuerdo no. 60, March 31, 1911, in Costa Rica Ministerio de Fomento, *Memoria* (1911), 11.

49. "Special Investigator's Report to the Promotor Fiscal," August 3, 1929, ANCR, Serie Congreso, 16360.

50. Declaration by Alfonso Zeledón Barrantes, July 8, 1932, ibid.

51. Described in Keith's memorial to the president, November 26, 1931, ibid.

52. Ibid.

53. Azofeifa to Juchem, January 28, 1921, ibid.

54. Juchem to White, March 7, 1921, ibid.

55. Hoffman to Juchem, January 29, 1921, ibid.

56. Sanford to Juchem, n.d., ibid. (between January 29 and January 30 reports).

57. Juchem to White, March 7, 1921, ibid.

58. Hoffman to Juchem, January 30, 1921, ibid.

59. Juchem to White, March 7, 1921, ibid.

60. Ibid.

61. Keith to president, November 26, 1931, ibid.

62. Juchem also gave evidence of his frustration with the U.S. government's inactivity in the case: "It will probably occur to you to ask why I did not ask the American legation for help. The reason is this: My experience has been that you are likely to lose your property and get yourself killed long before the State Dept and its rep's have finished their standard series of notes. If it should happen by any chance that we should be in the way of losing out after having exhausted every other resource, then I would say go to the legation; and, possibly, in the course of time something would be done. But at the same time I would cable you asking that you take the matter up with the State Department directly." Juchem to White, March 7, 1921, ibid.

63. Barboza to Aguacate Mine administrator, April 3, 1921. Another informer, José Prado, passed similar information to the mine administrator the next day. Prado to administrator, April 4, 1921. Both in ibid.

64. Aquiles Acosta, secretario de gobernación y policía, April 9, 1921, ibid.

65. Alex [illegible] to Juchem, May 1, 1922, ibid.

66. Keith to president, November 26, 1931, ibid.

67. Miguel Alvarado to jefe político of San Mateo, February 18, 1926, ibid.

68. Miguel Alvarado G., depositario, to jefe político of San Mateo, March 24, 1926, ibid.

69. "Secretaría de Gobernación recibe informes de haberse presentado un grave conflicto entre los vecinos de 'Llano Brenes' de San Mateo," newspaper article, n.d., ibid.

70. Jefe político of San Mateo to police chief of Mining Zone, February 28, 1929, ibid. This was the same police chief whom the Pérez brothers killed several months later. Ibid.

71. Keith to president, November 26, 1931, ibid.

72. Juchem to promotor fiscal, November 24, 1929, p. 6, ibid.

73. Ibid.

74. Investigador especial del Ministerio Público to promotor fiscal, August 3, 1929, ibid.

75. Juchem to promotor fiscal, November 24, 1929, pp. 6–7, ibid.

76. Investigador especial del Ministerio Público to promotor fiscal, August 3, 1929, ibid. Another description of these events can be found in Keith to president, November 26, 1931, ibid.

77. Investigador especial del Ministerio Público to promotor fiscal, August 3, 1929, ibid.

78. Juchem to promotor fiscal, November 24, 1929, p. 7, ibid.

79. Ibid., p. 8.

80. Ibid., p. 10, ANCR.

81. Ibid.

82. Ibid.

83. Ibid., p. 11. Contrary to Edelman, who argued that mining began to decline in importance in the 1920s (*Logic of the Latifundio,* 149–250), Juchem suggests that its character was changing: with the exhaustion of easily accessible veins, mining had to be carried out at greater depths, with correspondingly greater investment and greater need for timber. Juchem to promotor fiscal, November 24, 1929, p. 4, ANCR, Serie Congreso, 16360.

84. Juchem to Promotor Fiscal, November 24, 1929, ANCR, Serie Congreso, 16360.

85. Keith to president, November 26, 1931, ibid.

86. "Dificultades con los ocupantes. 1931," note attached to telegram from Sanford to Juchem, November 22, 1931, ibid.

87. ANCR, Serie Congreso, 16714, also published in *La Gaceta,* June 22, 1933, p. 139.

88. See Gudmundson, *Costa Rica before Coffee,* introduction, for a discussion of the origins and character of this ideology.

89. See Steven Paul Palmer, "A Liberal Discipline: Inventing Nations in Guatemala and Costa Rica, 1870–1900" (Ph.D. dissertation, Columbia University, 1990), and Avi Chomsky, "West Indian Workers in Costa Rican Radical and Nationalist Ideology 1900–1950," *Americas: A Quarterly Review of Inter-American Cultural History* 51, no. 1 (July 1994): 11–40.

CINDY FORSTER

Reforging National Revolution

Campesino Labor Struggles in Guatemala,

1944–1954

❂

Plantation workers unleashed powerful movements for social justice during Guatemala's national revolution from 1944 to 1954, called the October Revolution, which was that country's only era to date of genuine democracy. This article looks at two regions where the struggles of the poor erupted the moment the revolution began: the coffee belt of San Marcos and the United Fruit Company's banana zone in Tiquisate. The campesino histories of San Marcos and Tiquisate each offer a stunning metaphor for the revolution. Rural inequality lay at the root of oppression in Guatemala, and the desperate poverty of the rural majority was perpetuated by an economy in which coffee ranked as the largest export earner, followed by bananas. Further, to this day Guatemala has an Indian majority, and the question of race figures at the heart of any revolutionary project. Although the leaders of the October Revolution were assimilationist, rural Mayan laborers in San Marcos seized the moment to build a society that honored their ethnic identities. Non-Indian workers in Tiquisate also transformed the practice of revolution through their actions, trying to bring some accountability to the labor practices of a far-flung U.S. corporate empire. The different histories of the two regions profoundly question the usual characterization of the revolution as middle class or petty bourgeois, and the implied corollary that working people watched from the sidelines or acted as blind followers.

In San Marcos, collective worker initiative took place in an Indian cultural idiom. Indigenous identity infused the freedoms of the revolution with the memory of hundreds of years of resistance to forced labor. Even on the plantations this was true, where Mam-speaking workers were separated by one generation or more from the ethnic structures of highland villages. Strikes, work stoppages, and flight from labor contracts swept the coffee zone in San Marcos from 1945 forward. The evidence shows with great precision that worker agitation forced the state to deepen and honor its revolutionary promises.

In the township of Tiquisate, banana workers radically rewrote the labor rights of farmworkers nationwide, relying on the idiom of class. They struck for higher wages within weeks after the dictator fell. From that point forward, they organized the largest rural union in the country, participated loudly in grassroots pressure to win a higher wage and agrarian reform, and demanded dignity from their U.S. employer. Tiquisate fits the cross-national pattern of workers in banana enclaves who mounted strikes that redefined the state's relation to foreign corporations and governments. On a more personal level, banana workers understood their own freedom in opposition to North American managers who were accustomed to making and breaking presidents.

San Marcos and Tiquisate differed in size, ethnicity, and work patterns, but this dissimilarity is all the more reason to examine why both places nurtured vigorous local struggles. In both San Marcos and Tiquisate, unions were the single most powerful vehicle for collective action at the local level. Yet the poor of San Marcos have been wiped clean from the slate of national history, unlike the banana workers, who won national attention for reasons that will be explored later. This essay compares the formation, production routines, and labor struggles of the coffee and banana zones. It asks how race and class identity were reforged during the revolution and why particular issues emerged at the center of worker demands. The discussion reflects the overwhelmingly male discourse of working-class consciousness. (Elsewhere I have explored questions of gender identity among working-class women during the era in San Marcos.) With respect to sources, my point of departure consists of working-class memories collected as interviews that paint a portrait of a lost utopia, refracted through four decades of military terror since 1954. Most of the detail on labor struggle is drawn from local court documents and records of the Ministry of Labor. This new evidence, read through the lens of labor history, compels a very different analysis of the impact of local-level radicalism on national history.

For the majority of Guatemalans who lived through that era, the October Revolution is revered *not* because it brought more schools, free elections every six years, and social security legislation for urban workers; rather, it is remembered as a golden age for its conquest of a higher standard of living and dignity for the rural poor. Plantation workers unleashed the battle to achieve these dreams within several weeks of the revolution's start. Yet because the standard version of the revolution relies on urban and elite sources, it is often blind to the agency of nonelite actors. The traditional analysis accurately reflects the motives and hesitations of the revolution's main ideologues but leaves out vast areas of popular experience. In point of fact, indigenous peasants and workers rerouted the course of national history by altering the balance of power in the countryside, thereby forcing Guatemala City leaders to include them in the body politic. Campesino organizing created new freedoms of great beauty, which in turn fed the worst race hatreds and class fears of traditional society.

The Stakes of Revolution

Guatemala's national revolution began with urban protests in June 1944 that achieved the ouster of General Jorge Ubico, a dictator who was half-mad and monstrously efficient. He is said to have trusted two people on earth—his food taster and an ancient Indian woman renowned as a witch and charged with ferreting out the president's enemies.[1] Generals from the Ubico era assert that the dictator consulted his Ouija board before making any decision of significance, and a former bodyguard said Ubico could not bear the psychic power he imagined cats to possess and ordered all those in his presence to have their ears chopped off.[2] For fourteen long years, Ubico ruled the nation like clockwork. Each harvest, drafts of forced labor under the Vagrancy Law rounded up hundreds of thousands of Indian peasants to work on the coffee plantations. In the tradition of earlier dictatorships, Ubico also gave carte blanche to the U.S.-owned United Fruit Company, UFC, known to Guatemalans as "the Octopus." UFC expanded the reach of its banana and affiliated railroad empire to the Pacific beginning in 1936 and successfully conspired to inflate transport charges for everything *but* bananas to the most expensive freight rates in the world.[3] Meanwhile, the general froze wages at levels so low that the poor still remember the hunger of those days.[4]

After the ouster of President Ubico in June 1944, the dictator's hand-picked successor, Federico Ponce, tried to stifle the prodemocracy mobilization that was reaching the most remote corners of the country. Rumors flew of an impending military crackdown. The anti-Ubico forces took the offensive. On October 20, students, urban workers, professionals, and soldiers answered the call to arms, flooding the streets of the capital. They drove out Ubico's puppet. This uprising decisively launched the October Revolution, which provided the proverbial window of opportunity for urban and rural workers to challenge the terms of their poverty. Male suffrage and constitutional guarantees for basic labor rights tipped the balance in favor of the poor almost immediately. By 1945 a professor of education named Juan José Arevalo won the presidency with a mandate for democratization. In 1947, as a result of sustained grassroots organizing, workers' struggles received the blessing of the revolutionary state in the form of progressive labor legislation, which was, however, largely limited to urban workers. This urban bias was swept aside in 1951, when mass mobilization achieved a landslide victory for Colonel Jacobo Arbenz on a platform of agrarian reform. In 1952, the Agrarian Reform Law went into effect. It destroyed forever the hegemony of the agro-export elite. Amidst the ruins, planters had two choices: either accept a higher standard of living for the rural poor or else prevent it through terror. They chose the latter. Two years later, a coup conceived by the Central Intelligence Agency, with broad elite and middle-class support, forced out Arbenz. From that point to the present, only violence has preserved the rule of the planters.

Plantation Wealth and Human Geography

The "department," or province, of San Marcos borders Chiapas, Mexico, to the west and the Pacific Ocean to the south. In the south, the land rises from the tropical Pacific plain to 14,000-foot volcanoes, the highest mountains in Central America. The coffee zone stretches in a belt across the rising mountain face from roughly 2,000 to 6,000 feet. By contrast the banana zone of Tiquisate was a single township, or *municipio*. It lay several provinces to the east of San Marcos, in Escuintla, which was famous for the largest sugar plantations in the country. The province's capital, also called Escuintla, ranked as the third-largest town in Guatemala. The vast areas purchased by the Fruit Company in the municipio of Tiquisate fell entirely in the lowlands because bananas require a growing climate like a sauna.

Coffee production predated bananas by half a century, and coffee wealth gave birth to the so-called liberal state that drove Indians off the best lands and remade the nation's economy in the agro-export mold. The Liberals passed compulsory labor laws that drafted hundreds of thousands of Mayan campesinos every harvest and forced them to leave their villages in the highlands at 5,000 to 10,000 feet.[5] In sharp contrast to coffee, the genesis of the banana export sector was a Caribbean phenomenon, beginning at the turn of the century when U.S. entrepreneurs cast about for new production zones beyond Jamaica and competed to establish fruit plantations on the Central American mainland.

The Atlantic banana zone in Guatemala was cloned from the model of Fruit Company "divisions" elsewhere. UFC officials recruited thousands of black West Indian workers and inserted them into a grueling plantation regime that operated as a self-contained universe, far distant from the nation's capital, with company-run commissaries, housing, and clinics, as well as company allies in the pulpits and pulperias. Most of the workers on the Atlantic plantations were black, and lynch law reigned with perfect impunity to silence individual bursts of rage against white managers as well as collective worker actions. Labor conflict predictably took shape along divisions of race. UFC deftly manipulated native, non-Indian workers (called ladinos) against those of West Indian descent, driving a wedge of prejudice through the heart of the workforce. This policy backfired, however, because it inflamed prejudices that led the Guatemalan state to forbid West Indian immigration.[6]

Guatemala laid golden eggs for the company. The Atlantic and Pacific coast plantations together accounted for more than one-quarter of UFC's entire Latin American production during the October Revolution.[7] Because plant disease threatened the crop each harvest, the company hedged its bets by phasing in new Pacific coast plantations in the municipio of Tiquisate. UFC owned more than 180,000 acres in the township at the dawn of the revolution in 1944.[8] In its search for labor on the Pacific side, UFC was compelled to hire Guatemalans because of anti-immigrant legislation, but it disdained the strategies of Guatemalan planters. "Scientific" racism governed the company's thinking about which populations were most amenable to physically exhausting labor in the tropics. United Fruit did not recruit Indians from villages in the piedmont that for centuries had provided cane workers, nor did it send recruiters one day's walk to the cold-country Indian towns of the highlands. Instead, preferring Spanish-speaking workers, the company put out the word on their Atlantic coast plantations and sent labor contractors to the drought-bitten departments of the east. Wages were the greatest drawing power because employment as a banana "peon" paid twice as much as the prevailing wage for the largely Indian labor force on coffee and sugar plantations.[9]

By the late 1930s, the new plantations were bursting with ladino laborers. The first reliable census after the Fruit Company arrived, that of 1950, put the count at 1,810 Indians and 29,085 ladinos living in the township.[10] In contrast to all the country's other rural townships, men outnumbered women (by about 3,000).[11] Recruitment among ladinos was a wise management strategy on the company's part insofar as the workers were not tied to the Pacific coast region through centuries of cultivation, but instead viewed Tiquisate as a frontier in much the same way as their employer.[12] Uprooted from their communities of origin, workers were forced to re-create mutual loyalties from scratch. The harshness of the day's labor and the boomtown atmosphere of the Fruit Company operations defined a distinct working-class culture in Tiquisate with a self-contained, inward-looking population. Most social life took place in the brothels and cantinas in the town center or at dances on different company plantations. Rarely did Tiquisate workers cross paths with coffee or sugar workers some twenty miles away. Socially, they were remarkably isolated as compared to San Marcos laborers, even though geographically they lived in the same plantation zone.

In San Marcos, plantation labor was necessarily Indian because working-class ladinos were so few in number. Coffee planters, unlike the United Fruit Company, were eager to harness Indian labor, presumably because the burden of racism against the Indian majority permitted a lower wage and levels of exploitation not tolerated by ladino workers. Further, most planters did not possess the resources to pick and choose their workforce. The largest language group in San Marcos was Mam, and Mam speakers made up the vast majority of recruits to the plantation system. Culture and race were bitterly contested terrain. Planters saw labor power and nothing more in the "value" of an Indian. The colonial elite had invented the term *Indian* centuries earlier to transform conquered peoples into wards of the Crown and laboring subjects. The same economic logic prevailed 300 years later, when Liberal coffee growers conspired to harness the labor of the Indian majority. Yet Indians refused to assimilate to the hostile values of elite culture. They closely guarded an ethos, a language, a religious universe, and a distinct web of mutuality. Their labor could be forced but their identity could not be erased—hence they described labor relations under the Liberal state as "slavery." The word *slavery*, in fact, was used by Indians to describe the condition of the poor ever since the arrival of the Spaniards. Racial identity lies at the core of the investigation of labor history in San Marcos for the simple fact that race proved the first principle of unity among the poor. Indigenous values survived the separation from highland communities in *tierra fría* (or cold country) and formed the foundation of collective loyalties in the heart of plantation society.[13]

Mass action on the San Marcos plantations burst forth among people who called themselves campesinos, Indians, or workers, interchangeably, with maddening disregard for the finer meanings of each. Their bosses used the identical terms, along with more pejorative versions. Some scholars mistakenly suggest that permanent workers in Guatemala's coffee belt during the revolution were ladino, or non-Indian, in the belief that proletarianization had corroded cultural loyalties over the course of seven decades.[14] However, the picture is in fact the opposite: the Mam people, whose language is roughly coterminous with the boundaries of San Marcos and Quetzaltenango, supplied the plantation labor needs of those departments, giving way to K'ichee' and K'akchiquel peoples, who fed the labor streams to the east toward Escuintla, while additional gang labor was brought down to the south coast in specific arrangements with Kanjobal-, Ixil-, and even Kekchi-speaking municipalities in the departments of Huehuetenango, Quiché, and the Verapaces respectively. In the court and labor ministry records, Indian identity appears as a deep well of pride throughout the Pacific plantation piedmont despite humiliation and economic exploitation at the hands of non-Indian society. Decades of proletarianization had failed to instill ladino identity by the 1940s. But it did blur the distinctions *between* Indian peoples, because the stark class divide between planters and their labor pool reinforced a corresponding bipolar model of racism. Even today, laborers across the coffee belt continue to define themselves as Indian.

If race was the first principle of unity, campesino identity served as the second that knit together the rural poor. The term *campesino* was used with pride by those who worked the land, regardless of whether they owned the land they worked. Thus, by the turn of the century in San Marcos, a year-round semiproletariat lived on the plantations surrounded by a patchwork of smallholders and renters, most of whom drew their cultural nourishment from Indian roots, and all of these people called themselves campesinos. So did tens of thousands of migrants who descended from highland communities each harvest because the peasant economy did not sustain them (much of tierra fría in San Marcos is bitterly cold and as a result yields only one corn harvest a year rather than two). In other words, the majority of campesinos in the department were driven into the plantation economy as its seasonal labor force.[15]

On the plantations, a critical facet of campesino identity lay in usufruct rights that were jealously defended by year-round workers. The practice of granting permanent workers a parcel of land to cultivate the milpa (corn intercropped with beans, chile, and other greens) troubled revolutionaries in Guatemala City because they believed it promoted paternalism, or in their words, "feudal social relations." Free housing was another of the many vestiges of premodern labor relations that prevail in agriculture to the present. Less genteel survivals include child labor, legally sanctioned curtailment of labor standards, varieties of unfree labor, and a subminimum wage. For the wageworkers, their usufruct rights sustained a "campesino" connection to the land. They passionately defended the milpa—with or without title to it, and irrespective of the political designs promoted by national organizers.[16]

During the revolution, class and cultural solidarity as campesinos often overcame racial boundaries in San Marcos, uniting poor ladinos and poor Indians in dozens of labor struggles recounted in the court records. Race and class loyalties were neither mutually exclusive nor airtight categories. The milpa thus bound together wageworkers and petty producers in the countryside, while plantation production was familiar to many renters and small producers who would join the temporary labor pool picking coffee or cutting cane at peak season. (In Tiquisate, ladino union officials likewise joined forces with Indian revolutionaries in neighboring plantation sectors on the common basis of their "campesino" identity, but unlike in San Marcos, the association seemed to go no deeper than the leadership.)

The Work Regime and Prerevolutionary Habits of Resistance

From the 1870s until well into the revolutionary decade, the work regime for coffee pickers remained essentially unchanged. Plantation labor in San Marcos began at sunrise and ended at sundown. Labor in the coffee groves was organized by work gangs (rather than family production, which prevailed in Costa Rica, Colombia, and postabolition Brazil). The year-round laborers, in addition to using a farm plot as part of their wage, were also "tenants" housed on the plantation. Yet unlike tenants or sharecroppers, permanent coffee pickers were expected to render only their labor rather than money rents or crops in kind.[17] Most of the year they spent tending the coffee groves rather than their corn plots. During the harvest, which lasted from September through December, the pace was frantic. Work crews were brought in from the highlands and outnumbered the year-round workers by approximately four to one. Planters required that each adult select and harvest 100 to 150 pounds of ripe berries daily. In an older grove planted in less fertile soil, workers often had to comb through twice as many trees to pick the same piece rate. Everywhere the piece rate reigned supreme, which meant that the vagaries of production were absorbed by workers rather than employers. The piece rate functioned to accelerate production to each individual's maximum capacity, while foremen also maintained the work tempo at breakneck speed. This unrelenting pressure was often hardest on women and children, who always worked in the groves, especially during harvest, though in lesser proportions than adult men. Still, women and young children remain "invisible" in the written record because the entire family's earnings were usually paid to the male head of household. At the day's end, workers hauled their hundred weight from the grove to a mill that could be several kilometers distant, saving the planters the cost of mules or trucks and receiving no pay for their service as human transport.

Banana production was also bone-jarring and back-breaking labor. Harvesting bananas called for tremendous physical strength because the stem of about 100 bananas grown on a single stalk was the "unit of production," and a stem for U.S. consumption averaged eighty-eight pounds; the smaller fruit destined for Europe weighed some sixty pounds a stem.[18] One person climbed up to cut the stem, which then fell several feet onto the bent back of another person. The need to repeatedly catch, heave, and haul this weight through the course of a twelve-hour day meant that UFC never allowed women to work in the banana groves.[19] The worker who caught the plunging stem on his back would jog with his load to a waiting railroad car when the grove was near the track that formed the lifeline of the plantations. Mules and carts were provided when the grove was too distant from the track, and a second runner would relieve the first. Back injuries were frequent and virtually unavoidable across the span of a normal work life. Knife wounds were also frequent from various tools used to hack back the jungle growth and sever the banana stem from the tree. In addition, chemical exposure posed a health threat to all the workers who came in contact with the fruit because the company's zeal for scientific management, and its quest for the perfect banana to market to the U.S. public, required generous doses of a variety of toxins. Another incentive toward overuse of chemicals was fear of fungi and insects such as sigatoka and Panama disease, which had wiped out the crop in other zones.[20] The stems were packed directly into the railroad cars, then transported to Puerto Barrios on the Caribbean, where longshoremen loaded them into the holds of the Great White Fleet that sailed for New Orleans.

Anger against the punishing work regime on banana plantations often transmuted into anti-U.S. or "anti-imperialist" sentiment because UFC enjoyed the outspoken support of U.S. diplomats. The company also worked hard to inculcate "American" values, sometimes against the will of its workers. Examples include the promotion of condensed milk rather than breast milk for UFC babies, English-language directions for UFC field operations, and the company rule allowing forced entry to prevent immoral behavior in the homes of UFC workers.[21] Offended national pride, moreover, united UFC workers with unlikely allies in the universities, professional societies, and circles of artists and intellectuals who bitterly resented the humiliation of Ubico's *vendepatria* (selling out the country) concessions to United Fruit. After 1944, banana workers often saw themselves cast as anti-imperialist heroes in the mainstream media. To the leftist and labor press, they were giants. As a result, the consciousness of Fruit Company workers took shape in the warmth of cross-class solidarity and with a sharpened sense of obligation, as they played David to the international Goliath.

In San Marcos, the situation of wageworkers and campesinos had an international dimension as well, namely the presence of the border, which enhanced the workers' freedom to govern the terms under which they labored. Many highland Indians worked illegally on Mexican coffee plantations in neighboring Chiapas, where the wage was higher, though the risks of crossing the border without government permission entailed long jail terms.[22] Seasonal work in Chiapas often radicalized Guatemalan migrant workers by rendering them "criminals" for the simple fact of their seeking work. It also exposed them to a less violent plantation elite on the Mexican side, for reasons that obeyed patterns of modernization rather than the humanitarian sensibilities of the coffee growers.[23] Further, small-scale contrabandists who took advantage of the opportunity offered by the border numbered in the thousands; probably the entire population was in some measure complicit. The poor suffered ceaseless harassment by Treasury Police.[24] San Marcos campesinos chose to maintain commercial and labor networks in Chiapas that placed them in continual conflict with the Guatemalan state, which defined their activities as illegal. They also watched firsthand as the Mexican Revolution then the land reform of Lázaro Cárdenas shook the Chiapan countryside.

By the 1930s, the decade when Ubico's iron grip had supposedly reduced the population to utter docility, clandestine networks appeared on the San Marcos plantations.[25] This organizing merged seamlessly into the union struggles of the following decade. It was sparked by a family of partial Mexican descent that drew inspiration from the revolutionary precedents of Villa and Zapata. The ease with which this family established secret campesino networks is explained, in the first place, by the habits of independence or "rebelliousness" guarded by Indians in San Marcos and promoted by a border culture of contraband, and second, by the earth-shattering events then taking place in the Mexican countryside under President Cárdenas.

In Tiquisate, on the other hand, historical memories were much shorter. The necessary chemistry of popular radicalization was achieved through the combustion of anti-imperialist consciousness and United Fruit's arrogance. As one would expect, evidence of abusive managers did not lend itself to documentation until after 1944, when workers stood a chance of winning a sympathetic hearing from government officials. From that point forward, worker complaints belied company claims that their labor relations were uniquely humane. It is important to note in this respect that UFC vehemently denied charges, time and again, that were later proven true in the labor records.

Labor Struggles Compared

The single most striking quality of revolution as practiced by the poor was their definition of justice in the realm of economic, rather than political, liberties. At root, investigation of national history from the perspective of rural wage earners yields this fundamental observation, which counters the prevailing consensus that the revolution affected mainly the urban poor and middle-class except for a few brief years after the Agrarian Reform of 1952.[26] Beginning in 1944, the evidence shows that national laws—or the "revolution from above"—only achieved real substance when met with the strength and sacrifice of those on the bottom of the social pyramid. The comparison that follows of labor struggles in Tiquisate and San Marcos addresses four lacunae in the traditional record, then turns to the nature of "the enclave" in Tiquisate to discover the extent to which banana workers there deserve credit as a vanguard of sorts that sparked the organizing of other rural wage-workers.

Rural Agitation at the Dawn of Revolution

First, campesinos put ideas of equality into practice long before the same ideas entered the national legislature. In July 1944 as soon as the dictator stepped down, workers in San Marcos initiated a veritable avalanche of labor, land, and political struggles. Highland migrants, Indian colonos, ladino corn farmers, and hired hands on the coffee fincas flocked to the town plazas to celebrate the new era with marches and speeches. They described their demands as both "indigenous" and "campesino." Ubico's fall meant that they were free to demand a living wage. The poor also hoped the new government would divide up the land of the rich, as had happened in Mexico. Workers held union assemblies, elected officers, and collected dues. Unions and political parties formed at practically the same moment (they often shared leadership), in preparation for the first free presidential elections in fifteen years. Often the unions were led by individuals who had participated in the underground networks created during the dictatorship. Coffee pickers persuaded their coworkers to stand together against the bosses plantation by plantation, from the most central to the most remote regions of the coffee zone. The court records are full of labor disputes in which campesinos challenged the planters' monopoly of power years before the Labor Code was passed in 1947. Doing so was dangerous because during these years the coffee growers frequently called in the army. In San Marcos, wageworkers were better organized and more vocal than anywhere in the country except the banana zones of the United Fruit Company.

In Tiquisate as well the battle lines emerged quickly after Ubico stepped down. Within weeks workers founded a union, which signed up thousands of agricultural workers then decided to go on strike to protest frozen wages. After a fortnight they won a 15 percent pay hike but lost their leaders, who were jailed and then sent to serve prison terms in the rain forest of the Petén. As in San Marcos, the state sent in the army. Despite this unpropitious beginning, the fall of Ubico allowed banana workers to express opinions that contradicted the company's self-promotion as a corporate utopia in the tropics. From 1944 onward banana workers reported persecution at the hands of their supervisors and at the hands of the state when it used soldiers to break strikes. Strong socialist leadership in the department of Escuintla during the revolutionary decade gave workers an added advantage in much the same manner that secret networks organized during the 1930s in San Marcos prepared the ground for collective action. The mere presence of organized networks among the poor, regardless of ideology, goes far toward explaining why the two regions outpaced most other areas in the sheer quantity of grassroots committees and demands. Another crucial feature shared by both departments is structural, namely, their size: both departments claimed unusually large extensions of territory in the heart of the plantation zone, so the laws of probability dictated more labor conflicts.

Socialist theory led its practitioners to focus their energies on United Fruit enclaves on the premise that workers there were more proletarianized than other rural plantation workers and educated by experience to possess an anti-imperialist consciousness. Unlike the Atlantic coast plantations, Tiquisate's proximity to the capital meant that revolutionaries directly engaged in crafting national reform could drop in at a day's notice. Workers throughout the department of Escuintla were probably the most heavily courted of any plantation workers in the republic by revolutionaries from the capital. Most of the messengers of change were teachers, students, or more privileged urban workers. Banana workers in Tiquisate responded readily. They elected one of four outspoken congressional representatives, called "the worker's deputies," who took the lead in shaping egalitarian legislation for the poor. (San Marcos campesinos elected another one of the four, the same man who had begun the underground organizing of the Ubico era.) These leaders were often born outside Escuintla, yet their talk of rights and liberties found fertile soil in the aspirations of rural workers. National organizers would arrive for a weekend, convene meetings, then return to the capital to attend to a host of other local and national issues, leaving in their wake local structures and leadership to carry on the work. The people who performed the day-to-day tasks of the union were banana workers.

Rural unions in Escuintla also built networks that bridged the sugar, cattle, and banana sectors, on the basis of campesino issues that overrode racial barriers and joined people who owned their land with those who farmed the land of others. Agricultural workers were denied more rights than any other sector of the workforce, as is true of most class societies. In Escuintla campesinos closed ranks to combat their common enemy, the planter elite. Tiquisate's reputation for militancy is thus misleading insofar as other rural workers were behaving in exactly the same manner and risking their livelihoods to make identical demands. The chief difference lay in the peculiar situation of banana workers as direct employees of the "imperialist" Yankees. A second crucial difference is the question of size. The massive concentration of Tiquisate workers amplified their demands. Yet the union's size was a matter of official definition. Similar mass could have been achieved in coffee or cane had the government not insisted that unions in these sectors correspond to the productive unit defined by a single plantation. Workers on about 100 government-owned coffee plantations, for instance, lost their battle for recognition as a single union.

Amidst the explosion of popular enthusiasm for the revolution in San Marcos, one of the more intriguing developments concerned a widespread rumor that the rich would surrender their lands to the poor. A tremendous wave of hope swept the land (eight long years before the state decreed agrarian reform). It appears reflected in the funhouse mirrors of the elite, who made reports throughout the San Marcos coffee zone that peasants were plotting land invasions. Although the charge turned out to be false, it was based on real and widespread campesino rumors of immediate land reform, to be achieved by the rural unions. San Marcos campesinos did not wait for anyone's permission to build popular momentum at the first flush of freedom. With the same vigor, banana workers pursued a living wage while still facing the police and judges of the dictatorship. In both cases, the state responded by sending in soldiers to discourage popular organizing. With respect to the larger history, rural wageworkers called for the revolution's most thoroughgoing reforms long before talk of such reform gained credence in national discourse.

Mass Flight from the Plantation Economy

The second gap in the record concerns the mass flight of workers to achieve freedom as they understood it. In San Marcos, campesinos refused to honor their contracted obligations under the Vagrancy Law *before* the law was rescinded, not unlike thousands of slaves across the Americas in the nineteenth century who fled plantations *in advance* of emancipation. This process of mass resistance was the sum of thousands of individual decisions. Up to 36,000 contracted laborers in San Marcos chose not to honor their contracts for the harvest of 1945.[27] They either believed the rhetoric of social justice, or else chose to test it by refusing to leave their villages. Their decision was an act of cultural defiance: Indians chose to work in the more congenial world of highland milpas and to shun the prejudice and crass exploitation of the plantations. Because migrant workers outnumbered the year-round plantation labor force by about four to one, three-quarters of the coffee harvest would rot without their labor.[28] With the berries turning bloodred and ready to fall off the branch, the governor of San Marcos persuaded President Arevalo that migrant laborers had unleashed a national disaster and were threatening the country's economic foundation. The president decided to force people to work at gunpoint. Arevalo sent in the army, along with a commission of high-ranking ministers. Campesinos were persuaded by the threat to honor their contracts on the plantations and concluded that economic kinship bound the state more closely to the planters than to themselves. Yet the workers had altered the balance of power and given a good scare to the richest landowners in San Marcos by withholding their labor. Shortly thereafter, Congress repealed the Vagrancy Law. Like the first Tiquisate strike, these events launched the hopes of the laboring poor.

The whole episode in San Marcos does not even enter national histories. In fact, the migrant labor supply over the next decade grew thinner and thinner each year because a higher wage allowed campesinos to achieve subsistence and withdraw from the plantation harvest.[29] The same phenomenon occurred, as it turned out, across the country (except on the banana plantations, which did not rely on seasonal labor). Planters were thrown into a panic. Yet this was a very quiet panic that hardly entered the press as compared to similar shortages of the 1920s and 1930s. It was as though a pact of silence had been struck among landowners, in the knowledge they were no longer favored sons of the state. With a government that forbade excessive coercion, the obvious solution to the labor shortage was a higher wage, and the higher wage was exactly what rural unions made their central demand. Landowners avoided the wage question religiously. The discussion returns to the wage issue later on.

Governmental Fear of Union Strength

The third gap in the historical record concerns the tense relationship between union strength and official control. In 1945 campesinos in San Marcos rechanneled their energies into unions after the state doused the rumors of land reform and forced migrants to work the harvest. Workers seized the opportunity to organize up and down the length of the coffee belt and on small as well as large plantations. They did so in the knowledge that such activity practically guaranteed a jail sentence. Most of the San Marcos plantation disputes are remarkable in two respects: the absence of outside direction by revolutionaries from the capital and the cohesion of permanent and temporary wageworkers, who insisted time after time that everyone had arrived together at their decisions and if one were jailed, all would follow. Though unfamiliar with the phrase, they acted in the conviction that "an injury to one is an injury to all."

After 1944 the planter elite and the remnants of Ubico's judiciary carried on as though nothing had changed, which is hardly surprising. It is curious, however, that the new government made no attempt to

organize campesinos in state-sponsored or controlled unions. In its ora-
tory, Arevalo's government celebrated the common man, but it made no
real effort to mobilize the poor after receiving their votes, which would
suggest the state had little interest in populist alliances. Occasionally,
national organizers would drop in to deliver speeches and advice, but
most of them considered themselves labor advocates rather than "official" revolutionaries. Organizing in San Marcos built up speed under
the power of its own sails. This probably worked to the advantage
of campesinos insofar as their organizing embodied popular demands
rather than bureaucratic designs.

Within the first few years, the risks that workers took in standing up
to managers and police started to pay off. Landowners were forced to
shorten the workday long before the state possessed the means to police
the eight-hour day in San Marcos.[30] The wage climbed slowly under the
ceaseless pressure of work stoppages and strikes. Planters who ran their
estates like medieval fiefdoms now risked being reported by their employees when they overworked people, failed to meet customary obligations, provided decrepit plantation housing, abused the dignity of their
workers, or insulted the dignity of the revolutionary state (in numerous
instances, the old elite accused Arevalo of being a communist or threatened the president with different kinds of bodily degradation).

Ominously, labor rights in the countryside grew more fragile as the
organizing of rural workers gathered force. Planters declared war on
customary rights the instant that confrontational worker tactics began
to win improvements. In September 1945 the president moved to crimi-
nalize rural labor organizing, unless the workers at a given workplace
numbered 500 or more. This startling development revealed that the
state was deeply concerned by the fact that campesinos were changing
the face of social relations in the countryside. Because of their numbers,
UFC workers constituted the main exception to Arevalo's meltdown of
rural unions. The earlier militance of UFC workers surely acted as a
deterrent to the state's union-busting inclinations and affected the government's decision not to disband UFC unions. Probably the non-Indian
racial composition of the banana workers also shaped the administration's greater leniency. UFC employees were thus the *only* rural workers
whose unions could participate as political actors in the battles leading
to the passage of the 1947 Labor Code. By contrast, nonunionized rural
workers during these years could sway national policy through their

votes, but they were effectively prevented from more substantial participation by the absence of democratic worker organizations.

The banana workers held onto their legality because their numbers cloaked them in industrial and modern guise. Yet although government officials and banana workers shared racial commonalities and a common "imperialist" adversary, their points of similarity obscure more fundamental antagonisms. The Arevalo administration was annoyed by confrontational worker tactics and fearful of communism, which meant that the outspokenness of Tiquisate workers represented a real political threat.[31] Arevalo believed in gradual "dignification of the workers" through measures handed down by the state, rather than participatory or workplace democracy.[32] Above all he favored educational reform. His theory of "spiritual" as opposed to "materialist" socialism, which he had developed in exile as a professor of pedagogy, inclined him to distrust unions by definition because they focused their energies on material demands. Workers were to be seen but not heard: their "place" in the new era was to support democracy with their presence and their votes, but not to participate in actual governance. Yet owing to its size, the Tiquisate union was able to compel government recognition. It became the "elder statesman" among rural unions.

By 1947, the first year of the Labor Ministry's operations and hence the first year of surviving documentation, the Tiquisate union was collecting more than Q800 a month in dues (equivalent to U.S. $800) from well over 3,000 members. All the workers in Tiquisate belonged to a single union called SETCAG and all the workers in Izabal belonged to another called SETUFCO because technically the company was divided into two corporations, one on the Atlantic coast in the department of Izabal and the other on the Pacific. Each plantation laborer paid approximately twenty-five centavos per month while midlevel employees paid higher dues. The Tiquisate plantations with the largest union membership at that time were Jutiapa, Verapaz, and Izabal, which each counted hundreds of employees.[33] The remaining plantations collected dues from about 100 workers apiece. Hundreds of thousands of other plantation workers in Guatemala were fragmented into unions that never numbered more than several hundred each, owing to the government restrictions mentioned earlier that prohibited a single union from representing more than one workplace. The numerical strength of the Tiquisate and Izabal unions gave the banana workers exceptional political weight, as well as resources in union dues that allowed them to provide financial assistance to needy members and send a steady stream of union commissions to the capital and different plantations.[34] As a result, United Fruit workers formed the most powerful rural constituency in the country.

The prohibition of rural unions forms the backdrop to the debates that surrounded the passage of the Labor Code, which finally became law on May 1, 1947. The new code mandated the establishment of a Labor Ministry with local inspectors, and their effective presence in the countryside by 1948 dealt a crushing blow to planter autonomy. Yet in many ways the Labor Code hampered or hobbled worker organizing. It restricted the right to strike through the legal principle of "tutelary" state intervention, by which the government took a protective stance toward labor that in practice often functioned as corporatist control. By law, every strike was subject to government scrutiny on a case-by-case basis because official approval was required to declare a strike "legal." Major labor conflicts erupted in the Pacific banana zone in 1948, 1951, and 1952, some of them legal and some of them not; more minor conflicts were continuous. Among coffee workers, the antiunion prohibition was not even rescinded until a year after the Labor Code went into effect. In the meantime many San Marcos campesinos simply behaved as though they, too, were entitled to basic labor rights. They ignored the fact that such behavior usually led to criminal charges. In short, they forced the state to honor its rhetoric of social justice in much the same way that many among them had helped undermine the Vagrancy Law by deciding to break their contracts in 1945.

The Wage Struggle

The fourth gap in the record of national revolution concerns the wage struggle. Without local pressure, a higher wage probably never would have been won in the first place. It breathed life into the promise of economic justice. Necessity was the mother of the wage struggle because postwar prosperity arrived accompanied by inflation. The rural poor suffered a steady decline in their real wage at the same time that political democracy blossomed all across the land. Beginning in 1944, San Marcos campesinos demanded an increase in the minimum wage at each harvest, until finally it was written into law. But planters ignored the new law, which unleashed a wave of strikes up and down the San Marcos coffee belt that finally won compliance. This was a victory achieved at the grass roots, and thus it offers a clear example of how popular organizing drove national change.[35]

Both permanent workers and migrant laborers say that the sweetest victory of the revolution was the eighty-centavo wage.[36] In fact the wage struggle takes precedence over the land struggle in the oral histories. The higher wage entered into effect earlier than the agrarian reform, so perhaps its longer duration explains why the memory of the wage is so cherished. Further, the wage touched *everyone* who worked in the coffee harvest, as well as people on lowland cane, cattle, and banana plantations and even those bringing in the corn harvest on other people's land. It was the single reform that echoed most widely across the Indian highlands. By contrast, the agrarian reform unfolded mainly in the plantation belt, and among the boldest fraction of campesinos. The government wagered its future on agrarian reform, but essentially it abandoned the wage struggle to local initiative.

In Tiquisate, because the workers had won a single bargaining unit, the wage struggle on the banana plantations moved into the realm of negotiation after 1948, with work stoppages and strikes as a final resort. The proposed wage scale that year was voted on at a general union assembly and called for the largest raises for those on the bottom, which dramatically compressed the disparity between the best- and the worst-paid UFC employees.[37] Collective bargaining proved so beneficial that the UFC wage from that point forward always exceeded the national minimum.[38] Beginning in 1950 and continuing through 1951, Tiquisate workers joined with the United Fruit Company workers of the Atlantic coast—on the older plantations in the department of Izabal and also on the Atlantic docks of Puerto Barrios—to demand a single collective pact. When they finally succeeded, the workers achieved de facto recognition as one workforce in spite of the legal fiction that divided UFC into a number of different companies, a measure undertaken by the company with the idea of dividing employees into smaller and more manageable units and also avoiding antitrust laws.[39] The union thus managed to expose the illegality of UFC's corporate monopoly—and to curtail its power—years before a U.S. court delivered the same judgment. The UFC workers' strength acted as a buffer or shield for plantation workers across the country.

Tiquisate: The Enclave Reconsidered

Clearly, Tiquisate workers played a seminal role in the nation's labor history. Indeed, their presence adds a different twist to the notion of the enclave economy that has governed the study of other UFC zones. The company aspired to rule Tiquisate as a private fiefdom; however, the zone's isolation was more fictive than real. It was located in the web of a thriving regional economy, close to the largest industrial center of the south coast (the city of Escuintla) and only a few hours by car from the capital. Within half a day's travel in any direction, other workers fought the same battles. Workers across the department voted together to send "workers' deputies" to the National Assembly, and local union leaders visited back and forth on the business of regional confederations. In real terms, Tiquisate was not an enclave. Yet despite the unity of worker demands throughout Escuintla, the local record does not yield evidence of much cross-fertilization between the rank and file of different plantation sectors.

UFC employees acted like a labor aristocracy among plantation workers. They were self-consciously identified with the international market to a far greater degree than coffee workers ever envisioned their labor as integral to North Atlantic patterns of consumption. Banana workers built a social identity based on their function as an international rural proletariat. In this sense, United Fruit did effectively manufacture an enclave. The closed world of most Tiquisate workers stood in marked contrast to the fluidity of rural workers in San Marcos, whose freedom of movement and interaction across the wide boundaries of that department was so pronounced it suggests a sort of "rural urbanity"—a social universe of campesinos that bridged plantation and smallholding divides, not to mention the Mexican border.

Even in the peculiar example of Tiquisate, the most important feature of "the enclave" turns out to be foreign ownership. The organizing of banana workers inspired the Fruit Company to lobby for the intervention of the Central Intelligence Agency to oust the Guatemalan government. In fact, the Fruit Company's animosity began long before the Agrarian Reform Law of 1952, which is often cited as the principal reason for UFC opposition to the revolution. Beginning in 1944, UFC covered its flank by laying plans to undermine the national government.[40] It attacked banana workers as a proxy for the Guatemalan state. In the end, U.S. intervention proved the decisive factor in the 1954 coup that forced out Arbenz and ushered in four decades of state terror.[41] Elite opposition to Arbenz was so badly fractured and self-serving it never would have achieved the necessary cohesion or discipline to unseat Arbenz *without* the leadership and operational support of the CIA. The militance of banana workers thus altered the chemistry of relations between the Guatemalan government and the United States.

Banana workers personified Guatemala's national dignity. Under Arbenz, when the government supported the organizing efforts of Fruit Company workers, the national history ran counter to the more typical situation elsewhere in Central America, where a pattern of state cooperation with foreign capital prevailed.[42] The October Revolution offers an unusually sharp picture of anti-imperialist sentiments among the workforce because nationalism was actively encouraged by the Guatemalan government.

Another crucial aspect of "the enclave" was its ability to attract highly motivated outside organizers, inspired by nationalist or class ideology. Communists were attracted by what they believed to be a concurrence of revolutionary circumstances and in particular, the clear expression of economic subservience to the United States. In Tiquisate, like the Atlantic coast of Honduras and Costa Rica, the Communist Party was rooted among banana workers at different points in time. (During the October Revolution, the picture is complicated by the fact that communist leadership in Tiquisate may have been on the CIA payroll, while the competing, anticommunist labor leadership was allegedly bought for a handsome sum.)[43] While any area receiving such generous attention from organizers might well have responded in similar fashion, the UFC employees shook up national politics because they organized as a workforce of thousands.

Important distinctions separate Guatemala's Pacific Fruit Company plantations from other Caribbean plantation zones. Tiquisate's labor force was ladino and Central American from the start, not black or Caribbean, so the expression of contrary national or racial loyalties never emerged as a natural vehicle for working-class demands. Indeed, race never provided a cohesion similar to indigenous identity in San Marcos. In Tiquisate, probably a significant proportion of the individuals recruited by UFC were the children of West Indians who had married Guatemalans, yet the color line does not appear in the oral histories of the Pacific banana enclave and it was erased from the census, collapsed into the category of ladino. Tiquisate workers lived in their own country, free to speak their own language and practice their own culture without attracting the attention of xenophobes or racists. Given these differences, the fact that labor struggles in Tiquisate profoundly shaped national history in parallel fashion to other UFC enclaves argues for further comparative analysis of corporate plantation communities across international borders and a greater emphasis on the role of class as an explanatory factor, apart from or alongside the role of race as the case may be.

Conclusion

A number of conclusions emerge from the investigation of campesino history during Guatemala's national revolution. First, the "revolution from above" only set down roots when jealously defended, or "tended," by the poor, who usually risked losing their jobs when they struggled to implement national laws. From the vantage of labor history, this observation is self-evident, but from the vantage of national political history, independent worker initiative has remained largely invisible.

Second, the poor defined justice far more broadly than most bureaucrats, and in terms that reached beyond voting rights to demands for greater social equality. The disjunction between the language of local and national organizers is an argument for closer inspection of the ways workers challenged the revolutionary state. Their hopes gave birth to an utterly changed revolution.

Third, and perhaps most important, the revolution in the countryside seized crucial victories from a reluctant state. Coffee pickers in San Marcos spearheaded national demands for a higher minimum wage and more humane piece rates. Within a few years, they had maneuvered their escape from coercive labor relations through a higher wage on the plantations. Banana workers used their favored status to expand union and contract rights for all plantation workers. Their union fought like a lion in defense of labor rights, but so too did workers on the cane and coffee plantations, on cattle estates, and in the coffee and sugar mills, not to mention thousands of smallholders who joined the national campesino union and propelled the redistribution of the land to those who worked it. The agrarian reform marked the great turning point. It electrified San Marcos and Escuintla. Again, organizing networks allowed campesinos to play a central role in national events. The parceling out of the land brought down the fury of the United States as well as the landowners, which culminated in the 1954 invasion.

Insofar as the construction of any country's history is part and parcel of the nation-building task of the state, in Guatemala the consensus has held that the revolution's strengths were political because these were the freedoms that survived the invasion. By contrast, the history of the poor demonstrates that for them, the beauty of the revolution lay in its economic freedoms (which did not survive after the revolution was destroyed).

The aftermath of repression and exile scarred San Marcos, while it devastated Tiquisate, where trade unionists from up and down the south coast were machine-gunned into open trenches.[44] UFC vengeance seems to explain the ferocity of the counterrevolution in Tiquisate. The killing took place on one of their plantations and lasted five months, carried out by a commander of the invading forces who arranged for the victims to be seized from private as well as UFC plantations. The Fruit Company possessed considerable powers to suppress the evidence: the massacre went unreported and unremembered except by its survivors. In flashes it slipped into the national record, such as when a child left orphaned by the slaughter grew up and killed its principle perpetrator. With ghastly precision, the Tiquisate massacre serves as a metaphor for the substance, manner, and forbidden memory of four decades of state terror that have followed.

In Tiquisate, the banana groves have long since been planted in cotton, following the abrupt shutdown of UFC operations in the late 1950s when the antitrust suit first generated by the Arbenz government succeeded in New York courts. The workers scattered, taking their memories with them. Today, the cotton, sugar, and coffee plantations draw tens of thousands of highland migrants, who continue to organize for a better wage but under conditions of forced clandestinity best described as a species of war—though they have no weapons—because their employers mobilize soldiers, police, and private landowner armies against them.

As for San Marcos, since the late 1970s the department has been

a battleground. Following the destruction of campesino leagues in the
1960s, which had attracted many of the same individuals who fought
the union struggles of the 1940s, the region became home to one of four
allied guerrilla armies, the Organización Revolucionaria del Pueblo en
Armas (ORPA; Revolutionary Organization of the People in Arms).
ORPA is distinguished by its indigenous roots and its radio broadcasts
from the slopes of Volcán Tajumulco, which towers over the coffee
belt. (It also possesses a certain stellar quality because its highest commander, who is decidedly not indigenous, is the son of Nobel laureate
Miguel Angel Asturias. More recently, the death of an ORPA commander allegedly at the hands of a torturer on the CIA payroll has
raised, yet again, the issue of U.S. involvement in Guatemala's political violence.) One politically neutral resident in San Marcos describes
the planter regime today as a system of medieval fiefdoms where the
feudal lords fly about in helicopters and possess all the technology of
modern warfare.[45] Local military commissioners are largely drawn from
the plantation elite. However the comparison underrates the role of the
state: army soldiers and checkpoints are ubiquitous; helicopters hover
in the skies; squadrons of elite troops move through the coffee groves
like ghosts with combat-painted faces in search of guerrillas. Little girls
in one town in the middle of the coffee belt play an unusual form of tag,
in the privacy of the cemetery, racing back and forth and screaming,
"Run! Run! The soldiers are coming to kill you!" Usually the soldiers
do not find guerrillas. The military commissioners, however, are skilled
at locating and ridding themselves of campesino organizers who trouble
the social peace on plantations.

As in the days of Ubico, terror undergirds a plantation regime of vast
inequalities in Guatemala. Guerrillas have found fertile ground for the
same reasons that organizers during the 1940s lit sparks that turned into
a conflagration. In San Marcos, the Mam culture has promoted collective loyalties for half a millennia and continues to shape the character
of the rural poor, alongside more recent habits of resistance influenced
by the Mexican border. Among banana workers and their children,
on the other hand, the memory of their national strength during the
October Revolution has been submerged by relentless violence. Worker
resistance has moved into the realm of cautious, painstaking organizing
through unions whose leaders are targeted (one such leader was killed
in cold blood by company thugs in 1994).[46]

Cold war ideology has haunted the imagination of the landowning elite, then as now, and justified its worst crimes. By contrast this rhetoric was regarded by the poor as another expression of the poverty they suffered. The deadly language illustrates the abyss between the conceptions of the planters and their workers. In the words of one banana worker, "All those who claimed their rights, or who had a union, they called you communist. Or if you were a worker, for that they called you communist. They didn't like us. When is a boss ever going to like a union? Never!"[47] On the other side of the plantation belt in San Marcos, an Indian coffee worker who had benefited from the agrarian reform placed the thought in a larger context: "They always called us communists [during the days of Arevalo and Arbenz] and now they talk about the fall of communism. What do I care about some country called the Soviet Union—I've never been there. I don't even know where it is! But the problems we had then, those are still our problems now. And I tell you, when Arbenz divided up the land, that was the only time that campesinos were ever happy."[48]

Notes

I am both indebted and very grateful to two anonymous reviewers of an article on San Marcos that appeared in the Winter 1994 *Radical History Review*, as well as to Susan Besse, Michael Jimenez, Jeffrey Gould, Avi Chomsky, Cliff Welch, Carol Smith, and my dissertation advisors Tulio Halperin, Margarita Melville, and Linda Lewin for their comments on earlier versions of this essay.

1. The tall tales and true stories about Ubico are legion. These ones come from a member of the dictator's elite palace guard, secondhand, via a labor leader who lived with the guard decades later (Interview 60, September 1994). For more examples, see Kenneth Grieb, *Guatemalan Caudillo: The Regime of Jorge Ubico in Guatemala, 1931–1944* (Athens: Ohio University Press, 1979). All interviews where the speaker requested anonymity are identified by number and date. Socioeconomic information on the speaker is indicated in the note if it does not appear in the text.

2. Interview 35, July 1990, and Interview 60.

3. Paul J. Dosal, *Doing Business with the Dictators: A Political History of United Fruit in Guatemala, 1899–1944* (Wilmington, Del.: Scholarly Resources, 1993), 3 and chap. 11, "The United States versus United Fruit," 205–223.

4. See my oral histories from the province of San Marcos in "The Time of

Freedom": Campesinos and Workers in Guatemala's October Revolution, 1944 to 1954" (Ph.D dissertation, University of California, Berkeley, 1995), especially chap. 3.

5. On coffee labor during the Liberal era, see David McCreery, "Debt Servitude in Rural Guatemala, 1876–1936," *Hispanic American Historical Review*, 63, no. 4 (1983): 735–759, and more broadly, his *Rural Guatemala, 1760–1940* (Stanford, Calif.: Stanford University Press, 1994).

6. On the Guatemalan plantations, see Dosal, *Doing Business with the Dictators;* on UFC social policy more broadly, see Aviva Chomsky's *West Indian Workers and the United Fruit Company in Costa Rica, 1870–1940* (Baton Rouge: Louisiana State University Press, 1996).

7. Richard H. Immerman, *The CIA in Guatemala: The Foreign Policy of Intervention* (Austin: University of Texas Press, 1982), 72–73.

8. Ibid.

9. For wage rates, see severance form of May 20, Archivo General de Centroamerica (hereafter cited as AGCA), Inspección General de Trabajo, Correspondencia (hereafter cited as IGT-C), Sig B, leg. 48751, 1947.

10. Guatemala, Departamento de Estadística, *Censo general de la población* (Guatemala City: Tipografía Nacional, 1950), 13.

11. Ibid.

12. Interviews 38 and 39; both men were banana workers in Tiquisate during the revolutionary period, and each was interviewed on three separate occasions in May 1990.

13. Mayan identity in highland communities is often discussed in the anthropological literature in essentialist terms, implying that communities further from the traditional village model are less authentic. Insofar as the history of San Marcos does not support the logic of a necessary correlation between the physical and cultural loci of identity, this history may provide a window into the future of race relations in the central highlands of Guatemala, which are now experiencing at least the partial loss of language and indigenous dress that swept lowland San Marcos some fifty years ago. The circumstances Indians faced in San Marcos may also suggest the future of some 1 million Mayans driven from their home communities by the violence of the 1980s, who are now living as "internal refugees" on the coasts and in the cities. (This is the estimate of Archbishop Próspero Penados del Barrio, author's interview, July 27, 1990.)

14. See, for example, Jesús García Añoveros, *La reforma agraria de Arbenz en Guatemala* (Madrid: Ediciones Cultural Hispánica, Instituto de Cooperación Iberoamericana, 1988), 149.

15. Guatemala, Departamento de Estadística, 3 vols. *Censo agropecuario de 1950,* (Guatemala City: Tipografía Nacional, 1951), 1:86, 104 and 3:31, 8, 3.

16. Catherine LeGrand finds parallel complexities among banana workers

and peasants in the Santa Marta agro-export zone of Colombia ("Campesinos y asalariados en la zona bananera de Santa Marta, 1900-1935," *Anuario Colombiano de la Historia Social y de la Cultura*, 11 [1983]: 235-250), and Jeffrey Gould studying the Chinandegan countryside of Nicaragua likewise notes the encompassing value of the term *campesino* and describes a similar community of interest forged by wage earners and smallholders (*To Lead as Equals: Rural Protest and Political Consciousness in Chinandega, Nicaragua, 1912-1979* [Chapel Hill: University of North Carolina Press, 1990]).

17. Nathan Whetten, *Guatemala: The Land and the People* (New Haven, Conn.: Yale University Press, 1961), 100-101.

18. "La frutera sí puede pagar las demandas de los muelleros de Puerto Barrios," *Octubre* (January 17, 1952): 7.

19. Banana harvesting was not "women's work" in the modern conceptions of Fruit Company managers. Such gender distinctions are largely dictated by culture not capacity, insofar as the most physically demanding work in cane harvesting, for instance, was assigned to women slaves in the nineteenth-century Caribbean, whereas such tasks today are exclusively assigned to men. See Luis Figueroa, "Stirring up the Fields: Sugarcane Workers and American Colonial Capitalism in Guayama, Puerto Rico, 1898-1923," paper presented at the American Historical Association Meeting, panel on "U.S. Corporations and Labor Recruitment in the Periphery: Guatemala, Honduras and Puerto Rico in the Early 20th Century," San Francisco, January 1994.

20. See extensive documentation of complaints regarding fumigation work, for example, declaration of May 28, IGT-C, Sig B, leg. 48750, June 1947.

21. Letter of August 21, IGT-C, Sig B, leg. 48751, 1947. See also Avi Chomsky, "Health and Social Control: West Indian Workers and United Fruit Company Medical Policy in Central America, 1910-1930," paper presented at the American Historical Association, San Francisco, 1994.

22. Chiapas had been part of Guatemala until 1823.

23. Interviews with Fernando Cortés, Mexican labor organizer and communist, February 6, 7, and 9, 1990.

24. See Forster, "The Time of Freedom," chap. 4, "Justice, Poverty and Gender in San Marcos."

25. In addition to my oral histories for San Marcos noted earlier, see the testimony of Alfonso Solorzano in Stella de la Luz Quan Rossell, "Guatemala, una cultura de la ignominia (siete biografías y una entrevista)" (master's thesis in anthropological science, Escuela Nacional de Antropología e História, Mexico City: 1972), 141.

26. For examples of the traditional view, see Mario López Larrave (an urban labor lawyer assassinated by the military), *Breve historia del movimiento sindical guatemalteco* (Guatemala City: Editorial Universitaria, 1976), 26-27; Tomás

Herrera, *Guatemala: Revolución de Octubre* (San José: Editorial Universitaria Centroamericana, 1986), 88–99, 124–128; Robert Wasserstrom, "Revolution in Guatemala: Peasants and Politics under the Arbenz Government," *Comparative Studies in Society and History*, 17, no. 4 (1975): 443–478; Immerman, *The CIA in Guatemala*, chap. 3 and especially 54, 56–57; and Piero Gleijeses, *Shattered Hope: The Guatemalan Revolution and the United States, 1944–1954* (Princeton, N.J.: Princeton University Press, 1991), especially chaps. 7 and 13. Jim Handy has reformulated the traditional analysis; see "'A Sea of Indians': Ethnic Conflict and the Guatemalan Revolution," *Americas: Quarterly Review of Inter-American Cultural History*, 46, no. 2 (October 1989): 189–204, which explores labor and political organizing from the perspective of race hatred.

27. On the flight on migrant labor see AGCA, Hemeroteca, Hojas Sueltas, packets for 1945 and 1946; see also *Nuestro Diario*, February 5, 1946.

28. See, for example, the case of Finca Armenia in San Rafael, AGCA, Juzgado de Paz, Primera Instancia, San Marcos (hereafter cited as JP-SM), leg. 19-J, Pieza 2, 1946.

29. For reports of scarce labor based on a 1946 study, see Elizabeth Hoyt, "El trabajador indígena en las fincas cafetaleras de Guatemala," *Notas e informaciones, ciencias sociales, Unión Panamericana*, 6, no. 35 (October 1959): 259.

30. See JP-SM, leg. 19-J, Pieza 1, 1946, for example, on the eight-hour day.

31. Arévalo shut down a union training school in the capital called Claridad six months after it first opened its doors in 1945, because many of its founders were communist. He deported a number among them who were Central Americans in exile from neighboring dictatorships. See Graciela García L., *Las luchas revolucionarias de la nueva Guatemala* (Mexico City: n.p., 1952), 62–66, 79–95, 136, 145.

32. "El ministro de gobernación explica las razones que asistieron al gobierno para suspender temporalmente la actividad sindical en el campo," AGCA, Hermeroteca, Hojas Sueltas (bundled by year), 1947.

33. SETCAG financial report dated December 31, 1947, IGT-C, leg. 48753, January 1948. The company named its plantations after Guatemalan departments or towns.

34. Ibid. The only other unions in Guatemala that matched the size, and hence the political strength, of UFC employees were the railroad and teachers unions.

35. Copy of telegram dated November 8, 1947, IGT-C, leg. 48764, December 1948; August 1948, Acta, n.d., from Finca El Prado, IGT-C, leg. 48760; and Annual Report for San Marcos dated December 27, IGT-C, leg. 48764, December 1948. See also letter of June 18, IGT-C, leg. 48758, June 1948. In addition, see "Informe de ministro de economía y trabajo," in "Agricultura, ganadería, silvicultura y pesca," *Revista de Economía*, 1, no. 2–3 (1949): 135.

The nationwide inflation index for basic goods rose more than fifty-six points from 1946 to 1960; see García Añoveros, *La reforma agraria*, 80. According to a 1951 report by the International Bank for Reconstruction and Development, "Money wages have barely kept pace with the rise of the general price level." *The Economic Development of Guatemala* (Washington, D.C.: IBRD, n.d.), 255. On the strike wave, see letters, JP-SM, leg. 22-D, Pieza 1, 1947, and IGT-C, leg. 48820, September 1952; petition from Finca Las Conchitas, JP-SM, 48819, August 1952; letter of January 8, leg. 48824, January 1953; and Interviews 3 and 10, Indian coffee colonos and trade unionists, September 1990, and Interview 1, Indian wageworker in the coffee zone, November 1990.

36. See, for instance, Interviews 19 and 20, Indian colonos and unionists on the coffee plantations, September 1990; see also Interviews 1 and 10, ibid.

37. Letter of January 4, IGT-C, leg. 48804, May 1951.

38. López Larrave, *Breve historia*, 49.

39. Telegram of May 31, IGT-C, leg. 48804, May 1951. See also *Octubre*, 1, no. 2 (May 12, 1951): 4, and 1, no. 10 (July 9, 1951): 1.

40. Letter of August 21, 1944 from the Mexican ambassador to the Mexican secretary of foreign relations, Archivo Histórico de México, Secretaría de Relaciones Exteriores, núm. 287, Exp. 728.1/0.

41. Recent revisionist history, especially Jim Handy's work and that of Piero Gleijeses, has argued against the "Black Legend," as it were, of U.S. intervention destroying Guatemalan democracy in 1954. They have contributed a much needed counterweight with their analysis of the disintegration of elite and institutional support for Arbenz. Although not contesting their findings, I would argue that popular agitation was far more critical than usually credited in shaping national policy and U.S. counterpolicy and that U.S. intervention did ultimately swing the balance away from support of Arbenz.

42. See Aviva Chomsky, "West Indian Workers in Costa Rican Radical and Nationalist Ideology, 1900–1950," *Americas: A Quarterly Review of Inter-American Cultural History*, 51 (July 1994): 11–40; and Victor Meza, "Historia del movimiento obrero en Honduras," in *Historia del movimiento obrero en América Latina*, edited by Pablo González Casanova (Mexico City: Siglo Veintiuno Editores, 1985), 128–295.

43. See interview with Carlos Manuel Pellecer, October 11, 1990; Pellecer did not publicly disavow the Communist Party until after 1954. López Larrave, *Breve historia*, 32, and Antonio Obando Sánchez, *Memorias: la historia del movimiento obrero* (Guatemala: Editorial Universitaria, 1978), 122.

44. See Ricardo Falla, *Masacres de la Selva, Ixcan, Guatemala (1975–1982)* (Guatemala City: Editorial Universitaria, 1992), and Forster, "The Time of Freedom," 384–389. I have since collected corroborating interviews from others who lived in Tiquisate at the time.

45. Interview 2, ladino professional in the coffee zone, September 1990.

46. "Five Labor Activists Killed on Guatemalan Plantations," U.S./Guatemala Labor Education Campaign Update no. 12, November 1994, p. 3 (published by Amalgamated Clothing and Textile Workers Union, Chicago).

47. Interview 38, ladino banana worker, May 1990.

48. Interview 53, Indian coffee colono and agrarian reform beneficiary, January 1992.

The Hispanic Caribbean

EILEEN J. FINDLAY

Free Love and Domesticity

Sexuality and the Shaping of Working-Class
Feminism in Puerto Rico, 1900–1917

During the early twentieth century, the newly proletarianized sectors of the Puerto Rican population began to organize a labor movement that permanently changed the balance of power in Puerto Rican politics. Its activists produced new definitions of gender and sexuality; these in turn shaped the burgeoning movement's organizing strategies and social agendas. Working-class radicals' reconceptualization of moral norms and sexual practices became an important method of asserting their superiority over their opponents. Early leftists turned on their heads the accusations of plebeian promiscuity and disreputability that peppered elite discourses. The rich and the capitalist system that fed their wealth were immoral, early labor organizers insisted—not the poor. In fact, some argued, conscious rejection of the hegemonic honor code, which imposed artificial social hierarchies on women, in favor of the more inclusive values and sexual arrangements of the popular classes would help usher in an egalitarian utopia.

Such conceptions of sexuality marked a distinct break with the dominant sexual politics of the late nineteenth century. During the 1890s, Liberal planters and professionals based in the southern municipality of Ponce built a successful drive for autonomy from Spain. "Respectable" Ponce artisans struggling for a place in the emerging Puerto Rican body politic joined with male Liberal elites in excoriating urban plebeian women accused of prostitution. This moral consensus facilitated the consolidation of a Liberal-led cross-class male political alliance.[1]

The twentieth century witnessed a new convergence of politics and sexuality—one that openly challenged the dominant socioeconomic order. The Liberal-led compact shattered in 1898 with the United States' occupation of Puerto Rico and its consolidation of colonial rule there. The first decades of the twentieth century saw an explosion of working-class organization, agitation, and intellectual production in Puerto Rico. Fueled by accelerated proletarianization, hopes for democratic reforms under the new "progressive colonialism" of the United States, and the international circulation of socialist and anarchist ideas, Puerto Rican working women and men broke with the Liberal consensus of the 1890s and proudly began to articulate politics of their own.[2] No longer would laboring people allow the parameters of the island's political, economic, or cultural agendas to be set solely by elites.

This essay will explore the often striking reconceptualizations of gender and sexuality that formed an integral part of the newly self-conscious working-class politics and culture. It will also analyze the limits to the early labor movement's gender radicalism; the early Puerto Rican male Left was not uncompromisingly feminist, as most of its historians have claimed. For as Joan Scott has noted, although social change often entails the questioning of gendered norms, it can also produce attempts to preserve some semblance of stability in the face of disorder. Often this search for equilibrium is expressed in efforts to ensure the survival of a more-or-less familiar gender hierarchy.[3] As we shall see in this essay, many radical twentieth-century working men attempted to preserve some form of male-defined social order in Puerto Rico. Often, they advocated the return of women to an idealized domesticity, even as they defended women's rights to equal pay, suffrage, and freedom from sexual harassment. In addition, they generally remained silent about working-class men's role in the oppression of women. Instead, radical male workers laid the blame for women's subordinate social position solely on the shoulders of the capitalist system and the rich men who profited from it.

Only a handful of radical working women dared to break with this analysis and consistently challenge the gendered hierarchies *within* the working classes. These courageous women, epitomized by Luisa Capetillo, a working-class intellectual and organizer, asserted that the problems of plebeian men's sexual infidelity, economic abandonment, and physical violence were indeed pressing political issues. This chapter demonstrates that in the twentieth century's first decades, as today, such far-reaching critiques of power remained, for the most part, marginalized women's work.[4]

Finally, this essay traces the shifting politicization of sexuality within Puerto Rico's early labor movement. During the first decade of the twentieth century, a radical sexual ethics began to take hold among the movement's leaders and organizers. These plebeian intellectuals penned passionate defenses of prostitutes, whom they presented as the quintessential example of capitalist exploitation; developed critiques of marriage and women's sexual exploitation; and advocated the practice of free love. By the time the United States (and, consequently, Puerto Rico) entered the First World War in 1917, however, most of these radical discourses on sexuality had disappeared from the Left's lexicon. Only the issue of prostitution remained, a faint echo of the broader agenda for sexual reform that had briefly appeared in the creative birth pangs of Puerto Rico's radical working-class movement.

Emergence of the Puerto Rican Labor Movement

The U.S. invasion of Puerto Rico in 1898 unleashed intense debate within the laboring classes over the meaning of democracy, as well as ardent pressure for expanded civil rights.[5] The occupation also swept great economic changes across the island. With the influx of U.S. capital into sugar production, the transition to capitalism, which had begun during the 1870s, accelerated dramatically. Sugar rebounded from its moribund state of the 1890s to regain its previous position as the bedrock of the island's economy; by the 1920s, it comprised 65 percent of Puerto Rico's exports.[6] The great sugar *centrales* (mills) established by U.S. corporations devoured increasing amounts of land in their push for radically expanded production and profits; between 1900 and 1910, the land planted in sugar rose from 72,000 to 118,000 acres, while production levels soared from 61,000 to 285,000 tons. Thousands of men labored in the cane fields for low wages during planting and harvest seasons. Descendants of enslaved Africans who had cut cane for generations were joined by peasants pushed from their plots by the ever expanding sugar plantations and by thousands of migrants from the now stagnant coffee farms of the highlands.[7]

U.S. capital also transformed the cigar industry. Although tobacco farming remained in the hands of smallholders, U.S. companies focused their energies on taking over the processing and manufacturing stages of cigar production. Centered in Cayey, San Juan, Caguas, and Bayamón, with additional workshops and factories in Ponce and Arecibo, cigar production rapidly expanded in the early twentieth century and was soon reorganized on an industrial scale. Large factories, mainly owned by U.S. corporations and employing hundreds of male cigar-rollers and female stem-strippers, replaced small artisanal shops of three or four male *tabaqueros,* which had previously produced the bulk of Puerto Rico's cigars.[8]

Thousands of women entered the waged labor force during the great wave of proletarianization that swept the island in the first decades of U.S. rule. Between 1904 and 1920, the tobacco industry was the largest single employer of women, displacing domestic service, which had been women's primary source of employment in the late nineteenth century. Tobacco strippers' wages were even lower than those of their male counterparts; most women worked from ten to fourteen hours a day in the tobacco shops, earning forty cents or less for a full day's labor. Many women also canned fruits in factories, shelled coffee in warehouses, or made hats in their homes, where they could mesh income-earning with domestic labor.[9]

Out of this political ferment and accelerated economic change emerged working people's first attempts at islandwide organization. Puerto Rican workers formed their first general labor federation in October 1898, shortly after the U.S. occupation of the island. For the next few years, acute internal conflict rent the fledgling labor movement. By 1905, however, the Federación Libre de Trabajadores (FLT; Free Federation of Workers) had established itself as the preeminent labor organization on the island.[10]

In 1915, after more than a decade of organizing, the FLT founded the Socialist Party. For the next nine years, the Socialists enjoyed great electoral successes in Puerto Rico's coastal sugar regions, tobacco-producing centers, and urban areas. By 1920, the Socialist Party had built a substantial following in the majority of the island's municipalities; in that year, the party won more than 50 percent of the vote in ten municipalities and between 20 percent and 47 percent of the vote in thirty-one more.[11]

In these early years, and especially prior to 1911, the labor movement that coalesced around the FLT was quite diverse. Debates on political and organizing strategies raged between the two main tendencies within the movement: the young organizers and worker intellectuals

who embraced many tenets of anarchism, and those who controlled the
FLT's administration and advocated working for gradual reform in sal-
aries, working conditions, and civil rights.[12] And, as we shall see in the
areas of gender and sexuality, there was wide disagreement about the
ultimate goals of the movement even within each of these two factions.

Puerto Rican working women and men began to articulate their own
self-consciously political counterhegemonic discourses, which they developed and disseminated in public speeches and mass demonstrations.
The early labor movement also produced an intellectual and artistic explosion. Workers organized their own musical bands, literary competi-
tions, publishing presses, libraries, and local study circles. The *centros de
estudios*, which provided small libraries and regular discussions on theoretical and practical issues facing workers, had a surprisingly broad impact. The centros were coeducational and frequented by workers loyal
to the elite-led Unionista Party, as well as by socialists and anarchists.[13]
Working men and women wrote essays, novels, poetry, and plays, which
they read out loud and performed to large, enthusiastic audiences all
over the island in theaters, union halls, worker demonstrations, and
town squares. Worker newspapers mushroomed throughout the island
in addition to the FLT's official newspaper *Unión Obrera*.

Libertarian socialism, or anarchism, was the principal ideological current in the first decade of the Puerto Rican labor movement. Although
libertarian socialism was embraced fully by only a portion of the FLT's
leadership, Rubén Dávila Santiago points out that these dynamic anarchist organizer-intellectuals disseminated their ideas widely through
the newspapers, theaters, reading rooms, pamphlets, songs, and novels,
which they produced and which were quite popular among the working
classes.[14] This "organic [cultural] movement, . . . a socialist libertarian
aesthetic" was never a coherent, unified theory, but rather a wide variety
of rather diffuse discourses.[15]

A number of basic themes did arise consistently in the writings
of the early male worker intellectuals, however. Denunciations of
state and church control over social institutions and popular world-
views abounded. The radical plebeian authors scoffed at attempts by
proautonomy and nationalist planters to whip up patriotic sentiment
against U.S. colonial rule; the problems of Puerto Rico, labor leaders
insisted, would not be solved by creating a nation with the rich at the
helm and social hierarchies undisturbed. Their allegiance was solely to

all working people, regardless of national borders. Likewise, anarchists asserted, "bourgeois democracy" and the "freedoms" so touted by all political parties on the island were useless without a true redistribution of economic and political power. Otherwise, workers would remain "the slaves of the capitalists who rent them."[16] They argued that ownership of property should be collectivized and laborers should manage their places of work. Workers should organize and educate themselves in order to shed the individualistic, subservient practices and beliefs of the past. And, as we shall see, many among the early Puerto Rican male Left insisted that women should play a central role in the creation of this movement.

The epicenters of anarchist organizing and intellectual production were in the tobacco-processing cities of San Juan, Santurce, Caguas, and Bayamón.[17] It was in the tobacco-rolling shops that Puerto Rico's radical worker culture was born and most quickly flourished. The new militant proletarian politics grew out of a long tradition of autodidacticism in the tobacco industry, built around the institution of worker readers. The readers were hired by the tobacco workers themselves; they read out loud to the laborers newspapers, fiction, poetry, and essays by the great Latin American and European radical thinkers of the day. Passionate discussions of the merits of various organizing tactics or theoretical positions frequently broke out among the tobacco workers, lending a highly interactive nature to the already collectivized practice of workshop reading.[18] Workers who were initiated into this autonomous popular education in the tobacco shops were the first to found Puerto Rico's worker libraries, theater troupes, and centros de estudios of 1900 to 1910.

Gender and the New Working-Class Politics

It was probably no accident that the worker politics emerging out of Puerto Rico's tobacco factories demanded an end to women's oppression as well as to class hierarchies, private property, religion, and nationalism. Tobacco was one of the first industries to incorporate women as wageworkers on a large scale; unlike mass embroidery and clothing production, which was mainly performed by women in their homes until well into the 1930s, women's labor in tobacco was organized in collective workplaces.[19] Although they tended to be concentrated in the lower-paid tasks, such as stem stripping, and were often kept in separate rooms, female tobacco laborers did work in the same factories as men. In 1910, women comprised 27.8 percent of the tobacco industry's workforce, up from only 1.6 percent in 1899; by 1920, they had increased to 52.9 percent.[20]

FLT unions of women tobacco strippers, coffee processors, domestic servants, and laundresses were established throughout the island by 1907. Women organizers and union members not infrequently addressed FLT rallies of thousands of people. In Ponce, Santurce, Mayagüez, and Arecibo, girls and women often made up the majority of the performers in radical musical and dramatic presentations. They also attended the new workers' theater productions in large numbers, where they interacted enthusiastically with the plays, poems, and didactic "dialogues," hissing at the evil bourgeois characters and applauding the workers.[21]

However, despite their clear presence in the labor movement and the strong impetus they must have provided it, working women's voices are not well represented in the movement's historical record. The vast majority of the authors published in the early workers' newspapers were men, and virtually all the surviving novels and plays of the period were penned by men. Consequently, we can only hope to reconstruct a bare, skeletal sketch of how radical women attempted to shape the new working-class politics in Puerto Rico. The final section of this chapter will focus on female anarchist analyses of sexual politics. For now, however, we will turn to what radical men had to say about sexuality and definitions of womanhood.

Historians of the early Puerto Rican labor movement have long acknowledged that its leaders developed a new understanding of gender relations, especially in the tobacco sector. Influenced by the radical currents of Spanish, Cuban, and Argentinian anarchism, the story goes, the male Left leadership welcomed female workers into their movement. With their entrance into the world of collectivized waged labor, women were recognized as comrades in the struggle. From its inception, historians of the labor movement insist, the FLT committed itself to organizing the women swelling the tobacco labor force and advocated women's suffrage as well as equal pay for equal work. Women's emancipation was an integral part of the "tradition of dissent" forged in the early labor movement; this new gender vision "represented a negation of the *machista* ideology of the plantation culture's hierarchical paternalism."[22]

The FLT did undeniably spawn important new discourses on gender. The labor movement's newspapers and literature rejected the ideal image of the genteel, well-educated "angel of the home," which elite Liberal men had tried to popularize throughout the late nineteenth century. Instead, radical working-class male intellectuals celebrated plebeian women's historic feistiness. The working-class woman warrior became one of the early labor movement's feminine icons. Puerto Rican anarchists applauded revolutionary Barcelona women who "fought at the barricades, by the side of their husbands, brothers, and sons against the king's soldiers, sacrificing their beautiful blood and lives in the holocaust of a high, humanitarian ideal."[23] Equally praiseworthy were the "valiant, manly" Italian women who fought off strikebreakers in a Tampa tobacco factory—"now those are *real* women!" crowed the anarchist press.[24] As long as working women's aggressiveness was properly harnessed, it could serve the movement well.

The FLT also maintained an official position in favor of organizing female workers rather than attempting to exclude them from the labor force. Eugenio Sánchez, for example, a long-term organizer and union officer, insisted that women should be trained as cigar makers; as long as they were organized and demanded equal pay for their labor, they were no danger to male workers.[25] The FLT backed up its conviction by hiring women organizers.[26]

Stirring odes to the emancipation of women appeared in male workers' writings. Manifestos such as this one were not uncommon: "Today we proclaim that Woman is not ours; revolutionary men believe that she belongs to herself. As the old ideas crumble, we new men hope that those women who own themselves, and are our true and free comrades, will rip off their bonds, raise their heads to gaze at us fearlessly and love us as women, not as slaves."[27] Many labor leaders insisted that working women were comrades, companions, and sisters in the struggle— not simple sexual objects.[28]

For a few early male leftists, revolutionary women were the hope for resolving society's contradictions and ushering in an era of freedom and justice.[29] But another discourse was much more prevalent, and sexuality was key to it. Throughout the radical press and cultural production of the period, victimized, downtrodden working women came to symbolize the exploitation of the entire working class. The power of this imagery sprang in part from its joining of many aspects of the sexual and economic oppression that had in fact long haunted plebeian women.

A long line of impoverished widows, unfortunate single mothers, and desperate young female factory workers trudged through the pages of leftist publications and across the stages of anarchist dramatic productions. Deprived of male financial support by the premature deaths and political persecution of their husbands, bludgeoned by inhumanly low wages, and almost always raped or seduced and then abandoned to raise children alone by wealthy, immoral men, these representations of women became the quintessential symbols of the ravages of capitalism.[30]

Rape or sexual abuse at the hands of rich men was a constant theme, and it must have resonated strongly with many women's experiences. But male leftists were not solely denouncing actual abuses that occurred against plebeian women. Rubén Dávila Santiago points out that FLT organizers used this characterization of rape as a particularly powerful trope to "awaken a virile response from the [male] worker against the 'possession' of the most intimate capital."[31] José Limón de Arce's famous play *Redención* provides a striking example. Pedro, the charismatic labor organizer, and Tito, the vicious son of the local landowner, compete for the affections of the beautiful Clara. Pedro loves, respects, and hopes to marry Clara, whereas Tito "savagely" desires and attempts to rape her. Tito rages that the noble Pedro "wants to prevent men like me with money from buying a woman and possessing her, because he [Pedro] believes that no daughter of a worker should be the lover of a rich man."[32] Needless to say, Pedro wins Clara's hand in the end.

Thus, in the worker literature of the early twentieth century and quite possibly in workers' daily lives as well, class struggle between men was played out on the field of competing male "rights" to sexual possession of women. To radical Puerto Rican male workers of this period, female waged labor in factories meant both potential female political mobilization and women's increased economic and sexual vulnerability. It also translated into plebeian men's waning ability to sexually and economically control as well as to protect "their" women. The new working-class movement sought to strengthen laboring men's social position vis-à-vis both elite men and plebeian women. Radical men's construction of rape as always a cross-class act of domination, from which the noble working man would liberate "his" woman, neatly expressed these desires.

Unlike many late nineteenth-century Ponce male artisans, however, who had also feared their waning power over women, most of the new radical men did not openly call for the excoriation of women who stepped outside the "proper" bounds of the family. Instead, they condemned the capitalist system and the rich who directed it for destroying the fabric of working-class families. Thus, the early labor movement's gender politics diverged significantly from that of the misogynistic conservatism that dominated the political exchanges of 1890s Ponce. Nowhere is this clearer than in discussions of prostitution. The radical workers' discourse of the early twentieth century stands in stark contrast to male artisans' and elites' revulsion toward prostitutes and "rowdy women" during the late nineteenth century. In the new popular analysis of sexual politics, prostitution was not women's fault, as it had been constructed to be earlier. Rather, its roots lay in capitalism, which relegated women to such brutal poverty that they were forced to sell their bodies to survive. "Only misery creates whores," proclaimed an anarchist newspaper.[33]

Daughters and sisters of workers, prostitutes were an integral part of the laboring classes—not a "different type" of woman, to be isolated from respectable working folk. "The miserable prostitute is the proletarian's sister; her history, like his, is written with tears of blood. . . . Labor's flesh, prostitution's flesh—the same misfortune."[34]

Thus, the early Puerto Rican leftists resurrected and consciously politicized a more inclusive current in popular sexual norms that had been driven underground in Ponce by the moral panic of the 1890s. They recognized plebeian women's economic precariousness and publically acknowledged the impact this vulnerability could have on women's sexual practices. They consciously rejected rigid divisions between respectable and disreputable womanhood. And ultimately, they converted the prostitute, along with the woman warrior, into one of the central symbols of the Puerto Rican working classes.

This more accepting discourse on prostitution permeated the labor movement's press and literature. But it was not the Left's only innovation in sexual matters. A small group of anarchist leaders and organizers also began to articulate a politics of free love. Two Ponce labor organizers, Carmen Rosario and Francisco Santiago, publicly celebrated a "free and loving contract" in Ponce in 1907, presided over by Eugenio Sánchez, a national FLT officer. *Unión Obrera* announced it as "the first free love ceremony celebrated in Puerto Rico. It heralds a new, enlightened era."[35] Signs emblazoned with free love slogans hung on the walls of the Caguas anarchist study center directed by Juan Vilar.[36] Artisans in the sugar town of Guayama insisted on their right to live in "free union" with their partners, even when ordered to marry by local magistrates.[37] The mulato tobacco roller Emiliano Ramos from Cayey, who later edited an anarchist newspaper in Bayamón, was a widely recognized adherent of free love.[38] Julio Aybar, a leading FLT official, also publically affirmed his commitment to the ideology.[39]

Among early twentieth-century anarchists, "free love" had a very particular meaning. Like their counterparts in Spain, Argentina, and Brazil, Puerto Rican free love advocates rejected the dominant honor code and its sanctification of marriage. Marriage, they proclaimed, was built on social convenience or economic dependency, not on love and mutual compatibility. They declared that marriage also facilitated church and state control over the family and created false distinctions between "honorable" and "dissolute" women.[40] "It is well known that 'honor' is an empty word, invented to protect your privilege," the wife of a wealthy man accuses her husband in an anarchist short story.[41] Indeed, anarchists insisted that marriage was the ultimate form of prostitution, legitimized by the church and the state.[42] Ideal relationships, anarchists wrote, should not be built on economic considerations. Rather, men and women should unite "guided solely by love". Couples should form "naturally," with no intervention from either church or state. Unworkable relationships should be left at will by either partner.[43]

The advocates of free love drew on anarchist ideas from Europe and Argentina to develop their critique of marriage and the honor system. But these Puerto Rican sexual radicals were also building upon the moral norms of the popular classes within which they came of age. Female virginity was not so important to them as was women's fidelity once a couple had entered a relationship. Serial monogamy, rather than marriage, was the ideal form of heterosexual partnership. And the honor system, with its dichotomy between respectability and disreputability, existed only to support social hierarchies; women, especially, were damaged by such distinctions.[44]

Thus, during the first decades of the twentieth century, working people's protests against the abuses of the rich spawned a conscious politicization of popular classes' sexual norms, as well as public affirmation of these norms' superiority over those of the more privileged classes. An inclusive discourse on sexuality was briefly consolidated in the Puerto Rican labor movement prior to World War I, one that embraced prostitutes as comrades in suffering and which, at least in theory, rejected marriage and the distinctions it legitimized between "respectable" and "disreputable" women.

Gender, Sexuality, and the Limits of the Male Left

The early Left's discourses about women and sexuality did indeed mark an impressive shift when compared to the public prostitution-bashing and rigid definitions of female respectability of the 1890s. But close scrutiny of the sources indicates that there were important limits to the FLT's gender radicalism. Total consensus on the validity of the new sexual politics was never reached. In addition, male leaders of the labor movement rarely, if ever, acknowledged working-class men's role in the oppression of women. And many of the men who publicly advocated free love and "women's emancipation" hoped to construct a new domesticity within which to confine "their" women.

The cursory written record of the debate over death benefits at the FLT's 1910 Congress provides a glimpse at the conflicts over sexual norms that existed within the FLT itself. At issue at this islandwide gathering of delegates was which types of relationship the FLT would recognize as legitimate, that is, which types would entitle surviving female partners to male workers' death benefits. A group of union members, led by R. Alonso, Eugenio Sánchez (who had performed the 1907 free love ceremony in Ponce, hailed by *Unión Obrera*), Pedro San Miguel, and Blas González, proposed that consensual unions be included along with married couples for full death benefit compensation. Santiago Iglesias, Manuel F. Rojas, and Juan Gómez García (three men often credited with the shaping of the "mature" Socialist Party) and several others vehemently opposed the initial language of the proposal, which simply required that a couple have "lived together consensually". After a heated debate, a compromise was reached that recognized couples who had lived in "free and loving union" for at least five years, had children together, and in which the man had officially declared the woman as his partner.[45]

The basic principle of "free and loving union" had been officially recognized by the FLT, but not without days of debate—and in a much more limited form than originally proposed. The approved version codified a more conservative, male-dominant definition of popular sexual norms. Bearing a child to a man was made paramount, rather than partnership in and of itself. And without a man's official, public declaration of his commitment, women could be left with nothing in the way of financial compensation for the permanent loss of male income. Ultimately, the power of relationship definition—which could have serious material consequences for women—was left in the hands of men.

Likewise, in the very early years of the labor movement, there was clearly no consensus on the issue of women in the workplace. A San Juan workers' newspaper, which proudly called itself socialist and published articles by a Spanish anarchist feminist, insisted that women should not work in factories. Puerto Rico's economy was not strong enough to sustain both sexes as organized wage laborers; there was not even sufficient work for all men. Women, these writers warned, would replace male workers; the loss of male jobs and the public presence of women in factories would produce social disintegration and widespread immorality.[46]

Tobacco rollers, supposedly the most "enlightened" of all male workers, were not impervious to such ideas about women entering their industry and job categories either. In 1914, men in the tobacco unions complained of the threat posed by "invading women."[47] To its credit, the FLT, led by Eugenio Sánchez, eventually reaffirmed its official policy to organize, rather than exclude women. But in 1915, female workers still encountered frequent foot dragging and hostility from their male "comrades."[48] Clearly, then, neither gender-inclusive organizing nor sexual radicalism were uncontested positions among FLT male militants. The celebrated feminism of the early Puerto Rican male Left was far from unanimous.

In addition, even the most progressive male anarchists rarely acknowledged working men's role in the oppression of women. Instead, early twentieth-century working men's literature created stock villains of lecherous wealthy men, señoritos who sexually preyed upon plebeian women's economic vulnerability. Working-class unity was to be built around this sexually saturated excoriation of elite men.[49] In male anarchist writings, almost total silence surrounded questions of rapes by working men, the sexual double standard *within* the working class, plebeian men's infidelities, and their own abandonment of partners and children. Likewise, women's need for sexual and economic autonomy from men of their own class was a nonissue. FLT male militants attempted to legitimize their project by invoking a demonized, masculine "other," which allegedly threatened their own benevolent protection of "helpless" working women. In the end, radical male workers were no better than male elites at admitting their own sexual privilege or exploitation of women.[50]

J. Limón de Arce, the only male anarchist author to acknowledge (and briefly at that) working men's violence against women, insisted that this brutality was solely a product of the men's degradation under capitalism. In Limón de Arce's vision of the new socialist man, restored to true manhood by collective struggle and class consciousness, domestic violence would wither away. Plebeian men's abuse of working women was not an expression of male dominance independent of class exploitation.[51]

Thus, to male anarchists, capitalism, and capitalism alone was the cause of women's suffering. "It is [capitalism] which robs the virtue of future generations and the vitality of women. . . . it is the horrible house of immorality and the school of dishonor."[52] Capitalism bound women into a brutal double day of labor, in both the home and the shop. It destroyed families, forcing women to leave their children and sick, elderly parents alone.[53] And perhaps most threatening of all, women's double exploitation eroded relations between the sexes. Women "are no longer tender companions, idolized friends, but slaves, irreconcilable enemies of the worker."[54] But slaves of whom? Certainly not the working men for whom plebeian women washed, cooked, and cleaned each day. It was the rich who "have taught men and women to hate each other, to declare a war to the death against each other, to stupefy each other with unjust accusations; they have only divided homes more and more with their vile messages."[55] Many anarchist men, then, insisted that women's wage labor was destroying the sanctity of the domestic sphere.[56] Under capitalism and its allegedly newly imposed burden of wage labor, women were indomitable shrews; conflict within the home came from their constant complaints. Revolution would free them from wage labor to focus all their energies on the home and thus would sweeten and tame them.[57]

The utopian future, male anarchists trumpeted, held not only a society without private property, classes, states, or organized religion, but also a reconstituted, conflict-free working-class domesticity: "The wife happily awaits the arrival of her husband or beloved companion at the door of a comfortable home, not a miserable hovel, in order to shower him with tenderness and caresses after his long day's work, *not to make him suffer and embitter his existence.*[58] Thus, the same anarchists who advocated free love, female suffrage, and the organization of women workers also dreamed of a gender order not unlike the Liberal bourgeois ideal—a clear separation of domestic and "public," "productive" spheres, with women safely circumscribed within the former and men proudly owning the latter.

The novelist and organizer Santiago Valle y Vélez painted a bucolic picture of such an ideal relationship—after moving in with her lover, Valle's heroine Magdalena stops selling vegetables in the marketplace and herding sheep. She tends the family garden and peacefully dedicates herself to the "labors of her sex," while her lover, Pascual, earns all their income.[59] The anarchist free-lover Angel Dieppa concurred with this vision, insisting that "women are made naturally for childrearing and the home, better than for the rough labor to which the present system has condemned them."[60] Other anarchists asserted that women should be "converted into mothers" in order to make the home a "temple of instruction" for their children.[61] Nowhere in male Left writings was it suggested that women should not be economically dependent on men, that domestic labor be collectivized, or that men might do such work.

Thus, by and large, the early radical men avoided direct challenges to plebeian male privilege. Women's oppression and conflicts between working women and men always came from outside the working class—whether in the form of rapacious "señoritos" or from the economic structures of capitalism and the social institution of marriage. Although all these factors were indeed key elements in the reproduction of women's subordination, radical men consistently ignored or downplayed plebeian men's own responsibility for women's plight. For many male anarchists, the answer to the "woman question" lay in establishing a classless world of reconstituted separate gender spheres, where working men could be benevolent patriarchs, providing for, protecting, and guiding "their" women. This restoration of the "natural" order that had been destroyed by class exploitation would reinstate gender differences while eliminating class divisions.

And this "natural" order of things, not surprisingly, would legitimize male leadership of women. Women had to be educated out of their religious superstitions and ushered into class consciousness by radical

men.[62] The downtrodden female victims of capitalism would be transformed into female warriors through class struggle *led by men*. A poem
published in *Unión Obrera* perhaps said it best:

> Rise up, woman! . . .
> Be valiant! . . .
> *You learn from me. . . .*
> You are the muse who inspires me, the rebellious Walkyrie
> who encourages me in the struggle. . . .
> This, woman, is how I dreamed of you. . . .
> *This, woman, is how I conceived of you in my mind. . . .*[63]

Women's purpose, then, was to serve their men as muse and help-meets;
valiant, rebel working women were to challenge only the wealthy, never
men of their own class. The radical man, in turn, would shape the militant woman, even intellectually and politically "conceive" her.

Indeed, in the narratives spun by both early twentieth-century male
activists and late twentieth-century male historians, working-class
feminism itself became the creation of radical men. Ramón Romero
Rosa, one of the early Puerto Rican male leftists most concerned with
the recognition of women as productive intellectual beings, was careful to point out that *men* would liberate women. Working men "should
explain to her how much she is worth as a woman and an intelli-
gent being."[64] Early twentieth-century women's radicalism, we also are
told by male labor historians of recent years, sprang from male tobacco
workers and their farsighted organizing.[65]

But the limited historical record provides hints that female workers
were not only politicized by the radical workshop culture; they were
themselves instrumental in forging the relative egalitarianism of the
early labor movement's gender discourses. Female tobacco stemmers'
complaint to Ramón Romero Rosa that the union was ignoring female
workers prompted the FLT to begin to organize women in 1905.[66] Likewise, the FLT's 1908 call for women's suffrage (the first such proposal
in Puerto Rico) was initiated and pushed at its islandwide Congress by
female members, among them Luisa Capetillo.[67] And in 1915, a group
of female workers published a protest in *Unión Obrera* against some of
their male comrades' behavior. Working men were not true socialists,
the women insisted, if they tried to prevent women from joining labor
and political struggles, denied women their right to intellectual devel-

opment, or kept women from earning their own living. These female militants stated in no uncertain terms that working-class men helped reproduce women's subordination.[68]

It is clear, then, that at the very least, working women formed some of the initial incentives to broaden the labor movement's gender agenda. In addition, they underscored issues that even the most radical men of their day avoided, such as women's need for economic autonomy from men of their own class, and working men's attempts to maintain power over women. It is also possible that women's presence in the labor movement, and their acute understanding that little separated them from women who sold sex for a living, contributed to the FLT's progressive discourse on prostitution.[69]

Working women, apparently, had their own definitions of what revolutionary social change should mean. Some of their concerns were eventually incorporated into the Left's agenda and ultimately presented as men's innovations. Many more were probably silenced by the chorus of male voices and power struggles that dominated the labor movement.

Few sources remain that could provide us insight into the female world of the early Left. As noted earlier, women's voices were rare in the FLT and anarchist newspapers. The labor movement's talk of women's rights was usually carried on—at least in print—by men. Not one issue of Luisa Capetillo's newspaper for working women, which circulated for about a year in San Juan, has been preserved in Puerto Rican archives. Records of the accomplishments and ideas of female organizers such as Carmen Rosario, Martina González, and Paca Escabí have barely survived through scanty comments in FLT newspapers; none of these women wrote memoirs or series of essays as did male workers like Ramón Romero Rosa, Bernardo Vega, or Jesús Colón. Consequently, the richness of debate, ideas, and experience that surely existed among leftist women and between them and the men around them has largely been lost to history.

Fortunately for feminist historians, however, one working woman of this period did manage to leave a substantial historical record. Luisa Capetillo—anarchist, feminist, and labor activist—published four books from which can be gleaned a wealth of information about women's analysis of power relations and their dreams of justice. It is to her writings that we now turn.

Feminism "Desde la Mujer": Luisa Capetillo's Sexual Politics

Despite her unusual corpus of written intellectual production, Luisa Capetillo has only recently begun to receive serious political and scholarly attention. Yamila Azize began the recovery of Capetillo's feminist legacy in *La mujer en la lucha* (1985). Norma Valle Ferrer's biography of Capetillo and Julio Ramos's sensitive essay on her importance in Puerto Rican letters have also deepened considerably our understanding of Capetillo's politics and the challenges she faced in her day.[70] It is my hope that this brief discussion of her analysis of sexuality will aid in the collective project of establishing Luisa Capetillo among the ranks of great Puerto Rican popular intellectuals.

For Capetillo, sexual autonomy was as key to women's emancipation as economic self-sufficiency, education, and class struggle. By 1910, when she founded a newspaper in San Juan for working women, she had decided that her feminist campaign had to promote "women's freedom in *all* aspects of our lives."[71] This included opening discussion on "the sexual question" and placing it at the center of politics.[72] "In the modern age, women have been conceded rights and privileges, but they are still slaves. Enslaved, not in intelligence, nor in their labor, but by sex. In intelligence, women rival men; in their work, they are equal in activity, initiative, and perseverance. They have freedom and rights in everything, except in love, in the right to freely and frankly choose. This, male egotism still denies them."[73]

Capetillo's formulation of sexual politics marked a historical watershed. Although the early Left had already opened a space for such a discussion, and some anarchists had begun to articulate a radical sexual ethics, sexuality was not considered a *political priority* by the labor movement or left-wing parties. As we have seen, prostitution and cross-class sexual abuse were symbolically important in the movement's self-definition. Likewise, early radicals discussed the need to shift the terms of the sexual contract between men and women. However, these and related issues were not considered "truly political"; they were not formally acknowledged as organizing tenets of the workers' movement. Not one of the numerous official published platforms of the FLT or the Socialist Party, for example, ever mentioned the recognition of "free unions," divorce reform, or the rights of "illegitimate" children, despite the fact that these issues were of clear concern to working people and were debated within the labor movement itself, especially during its first decade. Despite their presence in the radical discourses of the period, these remained secondary questions, on the periphery of formal politics. Wages, working conditions, the right to organize workplace unions, worker education, debunking ruling-class nationalism, and later, electoral campaigns, on the other hand, were all given center stage by the male-led worker organizations and publications. In short, production, patriotism, and parties were "really" political, and therefore had priority over sexual issues.

Capetillo may have agreed with that platform during her first years in the Left. Her first collection of essays focused exclusively on restructuring the relations of production, although female workers loomed large in her analysis.[74] But by 1910, Capetillo was loudly asserting in no uncertain terms that sexuality *was* political, indeed central to a truly revolutionary agenda. Her play *Influencias de las ideas modernas* ends with a female worker exhorting women to reject the institution of marriage as a crowd of workers shouts, "Long live free, loving unions! An end to exploitation! An end to the reign of the wage!"[75] Thus, Capetillo tried to break the primacy of production; for her, bodily autonomy was essential to a broader liberatory project.

In addition, Capetillo was acutely aware that individual men, as well as institutions and structures, oppressed women. Certainly, horrifically low wages, terrible working conditions, and lack of democratic rights trapped working women in a cycle of poverty and powerlessness. However, men created and fought to maintain the laws, customs, and economic relations that perpetuated women's subordination. Men "are guilty of our ignorance, our slavery, of which they take advantage."[76] And not only wealthy men were to blame for plebeian women's misery.

Working men not infrequently abandoned their partners and children economically, but perhaps even more painful was their sexual betrayal of women. Capetillo opened her first feminist tract with a passionate denunciation of male infidelities and returned to the theme over and over again in subsequent essays and plays. She expressed the deep rage women of all classes felt at men's "right" to multiple sexual partners.[77]

Capetillo also sharply criticized men's preoccupation with the sexual control of women. Neither financial support nor marriage contracts gave men the right to own women and their bodies. Rather, men should control their own sexual drives; they should remain virgins—"not belong to a woman"—until fully mature and ready to settle down and create a family.[78] Those men who asserted sexual ownership of women, were unfaithful, or did not fully love their partners should be left, with no second thoughts.[79]

Luisa Capetillo, then, not only rejected the honor code's obsession with female virginity and fidelity, but actually applauded those women who stepped outside the bounds of propriety. Indeed, women had a responsibility to leave unsatisfactory or abusive relationships. Those who did not she deemed "stupid" or "idiots." Capetillo was especially contemptuous of women who hung on to the social and economic privilege gained by their attachment to men. These women, she scoffed, were weaklings who were willing to lose their dignity to avoid conflict and controversy.[80] This right to leave unworkable relationships was the essence of Capetillo's definition of free love.

Capetillo's vision of free love coincided in many ways with that advanced by her fellow male anarchists. However, unlike her male comrades, Capetillo was careful to point out that not only the permanence and coldly contractual nature of marriage sowed the seeds of conflict within couples. Men's refusal to treat women properly did so as well. Capetillo also discussed men's violence against women and its impact on children as well as on the battered women.[81]

And although Capetillo firmly advocated both men's and women's right to leave unworkable relationships, she also recognized women's particular economic vulnerabilities. Consequently, Capetillo insisted on men's economic responsibility for all their children, regardless of their relationship with the mother.[82] In addition, she repeatedly stressed the importance of women's economic self-sufficiency.[83] Again, Capetillo's contempt for the economic dependence of middle- and upper-class "ladies" was clear. "The woman who accepts slavery because she does not know how to work is an idiot."[84]

But economic issues were not the only area where Capetillo broke new ground. While advocating the control of male sexuality, she also spoke boldly of women's capacity for sexual pleasure and their right to experience it. Women, she insisted, "have strong sexual appetites, which, like in a man, are a great virtue."[85]

Thus, Luisa Capetillo broke the silences that preserved many aspects of male dominance within anarchist men's versions of free love.

In her reconceptualization of heterosexual relationships, she attempted to simultaneously address multiple aspects of women's concerns—economic vulnerability and the ability to escape male abuse; control of male sexual drives and women's right to experience their own. In Capetillo's feminism, women's autonomy was inseparable from male economic and sexual responsibility.

But how well received was Capetillo's feminist project? Plebeian women's responses to Capetillo's project are especially difficult to judge because we have lost sources such as her working women's newspaper. But despite her impassioned calls to solidarity among women, Luisa Capetillo's writings display little trace of the strong feminine network that sustained feminists in Europe, the United States, and among the upper classes in her own country. Rather, her words betray a strong undercurrent of frustration at society's lack of response to her ideas.[86]

It is entirely possible that Capetillo's assertion of both sexes' right to separation at any time was too frightening to working-class mothers. Plebeian women, especially those with children, faced deepening social and economic vulnerability with the increased mobility, fragmented communities, and shifting social relations of the early twentieth century. With no ability to count on state enforcement of child support outside of marital relationships, Capetillo's call for male economic responsibility was probably not nearly sufficient to counterbalance the fear—and ever present reality—of male desertion.

Capetillo's refusal to acknowledge the contradictions in women's lives may have limited her popular appeal as well. Her unrelenting scorn for all women, plebeian or wealthy, who depended on male income or feared to leave unsatisfactory relationships excluded great numbers of potential female allies. In some senses, judgment seems to have been easier for Luisa Capetillo than sympathy. She had braved single motherhood, poverty, and social condemnation with her head held high; those women who hesitated to follow her lead were not worthy of consideration.

Capetillo's stinging critiques of male dominance and the priority she gave to her sexual politics also contributed to her marginalization within the Left. Not surprisingly, resistance to Capetillo's feminist message was keen among working-class men. She bitterly complained that numerous working women stopped subscribing to her newspaper because self-described "enlightened" union men labeled it immoral.[87]

Luisa Capetillo, then, was fighting an extremely steep uphill battle in her campaign to "liberate women in all aspects of [their] lives." Although she gave public voice for the first time to many aspirations of plebeian women and exposed the silences that lurked in the counter-hegemonic sexual discourses of male anarchists, Capetillo's lonely feminist struggle was not enough to overturn the deeply entrenched structures and practices that supported male dominant sexual norms—of either the elites or the popular classes.

Her position must have been weakened even further by the decline of anarchism within the Puerto Rican labor movement. U.S. colonial officials carried out a sweeping repression against anarchists during 1911 and 1912, forcibly closing study centers and jailing key activists.[88] Many anarchist organizers fled Puerto Rico; Capetillo herself lived in exile in New York, Florida, and Cuba for several years following the crackdown. Concerted state repression against anarchists opened a space for the movement's dominance by "reformers." Men such as Santiago Iglesias and Eduardo Conde successfully consolidated their position as the principal leaders of the FLT during these years; Ruben Dávila charges that they failed to protest vigorously the state's crackdown against FLT anarchist members because it eliminated their competition.[89]

The new leadership bequeathed an uneven legacy to the Puerto Rican Left. They founded the Socialist Party and built it into a significant mass movement; the period between 1915 and 1930 is usually celebrated as the heyday of the Left in Puerto Rico. But the new leadership also tied the FLT firmly to the increasingly conservative American Federation of Labor in the United States. And perhaps most important for our purposes here, they closed the small but significant space that had opened for questioning gendered power relations within the Left.

Along with the anarchists was suppressed their broader critique of the family and sexual relations. With the exception of the Bayamón newspaper *El Comunista*, which circulated for a few short months during 1920, and Luisa Capetillo's last book, published in 1916, discussions within the labor movement of free love, the institution of marriage, and the sexual double standard all ceased during the second decade of the twentieth century. Even Juan Vilar, who allegedly supported free love and women's equality in his early days as an organizer, study center director, and children's theater producer in Caguas, made no mention of sexual issues in his book *Páginas libres*, which was published in 1914, after his release from a long stint in prison.

The broad analyses of the "woman question" that had been developed by Luisa Capetillo, and even by her male anarchist comrades, were effectively silenced. The focus on production, which had always marked the Puerto Rican Left's understanding of "the political," became even more pronounced and was eventually fused with its post-1915 prioritization of electoral politics.[90] Radical sexual reform was definitively eliminated from the labor movement's agenda—indeed, the suppression of such discussions may well have boosted the Left's popularity among the male electorate. Thus, with the institutionalization of the labor movement and the growth of its influence on the island's formal state structures was lost the fleeting historical moment when, in however conflictual and flawed a way, Puerto Rican working people's struggle for justice linked critiques of capitalism and sexual power relations.

Notes

1. For a detailed analysis of this process, see Eileen J. Findlay, "Domination, Decency, and Desire: The Politics of Sexuality in Ponce, Puerto Rico, 1870–1920" (Ph.D. dissertation, University of Wisconsin, Madison, 1995), chap. 4.

2. The United States was seen initially by Puerto Rico's poor as the bearer of democracy, political rights, and economic opportunity that would liberate them from Spanish repression and mitigate their exploitation by Puerto Rican elites. Fernando Picó, *1898: la guerra despúes de la guerra* (Río Piedras: Ediciones Huracán, 1987); Angel Quintero Rivera, *Conflictos de clase y política en Puerto Rico* (Río Piedras: Ediciones Huracán, 1977); Gervasio Luis García and A. G. Quintero Rivera, *Desafío y solidaridad: breve historia del movimiento obrero puertorriqueño* (Río Piedras: Ediciones Huracán, 1986).

3. Joan Scott, *Gender and the Politics of History* (New York: Columbia University Press, 1988), 49.

4. For examples of analogous limitations of male leftists' theory and practice elsewhere in the "Third World" and Europe, see the essays in Sonia Kruks, Rayna Rapp, and Marilyn B. Young, eds., *Promissory Notes: Women in the Transition to Socialism* (New York: Monthly Review Press, 1989); Mabel Bellucci, "Anarquismo, sexualidad y emancipación femenina: Argentina alrededor del 1900," *Nueva Sociedad*, 109 (September–October 1990): 148-157; Dora Barrancos, *Anarquismo, educación y costumbres en la Argentina de principios del siglo* (Buenos Aires: Editorial Contrapunto, 1990); María del Carmen Feijoo, "Las trabajadoras porteñas a comienzos del siglo," in *Mundo urbano y cultura popular: estudios de historia social argentina*, edited by Diego Armus (Buenos Aires: Edi-

torial Sudamérica, 1990): 181–311; Martha Ackelsberg, *Free Women of Spain: Anarchism and the Struggle for the Emancipation of Women* (Bloomington: Indiana University Press, 1991); and Joel Wolfe, *Working Women, Working Men: São Paulo and the Rise of Brazil's Industrial Working Class, 1900–1935* (Durham, N.C.: Duke University Press, 1993).

5. See, for example, "La Censura" from the artisan-supported Republican Party Ponce newspaper *La Patria,* April 10, 1899. In terms quite common for the period, this editorial described U.S.-sponsored liberty and justice in the form of an enraged woman, who strode through the streets whipping the "guilty rich" until they hung themselves "like Judas." For a few other examples of the relationship among democracy, civil rights, and economic justice, see "Abusar de la humildad," *La Democracia,* November 14, 1898; *La Democracia,* November 2, 1898, p. 3; "El cinismo de ayer," *La Justicia,* May 3, 1901; L. de Argensola, *Se despejó la incógnita,* loose pamphlet, September 15, 1902; "Al País," *El Aguila de Puerto Rico,* January 9, 1902, p. 1; "¿Serviles?" *El Aguila de Puerto Rico,* June 19, 1902, p. 2; and "Vaya el obrero al taller y la política al infierno," *Unión Obrera,* March 26, 1905, p. 1.

6. During the last decades of the nineteenth century, coffee had surpassed sugar as Puerto Rico's primary export. After the U.S. occupation, however, the coffee industry began to decline. Unlike sugar and tobacco, coffee did not enjoy tariff protection from "foreign" (non-U.S.) competition in U.S. markets. This factor, combined with the loss of its preferential access to traditional Cuban and Spanish markets, led to its demise. Francisco Scarano, *Puerto Rico: cinco siglos de historia* (San Juan: McGraw-Hill, 1993), 592–593.

7. Scarano, *Puerto Rico,* 584–590; García and Quintero Rivera, *Desafío y solidaridad,* 67–81. Ponce cane cutters' wages and working conditions are deplored in "Correspondencia de la isla—Ponce," *La Justicia,* January 30, 1915, p. 3.

8. Scarano, *Puerto Rico,* 590–592; Angel G. Quintero Rivera, "Socialista y tabaquero: la proletarización de los artesanos," *Sin nombre,* 8, no. 4 (March 1978): 12; Amílcar Tirado Avilés, "Notas sobre el desarrollo de la industria del tabaco en Puerto Rico y su impacto en la mujer puertorriqueña, 1898-1920," *Boletín del Centro de Estudios Puertorriqueños,* 2, no. 7 (Winter 1989–1990): 18–23.

9. Yamila Azize, *La mujer en la lucha* (Río Piedras: Editorial Cultural, 1985), 40–60; Marcia Rivera, "Incorporación de las mujeres al mercado de trabajo en el desarrollo del capitalismo," in *La mujer en la sociedad puertorriqueña,* edited by Edna Acosta Belén (Río Piedras: Ediciones Huracán, 1980), 41–65. For complaints about the low wages of female urban workers, see "Notas de Ponce," *Unión Obrera,* September 11, 1911, p. 3, and "La mujer obrera en Puerto Rico," *La Justicia,* February 6, 1915, p. 1.

10. See Quintero Rivera and García, *Desafío y solidaridad,* 34–81 for an over-

view of this period. Mariano Negrón Portilla discusses the violence between workers loyal to the Republican Party and FLT members in *Las turbas republicanas, 1900–1904* (Río Piedras: Ediciones Huracán, 1990). Rubén Dávila Santiago describes the short-lived attempt of a small group of workers to establish "moralizing circles" as an alternative to both the FLT and the Federación Regional in 1907. *El derribo de las murallas: orígenes intelectuales del socialismo en Puerto Rico* (Río Piedras: Editorial Cultural, 1988), 137–145.

11. Angel G. Quintero Rivera, *Patricios y plebeyos: burgueses, hacendados, artesanos y obreros. Las relaciones de clase en el Puerto Rico de cambio del siglo* (Río Piedras: Ediciones Huracán, 1988), 109.

12. Santiago Iglesias, often hailed as the father of Puerto Rican socialism, was the leader of the "reformist" group. Dávila Santiago, *El derribo*, 58–60, 88, 141–145.

13. Ibid., 201.

14. Ibid., 89.

15. Rubén Dávila Santiago, *Teatro obrero en Puerto Rico (1900–1920): antología* (Río Piedras: Editorial Edil, 1985), 12. Julio Ramos also characterizes the early radical worker culture in Puerto Rico as extremely heterogenous and felicitously "undisciplined." *Amor y anarquía: los escritos de Luisa Capetillo* (Río Piedras: Ediciones Huracán, 1992), 27.

16. "El ideal del siglo XX," *Voz Humana*, September 2, 1906, p. 1.

17. Dávila Santiago, *El derribo*, 130–168; Quintero Rivera, "Socialista y tabaquero," 100–137.

18. Julio Ramos provides a compelling portrait of this radical tobacco workers' culture that stretched throughout the Spanish-speaking Caribbean and its diaspora in Florida and New York City. He points out that owners of the tobacco factories fought to end the practice of worker readers. Employer attempts to eliminate these positions were even the focus of several strikes. *Amor y anarquía*, 19–27.

19. For discussions of women's labor in the textile industry, see Lydia Milagros González García, *Una puntada en el tiempo: la industria de la aguja en Puerto Rico (1900–1929)* (Río Piedras: CEREP, 1990); and the essays in María del Carmen Baerga Santini, ed., *Género y trabajo: la industria de la aguja en Puerto Rico y el Caribe hispánico* (Río Piedras: Editorial de la Universidad de Puerto Rico, 1993), and her "Women's Labor and the Domestic Unit: Industrial Homework in Puerto Rico during the 1930's," *Boletín del Centro de Estudios Puertorriqueños*, 2, no. 7 (Winter 1989–1990): 33–39, and "La articulación del trabajo asalariado y no asalariado: hacia una re-evaluación de la contribución femenina a la sociedad puertorriqueña (el caso de la industria de la aguja)" in *La mujer en Puerto Rico: ensayos de investigación*, edited by Yamila Azize Vargas (Río Piedras: Ediciones Huracán, 1987): 89–111.

20. Tirado Avilés, "Notas sobre el desarrollo," 23.

21. "El 1º de mayo de Ponce," *Unión Obrera* (Edición de San Juan), May 9, 1903, and "Movimiento obrero," ibid., p. 2; "Noticias," ibid., September 25, 1906, p. 3; "Noticias," ibid., March 4, 1907, p. 4; and ibid., March 7, 1907, p. 2, April 21, 1907, December 18, 1904, November 20, 1918, October 14, 1919, and May 7, 1907.

22. Quintero Rivera, "Socialista y tabaquero", p. 117, and *Patricios y plebeyos*, 267–274. Yamila Azize heartily concurs, from a feminist perspective. Azize insists that from the very beginning, most male tobacco workers had a "progressive attitude toward women" due to the men's "high cultural level." *La mujer en la lucha* (Río Piedras: Editorial Cultural, 1985), 50–94, 118–131. For other celebratory accounts of the early labor movement's gender inclusiveness, see Tirado, "Notas sobre el desarrollo", 23–29, and García and Quintero Rivera, *Desafío y solidaridad*, 75–78. The only exception I have found to this heroic feminist male Left narrative is Julio Ramos's insightful essay on Luisa Capetillo. *Amor y anarquía*, 30.

23. "Las calumnias oficiales," *Luz y Vida*, August 30, 1909, p. 5.

24. "Noticias," *El Combate*, December 3, 1910, p. 3. See also Edmundo Dantes [José Limón de Arce], *Redención* (San Juan: Tipografía "El Alba," 1906), reproduced in Dávila Santiago, *Teatro obrero*, 143, 183–202; Juan S. Marcano, "Páginas rojas," excerpted in *Lucha obrera en Puerto Rico* (Río Piedras: CEREP, 1972; article first published 1919), 67; Santiago Valle y Vélez, *Magdalena* (Mayagüez: Imprenta "Gloria," 1908), 27, 68; and Alejandro Sux, "Surge mujer!" *Unión Obrera*, September 7, 1911, p. 3.

25. "La huelga de Ponce," *Unión Obrera*, August 18, 1911, p. 1; "Meditando sobre el problema," ibid., August 31, 1911, p. 3.

26. This practice contrasted with the American Federation of Labor's (AFL) decidedly lukewarm relationship with the Women's Trade Union League (WTUL) in the United States during this period. Meredith Tax discusses the AFL's undercutting of the WTUL in *The Rising of the Women* (New York: Monthly Review Press, 1980), 102–109, 115–123.

27. "Dignificación de la mujer," *Unión Obrera*, August 21, 1906, p. 3. See also "Nuestra enseñanza," ibid., January 11, 1910, p. 2; Marcano, "Páginas Rojas," 66, 67; and Dantes, *Redención*, 171.

28. Jesús M. Balsac, "Primero de mayo" and Paca Escabí de Peña, "Nuestra misión," both in *Páginas del obrero* (Mayagüez: Imprenta la Protesta, 1904); Juan Vilar, *Páginas libres* (San Juan: Compañía Editorial Antillana), 77; Valle y Vélez, *Magdalena*, 57; Angel María Dieppa, *El porvenir de la sociedad humana* (San Juan: Tipografía "El Eco," 1915), 30; R. del Romeral [Ramón Romero Rosa], *Musarañas. Opúsculo sobre ciertas preocupaciones y costumbres que son un estorbo a los trabajadores puertorriqueños para la compenetración de los revindicadores ideales del obrerismo universal* (San Juan: Tipografía de El Carnaval, 1904), 43.

29. J. Elias Levis, "La huelga," *El Tipógrafo*, April 16, 1911, p. 2. See also the female characters in Magdaleno González's plays. In "Los crímenes sociales," Guita, a young working-class girl, persistently explains to her brother the nature of class exploitation and the need to develop strategic, collective forms of resistance. Juanita, the daughter of the local capitalist, sympathizes with the workers, defends hungry children from the police and wealthy bullies, and by the end of the drama cries out that she embraces the workers' cause. Magdaleno González, "Los crímenes sociales," in *Arte y rebeldía*, reproduced in Dávila Santiago, *Teatro obrero*, 319–320, 322–323, 327–329, 334 (play first published Caguas, 1920).

30. For some examples, see Juan de M. Vélez, "Ocho años depúes," *Unión Obrera*, April 2, 1905, and Juan Vilar, "Así está la sociedad," ibid., October 13, 1911, p. 3; and Magdaleno González, "Pelucín el limpiabotas a la obra del sistema capitalista," *Arte y rebeldía*, reproduced in Dávila, *Teatro obrero*, 341–354.

31. Dávila cites at least six plays and novels in which such rapes play a central role. *Teatro obrero*, 94. See also "A las uniones . . .", May 22, 1902 (unattributed flyer, in the Colección Puertorriqueña of the Universidad de Puerto Rico, Río Piedras); "¡¡No importa!!" *Unión Obrera*, November 21, 1906; "La hija del crimen," *Luz y Vida*, September 30, 1909, pp. 9–10; and "The Tyranny of the House of Delegates of Porto Rico," 1913, reprinted in Quintero Rivera, *Lucha obrera*, 50–51.

32. Dantes, *Redención*, p. 140.

33. "La ramera," *El Comunista*, December 18, 1920, p. 3. See also Dieppa, *El porvenir*, 29–31; "1º de mayo. '¿Civilizados?'" *Unión Obrera*, May 1, 1907; "2º Congreso obrero de Puerto Rico: labor que tiene que ejecutar," *Unión Obrera* (San Juan), July 19, 1903, p. 1; and "¿Quiénes somos?" *El Comunista*, July 10, 1920, p. 1.

34. Dieppa, *El porvenir*, 29, 31. See also Juan Vilar, "La ramera," in *Páginas libres* (San Juan: Compañía Editorial Antillana, 1914), 74–75.

35. "Lazo de amor libre," *Unión Obrera*, March 30, 1907, p. 1.

36. Dávila Santiago, *El derribo*, 182–184.

37. Luis Figueroa, personal communication, February 25, 1989.

38. Juan José Baldrich, personal communication, April 4, 1991.

39. Norma Valle Ferrer, *Luisa Capetillo: historia de una mujer proscrita* (Río Piedras: Editorial Cultural, 1990), 81.

40. Venancio Cruz, *Hacia el porvenir* (San Juan: Tipografía República Española, n.d.), 49, 99–105; Julio Camba, "Matrimonios", *El Comunista*, October 30, 1920, pp. 2–3; Dieppa, *El porvenir*, 30.

41. Julio Camba, "Matrimonios," *El Comunista*, October 30, 1920, p. 2.

42. Ibid., p. 3. See also Dieppa, *El porvenir*, 41, and Dávila Santiago, *El derribo*, 182.

43. Valle y Vélez, *Magdalena*, 57–58; Dieppa, *El porvenir*, 47, 50–55; Juan José

López, *Voces libertarias* (San Juan: Tipografía La Bomba, n.d.), 9; "Matrimonios y divorcio," *Unión Obrera*, March 7, 1907, p. 1; *Unión Obrera*, March 8, 1907, p. 1.

44. For a detailed discussion of Puerto Rican popular sexual norms, see Findlay, "Domination, Decency, and Desire." Of all the free lover anarchists, Luisa Capetillo was the most explicit in her references to Puerto Rican popular sexual norms. See *Mi opinión sobre las libertades, derechos, y deberes de la mujer, como compañera, madre, y ser independiente* (San Juan: Times Publishing Co., 1911), vii, 28–29, 78; "La influencia de las ideas modernas," in *Influencias de las ideas modernas: notas y apuntes, escenas de la vida* (San Juan: Tipografía Negrón Flores, 1916), 42–43; and "En el campo, amor libre," in *Influencias*, 181–185.

45. *Procedimientos del Sexto Congreso Obrero de la Federación Libre de Trabajadores de Puerto Rico, celebrado del 18 al 24 de marzo de 1910, en la ciudad de Juncos* (San Juan: Tipografía de M. Burillo and Co., 1910), 102–103.

46. "Adelanto y desmoralización," *Federación Obrera*, February 4, 1899, p. 3. See also "Don Simón: ¿Va usté mirando?", "¡Siempre socialista!", and "Triqui-Traque," ibid., January 21, 1899. This more conservative vision should not come as any surprise, even within anarchosyndicalist circles. A similar gender worldview was articulated by Pierre-Joseph Proudhon, and it was further developed by Ricardo Mella in Spain. Proudhon and Mella saw women primarily as reproducers, whose roles in the domestic sphere should be enhanced in value but whose work outside the home should be decidedly secondary to men's. Mikhail Aleksandrovich Bakunin, followed by the Spanish anarchist Isaac Puente, argued against such conceptualizations of gender roles. Like Puerto Ricans such as Ramón Romero Rosa and Luisa Capetillo, Bakunin and Puente insisted that women were equal to men and that their full and equal incorporation into the waged labor force was the key to their emancipation. Ackelsberg, *Free Women*, 25; Mary Nash, "Estudio Preliminar," *Mujeres libres: España, 1936–39* (Barcelona: Tusquets, 1976), 10–11.

47. Federación Libre de los Trabajadores de Puerto Rico, *Actuaciones de la Segunda y Tercera Asambleas Regulares de Tabaqueros de Puerto Rico* (San Juan: Tipografía Murillo, 1914), 48.

48. *Unión Obrera*, November 10, 1915, cited in Azize, *La Mujer*, 70; "La independencia de la mujer del siglo XX," *La Justicia*, June 26, 1915.

49. "2° congreso obrero de Puerto Rico: labor que tiene que ejecutar," *Unión Obrera* (San Juan), July 19, 1903, p. 1; R. del Romeral [Ramón Romero Rosa], "En serio y en broma," ibid. (San Juan), June 14, 1903; Dantes, *Redención*, 141; "¡¡No importa!!" *Unión Obrera*, November 21, 1906, p. 2; Torres de Solón, "La hija del crimen," *Luz y Vida*, September 30, 1909, pp. 9–10; "Ironía de patricios," *Unión Obrera*, January 25, 1910, p. 1; Vilar, *Páginas libres*, pp. 74–75; "¿Quiénes somos?" *El Comunista*, July 10, 1920.

50. Ramón Romero Rosa was the one exception. He discussed male artisans'

sexual objectification of women in their nineteenth-century casinos and social events. However, his treatment of this "contradiction" within the working class implied that he saw it as a practice rooted in a prepolitical, unenlightened age, now quickly passing from the stage of history. *Musarañas*, 11-12.

51. Dantes, *Redención*, 164-175.

52. "El infierno del gobierno invisible en Puerto Rico," *La Justicia*, July 28, 1924, p. 6.

53. Dieppa, *El porvenir;* R. del Romeral [Ramón Romero Rosa] *Unión Obrera* (San Juan), March 1, 1903, p. 1; Marcano, *Páginas rojas*, 66.

54. Dieppa, *El porvenir*, 47.

55. Cruz, *Hacia el porvenir*, 40. See also Dieppa, *El porvenir*, 47.

56. Again, the exception was Ramón Romero Rosa, who wrote enthusiastically that "Puerto Rico will become great, with its women's work in workshops and factories, which will moralize our society. . . . We have to put an end to what was said until very recently—that women were only good for household chores." R. del Romeral [Ramón Romero Rosa], "En serio y en broma," *Unión Obrera* (San Juan), May 17, 1903, p. 2.

57. *Luz y Vida*, September 15, 1909, p. 6.

58. "Casos y cosas," *Luz y Vida*, December 30, 1909, p. 6; emphasis added.

59. Valle y Vélez, *Magdalena*, 57. See also Dieppa, *El porvenir*, 47.

60. Dieppa, *El porvenir*, 47.

61. Vilar, *Páginas libres*, 36; Dieppa, *El porvenir*, 47.

62. Alfonso Torres, "El amor y el ideal," *Luz y Vida*, August 30, 1909, p. 4; Juan Marcano, "Páginas rojas," 67.

63. "¡Surge, mujer!" *Unión Obrera*, September 7, 1911, p. 3.

64. R. del Romeral, *Musarañas*, 11.

65. Amílcar Tirado Avilés asserts that atheism, the necessity of class struggle, and the importance of worker education were all absorbed by women through their exposure to radical male·tobacco culture. By implication, then, women were simply receptors of male ideas, not intellectuals and historical actors in their own right. Tirado reduces even Luisa Capetillo, who clearly acknowledged her intellectual and political debts to other women, to an example of a woman radicalized solely by her contact with the male-led and conceptualized labor movement. Tirado quotes only one female worker in his article; she recounted in properly feminine form: "Basilio taught me how to understand our problems, and when he died, he left me with a different consciousness." "Notas sobre el desarrollo," 26. Angel Quintero Rivera, Gervasio García, and Rubén Dávila Santiago also see the early Puerto Rican Left in this light. Quintero and Dávila should be given credit for making Capetillo's work available to the general public; they included excerpts from her plays in their collections of worker's writings. See *Lucha obrera* and *Teatro obrero*. However, none of these scholars

even mentions Luisa Capetillo or her female compatriots in his own historical analyses, which have been crucial in reconstructing the history of the early Puerto Rican Left. This virtual silence on women's contributions is striking, particularly because Capetillo left behind such a substantial published corpus.

66. Azize, *La Mujer,* 50.

67. Ibid., 93–94; Valle Ferrer, *Luisa Capetillo,* 67.

68. *Unión Obrera,* November 10, 1915, cited in Azize, *La Mujer,* 70.

69. Female workers' broadening of male anarchists' organizing and discursive strategies did not only take place in Puerto Rico. Joel Wolfe discusses a dramatic example of this process in São Paulo. "Anarchist Ideology, Worker Practice: The 1917 General Strike and the Formation of São Paulo's Working Class," *Hispanic American Historical Review,* 71, no. 4 (1991): 809–846.

70. Valle Ferrer, *Luisa Capetillo;* Ramos, *Amor y anarquía,* 11–69.

71. *Influencias,* prologue.

72. *Mi opinión,* 182.

73. "La mujer en la época primitiva," in *Mi opinión,* 148.

74. Luisa Capetillo, *Ensayos libertarios* (Arecibo: Imprenta Unión Obrera, 1907). The essays contained in this collection were written between 1904 and 1907. Julio Ramos notes the shift in Capetillo's thinking to include nonproduction issues; he contends that Capetillo was the first proletarian woman to infuse the question of woman's role with "specificity and autonomy." *Amor y anarquía,* 51–53. Martha Ackelsberg also noted that the elderly Spanish anarchist women she interviewed during the 1970s and 1980s often expressed disdain for second-wave feminists' "fixation" on sexuality. These women took it for granted that a woman's body should be her own, but scoffed at the notion that this was a "political" issue. Prostitution, however, was another matter, for it clearly displayed women's class exploitation. *Free Women,* 3, 133–140. Prostitution was also the only sexual issue deemed to be "political" by Argentinian male anarchists in the early twentieth century. Maxine Molyneux, "No God, No Boss, No Husband: Anarchist Feminism in Nineteenth-Century Argentina," *Latin American Perspectives* 13, no. 1 (Winter 1986): 119–146, esp. 136–137.

75. "Influencias de las ideas modernas," in *Influencias,* 50. See also "Recuerdo a la Federación Libre," in *Mi opinión,* 182.

76. "La mujer en la época primitiva," in *Mi opinión,* 150. See also her "Notas, apuntes, pensamientos, conceptos, definiciones, sentencias y reflexiones filosóficas, naturistas, psicológicas, moralistas," in *Influencias,* 53, 56, 92–93; "Influencias," in ibid., 41; *Mi opinión,* 15–16.

77. "La corrupción de los ricos y la de los pobres, o como se prostituye una rica y una pobre," in *Influencias,* 179; *Mi opinión,* 6–10, 16–19, 26–29, 30–32, 74–78; "Notas," in *Influencias,* 53; *Influencias,* 76, 93.

78. *Mi opinión,* 7, 28–36, 51, 74–78; *Influencias,* 41, 91–93.

79. *Mi opinión,* 7–9, 16–17; "Influencias," in *Influencias,* 49.

80. *Mi opinión,* 9, 17–18.

81. Ibid., 11–12; "Notas," in *Influencias,* 56.

82. *Mi opinión,* 9–10, 13, 17–19, 27–28; "La influencia," in *Influencias,* 49, 93.

83. *Mi opinión,* 9, 17, 31; "Notas," in *Influencias,* 56; and *Influencias,* 93.

84. *Mi opinión,* 17.

85. Quote from Magdalena Vernet, "El amor libre," reprinted in *Mi opinión,* 38–55. See also "Notas," in *Influencias,* 66, and *Influencias,* 93.

86. *Mi opinión,* xi; "Influencias," in ibid., 41; "Notas," in ibid., 56.

87. *Mi opinión,* 183, and "Cartas interesantes de un ácrata de Panamá," in ibid., 150–151. Interviews with Capetillo's male contemporaries confirm her complaints. Valle Ferrer, *Luisa Capetillo,* 77–78, 80, 100–101; Quintero Rivera, *Luchas obreras,* 34.

88. See Dávila Santiago, *El derribo,* 181–216 for a discussion of this repression and its role in the consolidation of the reformist leadership's power within the Puerto Rican Left.

89. Ibid., 192–203.

90. Historians of Argentinian working-class feminism have noted a similar pattern. With the emergence of socialism as the dominant force within the Left, anarchist critiques of the family, male dominance, and authoritarian power more generally were all dropped. Molyneux, "No God," 139–141; Feijoo, "Las trabajadoras porteñas," 305–309.

BARRY CARR

"Omnipotent and Omnipresent"?

Labor Shortages, Worker Mobility, and Employer Control in the Cuban Sugar Industry, 1910–1934

⁙

For more than 200 years, sugar has been Cuba's main agricultural crop and export, shaping the island's political and social life and patterning the development of the island's ports, roads, and railroads.[1] Sugar called into being and then shaped new labor forms based on slavery as well as on indentured and free labor. It massively altered the geographical and demographic structure of the island and reworked land tenure arrangements in a whirlwind of land clearances and mill construction. Finally, "Sugar Power"'s explosion of gold and green deepened Cuba's insertion into the circuits of international capitalism, introduced new social relations of production, and, in so doing, traumatized entire social classes, fueled the nationalism and anti-imperialism of planters and workers, and, finally, ruptured state and civil society.

By 1870, sixteen years before the formal abolition of slavery, Cuban sugar mills employed a mix of free, indentured, and slave labor. But the unwillingness of slaves to reproduce themselves in adequate numbers, the high cost of slaves, the technical sophistication of the most advanced sugar *fábricas* (factories), and the huge capital requirements flowing from the modernization of the mills reduced the attractiveness of servile labor and forced an epochal reorganization of the ways sugar was produced and milled. There were two crucial features of this reorganization. First was the creation of a system of sugar factories, known as *centrales*.[2] Many of these new "factories in the fields" were financed by U.S. and British capital through credit and loans advanced by sugar merchants and sugar mill equipment manufacturers. The second feature was the emergence of the *colonato* system. As sugar growing and milling became increasingly separate activities, the work of sugar cultivation (as opposed to milling) was handed over to a class of independent planters and *colonos* (tenant farmers).

As the end of the century approached, the number of mills of all kinds fell sharply, although their size had grown substantially. Sugar output also exploded, driven by the new *central* system, further technical improvements in sugar extraction, and tariff changes that made the United States the most important market for Cuba's sugar. The disruption of the sugar fields and population losses caused by the independence struggles of 1895 to 1898 wrought havoc in the sugar sector. As ruined Cuban and Spanish planters went bankrupt and sold off their properties, more mills passed into foreign hands. But peace and the signing of the U.S.-Cuban Reciprocity Treaty in 1903 restored Cuban production to preindependence levels.[3] One year before the First World War erupted, Cuban mills pushed production over the 2-million-tons mark. In that same year, U.S. investment in Cuban sugar hovered around $200 million. In the virgin lands and forests of eastern Cuba, regions with little prior history of sugar cultivation, American companies such as the Rionda family's Cuba Cane, the Cuba Company, the Cuban American Sugar Company, the West Indies Finance Corporation, and the United Fruit Company constructed, acquired, or expanded many of the most dynamic centrales, the "colossi" of twentieth-century Cuba.

War was a great catalyst for the Cuban economy. Spurred by dramatic increases in the world price (sugar prices doubled in the first three months of the war), Cuba entered its most spectacular period of economic growth. Whereas its nearest rival, Java, produced two and a half times as much sugar as Cuba did in 1899, over the next ten years Cuba overtook its competitor and, by 1924, its sugar output was two and a half times that of Java's.[4]

The sugar boom was not without its challenges. Maintaining an adequate supply of labor was an especially intractable problem. In particular, the close association between fieldwork and coerced labor (slavery and indentured labor) obstructed the recruitment of free laborers well into the first decades of the twentieth century.[5] When the new mills of Camaguey and Oriente provinces increased the demand for labor, the traditional sources of field labor—Cuba-born workers, Spanish immigrants, and specially authorized contingents of Caribbean braceros—could not cope. Pressure from mill owners and from the U.S. Food Administration Agency soon forced the government to authorize, for the first time, unlimited importation of contract laborers.

Recruiting sufficient labor for cane cutting was a symptom of a more general problem. During the expansionary period, employers not only experienced labor "shortages"; they also confronted a high degree of labor mobility. The vast new agroindustrial complexes in eastern Cuba, for all their pretensions to constitute independent fiefdoms and centralized and isolated zones of employer authority, never succeeded in totally dominating their workforces. This chapter examines the reasons for this failure of hegemony. It shows how the structure of the sugar mill complexes, high levels of worker mobility, and the survival of subsistence alternatives to exclusive dependence on wage labor constrained employer ambitions. Centrales were rightly condemned for their arbitrary, exploitative, and often violent practices. But this should not conceal the complex forms of worker resistance and accommodation.

Agriculture and Industry: Fields and Batey

Sugar's industrial sector was concentrated within and around the *batey*, or central yard. In some areas, especially the eastern provinces, where centrales were often a long way from the nearest town, the batey resembled a small city, supplying many of the services that might have been provided by established towns in older provinces such as Las Villas, Matanzas, Havana, and Pinar del Río.[6] As a bare minimum the batey incorporated the buildings involved in the processing of sugarcane, administrative offices, a sugar laboratory, foundries, carpentry and machine shops, a distillery, facilities for handling and servicing railroad equipment, and electricity-generating plants. Centrales would often have their own post offices and an army post or buildings dedicated to the use of detachments of *guardajurados* (sworn guards). Where centrales had their own port facilities, the docks and their associated labor force formed part of the industrial sector of the batey.[7] In some cases, especially in the older sugar provinces such as Las Villas, proximity to well-established towns produced bateyes with no commercial facilities and little or no housing for workers, who instead commuted to work from neighboring towns such as Sagua, Encrucijada, and Cruces in central Cuba, and Morón and Ciego de Avila in Camagüey.[8]

The worst housing was always found in the smaller batey settlements located near the residences of middling and large colonos or, in the case of mill-controlled land, near the office that administered particular sections of administration cane (sugar cultivated directly under the management of the mill, as opposed to on land owned by colonos). In contrast with the architecturally planned and ordered housing of the central batey, these satellite population nuclei contained more rustic and less uniform housing. Even smaller population settlements sprung up spontaneously around the *chuchos* (rail junctions); they housed field laborers and workers involved in transporting sugar, as well as carters and rail workers.[9] Sugar estates, therefore, especially in Camagüey and Oriente, were characterized by dispersed patterns of settlement in spite of the massively conspicuous buildings that dominated the central batey area and which could easily give casual visitors a misleading impression of extreme centralization of authority and settlement.

This dispersed pattern of population distribution gave workers opportunities to evade or resist the hegemonic pretensions of mill authorities. But it also made it difficult for collective labor action to incorporate workers residing in all the locations scattered throughout the biggest estates. Thus, care has to be taken when referring to the large eastern sugar estates as sugar plantations. The word *plantation* conjures up images of huge integrated estates and mills, and this was unquestionably a feature of the central complexes. However, land ownership should not be confused with land use. With the exception of the so-called administration land, owned and managed by mill corporations (especially common in the East), most sugarcane was grown on a patchwork of *colonias* (farms) cultivated by the farm owners and tenants supplying each mill. This patchwork arrangement meant that fieldworkers, rather than confronting a single monolithic sugar mill complex, treated with one of the more modest tenant farmers or independent cane growers who supplied the central. Although colonos could be as authoritarian and exploitative as the most miserly central, relations between colonos and their fieldworker employees were generally marked by the more paternalistic tone characteristic of face-to-face encounters. On occasion this would produce significant, if short-lived and very unstable, coincidences of interest between colonos and fieldworkers, especially during times of economic hardship when conflicts between colonos and central management coincided with worker insurgency.

Of the fieldworkers, only 10 percent to 15 percent were permanent
or semipermanent agricultural laborers who had alternative employment during the *tiempo muerto* ("dead season") in cleaning, sowing,
and preparation of the soil and cane. The bulk of the remaining workforce was made up of seasonal workers who either farmed and harvested
other crops or cultivated their own plots of land, known as *conucos*. This
larger group, then, constituted a semiproletariat, resembling poor peasants but with links to agroindustrial sugar complexes that made them
more susceptible to social and political influences coming from the more
thoroughly proletarianized mill workers, engineers, and railroad men.[10]

Women were not widely employed in the fields in the twentieth century, although their presence in the workforce was more common in the
western provinces of Cuba than anywhere else and they had been widely
used under slavery and up to the last decade of the nineteenth century.
It is possible that the withdrawal of women and children from fieldwork may have been part of a worker-inspired strategy to reduce the
scale of employer control over the disposition of labor, whereas under
slavery work had often been imposed on planters in the form of family
labor.[11] The sex ratio among workers who emigrated to new sugar estates in the East may also have been skewed more heavily toward men
than had been the case in the older sugar-producing regions. Moreover,
in the East, imported bracero labor predominated, and it is known that
the first wave of emigrants from the British West Indies and Haiti contained a majority of males.[12] Nevertheless, oral evidence suggests that
in such areas as the Guantánamo valley, *cuadrillas* (labor gangs) of East
Indian women, contracted as seasonal workers, labored in the sugar
fields before the First World War.[13]

Labor Mobility

The central and the lands that supplied it were the "social territory" of
the estate and constituted a contested terrain in which mill owners and
work supervisors, factory and field workers, struggled to control space,
leisure, and production.[14] Certainly, arguments that sugar estates were
"omnipotent and omnipresent" institutions need to be questioned.[15] Although the contest between owners, managers, and workers was uneven
and the eventual outcome was often predictable, confrontation and re-

sistance were common and employers' power was never total. Although it is common to see references to centrales that present the sugar mills as semifeudal "closed" formations in which employers exercised private justice, engaged in coercive labor practices, and limited the mobility of workers, documentary and oral evidence suggests that this picture, especially the issue of worker mobility, needs modification.[16] Ever since the abolition of the final vestiges of slavery in 1886, when ethnic segregation ended in the sugar fields, a labor force of former slaves, downwardly mobile small *ingenio* (nineteenth-century sugar-milling unit, before the establishment of centrales) owners, impoverished smallholders, and immigrants from Spain, China, and later the West Indies had fluctuated in size from season to season and moved freely in and out of the bateyes and fields.[17]

Historians have systematically underestimated the mobility of the sugar labor force. The rapid expansion of the industry created a restless and mobile labor force that, until the early 1920s, was able to exploit the opportunities made available by the expanding sugar frontier, on which mill owners and planters scrambled to locate secure supplies of labor. The nuclei of the centrales in Havana, Matanzas, and Las Villas provinces were often older mills that had been modernized and expanded. These mills filled their increased demand for labor with workers from local sources—a traditional labor force inherited from the immediate postemancipation period—or with laborers recruited from the dense network of towns and communities that peppered these provinces. The newer and much larger centrales built in Camaguey and Oriente had no such luck, being located in areas of low population density. These mills were forced to import labor, both from other areas of Cuba and from the greater Caribbean.

During the boom period of the *vacas gordas* (literally "fat cows," i.e., boom time) which ended in late 1920, many Cuban sugar workers, like their confreres in the Dominican Republic, moved from mill to mill every three or four years, sometimes in response to ill-treatment, other times in a search for better work environments.[18] This migratory tendency was not new; after the abolition of slavery workers soon realized that mobility was one way of counteracting falls in wages.[19] Although conditions during the tiempo muerto were appalling, especially in the late 1920s and early 1930s, when the *zafra* (sugarcane harvest) was massively shortened, some workers found limited opportunities for work in nearby towns or even, in the case of mills in the central and western provinces, in the capital, Havana.[20] As late as 1933, at the most critical point of the Depression, organizational problems created by workers' continuing geographical mobility were still at the center of debate.[21]

Cuban crop cycles also encouraged a degree of labor mobility. Field-workers, especially Haitian immigrants, could combine activity in the sugar sector with work in other agricultural zones, most notably in tobacco growing in central Las Villas (where the *escogidas* [tobacco harvesting] took place between June and September, i.e., the tiempo muerto) and later in the booming coffee industry of the 1920s in the southern portion of Oriente province.[22] Coffee picking offered additional benefits. Payment was made to individuals rather than to the work teams used in cutting cane, where such abuses as illegal discounting of task payments proliferated. Thus incentives and rewards for hard work were more substantial than in the sugar fields, and laboring on the coffee farms was not as physically unpleasant. Coffee picking was also attractive because entire families could take part; among the Haitian immigrants, only the elderly and the sick did not make the trek from the heat of the cane fields to the cooler temperatures of the sierra region of Oriente in September and October each year.[23] The small amounts of capital and labor needed to initiate and manage a coffee farm (relative to the heavy capital investments and large labor forces required for even a small sugar colonia) meant that Haitian braceros were sometimes able to accumulate enough resources to become small colonos in the highland areas of southern Oriente, parts of which surely reminded immigrants of the rugged land surface of their homeland.[24]

Shortages of field labor were the norm right until the early 1930s, after which restricted production and a depressed economy produced a domestic labor surplus. However, employer complaints about labor scarcity and the poor discipline of native Cuban workers were as much a reflection of the harsh and arbitrary conditions dominating the sugar industry as they were well-founded statements about the Cuban labor market. As Michael Taussig has pointed out, in a different context, references to labor scarcity are frequently statements that labor will "not work appropriately, and this is a socio-political and cultural issue, not a demographic one."[25]

Nevertheless, labor shortages, whether caused by scarcity of people or unattractive remuneration and conditions, were serious matters especially for the largest mills, which required the output of several hundred acres a day to maintain efficiency. Centrales could not afford to pause during the zafra, and such events as cane fires, technical breakdowns in machinery, and delays in delivering cane, whether due to strikes or incompetence, were always a disaster. Interruptions to fieldwork caused by bad weather were also enough to cause sudden hemorrhages of labor as workers melted away to the drier fields of rival mills.[26]

Sugar Moves East

The demand for labor grew enormously during the sugar boom of the First World War, the "Dance of the Millions." Between 1900 and 1913, seventeen new mills were constructed; but over the period of 1914 to 1918 a further twenty-five mills were built, and existing mills doubled their capacity as the ferryboats from Key West brought in weekly shipments of sugarhouse machinery to meet the expansion and modernization.[27] The new eastern mills produced huge quantities of sugar. The combined production of just two mills, Vertientes and Morón, exceeded the total annual output of South Africa and Mauritius.[28] In 1925, Camaguey and Oriente produced over 53 percent of Cuba's total sugar, compared with 20 percent in 1904.[29]

Land for the new eastern mills was cleared by burning forests. Then the soil had to be prepared for planting while central buildings were being constructed. Forest clearance and other preparatory work for the building of the large Manatí mill in 1912 required 3,000 workmen to clear the 9,000 acres of forest; to attract laborers in a labor-scarce area "extra high wages" were "promptly paid."[30] In the area around central Stewart the clearing and preparation of 2,000 caballerías (1 caballería is equal to 33.3 hectares) of mainly wooded land employed nearly 10,000 men by early 1917.[31] Even after the disastrous collapse of the market in late 1920, mills continued to clear virgin land in the hope that the surprisingly buoyant condition of the world market, which enabled Cuba to sell a record crop in 1922, would continue. Deforestation only ended in 1926, when the Verdeja Crop Restriction Bill prohibited the clearing of virgin forest land for sugar planting.

The new and expanded mills consumed huge amounts of field labor. At Manatí, for example, 6,600 men were involved in cutting cane at the beginning of the 1927 zafra, while at Chaparra the extraordinary number of 10,000 workers were employed in the zafra.[32] Native-born workers could not or would not meet this increased demand for field labor. Instead, the appetite for labor was satisfied largely through immigration, first from Spain and the Canary Islands and then from Jamaica, Barbados, and Haiti.[33] By the early 1930s there were between 150,000 and 200,000 Caribbean braceros in Cuba.

Whatever the national origin of field labor, mill administrators during the boom years to 1920 never ceased complaining about the unreliability of their labor force. The superiority of Spanish workers, especially those with families, was a frequent refrain. But increasingly, as the immigrants became more assertive in defending their rights, the association between Spanish laborers and labor resistance made employers wary of these "disturbing" elements. Manuel Rionda, one of the most powerful sugar barons, argued that Puerto Ricans could not be trusted as they were U.S. citizens and might introduce American customs such as labor unions. He concluded that the ideal laborers were the Chinese. "They remain in the country; they never leave it; they don't go to dances and into the towns at night."[34]

Even after the initial burst of demand for labor during the opening up of new mills and sugar lands, difficulties in securing workers persisted. Mills in the older western and central provinces, with a dense population of colonos, had fewer problems either because many colonos provided family labor for agricultural tasks or because the work of recruiting labor was placed on the shoulders of colonos, who generally found it easier to obtain them. In the east, new entrants were forced to pay premium wages to attract a labor force—as at Tacajó, which had to compete with the huge mills of the United Fruit Company (UFC) nearby in the Antilla region in its first zafra.[35] But the new mills' voracious appetite for workers was difficult to satisfy on account of a more basic problem. The two eastern provinces, the traditionally pastoral Camaguey and Oriente, were sparsely populated in comparison with the older sugar-growing regions of the center and west. Farmers here had long been engaged in small-scale independent cultivation and were reluctant to lose their autonomy by becoming drawn into wage labor. On the eve of independence, in fact, the agriculture of Oriente province was easily the most diversified in Cuba. Sugar occupied 34 percent of all cultivated land, but the rest was occupied by a wide range of other crops including corn (12 percent), potatoes and yams (11.5 percent), manioc (6.4 percent), cocoa (5.9 percent), coffee (4.7 percent), coconut (5.2 percent), and bananas (15.5 percent).[36] The last two items were mostly grown on estates; all the remaining items were compatible with small-scale cultivation.

At the beginning of the century, Oriente's agriculture was relatively unaffected by the transformation in sugar technology that had appeared further west, and peasant smallholdings and rental arrangements were more prevalent. The number of Oriente farms halved between 1899 and 1904 as sugar cultivation expanded, new mills sprung up, and large corporations launched an assault on joint ownership of land, known as the hacienda *comunera* system, which was particularly prominent in eastern Cuba.[37] Nevertheless, the eastward drive of sugar capital took time to digest its prey, and diversity was still a feature of the eastern economy until the beginning of the Great War.

The challenge posed by the existence of a significant peasant sector and an insatiable demand for field and construction labor could only be met by immigration from other areas of Cuba and from outside of the island.[38] Low population densities and geographical remoteness also contributed to the demand for immigrant labor, as the general manager of the Tánamo mill in Sagua de Tánamo (Oriente province) explained in a worried letter to President Machado. In addition to the small population of the area around the mill, the manager complained, the peak labor demands for the tobacco-growing Cuban small farmers, who dominated agriculture in the area, coincided with the height of the equally labor-hungry sugar zafra, forcing Tánamo to import 4,000 Haitians as macheteros.[39] The preference for subsistence cultivation shown by poor rural cultivators in water-deprived areas of the central region of Oriente within the triangle formed by the towns of Holguín, Bayamo, and Palma Soriano was also a factor that made the supply of labor more precarious.[40]

Capturing Labor

The struggle to secure labor shattered efforts to create a solid planter and mill owner lobby. Even during strikes, such as the one held over demands for union recognition and an eight-hour day in mills in Santa

Clara and Camaguey in 1917, labor-hungry centrales and companies directing the construction boom in the sugar industry sent labor contractors by the dozen to "poach" striking *mecánicos* (mechanics or engineers).[41] On those occasions when civil insurrections occurred—the Liberal insurrection of 1906, the 1912 rebellion directed by the Partido Independiente de Color (Independent Party of Color), and the Liberal-led Chambelona (a rebellion that took place from February to May 1917)—labor discipline collapsed as workers joined the warring factions or vanished in the chaos provoked by the fighting.[42] In August and September 1906, for example, planters complained that cleaning and preparation of cane fields had become almost impossible because of the insurrection launched earlier that year in protest of the fraudulent reelection of President Tomás Estrada Palma. Field laborers fled the countryside to avoid being drafted by the warring parties or joined the ranks of the government forces for a daily pay of two dollars plus meals. Spanish immigrants were also reported to be wary of returning to Cuba for the new season because of the fighting.[43] In January and February 1917, when another Liberal rebellion seemed to threaten ruin, some colonos at Manatí were left without cart drivers, most of whom were "Negroes who are Liberals and they have had to leave."[44] At Francisco, the zafra was secured by a large contingent of Haitians and Jamaicans, who were convinced to stay by promises that they would be paid for any cane they cut even if it couldn't be loaded onto carts.[45]

Even in times of acute crisis and unemployment, mills and colonos complained of labor shortages. Thus, the U.S. consul at Nuevitas (on the coast of northeastern Camagüey) noted in February 1931 that wages were so low that the authorities were reduced to rounding up vagrants and locking them up in police stations after which they were given the option of working in nearby cane fields.[46] Two years later, the administrator of Céspedes complained that the mill's colonias retained only 300 of the 900 men who normally cut cane.[47] Moreover, the cultural and leisure pursuits of laborers in the postemancipation era continued to concern employers. In 1914, the minister of the interior, Carlos Hevia, was sufficiently worried by planter complaints that he issued a proclamation banning the holding of cockfights on working days in an attempt to promote greater discipline and lessen alleged worker indolence.[48]

Employer responses to labor shortages varied enormously. Domestic options were limited. In contrast to the sugar industries of northwestern

Argentina and the coast of northern Peru, Cuba possessed no reservoirs of indigenous labor capable of being mobilized either through *enganche* (labor contracting) or purchases of existing agricultural estates to tap the labor of their tenant smallholders.[49] Neither could Cuban planto-crats draw on servile forms of labor such as indentured immigration, the remnants of which survived in Guyana and Trinidad as late as 1917. The international "free" labor market proved much more promising. Immi-gration from Europe and the Caribbean was a major option to which employers had recourse in order to maintain a labor pool big enough to cover their fluctuating labor needs, which varied according to the sea-son, week, or even time of day.[50]

The absence of a domestic reservoir of precapitalist labor or overseas sources of semiservile labor was not the only obstacle; interplantation competition for labor also limited the mills' hegemonic aspirations.[51] This predicament made protection of their existing labor forces an urgent priority. Hence there were frequent proposals to restrict labor mobility in sugar areas and prohibit emigration. A meeting of the Asso-ciation for the Promotion of Immigration in November 1917 moved to petition the government to make able-bodied vendors of lottery tick-ets abandon "this easy method of making a living and be sent to the cane fields." In this way, the association believed, an additional 20,000 cane cutters could be obtained.[52] Much time was also spent in devising methods to curb the dishonest practices of contractors and moneylen-ders at the immigrant disembarkation points.[53]

Mill employers and the larger colonos were also notorious for poach-ing labor from rivals. A manager of the large U.S.-controlled Cuba Company, the desperate Mr. Whigham, noted that

of course there is not enough labor to go around, so one sugar mill has to steal from another. Every week or so I have had to bring in more people and have had to take a lot of surprising precautions to keep other mills from taking our people. As there is a public town here in front of the batey I cannot touch the labor contractors who are continuously here looking for people, unless they should go out of the town limits, when I see that they get their deserts.[54]

In newly opened regions, competition for labor allowed workers and labor contractors to devise elaborate scams. At Manatí in 1917, the man-ager, the elegant Spanish Marquis Eduardo Díaz de Ulzurrún, reported the discovery of a "trick" by which labor agents would deliver men and pocket the commission, subsequently "recycling" the same workers around several colonos, often in league with the lucky recruits.[55] In the period before the First World War, when European labor was still actively sought, labor recruiters hovered around the Triscornia quarantine station in Havana, ready to "capture" immigrants from Spain as they landed from ships and entice them to particular mills with promises of free transport and expenses. Even then, one planter sadly noted, "of every 100 who set out . . . possibly thirty actually work on the estate to which they depart from Triscornia. . . . they go their own sweet way and leave him pensive." [56] In order to avoid these problems the powerful sugar baron, Manuel Rionda, proposed the introduction of legislation requiring immigrants to carry *cédulas* recording personal details and a record of all monies advanced and work done together with the names and addresses of employers.[57]

Some employers, like the powerful UFC, fought hard, but not always successfully, to enforce uniform wage scales in their areas; in the case of the UFC, this effort required cooperation from banana growers, the only significant force competing for labor in the Banes and Nipe regions.[58] Other employers thought carefully about how the positioning of private rail spurs between their mills and public railroads might lessen labor recruitment problems.[59] And during the peak labor demand generated by the world war, employers worried over whether differences in pay and conditions between their mills and those of rival producers might provoke worker dissatisfaction.[60] Where all else failed, violence was used to persuade men, particularly cane cutters, to remain on estates. Thus, in a case that made it into the courts, several Haitian workers were killed in 1924 during an attempt by an administrator and *mayoral* (overseer) to prevent them from leaving a colonia during an acute labor shortage.[61]

Labor mobility could be slowed down by paying wages in the form of scrip or tokens or by advancing credit and thereby ensuring "fixity" through debt. Although there is abundant evidence of the widespread use of *vales* (tokens) until well into the 1920s, the scale of worker indebtedness achieved through the use of estate stores has not yet been clearly established.[62]

Finally, colonos deliberately set fire to their cane in order to accelerate harvesting and jump the queue in the rush with other colonos for scarce labor; burned cane needs to be harvested immediately, and mills gave it priority for processing.[63] Contracts between colonos and mills frequently stipulated that in the event of fires other colonos were obliged to assist the victim with their workers, carts, and equipment.[64]

Controlling Labor

Maintaining tight labor discipline was vital. It was also extremely difficult. There was no way to mimic the cultural, physical, and psychological mechanisms that maintained slavery or the coerced labor provided by Chinese indentured laborers. Therefore, in the free labor system, planters and mills depended on a mix of techniques to discipline their labor force. Like a palimpsest, a document overwritten many times with traces of each overlay, the system of labor control could be very complex. Internal order could be maintained by the use of army personnel, especially members of the Guardia Rural (Rural Guard), stationed on mill lands. Where this was not sufficient to preserve order, U.S.-controlled mills requested and received the protection of companies of American cavalry or marines on those frequent occasions when U.S. military forces occupied Cuban territory.[65] More commonly, estates could count on the protection of the guardajurados, who received accommodation and food directly from the mills' payrolls.[66] These special agents of the state were viewed with particular hatred by workers, so it comes as no surprise that workers vented their anger by burning down the guardajurado posts during the worker revolts of the summer of 1933. At Santa Lucía, workers from a nearby mill set fire to the guards' *caseta* and then tore down the chains that had controlled access to the batey ever since Spanish colonial times, jubilantly carrying this symbol of managerial power back to their union office.[67]

Although the use of force was never abandoned by even the most "modern" mills, there seems to have been a transition (in the decade before the First World War) in which mill and field production was increasingly regulated not only by despotic means but by methods in which the securing of consent was of great importance.[68] Progressive mills, for example, increasingly practiced a "paternalism of perquisites" ("enlightened selfishness" was the label used by Irene Wright to describe the attitudes of the U F C) by investing in schooling and health facilities in order to retain a healthy and therefore hopefully a loyal and grateful labor force.[69] Recreation was also provided. To help workers fill their "free time" during the dead season, Salvador Rionda of Manatí opted to build a sports field for baseball and football, although his New York–based uncle Manuel testily argued that workers would do better to spend their leisure time raising vegetables and flowers—a healthier and, he was quick to add, cheaper option.[70] The same urgent concern with labor capture and retention led mill managers to criticize price gouging by independent merchants because high prices inflamed the legitimate grievances of workers and might promote unrest. The solution, managers frequently argued, was for mills to set up their own commercial departments and, in the process, strengthen the vertical ties binding "loyal" workers to the mill.[71]

Although the commercial departments of those mills that most resembled enclave economies managed to recover a large part of the value of workers' wages, mill management personnel knew that high shop prices angered the labor force, encouraged demands for higher wages, and caused problems in recruitment.[72] In 1917, the most inflationary year of the Great War, Canary Islanders abandoned several colonias of Manatí complaining of unbearably high prices charged by the colono Edgardo Rabel. Manatí's administrator admitted that Rabel used his store to boost profits and insisted that other colonos who refused to speculate with their *tiendas* (stores) and gave workers freedom to make their purchases wherever they liked had no problems in keeping their laborers happy.[73] Whether prices charged at the mill stores were higher or lower than those of nearby competitors is impossible to establish as the situation varied immensely according to geographical location, differing costs of transporting merchandise, and whether the stores were owned by the mills or leased to third parties. But the stores certainly offered easy credit to their customers and enhanced the power domain of the mill's management over the batey and field labor forces.

These examples of employer action are a reminder of how paternalistic management styles functioned as a powerful mechanism of control. A combination of benign parent-child concern and firm responses to "inappropriate" worker behavior was at the core of managerialism. For the absolute authority of managers to function properly they needed "to have an overpowering presence, and for the worker to be made to feel it," a process of "magnification" as Dipesh Chakrabarty has put it in his study of Bengali jute workers.[74]

The living accommodations and style of managers were crucial to the reproduction of a quasi-colonial ruling-class culture. The class and ethnic differentiation of housing in the bateyes of eastern Cuba were exemplary features of this system of rigid class-color stratification. Cuban centrales, unlike the Indian jute mills examined by Chakrabarty, functioned in a formally independent country. Nevertheless, many of the newer and bigger sugar estates, especially those controlled by non-Cuban capital, were unashamedly enclaves—wedges of foreignness inserted into Cuban territory—and certainly displayed some of the paraphernalia of colonial nabobery. On these newer estates, most of them built in areas that had been on the margins of the sugar economy under slavery, there was little of the face-to-face relationship sometimes encountered in the older and often much smaller and Cuban-owned mills and estates of the central and western provinces.

The spatial and architectural characteristics of the bateyes constructed by the larger U.S.-controlled mills followed a common pattern—a "tropicalized Anglo-Saxon" clustering of private schools, churches, and recreational centers and a residential zone for management employees (referred to as "first-class Anglo-Saxon employees" by the UFC), the entire complex commonly known as the *barrio americano*. At the UFC's Preston mill, this zone was given the name *New York*—distinguishing it from the rather more proletarian-sounding "Brooklyn" barrio that housed ordinary workers.[75] Housing in the batey area, therefore, was strictly segregated along racial and socioeconomic lines. The senior administrator and *altos empleados* (white-collar employees) lived in detached houses or, if they were of sufficient rank, in more handsome dwellings often known as chalets, an attempt to inject a touch of bucolic elegance into these substantial buildings with their fine decorations and furniture. These labeling practices also established a linguistic barrier between the quarters of the better-off (and generally foreign) employees and the more indigenous, dusty and pungent accommodation provided (sometimes free of charge—in other cases for a small rent) for the semi-skilled and unskilled mill workers.[76] Caribbean migrant workers, on the other hand, were housed in specially equipped *barracones*, or barracks— recalling the slave quarters that served as the distant model for these long, single-story buildings of twenty or more rooms—as in the aptly named Barrio de los Jamaiquinos at Baraguá or in the UFC's "Brooklyn" at Preston.[77]

Elaborate houses, an abundance of servants, the preparation and serving of lavish meals—what Chakrabarty calls the "ritualised expression of a colonial ruling-class culture" and making a "spectacle of oneself"— were important parts of managerial power in the Cuban sugar industry.[78] No event was invested with more sparkle and spectacle than the opening of the zafra. Industrial and field workers awaited the start of the harvest season with enormous anxiety. Cleaners spruced up the mill's administrative buildings, and servants prepared the better-class houses to receive the technicians and senior managers flooding in by train and boat. The signal that the zafra had begun was given by a steam-driven whistle. Even in the depths of the depression, no expense was spared in organizing the public display to accompany the launching of the harvest. Distinguished guests might be invited for the occasion as at Senado, a major Camaguey mill, where the spectacle (and the prospect of bringing home exotic candies made of raw sugar) tempted the American society lady, Iona Garrison, to leave her West Palm Beach winter holiday home to operate the factory siren.[79]

Family Subsistence

More important than wages for sugar workers was the length of the zafra, which got progressively shorter in the 1920s or early 1930s. In the boom period the zafra could last eight or even nine months; Irene Wright noted that grinding at the United Fruit centrales of Boston and Preston in 1909 began on December 20 "and should go on continuously until mid-September."[80] In 1926, the average grinding period was 135 days.[81] By 1933 it had fallen to sixty-six days. In these circumstances workers could do little more than flee to the cities and draw on their subsistence fund.

Subsistence plots were the most common way of supplementing money wages. Studies of sugar agriculture in the decades following abolition in the Anglophone and Spanish-speaking Caribbean have emphasized the survival of precapitalist structures and relations of production within the increasingly capitalist mode of production that characterized the sugar sector. This nonlinear and highly uneven combination of forms and relations of production had important consequences for the political and sociocultural development of sugar labor forces. The survival and even flourishing of alternatives to exclusive dependence on wage labor available to fieldworkers would substantially shape patterns of worker resistance, accommodation, and strategies for maximizing well-being and autonomy. Just as the availability of a multiplicity of employment possibilities altered the dynamic of workers' relations with centrales and large colonos, so access by sugar workers to some means of production under their own control—even modest access could be crucial—might constrain the power of employers and strengthen the hand of workers.

The availability of nonwage forms of subsistence to workers embedded in wage labor systems has been little studied in Cuba, at least for the twentieth-century history of sugar. The dynamic character of sugar capitalism in the island, which made the colossal new centrales the epitome of the corporate land and factory combines discussed by Sidney Mintz, the eastward shift of cultivation and labor to virgin lands in Oriente and Camagüey provinces (which eroded the pre-boom-era traditions of small-cultivator autonomy), and the prominent role immigrant Haitians and British West Indians (who were supposedly without access to "local" histories of independent cultivation and nonwage labor) played in field labor may have all suggested that this is not a valid topic.

Some of these assumptions need major qualification. Jamaican immigrant workers came from a society in which many wage laborers still owned small properties; indeed, among Jamaicans "the legacy of land holding remained a powerful aspect of working class organization."[82] As for Haitian braceros, these immigrants of rural origin came from a Caribbean society with a long tradition of peasant smallholding agriculture. Moreover, the desperate need to secure a stable labor force led colonos and mills to cede small land plots to their Haitian labor force.[83] Certainly, the significance of subsistence resources for fieldworkers must have varied enormously according to factors such as the availability of land, the density of central construction in particular areas, and the degree of central monopoly over alternative forms of cultivation. But there is enough evidence to suggest that this is a promising trail to research.

As late as the mid-1930s some agricultural wage workers cultivated two to five acres of land, whose products supplemented family diets. The family surveys carried out by a research team in 1934 found this practice to be common and associated it with better-than-average diet and family welfare.[84] Access to extended families with land away from the cane areas may sometimes have alleviated hunger during the dead season. For example, Ursinio Rojas, later a Communist union official, recalls how when the zafra was over, he and his brother were sent to a small *finca* (farm) in a suburb of Holguín owned by their grandparents.[85] Even the most fragile degree of access to production could provide workers with opportunities to resist the hegemonic pretensions of employers.[86]

Many more workers had access to *conucos*, on which maize and *viandas* (root crops) were grown to supplement the family diet.[87] The conuco system's tributaries are to be found in the era of slavery when slaves produced portions of their own subsistence needs, constituting the beginnings of "protopeasantries."[88] The farming of slave provision grounds granted the plot owners a degree of autonomy and a group and individual identity that was separate from the overarching "unfreedom" in which they worked. Provision grounds have understandably been seen as "breaches" or points of vulnerability in a master-dominated world, instances that might have allowed slaves to gradually expand their fragile hold over independent spaces of cultivation to take control of production, marketing, and culture. As the Cuban runaway slave Esteban Montejo noted, "[conucos] were the salvation of many slaves, where they got their real nourishment from."[89] After abolition, however, Montejo noted, conucos were less common.[90] Nevertheless, as Rebecca Scott has reminded us, "the conuco . . . remained a model for subsequent agricultural activity" and reinforced the possibility of combining wage labor in the sugar fields with cultivation of food crops.[91] Writing in 1902, the U.S. labor specialist Victor S. Clark was also struck by how the reliance of Cuban field hands on "garden patches and other small holdings for their subsistence" during the dead season increased their tactical independence and unreliability as a source of labor.[92]

Even when conucos vanished, colonos sometimes raised sweet potatoes in the fire lanes on their lands. The colonias where these subsistence crops were grown were particularly attractive to macheteros, in particular Haitian braceros, because they promised to greatly cheapen living costs.[93] No group was better able to squeeze value out of the tiniest land plot. Haitian peasants, after all, brought with them an intensely microfundista consciousness born of a century of land subdivision in a country with an ever diminishing quantity of land in peasant hands. Moreover, Haitian workers were masters of the art of growing subsistence crops on poor soil and stony land using the pockets of moisture trapped in between impermeable rocks, a technique they developed in the mountainous areas of southern Haiti.[94] The remnants of this tradition of cultivating "plants," as the Haitians called them, were still visible in the 1970s. In addition, Haitians raised pigs and farm birds and manufactured charcoal—sometimes for sale—in imitation of traditional Haitian practices.[95]

The emergence and survival of subsistence plots responded to a set of complex circumstances—the availability of land; population densities; the cost to landowners, transmitted through wage demands, of feeding their workforces with imported foodstuffs or local subsistence production; and the changing profitability of sugar production. Periods of low prices for sugar and the brutal cuts in wages that accompanied such crises generated greater interest in locally produced subsistence crops by both owners and workers. Subsistence plots, therefore, became a lot more important during the depression, when conucos multiplied everywhere.[96] There was even considerable government propaganda to increase this kind of cultivation. The Cuban Congress spent a good part of early 1918 discussing the question of making cultivation of staples and truck crops obligatory in order to make laborers independent in foodstuffs at a time of rapidly inflating prices for imported food.[97]

Some mill owners, such as Manuel Rionda, had long encouraged the development of family plots. As early as 1917 the management of Francisco had tried to combat the sharply inflated food costs generated during the Great War by planting white potatoes, cabbages, yucca, and pumpkins and encouraging colonos to plant sweet potatoes and corn.[98] Conucos also multiplied at Francisco to cover virtually all the strips of land separating the cane rows, or *guardarrayas* (firebreaks), which were planted with *frutos menores* (common fruits i.e., of no commercial value), viandas, and grains.[99] The hope expressed by company managers was that eventually at Manatí and Francisco ("where the labor stays all the year round") "we will be in a position where most of our labor will be able to live cheaply and practically support themselves during the Dead Season."[100] *Problems of the New Cuba* noted that some mills in the winter of 1933 "had plowed up the cane rows and other spare land and had even made the workers plant subsistence crops."[101]

Although fieldworkers were the principal cultivars of subsistence plots, workers employed in the central and its industrial surrounds could also be involved in cultivation. Thus, at the end of the 1931 zafra, the

manager of the Báguanos and Tacajó Sugar Estates offered land to all of
its workers who were permanently situated in the batey. After some initial hesitation, the offer was taken up by families of all nationalities. The
company claimed that it gave out most of the pasture land around the
batey and provided ploughs and bulls free of charge, thereby enabling
its workforce to survive through the 1931 and 1932 tiempos muertos.[102]
Long after the worst effects of the depression were over, a few large
sugar companies institutionalized the practice of renting subsistence
farms to their batey workers. Mainly, it seems from the best-known case
—involving the UFC—this practice was designed to stabilize the labor
force and reduce pressure on wages by encouraging workers to produce
a portion of their own subsistence. By the early 1940s, the UFC, in addition to renting land to its more than 1,100 fieldworker tenants, leased
land to 750 tenants, who were described as "largely mill hands, over-
seers and skilled workers"—with plots averaging five acres per tenant.[103]

The fall in money wages and the drop in national income during the
depression led to a sharp increase in individual and small-scale food
and clothing production, which may have generated some income for
a portion of the rural population, either in the countryside or in small
towns.[104] Nevertheless, it is important not to exaggerate the availability
of nonsugar-based sources of income and food. Many mills, especially
U.S.-owned properties, were reported to be reluctant to allow their
workers, particularly in the batey, to engage in cultivation for fear that
access to subsistence farming would make them less willing to work.[105]
And where land plots were allowed, the conditions imposed by employers were often onerous (including a requirement that workers hand
over a portion of product cropped) and provoked conflict.[106] Thus, although any access to forms of subsistence production would confer
benefits to fieldworkers and other wageworkers, the degree of autonomy
and increased leverage in bargaining that it conveyed were much less on
land plots that were rented from mills or colonos, who in effect could
function both as employers and "benevolent" landlords. There were also
frequent employer and government complaints about the reluctance of
cane cutters in particular to plant food items on their conucos.[107] Finally,
signs of recovery in sugar prices often led mill companies to abandon
their interest in encouraging worker-cultivated subsistence plots.[108]

Conclusion

Descriptions of the sugar mill's socioeconomic and cultural system have often drawn on metaphors taken from feudal society. Thus Francisco Pérez de la Riva refers to the "semifeudal" character of the batey, in which ingenios and later centrales minted their own currency and maintained company stores. Juan Pérez de la Riva, in his otherwise excellent study of Caribbean migration to Cuba, refers to the "feudal microsystem" created by large foreign sugar companies, a world in which the Haitian immigrant worker was the *homme-lige* of the labor contractor, who owed loyalty to the colono, who in turn was dependent on the mill administrator.[109]

The chains of dependency binding workers to the mill complex were indeed substantial and omnipresent. But this should not blind us to the very real opportunities for maneuver and negotiation that workers could enjoy. This chapter has explored some of the ways in which workers could expand their autonomy during the period of expansion of the sugar industry.

The coming of the depression, whose periodization in Cuba is different from that in the rest of Latin America (it arrived earlier and hit harder than in any other country—with the exception of Chile), reduced the margins of manoeuver available to sugar workers. At this point workers developed more formal mechanisms of collective struggle (unions, parties), which were slow to develop in the sugar sector. The worker insurgency peaked in 1933, during the worker occupations of sugar mills. Although these actions might be (erroneously) viewed as unproblematic markers of political "modernity," they also incorporated forms of contestation that drew on earlier traditions—imported from the black Caribbean (Haiti and Jamaica), and also retained from local experiences of autonomy.

Notes

1. The paragraphs in this section draw on the work of Manuel Moreno Fraginals, *The Sugar Mill: The Socio-Economic Complex of Sugar in Cuba*, translated by Cedric Belfrage (New York: Monthly Review, 1976); Herbert Klein, *African Slavery in Latin America and the Caribbean* (New York: Oxford University

Press, 1986); Jules Benjamin, *The United States and Cuba: Hegemony and Dependent Development, 1880–1934* (Pittsburgh: University of Pittsburgh Press, 1977), chap. 1; Ramiro Guerra y Sánchez, *Sugar and Society in the Caribbean* (New Haven, Conn.: Yale University Press, 1964); and Julio Le Riverend, *Historia económica de Cuba* (Barcelona: Ediciones Ariel, 1972).

2. On the diffusion of central factories in the Caribbean, see Christian Schnakenbourg, "From Sugar Estate to Central Factory: The Industrial Revolution in the Caribbean (1840–1905)," in *Crisis and Change in the International Sugar Economy 1860–1914*, edited by Bill Albert and Adrian Graves (Norwich, England: ISC Press, 1984), 83–93. See also César J. Ayala, "Social and Economic Aspects of Sugar Production in Cuba, 1880–1930," *Latin American Research Review*, 30, no. 1 (1995): 95–99.

3. Manuel Moreno Fraginals, "Plantations in the Caribbean: Cuba, Puerto Rico, and the Dominican Republic in the late Nineteenth Century," in *Between Slavery and Free Labor: The Spanish-Speaking Caribbean in the Nineteenth Century*, edited by Manuel Moreno Fraginals, Frank Moya Pons, and Stanley L. Engerman (Baltimore: Johns Hopkins University Press, 1985), 20–21.

4. Francis Maxwell, *Economic Aspects of Cane Sugar Production* (London: Norman Rodger, 1928), 103.

5. Manuel Moreno Fraginals, "Migraciones asiáticas a Cuba: 1849–1959," in *La historia como arma y otros estudios sobre esclavos, ingenios y plantaciones* (Barcelona: Editorial Crítica, 1983), 118–144; Denise Helly, *Idéologie et ethnicité: les chinois macao à Cuba: 1847–1886* (Montreal: Les Presses de l'Université de Montréal, 1979).

6. *Batey*, a word of Indian origin, has two meanings, referring both to the central yard and associated buildings attached to a sugar mill and also the clustering of dwellings used by workers employed on the cane farms known as *colonias*. See Andrzej Dembicz, *Plantaciones cañeras y poblamiento en Cuba* (Havana: Editorial de Ciencias Sociales, 1989).

7. Most centrales, however, exported their production through multiuser ports like Nuevitas, Antilla, Puerto Padre, Caibarién, Cienfuegos, Caimanera, and Manzanillo.

8. José Ramón Cabrera y Pérez, *Memoria explicativa e ilustrada de varios centrales de Ciego de Avila, Camaguey—año 1919* (Havana: Montalvo, 1920), 51.

9. Dembicz, *Plantaciones cañeras*, 95; Oscar Zanetti and Alejandro García, *United Fruit Company: un caso del dominio imperialista en Cuba* (Havana: Editorial de Ciencias Sociales, 1976), 303.

10. This description of fieldworker composition summarizes the argument and data of Lionel Soto, *La revolución de 1933* (Havana: Pueblo y Educación, 1979), 1:235–236.

11. See the arguments (for the Guyana case) of Walter Rodney, "Plantation Society in Guyana," *Review*, 4, no. 4 (Spring 1981): 650–651.

12. Haitian women took part in cane cutting according to the authors of a study of one Haitian community in Camaguey. Jesús Guanche and Dennis Moreno, *Caidije* (Santiago: Editorial Oriente, 1988), 28. On female fieldworkers at the Rosario mill in Havana province, see *Historia del central Rubén Martínez Villena* (n.p., 1972), 41. An American report in 1917 estimated female and child labor as 5 percent of the total agricultural labor force, but this is an aggregate figure and it is not possible to establish the figures for female involvement in the sugar sector. U.S. Department of Commerce, Bureau of Foreign and Domestic Commerce. *The Cane Sugar Industry: Agricultural, Manufacturing, and Marketing Costs in Hawaii, Porto Rico, Louisiana, and Cuba,* Miscellaneous Series no. 53 (Washington: Government Printing Office, 1917), 63.

13. Jaime Sarusky, *Los fantasmas de Omaja* (Havana: Girón, 1986), 75.

14. I take the term *social territory* from Marta Petrusewicz, "Wage-Earners but Not Proletarians: Wage Labor and Social Relations in the Nineteenth Century Calabrian Latifondo," *Review* (Fernand Braudel Center), 10, no. 3 (Winter 1987): 477.

15. Contrast this opinion with George L. Beckford, *Persistent Poverty: Underdevelopment in Plantation Economies of the Third World* (New York: Oxford University Press, 1972), 55.

16. See, for example, Francisco Pérez de la Riva, "La habitación rural en Cuba," *Revista de Arqueología y Etnología*, 7, nos. 15-16 (1952): 305, and Juan Pérez de la Riva, "Cuba y la migración antillana 1900-1931," in *La república neocolonial: anuario de estudios cubanos*, vol. 2 (Havana: Editorial de Ciencias Sociales, 1979), 51-52.

17. Abolition was decreed in 1880, but a transitional period was introduced, guaranteeing mill owners a tied labor force at below-market prices. Rebecca J. Scott, "Class Relations in Sugar and Political Mobilization in Cuba 1868-1898," *Cuban Studies,* 15, no. 1 (Winter 1985): 23, and her "Defining the Boundaries of Freedom in the World of Cane: Cuba, Brazil and Louisiana after Emancipation," *American Historical Review*, 99, no. 1 (February 1994): 86, 87, 89.

18. See the accounts in Ana Núñez Machón, *Memoria amarga del azúcar* (Havana: Editorial de Ciencias Sociales, 1981). For confirmation of this feature at an earlier period of Cuban sugar history, see Scott, "Defining the Boundaries," 89.

19. Martín Duarte Hurtado, "La abolición de la esclavitud y las discusiones en torno a la repercusión de este hecho en la oferta de fuerza de trabajo," *Santiago*, no. 61 (March 1986): 145-146.

20. See, for example, the memoirs of Francisco García, *Tiempo muerto: memorias de un trabajador azucarero* (Havana: Instituto del Libro, 1969), 50-67. García, born in 1907, worked mostly in mills in the Santa Clara region.

21. "Un éxito: la Segunda Conferencia Nacional Azucarera," *El Trabajador*, 3, no. 4 (August 1, 1933): 8.

22. Juan Portilla, *Jesús Menéndez y su tiempo* (Havana: Editorial de Ciencias Sociales, 1987), 23. Some sugar estates, such as San Germán in Oriente province, were surrounded by coffee farms. Few Cubans worked in the coffee sector, according to Alberto Arredondo. Alberto Arredondo, *Cuba: tierra indefensa* (Havana: Editorial Lex, 1945), 347–349.

23. Guanche and Moreno, *Caidije,* 26–27. Wages for picking coffee were twice those earned cutting cane.

24. Joel James, José Millet, and Alexis Alarcón, *El vodú en Cuba* (Santo Domingo: Ediciones CEDEE/Casa del Caribe, 1992), 65.

25. Michael Taussig, *Shamanism, Colonialism, and the Wild Man: A Study in Terror and Healing* (Chicago: University of Chicago Press, 1987), 54.

26. This was a complaint at Tacajó in February 1918, where three solid weeks of rain the previous December had enabled rival mills (especially Chaparra) to poach labor. Manuel Rionda to Alfred Jaretzki, February 13, 1918, *Braga Papers,* University of Florida, Gainesville (hereafter cited as *Braga Papers*), RG II, Series 10A.

27. *Louisiana Planter,* 59, no. 17 (October 27, 1917): 264; Luis Aguilar, *Cuba 1933* (Ithaca, N.Y.: Cornell University Press, 1972), 41.

28. Maxwell, *Economic Aspects,* 65.

29. Brian Pollitt, "The Cuban Sugar Economy and the Great Depression," *Bulletin of Latin American Research,* 3, no. 2 (1984): 4.

30. *Louisiana Planter,* 1, no. 12 (March 22, 1913): 185–186. Construction work in general paid much higher wages than cane cutting, whereas planting new cane was paid for at even higher rates. However, after the 1920 crash, construction of new mills slowed greatly (the last new mill, Andorra, was built in 1927), and this particular source of pressure on the labor market disappeared. W. W. Craib (Jatibonico) to J. H. Whigham, June 1, 1915. *Cuba Company Papers,* University of Maryland, College Park (hereafter cited as *Cuba Company*), box 21, folder 37. Silvestre Rionda to Manuel Rionda, April 6, 1915, *Braga Papers,* RG II, Series 1, Silvestre Rionda/Colonia "La Esperanza". See also Ayala, "Sugar Production in Cuba," 115–118.

31. J. G. Ríos to Manuel Rionda, April 4, 1917, *Braga Papers,* RG II, Series 10A, Box 5, folder 11, Jaretzke, Alfredo 1916–1919.

32. Salvador Rionda to Manuel Rionda, February 19, 1929, *Braga Papers,* RG II, Series 10C, Manatí, Rionda, Salvador, General Manager, 1927. On Chaparra, see José Luis Luzón, *Economía, población y territorio en Cuba (1899–1983)* (Madrid: Ediciones Cultura Hispánica del Instituto de Cooperación Iberoamericana, 1987), 42.

33. One estimate is that the 1902 zafra required 4,500 *macheteros* whereas the 1913 harvest demanded 21,000. Pérez de la Riva, "Cuba y la migración antillana," 26.

34. Manuel Rionda to Victor Zevallos, August 6, 1917, *Braga Papers,* RG II, Series 2, vol. 43, letters from July 1917 to December 4, 1917.

35. Ursinio Rojas, *Las luchas obreras en el central Tacajó* (Havana: Editora Política, 1979), 153, n. 4; Zanetti et al., *United Fruit Company,* 243–244.

36. Robert Hoernel, "Sugar and Social Change in Oriente, Cuba 1898–1946," *Journal of Latin American Studies,* 8 (November 1976): 220–230.

37. Louis A. Pérez, "Insurrection, Intervention, and the Transformation of Land Tenure Systems in Cuba, 1895–1902," *Hispanic American Historical Review,* 65, no. 2 (1985): 245–254. Haciendas comuneras were land tracts owned by several individuals, whose rights were backed by shares (known as *pesos de posesión*) guaranteeing owners a share of the land and its value but not exact title to any particular piece of land. Over time families divided and subdivided their pesos de posesión until some haciendas had hundreds of co-owners. This Cuban form of *minifundismo* sustained thousands of smallholders in Oriente and Camaguey, imposing a barrier to the expansion of the sugar latifundium, which was removed by the passage of Civil Order no. 62 during the last year of the U.S. military occupation of the island.

38. On the peculiarities of the demographic and land tenure structure of Oriente, see Hoernel, "Sugar and Social Change," 220–230.

39. Eardley G. Middleton to President Machado, March 22, 1928, Archivo Nacional de Cuba, Havana (hereafter ANC), Secretaría de la Presidencia 121/66.

40. Rogelio Pina y Estrada, "Informe rendido por el Dr. Rogelio Pina y Estrada al Hon. Sr. Presidente de la República al Consejo de Secretarios Sobre la Inmigración, Haitiana y Jamaicana, June 29, 1934," 13, ANC, Secretaría de la Presidencia, 121/84.

41. John Dumoulin, *Azúcar y lucha de clases, 1917* (Havana: Editorial de Ciencias Sociales, 1980), 111.

42. Manuel Rionda to Bernardo Braga and Manuel Enrique Rionda, February 22, 1917, *Braga Papers,* RG II, Series 12, January–March 1917. Even the presence of U.S. Marines attached to sugar estates failed to stop rebel burning of cane, theft, and so forth. Mr. Gerard Smith to L. J. Rionda, March 12, 1917, ibid. For the vanishing trick played by skilled sugar mill workers in the Cruces and Cienfuegos region of Santa Clara province, see Dumoulin, *Azúcar y lucha de clases,* 111–112, and Louis A. Pérez Jr., *Lords of the Mountain: Social Banditry and Peasant Protest in Cuba, 1878–1918* (Pittsburgh: University of Pittsburgh Press, 1989), 180–188.

43. *Louisiana Planter,* vol. 37, no. 10 (September 8, 1906): 153, no. 11 (September 15, 1906): 168, and no. 13 (September 29, 1906), no. 18 (November 3, 1906): 282. For a report on the impact of the 1912 Estenoz revolt on labor conditions, see *Louisiana Planter,* 49, no. 3 (July 20, 1912): 44.

44. Eduardo de Ulzurrún to Regino Truffin, February 6, 1917, *Braga Papers,* Series 4, Confidential Letter Book, vol. 2. A June report noted that Francisco produced 196,000 bags as against an expected 375,000 bags and Elia produced 68,000 as opposed to 125,000 bags.

45. F. Gerard Smith to L. J. Rionda, February 15, 1917, *Braga Papers,* Series 4, Confidential Letter Book, vol. 2. Notwithstanding the labor shortages and insurrection, the 1917 sugar harvest was a record. American diplomats, U.S. Food Administration officials, and U.S.-owned mills unquestionably exaggerated the extent of the disruption to the sugar crop to justify military intervention and a relaxation of the Cuban government's restrictions on the importation of braceros. See Dumoulin, *Azúcar y lucha de clases,* 30–32.

46. E. A. Wakefield, "Political Situation in Nuevitas Consular District," February 6, 1931, U.S. National Archives, Washington (hereafter cited as USNA), RG 84, Havana Post Records, pt. 10, 1931, 800 Cuba.

47. "Extracto de carta dirigida a Barro por Douglas," February 4, 1933, *Braga Papers,* RG II, Series 11, Internal Correspondence 1933–1935, folder 2, December 21, 1933 to March 31, 1934.

48. *Louisiana Planter,* 52, no. 10 (March 7, 1914): 151. Judging by the memoirs of Esteban Montejo, both workers and colonos were equally addicted to cockfighting. Esteban Montejo, *The Autobiography of a Runaway Slave* (London: Bodley Head, 1968), 72–73, 98. For earlier (1888) employer interest in restricting cockfighting, see Rebecca Scott, *Slave Emancipation in Cuba: The Transition to Free Labor, 1860–1899* (Princeton, N.J.: Princeton University Press, 1985), 236.

49. Daniel J. Santamaría, *Azúcar y sociedad en el noroeste argentino* (Buenos Aires: Ediciones del IDES, 1986), 97; Bill Albert, "The Labor Force on Peru's Sugar Plantations 1820–1930: A Survey," in Albert and Graves, *Crisis and Change,* 203–207.

50. Rain and cane fires might generate sudden leaps (or contractions) in the demand for labor.

51. On indentured labor in the Hawaiian case, see Gary Y. Okihiro, *Cane Fires: The Anti-Japanese Movement in Hawaii, 1865–1945* (Philadelphia: Temple University Press, 1991), 59.

52. *Louisiana Planter,* 59, no. 22 (December 1, 1917): 342.

53. Ibid., 62, no. 3 (January 18, 1919): 38.

54. L. M. Evans (Superintendent Jobabo) to George Whigham, March 2, 1913, *Cuba Company,* box 31, folder 124. In May 1915, at the end of the zafra, the administrator of Jobabo mill accused the Manatí mill of paying twice the regular wage to get their cutting and planting done. Mr. Evans (Jobabo) to W. W. Craib, June 2, 1915, *Cuba Company,* box 21, folder 37. Jobabo also seems to have been able to siphon off labor from its rivals like the UFC mills

at Boston and Preston. *Louisiana Planter*, 1, no. 1 (January 4, 1913): 8. In the immediate aftermath of the independence war (when labor supplies had been greatly disrupted), poaching was also the norm. According to the testimony of a Louisiana congressman in 1902, "every planter seeks to get the laborer of his neighbor unless his neighbor is a friend of his." Testimony of R. F. Broussard in U.S. Senate, Committee on Relations with Cuba, *Cuban Sugar Sales* (Washington: n.p., 1902), pts. 1-7, 292. On interestate competition for labor in Hawaii, where planters used "runners" to raid workers employed on sugar estates with bad reputations, see Edward D. Beechert, *Working in Hawaii: A Labor History* (Honolulu: University of Hawaii Press, 1985), 108, 136.

55. Mr. E. D. de Ulzurrún to Regino Truffin, January 19, 1917, *Braga Papers*, RGII/10A, Manatí Sugar Company 1915-1917. For evidence of how Peruvian workers managed to swindle contractors by accepting advances from several rival enganchadores at the same time, with apparent impunity, see Michael González, *Plantation Agriculture and Social Control in Northern Peru 1875-1933* (Austin: University of Texas Press, 1985), 142.

56. *Louisiana Planter*, 1, no. 4 (January 25, 1913): 58-59.

57. Manuel Rionda to Victor (Zavallos) and Higinio (Fanjul), August 21, 1917, *Braga Papers*, RG II, Series 2, vol. 43, Letters from July 19, 1917, to December 4, 1917.

58. Zanetti and García, *United Fruit Company*, 239. The power of the UFC was such that it attempted to force other employers to act together on wage policy.

59. R. Truffin to Manuel Rionda, March 28, 1913, *Braga Papers*, RG II, Series 10A, folder 23. Manatí Sugar Co., 1911-1913. In 1913, the administrator of the newly constructed Manatí central in the extreme northwestern corner of Oriente province thought, for example, that building a rail link south to Victoria de las Tunas would exploit Manatí's geographical location as the "first [mill] to be reached at the entrance of the province of Santiago de Cuba" and give the plantation advantages over rival mills (farther to the east) like Chaparra, Preston, Boston, and Santa Lucía.

60. W. C. Van Horne to W. W. Whigham, January 6, 1915, *Cuba Company*, File 131, box 32.

61. *Gaceta Oficial*, 30, no. 123 (May 27, 1932): 98, 89-91.

62. Rebecca Scott, "The Transformation of Sugar Production in Cuba after Emancipation, 1880-1900: Planters, Colonos and Former Slaves," in Albert Graves, *Crisis and Change*, 114-126.

63. See the interesting report on sugarcane burning provided by a U.S. soldier in 1906. Captain J. A. Ryan to chief of staff, Army of Cuban Pacification, December 28, 1906, USNA, RG 350 (Bureau of Insular Affairs), Entry 5, General Classified Files, File 1495/11. See also Katherine Steele Ponvert, *Cuban*

Chronicle: The Story of Central Hormiguero in the Province of Las Villas, Cuba (Limited Edition, privately published, 1961), 38–39.

64. See the model contract published in Guerra y Sánchez, *Sugar and Society*, 199–200.

65. During the U.S. occupation of 1906 to 1909, U.S. troops were stationed at the Atkinses' Soledad mill, where they "added to the gaiety and interest of our lives" as noted in Edwin Atkins's memoirs. Edward F. Atkins, *Sixty Years in Cuba: Reminiscences of Edwin F. Atkins* (Cambridge: Riverside Press, 1926), 340.

66. Even when the Guardia Rural members made exorbitant and dishonest demands for financial help, sugar companies thought that they could "afford to treat them well" in order "to be on good terms with them." W. W. Craib (Jatibonico) to George F. Whigham, October 25, 1913, *Cuba Company*, box 31, folder 119.

67. Rojas, *Las Luchas obreras*, 82.

68. The terminology used here is from Michael Buroway, "Between the Labor Process and the State: The Changing Face of Factory Regimes under Advanced Capitalism," *American Sociological Review*, 48, no. 5 (1983): 587–605.

69. On schooling at Manatí, see *Braga Papers*, 10C, no. 3. Salvador Rionda to Manuel Rionda, April 26, 1928, Manatí, Rionda, Salvador C., general manager, 1928. A decision to allocate money for additional school accommodation at Manatí was clearly motivated, in part, by embarrassment at the unflattering comparison between its facilities and purpose-built schoolhouses constructed at the neighboring estates of Delicias, Chaparra, and Jobabo; Irene A. Wright, *Cuba* (New York: Macmillan, 1910), 483.

70. Salvador Rionda to Manuel Rionda, April 11, 1928, and Manuel Rionda to Salvador Rionda, April 26, 1928, *Braga Papers*, 10C, no. 3. Manatí, Rionda, Salvador C., General Manager, 1928.

71. William W. Craib (Jatibonico) to George E. Whigham, January 17, 1915, *Cuba Company*, File 131, box 32, folder 131.

72. In the case of the UFC properties in northern Oriente province, this percentage reached 50, Zanetti and García, *United Fruit Company*, 304–310. At the turn of the century, informants told the U.S. agricultural analyst Victor Clark that company stores were viewed as a source of profit. Victor S. Clark, "Labor Conditions in Cuba," *Bulletin: Department of Labor*, 7, no. 41 (July 1902): 697. For Francisco, see Gerard Smith to Higinio Fanjul, October 12, 1917, *Braga Papers*, Series 2, Smith, Gerard F., 1917 (Francisco Sugar Co.).

73. Ulzurrún to Manuel Rionda, June 3, 1917, *Braga Papers*, RG II, Series 1, box 26, Ulzurrún, Eduardo D de 1/1917–5/1917.

74. Dipesh Chakrabarty, *Rethinking Working Class History: Bengal 1890–1940* (Princeton: Princeton University Press, 1989), 166–167.

75. José Vega Suñol, "La colonización norteamericana en el territorio nor-

oriental de Cuba: 1898–1933," *Anales del Caribe*, 10 (1990): 220; Zanetti et al., *United Fruit Company*, 303.

76. Laborers at Manatí were charged for both housing and lighting. Salvador Rionda to Manuel Rionda, April 11, 1928, *Braga Papers*, 10C, no. 3. Manatí, Rionda, Salvador C. General Manager 1928.

77. Cabrera y Pérez, *Memoria explicativa*, 11. For the black and Caribbean worker zone ("Colored Section") maintained at the United Fruit Company's Preston mill, see José Yglesias, *In the Fist of the Revolution: Life in Castro's Cuba* (Harmondsworth, England: Penguin, 1968), 120–122, 162, and Zanetti et al., *United Fruit Company*, 303.

78. Yglesias, *In the Fist of the Revolution*, 167, 170.

79. *La Región* (Camagüey), January 16, 1932, p. 1.

80. Wright, *Cuba*, 481–482.

81. Foreign Policy Association, *Problems of the New Cuba* (New York: Foreign Policy Association, 1935), 281.

82. Abigail B. Bakan, *Ideology and Class Conflict in Jamaica* (Montreal: McGill-Queen's University Press, 1990), 9.

83. Guanche and Moreno, *Caidije*, 8.

84. Thus, in the case of family no. 15 from Santa Clara province, which was headed "by a field worker and carter who cultivates three and a half acres during the dead season," the team commented there was "only one worker in family of seven but his farming enabled them to have meat once a week even in the dead season." Family no. 33 (also from Santa Clara) was headed by "a field hand in cane and subsistence farmer during depression," which meant that the "diet [was] freely chosen now due to farming." Foreign Policy Association, *Problems*, 83, 85.

85. Rojas, *Las luchas obreras*, 41.

86. Jeff Gould discusses the politics of retreats to subsistence production (the "march to the parcela," he calls it) in his study of sugar workers in Chinandega. Jeffrey L. Gould, *To Lead as Equals: Rural Protest and Political Consciousness in Chinadega, Nicaragua, 1912–1979* (Chapel Hill: University of North Carolina Press, 1990), 27–28.

87. Rojas, *Las luchas obreras*, 22, 28, 41, 44.

88. Sidney W. Mintz, "From Plantations to Peasantries in the Caribbean" in *Caribbean Contours*, edited by Sidney W. Mintz and Sally Price (Baltimore: Johns Hopkins University Press, 1985), 134–135. On the significance of conucos for Cuban slaves, see also Scott, *Slave Emancipation*, 16–17, 149–150, 183.

89. Montejo, *The Autobiography*, 24.

90. Ibid., 97. Montejo notes that he never had a conuco himself "because I didn't have a family."

91. Scott, *Slave Emancipation*, 245.

92. Victor Clark, "Labor Conditions in Cuba," *Bulletin, Department of Labor,* 7, no. 41 (July 1902), 694.

93. Manuel Rionda to E. D. Ulzurrún, June 8, 1925, carta no. 19, *Braga Papers,* RG II, Series 10C, box 37, folder 9, Manatí, Ulzurrún, E.D. de 1926, Correspondence.

94. Guanche and Moreno, *Caidije,* 28–29.

95. Ibid., 30–32.

96. Rojas, *Las luchas obreras,* 44.

97. *Louisiana Planter,* vol. 60, no. 21 (May 25, 1919): 325.

98. Gerard Smith to Higinio Fanjul, October 12, 1917, *Braga Papers,* Series 2, Smith, Gerard F., 1917 (San Francisco Sugar Co.).

99. Ibid., 21, 41, 44. But not all mills allowed frutos menores in the guardarayas. On vegetable plots farmed by cane workers in the middle 1940s, see Lowry Nelson, *Rural Cuba* (Minneapolis: University of Minnesota Press, 1950), 66–67.

100. Salvador Rionda to Manuel Rionda, April 26, 1928, *Braga Papers,* 10CC., folder 3, Manatí, Rionda, Salvador C. General Manager 1928, Letter No. 24.

101. Foreign Policy Association, *Problems,* 78.

102. Mr. Grant Watson to London, July 31, 1933, Foreign Office Records, Public Records Office, London (hereafter PRO), FO 369, K9757/5888/214.

103. J. Merle Davis, *The Cuban Church in a Sugar Economy* (New York: Department of Social and Economic Research and Council, 1942), 122.

104. United States Department of Commerce, Bureau of Foreign and Domestic Commerce, *Cuban Readjustment to Current Economic Forces.* Information Bulletin no. 725 (Washington: Government Printing Office, 1930). "Cuban Readjustment," 8. This production was probably unrecorded in the official statistics.

105. Grant Watson to Foreign Office, London, February 21, 1934, PRO, FO 371, A 82031/211/14.

106. Batey-based workers at the Socorro and Conchita mills in Santa Clara province reported in mid-1931 that they had never been allowed to grow frutos menores. Leonardo Fernández Sánchez, "La desocupación y las marchas de hambre en Cuba," *Mundo Obrero* 1, no. 1 (August 1, 1931). The young Leví Marrero reported in early 1934 that workers at the huge Vertientes central were prohibited from planting frutos menores in the guardarayas of the cane fields or in any other area devoted to sugar. Leví Marrero, "Misería, acero y sangre: la rebelión campesina," *Bohemia,* 26, no. 7 (February 25, 1934): 21. Batey workers in the Jaguey Grande area reported in 1931 that they had been allowed to plant sugarcane for the first time in exchange for handing over one-third of the crop. "El terror blanco en los campos de Jaguey Grande, Cuba," *Mundo Obrero,* 1, no. 3 (October 1, 1931).

107. The *Problems of the New Cuba* research team suggested that scarce dead season work should be given first to those workers who were prepared to engage in subsistence food production. Foreign Policy Association, *Problems*, 446.

108. Ibid., 75.

109. Francisco Pérez de la Riva, "La habitación rural," 305; Juan Pérez de la Riva, "Cuba y la migración antillana," 51–52.

RICHARD L. TURITS

The Foundations of Despotism

Agrarian Reform, Rural Transformation, and Peasant-State Compromise in Trujillo's Dominican Republic, 1930–1944

❀

From 1930 until his assassination in 1961, Rafael Trujillo Molina ruled the Dominican Republic. His regime proved to be one of the most ruthless and long-reigning tyrannies in the history of Latin America. Given the stability of the regime and the enormous power Trujillo exerted throughout the country, one would expect to find that his rule was backed by key elements of Dominican society. Yet the existing literature has stressed only coercion and terror as the explanation for Trujillo's long, stable rule.[1] Both comparative and case studies of the regime have portrayed the state as being almost all-powerful, with its leader exercising nearly unlimited discretion, while, paradoxically, having no social base that would help explain Trujillo's exceptional power and longevity. The historiography of the Trujillo state thus contrasts sharply with that of most authoritarian regimes, in which scholars have found powerful or even broad sectors of society accepting dictatorial rule as a means of providing order, mediating social conflict, and controlling (or impelling) social and economic change. The putative state autonomy and absolute discretion of Trujillo's reign has made it appear to fit the ideal type of despotic or "sultanistic" rule as formulated by the social scientist Juan Linz; in fact, the contrast of the Trujillo regime with Francisco Franco's "highly institutionalized" dictatorship in Spain (1939–1975) served as the inspiration for Linz's model.[2]

Yet this essay suggests that even regimes such as Trujillo's, which have been classified as purely despotic and repressive, in fact depended on a social base and spheres of hegemony. Historians have tended to disavow the degree of popular support for Trujillo's policies in light of the totalitarian features and inhumane characteristics of his rule. I show, however, that Trujillo's efforts to achieve a type of rural populism and foster paternalistic policies were far more substantial than previously assumed. They were backed by concrete government actions and material benefits for those willing to offer both loyalty and productivity in return. Contrary to conventional assumptions, the regime distributed, and maintained peasant access to, large amounts of the nation's lands and thereby helped secure political loyalty or acquiescence among the peasantry.[3] Careful examination of this land distribution campaign, never before studied in depth, demonstrates how power was exercised under Trujillo less by autocratic decree than by a heterogeneous state, constant negotiation with elites, and exchanges, however unequal, with popular sectors. This system of rule suggests that power even in highly authoritarian regimes may be far more dispersed and conditional than has generally been assumed. Squatters, peasants, landowners, foreign corporations, local officials, and members of the central state all competed to shape both the intent and outcome of Dominican rural policies. Although the land campaign responded to the balance of power and interests in each particular situation, overall the policies that emerged were ones that were relatively appealing to broad sectors of the rural population.

Peasant support for the regime's policies developed only in light of the dramatic transformations in early twentieth-century Dominican society that were rapidly diminishing free access to land and constraining peasants' traditional ways of life. Unlike most Latin American peasantries with pre-Columbian histories and collective identities, the Dominican peasantry had been "reconstituted" from freed and runaway slaves and poor and marginalized Spanish colonists; the peasants were relatively independent and highly dispersed.[4] Until the twentieth century, peasants had found ample space for free land access in a country of negligible capitalist development and commercial agriculture, contrasting sharply with the Caribbean plantation model. At the onset of Trujillo's rule, however, the Dominican peasantry faced ominous changes in property relations and land tenure that threatened to eliminate its traditional free access to land. In the 1900 to 1930 period, growing enclaves of commercial farming and rising land values in certain areas had led to increasing efforts by those with means (and prescience) to enclose, survey, and claim lands without clear ownership, as will be discussed further. And new forms of individualized, private property were consolidated through legislation promulgated under the United States occupation (1916 to 1924).[5] By 1930 in the eastern region near the cities of San Pedro de Macorís and La Romana, thousands had been displaced by U.S. sugar companies, which had accumulated vast tracts of land. Peasants had traditionally used this land collectively for hunting and raising animals and individually for small-scale, shifting agriculture.

Confronting this critical juncture, the Trujillo regime engaged in a massive campaign of land distribution and property reform in an effort both to increase agrarian production for the domestic market and possible export and to garner political loyalty among the peasantry. The state sought to prevent further land concentration and peasant dispossessions and to impede the rise of a rural oligarchy characteristic of other Latin American countries at the time. The regime attempted instead to create a "peasant road to modernity" to satisfy both peasant interests in continued free access to land and elite demands for increased agricultural output, national economic development, and the establishment of "modern" farming techniques. The relative ease with which the Trujillo regime was able to implement its "land to the tiller" program was due to the abundance of uncleared public and private lands and to the lack of clear and definitive land titles in most of the country. These conditions meant that the regime's agrarian reform required few expropriations of utilized land.

The Trujillo regime offered land and eventually property rights to peasants—almost none of whom had previously had title to the land they used—on the condition that they cultivate the plots as productively as the government demanded. Otherwise the land would be distributed to other "poor agriculturists." Laws that classified any peasant cultivating less than ten *tareas* (.63 hectare) of land as "vagrant" were vigorously enforced throughout the country.[6] The state engaged in a massive, all-encompassing effort to ensure that plots were carefully maintained, to supply basic tools and agricultural inputs, to improve market access, and to end what had been the traditional mode of existence based on open range hunting and animal raising combined with shifting, slash-and-burn agriculture on tiny, subsistence plots (often only five tareas in size). Land reform distributed woods and pasture that previously had been used in common for grazing, hunting, and foraging as well for itinerant farming. It thereby accelerated the demise of open range animal raising, increasingly forced peasants to expand agricultural production in order to subsist, and impelled the transition from an agropastoral to agricultural economy.

In the past peasants had eschewed more extensive and sedentary farming, in part because transport to markets had been prohibitively expensive due to few or inadequate roads, and also because livestock had been permitted to graze unenclosed in most areas, thus forcing peasants to spend time (and sometimes money) building fences to protect their crops. Outside the highly fertile Cibao region, moreover, vast, untamed lands had been readily available in much of the country. This allowed peasants free access to pasture, wild animals, timber, and fruit, and an open frontier on which to shift plots every few years as land became less fertile, plots became overgrown with weeds, and wood fences rotted. One could thus secure subsistence without any need for more intensive cultivation, and a surplus remained, to a large extent, both economically and culturally unnecessary for most peasants. Yet, with land in much of the country being accumulated and enclosed for the first time, and animal fencing being legally required in widening areas, traditional economic practices were becoming problematic. In this context, the Trujillo state orchestrated various large-scale campaigns to distribute, legalize, or at least temporarily cede to peasants lands they desired or were already cultivating without title. In exchange, peasants were obligated to farm in a more sedentary and productive manner.

This process required peasants to sacrifice aspects of their way of life that they had been unwilling to renounce in the past. During the previous 150 years, intellectual and state elites had excoriated the traditional peasant economy as the prime cause of the nation's poverty and "backwardness."[7] It was purely subsistence oriented and provided no surplus to feed the cities, let alone provide exports to build state revenues and economic development. Yet a variety of state efforts throughout the nineteenth century to eliminate peasants' autarky and force them into either commercial farming or wage labor had failed almost entirely (except in the Cibao, where production for the market did expand, although generally not at the expense of peasants' self-sufficiency).[8] In most of the country peasant existence remained largely independent of commercial agriculture; and this "resistance" had been fostered by continuing access to the means of both production (land) and destruction (guns). However, following the U.S. military dictatorship's disarmament of the population and in the wake of increasing enclosures and evictions, peasants faced possible elimination of their means of survival if they failed to forge an effective alliance with the state. No longer, moreover, were there local *caudillos* (leaders or strongmen) competing for peasant loyalty and able to provide protection and assistance in return; rather, peasants faced a centralized state with a powerful army developed under the U.S. occupation. State-protected land use combined with agricultural assistance and new market access made sedentary, intensive farming attractive to the peasantry for the first time in Dominican history. A peasant-state compromise thus became possible given the alternative prospect of landlessness for many peasants.

Trujillo sought to augment peasant production through legal action and official policies that reflected the dual nature of the government's "protection" of the peasantry. The state distributed rewards to those it deemed "men of work" by providing them with land, irrigation, seeds, tools, pesticides, credit, breeding animals, and instruction in new growing techniques, while it severely punished with vagrancy penalties and withdrawal of usufruct rights those it considered to be "idle." At the same time, the regime vastly expanded the nation's infrastructure of roads and bridges, which permitted the circulation of commodities, to a large extent for the first time. Judging by the statistics, as well as peasants' own recollections, the regime's efforts at economic development and land distribution were fruitful. National self-sufficiency and per capita agricultural production increased under Trujillo,[9] and elderly peasants generally recall Trujillo as having carried out agrarian policies that they perceived to be relatively beneficial to them.[10]

The Origins of Trujillo's Land Distribution

In the early 1930s, lands of mostly ambiguous ownership in the Dominican countryside (state lands and *terrenos comuneros*)[11] were being increasingly cordoned off by owners or would-be owners, either elites or better-off peasants, through various forms of fences and enclosures, such as *trochas* and *carriles* (both words for cleared paths marking possession). Thus peasants were increasingly being denied access to uncultivated lands, in most areas for the first time in Dominican history. Local authorities condemned the fact that most of the enclosed land remained uncultivated by its "owners" while a large group of peasants wishing to farm (or raise animals) no longer had access to these erstwhile available lands. One rural authority in the Cibao complained to Trujillo in March 1934 that "it is well known that a large portion of those who claim to be landowners neither work their land nor let others do so." In response to this situation, he explained, he had, with the approval of the Santiago governor, provided many landless peasants with uncultivated lands in nearby Maimón, Esperanza. Around the same time, the governor of San Pedro de Macorís commanded the army to stop peasant evictions by large Dominican landowners near Juandolio and Guayacanes. He asked the central state to assist those who had already been dispossessed, including more than 150 families, as they represented a problem of "public order." Local authorities thus pressured the state to address land tenure concerns that were seen as stymieing production and piquing rural instability.[12]

Individual members of Trujillo's cabinet began to shape a national policy to address these issues, pushing the state in novel directions in terms of both land distribution and property rights. Secretary of Agriculture César Tolentino Rojas was one of the main forces behind emerging policies to ensure peasant land access. He had been an important nationalist leader and was persecuted for his opposition to the U.S. military dictatorship; under Trujillo he became an advocate for the lower classes. As early as December 1933, Tolentino made several public speeches in which he purportedly encouraged "the movement of squatters" onto private lands, including those of the U.S.-owned sugar company the Central Romana. The U.S. State Department received complaints from the company lawyer that "under recent presidential decree Dominican citizens were permitted to enter and occupy unused lands in the Republic."[13] The U.S. legation in Santo Domingo stated that its sources were "hopeful that when this matter comes to the attention of President Trujillo, Señor Tolentino's enthusiasm for the interests of squatters and the poor classes generally, would take a more rational form." However, the powerful Italian Dominican Vicini family, the owners of the largest sugar conglomerate after those belonging to U.S. corporations, had reportedly already protested to Tolentino only to receive a firm reply by him defending "his speeches and the action of the squatters in pursuance of the speeches."[14]

Nonetheless, the state eventually retreated. Pressure from the Central Romana forced a reluctant Tolentino to issue a circular to local officials in the East disavowing "misinterpretations" of his comments concerning

the plan for the distribution of state lands . . . which reflects the interest of the Dominican Government in improving the present condition of the peasants, [and] being able to make a landowner of each man of work and good will. . . . Often complaints are communicated to this Department from agriculturists who occupy lands that have been adjudicated in favor of sugar companies. . . . In this regard, it must be borne in mind that the agrarian policy which this Department has put into practice cannot be interpreted in a way that hinders the operation of justice.[15]

Although ostensibly bowing to powerful foreign sugar interests, the government would later that year inaugurate a new land distribution policy—sponsored by Tolentino—which would essentially legalize throughout the country what Tolentino had earlier adumbrated. Distributing land and legalizing squatter occupations would become the heart of subsequent rural policy, especially during the next few years.

It is likely that the actions of peasants themselves also helped shape Trujillo's rural policies. At a time when Trujillo's propeasant rhetoric remained vague or focused solely on production,[16] peasants were already petitioning directly to Trujillo for help in securing land access. For example, in 1934 Fidelio Trinidad, a peasant from the East, explained that he had been farming for four years on uncultivated lands belonging to the Ingenio (Sugar Mill) Santa Fé, a subsidiary of the Central Romana, when he was suddenly prevented from working there. He recounted his plight to Trujillo, addressing him as the peasantry's *palanca* (patron or friend with pull):

Where there is an immense amount of [unused] land . . . we, the residents of these parts, eager for work, decided to cultivate certain farms in this land. But we have been stopped by employees of this company [the Santa Fé].

Knowing . . . that you are the true patron of the agriculturalist obliges me to write to you . . . to see if by your efforts we could obtain from this company permission to farm these lands, even it were under a Contract, one that may be favorable to us, since we are not unaware that the land belongs to said company.

There are more than two hundred of us, seeming like vagrants; even though we are genuinely men of work, we cannot find any place to earn a living and provide for our families. Also, we want to make clear that these lands . . . are superb for the production of rice, corn and beans, which are what we need.[17]

At the time that the letter was received, the state had just retreated from any encouragement of squatters on sugar company property in the manner described earlier, and the land distribution campaign had not yet been initiated. The secretary of agriculture informed the secretary of the president that the former could not force the Ingenio Santa Fé to cede its lands.[18] Nonetheless, the regime's emerging land distribution policies would subsequently seek to assist agriculturists in exactly the manner that Trinidad had requested. And Trujillo would begin to disseminate what would become, to this day, the regime's most enduring propaganda in the countryside: that Trujillo's "best friends" were the "men of work." It was the peasantry, moreover, that adroitly inverted such statements by Trujillo from an exhortation to work harder into a petition for *protección,* or support, for the hard-working class, namely, the peasantry. Deference to this paternalist discourse became a disingenuous means of demanding benefits: "Knowing that you are the patron of the agriculturist," our benefactor and best friend, we know you will help us in this hour of need.[19]

The Trujillo regime's land distribution campaign commenced in the autumn of 1934. It was then that Trujillo commissioned Major Rafael Carretero to travel to the southwestern region of Barahona to investigate and try to reform land tenure problems existing there in order to maximize both distribution and production. Like Tolentino, Carretero appears to have been an effective force in moving the regime's rural policies in a direction beneficial to the maintenance of a semi-independent peasantry, despite the seemingly unipersonal character of Trujillo's rule as well as the corruption and brutality of many exercising power within the regime. After several weeks in the Southwest, Carretero wrote to Tolentino that he had appropriated and distributed 912 hectares in nearby Neyba, despite the carriles that had been established on them by would-be owners "who could never have cultivated them even in fifty years."[20] He distributed these lands to agriculturists "ready to work them immediately," some of whom had come from as far as El Cercado to obtain them.

During the next month, Carretero distributed 6,975 hectares to 2,217 persons (the plots varied substantially in size but averaged three hectares each) in this same area of Neyba and Barahona. As large parts of these lands had previously been marked off and claimed by various landowners, Carretero wrote to Secretary Tolentino: "I would like you to know that many persons in this area had possessed huge extensions of land marked off with trochas that they would never have been able to cultivate, and I have given out contracts for some of that land. Some unfounded complaints may therefore reach this Secretary of State, as these *trochadores* have always lived by exploiting the poor." Comparable circumstances existed in neighboring Enriquillo, from where Carretero filed a similar report in early February. He wrote that many who claimed to be landowners had opened trochas around *montes* (uncleared areas) in terrenos comuneros, carving out vast "extensions of land that they could never cultivate in their lives . . . [and which] are requested by peasants who wish to work them but have been restricted from doing so."[21]

In fact, throughout most of the country, land grabbing had become a major problem, an obstacle to Trujillo's goal of expanding production and the regime's aspirations of creating a nation of small farmers. The forest ranger for the southern commune of San José de Ocoa, Francisco Paulino, protested to Major Carretero that "the people cannot open up new farms in accordance with the desires of the Honorable President Trujillo because they do not have access to lands. The local bosses have all the lands marked off with trochas, seemingly for the purpose of making the poor unable to live." The ranger of the northwest commune of Monte Cristy wrote of a similar situation, in which "the ambition for woods among some owners [had led them to] cordon off immense areas with two cords of wire and wood fences. . . . These are places where there has never been a land survey. The small agriculturists are complaining, saying why are these montes being *trancados* [cordoned off] if they are producing no crops, and the result is that there is less area for raising animals (as these areas are considered *zona de crianza* [open range])."[22]

To confront these and other land problems, Tolentino recommended to Trujillo that Carretero's "highly beneficial plan for the distribution of lands among the rural poor" be extended throughout the country, "with the assistance of an Agricultural Instructor, a work team, seeds and the necessary [growing] techniques."[23] The bureaucratic structure responsible for the campaign would be the recently created "juntas for the protection and assistance of agriculture," now placed under Carretero's supervision and established in every *sección* (submunicipality). These juntas would attempt to provide free access to idle terrains on the basis of contracts whose conditions, as will be described, depended on whether the lands in question were terrenos comuneros, state lands, or privately owned.

The campaign to distribute land would be one of the regime's most dramatic and profound policies. It reflected many of its fundamental objectives. From the onset of the regime, a primary goal was to expand agricultural production and further national self-sufficiency through increased concentration on farming and improved cultivation techniques. To do so, the government sought to free up the forces of production and maximize output in a situation of supposedly idle labor, excess land, and capital shortage. "To move men to work and make idle soil productive in our fundamentally agricultural country" was the essence of the new campaign, one journalist argued. With this "socialization of the land . . . the Republic [will attain] the maximum development of its economic potential!" Perhaps the baldest statement of the regime's productivist telos was Carretero's instruction to one junta leader: "Double the agricultural work of each inhabitant and put in good condition all the abandoned plots" that were the consequence of swidden agriculture.[24]

Notably, the perennial elite critique of rural "vagrancy" was no longer cast as simply the consequence of an inexorable laziness as frequently had been argued in the nineteenth century, but rather of primarily material constraints on the peasantry, namely a lack of secure land access, as well as inadequate markets, infrastructure, irrigation, and growing techniques. In 1935, an editorial in the nation's most prominent newspaper, *Listín Diario,* exemplified this discourse: "The new southern usufructuaries having been provided for, the Commissioner of President Trujillo [Carretero] is at present in the Communes of the East, carrying out the same program and winning the grateful applause, for the incomparable Chief, of the legion of country people who had been leading an idle life for lack of four clumps of soil to cultivate in order to meet the needs of themselves and their families." Although the regime loudly condemned the problem of "vagrancy" as characterizing a small minority, the peasantry, in general, was praised far more strongly and consistently than ever before. Peasants were frequently referred to as the "men of work," as those who "fertilize the nation by the sweat of their brow," and as those who are the "worthy toilers for the welfare of the nation." On the other hand, those who did not readily accept the regime's modus vivendi—"protection" in return for production—were arrested as vagrants, assigned ten tareas to cultivate immediately, and then, no doubt, carefully scrutinized.[25]

In addition to the desire to further production, the regime's efforts at land distribution reflected its fundamental commitment to modernization via small-scale agriculture rather than large-scale agribusiness. Since the second half of the nineteenth century, debate had raged between these two imagined paths to "progress." The model for large-scale foreign agribusiness that transpired in the sugar areas of the East had been severely disillusioning. Critics viewed with misgiving not only the deleterious effects on the food supply and on national pride of the foreign sugar enclave, but also the more everyday forms of what they saw as the "barbarism" resulting from proletarianization and unemployment: poverty, social dislocation, novel forms of "vagrancy," and growing rural unrest and "banditry."[26] In 1935, one journalist lamented peasants' abandonment of their farms and their transformation into "miserable wage laborers whose only future was to swell the ranks of those who would become beggars in their old age."[27]

The intelligentsia also feared the economic and cultural consequences of a growing peasant "exodus" to the cities in wake of land concentration and capitalist agriculture. In 1935, the editors of *Listín Diario* wrote:

On many occasions we have discussed the important problem of the peasant exodus, an uncontrollable hemorrhage which is significantly weakening the social body, . . . increasing poverty and decreasing public and private wealth. . . . Within a few months [in the city], the misguided peasants are besieged with the most complete failure . . . often ending up in prison. . . .

With the current distribution of lands that is being systematically carried out in the twelve Provinces, the afflictions that we suffered before will disappear. . . . Having land to cultivate as their own, assured of good, productive crops, the attraction of a modest wage offered by the nearest estate disappears, as does the asphyxiating atmosphere created by latifundistas monopolizing all the land, which forces erstwhile landholders to become humble farm workers or to migrate [to the city] and be crushed by disillusionment.[28]

An analogous mixture of conservativism and populism was evinced in an authoritative missive from Tolentino and his colleagues, in which they counseled Trujillo that "the return to the countryside of the agricultural worker is what is needed for our Country so as to foster the small independent producer who loves the land which is cultivated with one's own hands. . . . the small landowners are the pillars of the social order and the basis for the Nation's wealth."[29]

It was already a long-standing belief that political stability required a nation of small farmers rather than of "nomadic" peasants or landless and underemployed workers.[30] Without ties to property, these groups had been seen as ready recruits for powerful caudillos, who sought to gain control of state power or patronage, and for rebellious *gavilleros* (regional strongmen, political gangs, and bandits), who repudiated, and remained outside of, central state authority.[31] In support of the land distribution campaign, the editors of the important national newspaper, *La Opinión*, stated: "The Government has as its highest ideal the hope that the day will soon arrive when every Dominican family has its own farm and its own home . . . [then] there will be no more revolutionary commotions."[32]

Listín Diario extolled the distribution campaign in perhaps the broadest and most turgid terms:

The Generalissimo . . . is carrying out with unflagging energy . . . the socialization of Dominican lands. Without violent outbursts, without erudite speeches, without noise, President Trujillo is bringing about the success of one of the most vital measures of a true, modern statesman: reforming the land to meet collective and private needs. Possession will come to correspond with those who cultivate [the land], awakening it from the heavy sleep of inertia and unproductivity. That infliction of degenerate capitalism which has cost humanity so many rivers of blood and so many tears, the latifundium, is being fought and steadily overcome.[33]

Modernization as had transpired in the East via large-scale sugar development and foreign investment was seen as a hollow and invidious "progress." It was based on "latifundia and a miserable proletariat . . . [on] ephemeral foundations . . . out of which quickly grow class hatred, discontent and desperation."[34] Trujillo's agrarian reforms, one state official proclaimed, preempted the need for peasant revolution, which would otherwise be required to counter an inexorable growth in latifundia.[35] With this perspective, the regime adopted land and property policies to foster small peasant production. On the one hand, peasant access to land was guaranteed; on the other, peasants were required to farm more extensively, and without shifting at will to new plots every few years, or else be arrested for vagrancy. Like most agrarian reforms, production and distribution were inseparable goals, not only representing land to the tiller, but also "use land efficiently, or be dispossessed."

Nationalist elements dovetailed with the regime's idealization of the small farmer and efforts at agrarian reform. Declining world commodity prices since the 1920s had further disillusioned policymakers with the sugar sector, impelled the regime to a politics of self-sufficiency (rice, for instance, would change from a major import to an export in a few years), and intensified nationalist sentiments against foreign agribusiness and latifundia.[36] In his 1936 annual report, Secretary of Agriculture Rafael Espaillat praised the land distribution campaign as a "model of prudent, nationalist politics with imponderable benefits for the well-being, unity, and independence of the Republic. . . . Peoples divested of dominion over their land are enslaved peoples." Espaillat had been an impassioned advocate of land reform, small peasant production, and restrictions on the sugar industry since the 1920s, when he had also been secretary of agriculture (as well as a consistent opponent of then general Trujillo). Like Tolentino and Carretero, Espaillat moved the Trujillo regime in reformist directions. Indeed, he even compared the land distribution campaign with the Mexican Revolution's commitment to the "most abandoned members of the Mexican citizenry: the country's Indians and poor agriculturists."[37]

The aim of Trujillo's land reform was not only to promote the stability associated with a class of small landowners, but to wrap the regime in a type of rural populism or paternalism. In fact, the aforementioned letter from Tolentino and his colleagues counseling Trujillo appears to have been in response to the latter's expressed interest in gaining support among the popular classes, which the "Benefactor of the New Country," as he was called, may have first imagined in an urban context. Toletino et al. continued their letter to Trujillo with this forceful recommendation:

Our country is not industrial and at present there does not exist a class of industrial laborers that need the immediate assistance of the State to improve their living conditions. The construction of housing for workers is justified . . . in the big cities that live on industrial factories. Our country, on the contrary, is essentially agricultural. . . . Therefore we believe that whatever investment . . .

is made by the State in terms of helping the working people should be used for fostering agriculturists, creating small property owners, [and] stimulating and furthering production from the land. . . . the industrial workers will not be excluded from agricultural distributions. Any worker can acquire a farm.[38]

Throughout the land distribution campaign, Carretero directly corresponded with Trujillo regarding its progress. Interestingly, Carretero's accounts of popular acclaim for Trujillo are sufficiently consistent and effusive as to stand out from most intrastate missives and suggest that Trujillo was eager to hear of popular support in this regard. In December 1934, at the outset of the campaign, Carretero telegrammed Trujillo: "The future small proprietors [of Azua] are overtaken with gratitude . . . [and] deliriously acclaim your name." Other examples abound, such as "The inhabitants of these areas regard you with love and admiration, repeatedly cheering your name"; "I can assure you that the peasants genuinely thank you for this help"; and "I have spoken at length [to them] about the protection and aid you offer men of work, and . . . [have told them that] I came at your behest to resolve their problems and offer them help." Often, when Carretero gave out plots, he also distributed photographs and portraits of Trujillo to his "peasant friends," reflecting Trujillo's wish to be associated personally with the land "gifts" and thus be "loved" as well as feared. The distribution of benefits under Trujillo thus served to dramatize the dictator's personal power, as they were represented more as donations than constitutional or impersonal rights.[39]

By June 30, 1936, 107,202 hectares had been distributed by the juntas to 54,494 agriculturists, representing 6 percent of occupied land and an impressive 29 percent of the nation's farms. The land campaign quickly brought dramatic results in virtually every province of the country.[40] The precipitous operation also soon realized much of its potential, even though its significance would continue, to some extent, throughout the regime. Half of all distributions occurred between December 1934 and June 1936 while Carretero was spearheading the campaign and while Tolentino and subsequently Rafael Espaillat were secretaries of agriculture. By 1955, 222,016 hectares had reportedly been distributed to 104,707 persons, representing 10 percent of occupied land and some 31 percent of rural producers (farms).[41] This amount increases to roughly 18 percent of land and 36 percent of producers if one includes the permanent distribution of lands provided by the regime's agricultural colonization program—founded by Espaillat under President Horacio Vásquez in the late 1920s. (Colonization and irrigation efforts, in some senses, supplanted the land distribution campaign in the latter half of the regime as fertile, nearby terrains became unavailable.)[42]

Yet what exactly was this land distribution campaign, which involved the allocation of millions of tareas within a few years to tens of thousands of landless peasants? What land was distributed and under what conditions? The answers are as complex as were the various forms of property in the country and the contradictory power relations within the Trujillo regime. In fact, the land distribution was neither the straightforward agrarian reform that supporters claimed nor the illusory manipulation only favoring landowners that critics have implied in brief references to it.[43] The campaign was the opposite of a uniform policy. It was flexible, experimental, and varied widely in its scope and meaning across the diverse regions of the country and in response to a multiplicity of distinct land tenure problems and power relations. In addition, the campaign was sometimes blurred with the colonization program, which also distributed land to peasants. Essentially, however, there were three types of property distributed: comunero, state, and private, each of which had its own dynamics and conditions. Technically, almost all of these distributions were made via a contract between the owner and the beneficiary in which the latter agreed to return the land to the owner after a certain number of years. However, the evidence suggests that in the majority of cases, land never had to be returned and property rights were consolidated by the tenant.[44]

During the height of the campaign, 1935 to 1940, cropland increased by a dramatic 47 percent.[45] Peasants had secured free access to land that "owners" were claiming but not using; and, in return, the state was able to exact more intensive land use and peasant agricultural production. Although many had to eke out a meager subsistence on tiny plots during the Trujillo regime, the vast majority of rural denizens owed no land tribute, rarely worked as paid laborers, and paid only modest taxes.[46]

Distribution of Terrenos Comuneros

Terrenos comuneros represented the largest type of property in the Dominican Republic at the time Trujillo seized power.[47] These properties had been spawned during the colonial period from single estates whose general boundaries had been documented in royal land concessions or *amparos reales* (provisional titles from the Crown), or, in other cases, by custom and oral tradition. Terrenos comuneros were not "common lands" in any conventional sense, but rather sites traditionally claimed by a limited association of co-owners all holding varying quantities of titles denominated in "pesos" or "land pesos." The titles did not refer to a specific plot or amount of land. Instead, they supported rights to utilize any unused area within a site's vaguely defined parameters, whether for private agricultural purposes or for collective herding, hunting, and foraging, as had traditionally been a predominant part of the rural economy. There had been no norms regulating amounts of land use, and historically this had not been an issue given the country's sparse population, colonial neglect, and general poverty.

Yet when commercial agriculture spread in certain provinces of the country (parts of the Cibao and the East), land became valorized in those regions, and widening areas of terrenos comuneros began to be claimed through enclosures and surveys. In other cases, all the co-owners were assembled, and the land was legally divided among them in proportion to the share of total land pesos one held. Various concepts of property collided. Should land be given to the persons who had claimed it via enclosures and other signs of possession or on the basis of their peso share? What precisely should be considered "possession"? Most important, were claims clearly limited to those with peso titles?

In practice, terrenos comuneros had always been used almost equally by those without any peso titles as by those with them. And although efforts had been made throughout the nineteenth century to eliminate "squatters" and restrict use to *accionistas* (co-owners) — generally better-off ranchers or town elites sometimes not using the land at all — the numbers of titleless occupants only grew. Initially these occupants were ignored, and the laws favored allocating property simply in proportion to one's peso share. But during the U.S. occupation (1916 to 1924), property rights were largely redefined, emphasizing rights based on possession rather than on existing titles. "Possession" — demonstrated by cultivation, pasture, surveying, or enclosure — would give one certain preferential rights to own or purchase land that superseded all other claims. Drawing on the Dominican Civil Code, the new laws permitted those who had "possessed" territory under conditions as if one were the owner (i.e., without paying rent of any kind) for an uninterrupted period of ten to thirty years, depending on various other conditions, to ipso facto acquire title to it on the basis of "prescription."[48] This rule would obtain not only for residual areas belonging to the state, as prescription laws had always been interpreted, but in terrenos comuneros as well. Now only those areas not "prescribed" within a comunero site could be divided up in proportion to peso titles.

On the one hand, this new property system was potentially of great benefit to squatters. It allowed them to prevail over holders of peso titles, as long as the occupants had completed the necessary period for prescription before co-owners were able to execute a land division and obtain a court adjudication of property (known in the Dominican Republic as a *saneamiento*). On the other hand, it could also be of great benefit to large landowners such as those sugar companies that early on had surveyed and enclosed vast tracts of land (or that had purchased areas from those that had). Indeed, simply on that basis the companies were able to gain property rights, even at the expense of individuals who had occupied the same plot but without sufficient time for prescription.

When Trujillo came to power, much of the East had already been awarded by irrevocable titles to the sugar companies, often on the basis of prescription dating back to early surveys and enclosures (trochas and fences) from the turn of the century.[49] In most of the rest of the country, however, such "symbolic" forms of possession (as opposed to actual land use) were only beginning to be utilized and, as described earlier, were generally disregarded by state officials wishing to redistribute territory. In addition, private, individual surveys had been prohibited since 1920 (notably, once the sugar companies already had completed theirs). Thus, the only extant threat to peasant land access was that of peso title owners proceeding with a land division in unoccupied areas or, worse still, where existing occupants had not yet consolidated prescription rights. In this regard, the greatest constraint for peasants was that in much of the country they had practiced shifting agriculture in conjunction with hunting, foraging, and raising animals in unenclosed areas. As they moved every two or three years to clear a new plot, they would not have remained in any one place long enough to gain prescription rights; nor was prescription possible in the unenclosed areas that had been collectively used.

During the 1930s and 1940s, the Trujillo regime distributed idle lands and woods in comunero sites to landless peasants and also provided

AGRARIAN REFORM IN DOMINICAN REPUBLIC

titleless occupants with contracts guaranteeing their possession of the plots they were already cultivating. The state thus slowly dismantled the comunero system of property by assigning fixed plots of land to specific individuals or families who could eventually obtain prescription rights to them (at the expense of absentee and "underutilizing" co-owners of these sites). Prescription could now be obtained when peasants remained for extended durations on their allotted lands and practiced sedentary agriculture as the state had so long desired them to do. Simultaneously, the government prohibited privately initiated requests for land divisions, whereas the state itself underwrote relatively few such efforts, and certainly none that would undermine official land distribution and squatting concerns.[50] These policies greatly slowed down the already lengthy process of adjudicating land titles in the country and thereby helped peasants extend their occupations until they could obtain property rights via prescription. Unless co-owners had already completed the legal steps necessary for the division and saneamiento of a particular comunero site—something that was thwarted by the Trujillo regime—local officials treated the area as if it were simply state owned. The state thus effectively nullified future peso title claims and secured the rights of existing squatters to the land they cultivated without titles. Given the predominance of terrenos comuneros and the only recent emergence of clearly defined private property, it is probable that the greatest amount of distributed terrains were terrenos comuneros.

Interestingly, official policy of treating comunero areas, when not yet legally divided, as if they were state lands can be seen as a reflection by the state of traditional peasant attitudes that viewed all unoccupied lands as "comunero," not in the sense of belonging to a limited association of co-owners holding peso titles, but rather of being "nobody's lands" accessible to all on a first-come-first-served basis. It is striking that these once very different categories had become virtually synonymous among state functionaries, as they had long been at a popular level. Thus, when the *juez alcalde* (justice of the peace) reported a cumulative distribution of 1,542 hectares in Enriquillo, he stated without differentiation that these lands were all "comunero or state land." In this context, "terrenos comuneros" referred to any terrain without clear private ownership, whether historically state land or not, all of which was subject to unilateral distribution by the government. In a similar conflation of state and comunero property, Carretero asked the San

Cristóbal junta president for a report of all lands either "offered [i.e., private] or comuneras" so that they could be distributed by him.[51]

Only in a few cases did the state ultimately offer preferential treatment toward elite *accionistas*. Otherwise comunero sites were distributed to landless peasants as if they were state lands. In the process, peso title owners were not recognized as having any rights to lands that they were not already using. On the bureaucratic forms and contracts documenting distributed plots, the "owners" of comunero sites were generally listed either as "comunero" or, paradoxically, as the recipients themselves. In Villa Tenares, for instance, of the thousand hectares given out by November 1936, 301 had been listed with the owner as "comunero."[52] In another commune, 400 recipients were listed simultaneously as the "owners" of some 465 hectares they received in April and May of 1936.[53] Ownership was also frequently ascribed to "the junta" that organized the distributions or else simply left blank.[54] These contracts were often for ten to twenty years; but, most likely, as there were no recognized owners other than the state or the recipients themselves, the lands never had to be returned and became the property of the beneficiaries through prescription.[55]

The essence of Trujillo's agrarian reform was that through the regime's complementary land and property policies most cultivators of land—both distribution recipients and "squatters"—were able to eventually consolidate property rights in terrenos comuneros (as well as in state lands, as will be discussed). At the same time, accionistas were prevented from gaining property rights simply on the basis of their titles, while the shrewd and powerful were impeded from enclosing, accumulating, and speculating with the nation's erstwhile unoccupied territory. Such areas were "nobody's lands" to the regime. And, as such, they were highly instrumental in its plan to develop the country via a type of small-farmer road to "modernization" rather than one of large-scale agribusiness, proletarianization, and a monocrop export economy. Trujillo's policies helped impede the transformation of terrenos comuneros into large latifundia as had already occurred in a large part of the East. Instead, the state sought the quickest possible transformation of idle and abandoned lands and of areas collectively utilized for shifting agriculture and open range herding into private lands for sedentary farming or enclosed ranching.

In the years prior to Trujillo's rule, those claiming land with peso titles or enclosures had in certain instances required peasants to share-crop or, less frequently, to pay rent. Land "distribution" often served to eliminate such practices.[56] The regime's ideology of establishing a nation of small, independent agriculturists clashed with the practice of sharecropping, which was perceived as inequitable and a disincentive to expanding production beyond subsistence needs. Throughout the three decades of the Trujillo regime, state officials frequently referred to sharecropping as "exploitation" and a "noxious practice" at odds with peasant independence. In 1935, for example, Carretero complained to Trujillo of the "landlords who exploit the humble charging them 25 percent and 50 percent of the crops harvested."[57] With few exceptions at this time, the state's agricultural juntas distributed both public and private lands without any sharecropping or monetary obligations.

When Dulce Echevarría of Azua demanded a fourth of the crop from occupants of the land she claimed by virtue of peso titles, Carre-tero responded that her land was validated only by an individual survey insufficient for claiming territory on terrenos comuneros. Carretero re-jected those demanding various forms of tribute from peasants for land claimed without absolute titles via a saneamiento, and he excoriated the "abuses that certain powerful individuals committed . . . [against] poor agriculturists because . . . the powerful . . . had some documents to a piece of land that had never been surveyed [and *saneado*]." Interestingly, Carretero explained to Trujillo that it was because of these traditional practices that the peasantry was now so grateful to him that he was "proclaimed in all of the South as the savior and *protector* [patron] of agriculture." As other peasants heard about the land distribution cam-paign, they demanded the same rent-free conditions for themselves and appealed to the state for assistance in this regard. Such appeals were forwarded from the secretary of agriculture to Carretero, who asserted that "these situations will be resolved and the peasants will be pleased with the elimination of those obstacles that are being placed before them and hindering their labor."[58]

Distribution of State Lands

State lands were essentially a residual category consisting of areas that had neither been ceded by the Crown in colonial times (lands that had evolved into terrenos comuneros in virtually all cases), nor had occupants of sufficient duration to have acquired the basis for private property via prescription. During the Trujillo regime, local juntas oversaw the distribution of state lands to peasants who were either immediately given property rights or who entered into contracts to "rent" the land free of charge for periods generally lasting, in principle, ten to twenty years.[59] These contracts listed as "owners" of the distributed lands either the state or the recipients themselves. In most instances, occupants would be able to maintain possession for a period of time sufficient to consolidate their property rights via prescription.

When Carretero commenced his campaign in the Southwest (Barahona), the lands he first assigned to peasants were mostly in areas assumed to be state property. Distributions in the region during 1936 continued to be listed as taken from predominantly state lands. In Duvergé, for instance, one monthly report documented a distribution of 768 hectares of state land compared with only 12 hectares of private land. Throughout the country, varying amounts of state land were made available. Near Jima Abajo in the Cibao, for instance, 262 hectares of state lands were given to 110 individuals in one two-month period, with the plots ranging from one to six hectares. Although the contracts were for ten years, a recipient from this distribution informed me that the land never had to be returned, but rather became the property of recipients. The varying plot sizes in Jima Abajo reportedly reflected the beneficiaries' different resources (family size, above all).[60]

In other instances, when a wide variance existed in the size of distributed plots, it may have indicated preferential consideration or that the grants were "legalizations" of preexisting occupations by squatters. Legalization protected occupants from the possibility of eviction and permitted the eventual consolidation of property rights by those occupying and cultivating the land. For instance, at the end of 1934, the state planned to "distribute" its lands in Pedro García near Santiago by demarcating the actual cultivations of some 200 persons already occupying plots there. Free tenancy contracts would be given to occupants for the area of actual cultivation and the remaining territory would be distributed to others, regardless of whether or not they were enclosed.[61] For the many people already utilizing the area, this was more a legalization than a distribution of land, as squatters became secure occupants and potential owners of private property.

The state acted similarly in Enjuagador in the commune of Guerra.

Saturno Pagán, a Puerto Rican immigrant, claimed nearly 188 hectares, which he had begun clearing around 1912 mainly for cattle grazing. Over time, squatters increasingly entered "his" land. In 1934, some inhabitants complained to the state that Pagán had threatened to let his animals ravage their crops if they did not leave. Tolentino defended the squatters, informing Pagán rhetorically that he knew this "rumor could not be true" and that the Department of Agriculture was rethinking "the situation of these state lands and how they can be better utilized." Subsequently, the department made plans to "distribute" the lands to existing occupants as part of an "agricultural colony."[62]

In many areas, land distribution was thus as much about guaranteeing possession and property rights as it was about providing land. Peasants had traditionally had access to most state, as well as comunero, lands, but now they were acquiring the basis for private property. Antonio Taveras from the sección La Romana, in the town of Jima Abajo, was one of thousands of recipients listed in the Department of Agriculture records for land distribution.[63] When I spoke to him in 1994, he explained that for years he had used what he thought were state lands before he was given his plot by Trujillo in the same area. He told me that he was grateful for the fifty tareas (three hectares) he received because having his own property was "more appealing and had more value" than using other lands. In the past he said he never knew if the land he used actually belonged to someone else and whether it might be taken from him.

In addition to distributing uncleared state lands, and legalizing areas already held by squatters, the secretary of agriculture acquired substantial new lands to distribute from areas appropriated from private owners in return for public irrigation and also as reimbursement for state-sponsored surveying (and title adjudication). Those acquired in return for irrigation represented the most valuable lands distributed. Whenever the government built a new irrigation project, private landowners were obligated to pay one-fourth of all cultivated lands and one-half of idle areas that were reached by the canal, regardless of whether they wished to use such irrigation. According to the law establishing this policy, the lands acquired were supposed to be distributed to "poor agriculturists, with preference given to Dominican residents in the area of the canal." In practice it appears that under Trujillo, priority was generally given to such peasants, many of whom helped build the canal as *prestatarios*.[64]

The "fourth-part" policy dated back to Law no. 961 of 1928, before

Trujillo's seizure of power, and had antecedents as well in legislation under the U.S. military dictatorship. However, the state built few aqueducts at that time, and defiant landowners refused to cede then what terrains they did owe; thus, the policy's impact was felt primarily during Trujillo's rule.[65] Public irrigation was a key feature of the regime's campaign to vastly augment agricultural productivity. Whereas in 1935 only 3,000 hectares had been irrigated, by 1955 "constructed or almost complete" canals reached 165,000 hectares of land as a result of over $20 million in state investment and the unpaid labor of prestatarios, who provided much of the workforce. In return, the regime must have accumulated some 40,000 to 80,000 hectares of highly desirable, irrigated lands to distribute.[66] Furthermore, Trujillo had substantially modified the original legislation that had permitted state appropriations of irrigated private lands only "after sixteen years of uninterrupted irrigation." From the onset of the regime, this stipulation was ignored—as Vásquez had tried unsuccessfully to do—and it was legally suppressed in a 1942 legal reform. In addition, the original law stipulated that in idle areas comprising less than 1,000 tareas (63 hectares), only one-fourth of the area had to be ceded, whereas the new legislation required one-half of all idle lands to be relinquished.[67]

The Department of Agriculture files in the Archivo General de la Nación (National Archives) show a myriad of land distributions from areas appropriated in return for public irrigation. The vast majority of these were small plots. In the Baní region, for example, a multitude of squatters and sharecroppers requested and received small irrigated plots (.5 hectare to 3 hectares) from the state.[68] Similarly, in Valverde some 440 hectares were appropriated from six "co-owners" and then distributed in plots of ten tareas each to hundreds of recipients. In this case, the distributions involved "legalizing" the possessions of 412 squatters. These occupants thus became overnight legal occupants of irrigated lands rather than squatters on arid terrenos comuneros, for which they may or may not have been eligible for prescription rights prevailing over the peso title claims of the site's co-owners. In addition, the government hoped to place almost 300 new occupants on the land from requests it had received.[69]

The new irrigated lands were valuable and widely sought after, including by powerful individuals for whom the lands were not supposedly intended but who in some cases may have attained them through connections to the political elite. Indeed, the president of the Las Matas de Farfán junta, Santiago Rodríguez, was forced to defend himself to the new supervisor of the agricultural juntas, Bayoán de Hostos (who replaced Carretero in 1936) regarding his failure to respond to a request by "JY," presumably a man of influence. "JY" had asked for a sizable amount of land in the newly irrigated El Llano area. Rodríguez explained:

Everyone wants some of the lands in El Llano. Requests are coming in all the time . . . but no one can be promised or given anything since the Junta must attend to the over two thousand prestatarios who are the ones who labored in the removal of the land to build the canal, and who did so without even any sustenance provided to them. . . . It seems to this Junta that when it succeeds in obtaining the 50 percent of the lands owed [to it], that it should be distributed to the poor agriculturists who fertilized these lands with the sweat of their brow, and thus it will fulfill the desires of the Generalissimo. . . . If, for example, four hundred tareas [twenty-five hectares] were conceded to him ["JY"] that would deprive forty needy prestatarios of the urgent government assistance they are requesting.[70]

Although the denouement of this case is not certain, Rodríguez's insistence on official goals for assisting the poor suggests the space for individual state actors to shape the local consequences of distribution. Furthermore, Rodríguez's need to defend his actions in favor of "poor agriculturists" implies that it was not unusual for the well connected to obtain lands.

In some instances, plots were indeed offered to the regime's clients or sold to the affluent. Especially with irrigated lands, leading state figures sometimes demanded that they be awarded to particular individuals, thus bypassing the normal process of local selection and approval, generally by the alcalde *pedáneo* (ex officio, head of the local agricultural junta), the authority in charge of each sección. For example, Luciano A. Díaz of Santiago wrote to his friend Huberto Bogaert, then secretary of agriculture: "My dear compadre, the youth Gerardo Polanco would like [to obtain] from this Secretary land in one of the irrigated zones closest to Santiago in order to grow rice. He is the son-in-law of Abrahán de León, whom you know, and I recommend him as a man of work. I am writing to you in the hope of obtaining this wish for [him]." Nine days later, Secretary Bogaert replied that he had directed the chief of the Santiago district to offer Polanco a plot by the Presidente Trujillo canal with the usual condition that it be entirely cultivated within two months. He explained to Díaz that the size of his plot would depend on land availability and Polanco's resources.[71]

Although powerful elites sometimes benefited from corruption within the land distribution system, more typically land was given in small plots to peasants without any political power. Not infrequently, the "fourth part" was taken from medium and even small landholdings (two to three hectares). The distribution of such tiny plots was of interest only to the poor, not the regime's powerful clients.[72] Although exceptions were made for the narrow inner circle around Trujillo, the regime's policy of preserving hegemony in the countryside depended more on securing many humble clients than on an elite few. For the era of Trujillo, a distinction—however blurry—can be drawn between a state with a relatively well-developed and responsible bureaucracy that generally followed more or less legitimate and popular rural policies, and a regime that operated on highly corrupt, terroristic, and arbitrary principles. Although the latter could intervene in the policy of and supersede the former, a sense of order appears nonetheless to have been predominant among peasants in everyday rural life under Trujillo.[73]

The above limitations notwithstanding, the fourth-part policies essentially functioned in the interests of more equitable land distribution and the fostering of small farmers. In twentieth-century Latin America, few governments would probably have been willing and able to unilaterally appropriate this large a portion of the nation's lands in return for new public irrigation. It should be noted that irrigation was not necessarily desired. Some large cattle ranchers preferred to maintain their estates undivided and unreduced, rather than have them irrigated, as irrigation was more beneficial to agricultural production, such as rice. In fact, tension over this policy was reportedly one of the triggers for the regime's most notorious and dangerous conflict with a member of the rural elite, Juan (Juancito) Rodríguez García, who had been perhaps the largest rancher in the country.[74]

Clearly, the state's constant mediation of peasant access to the means of production provided a high level of social control. All individuals who wished to obtain land had to supply a certificate of approval and "good conduct" from the neighborhood authority, from the alcalde pedáneo, or from one of various other local state representatives (agricultural district supervisors, colony administrators, or army officials). Certainly, anyone suspected of political "disloyalty" as well as anyone not considered hard working would be excluded from the regime's provision of land security. To a far lesser extent, officials exercised a degree of clientelism or petty corruption in their organization and approval of land distribution. This was limited not only because most corruption under Trujillo occurred among the elite, but, above all, because the campaign represented a broad policy intended to predicate the regime's political and economic fortunes on successful, small peasant production. The campaign involved too many recipients for them all to have been elite clients. And its goals transcended simple charity and favoritism (even though these were aspects of this and other state operations).

Finally, with the exception of taxes on rice grown on irrigated lands, the state collected no direct revenues from its irrigation, appropriation, and distribution of private lands. One official had recommended instead that those who had received irrigated land should begin paying an annual rent and that in the future the government should not appropriate territory and distribute it but rather exact payment for public irrigation. Considering the revenue that this reform could have produced, it is notable that the regime chose not to adopt it.[75] Rather the fourth-part law remained for many years a key part of the regime's reformist, agrarian policies designed to increase national wealth while shoring up social and political stability through distributionist and, to some extent, clientelist policies.

Distribution of Private Lands

Outside of the East, most of the country's territory and landholdings remained without clear ownership in the mid-1930s.[76] Nonetheless, private lands did represent a significant part of the country; and they contributed a substantial portion to the distribution campaign. However, the terms of these grants were very different from state and comunero cessions. Authorities pressured owners to provide peasants with idle areas for limited, renewable periods, generally around five years. After that time, owners with clear property titles had the legal right to evict tenants if the former were ready to utilize their plots but had to offer occupants land elsewhere if they still had idle territory. Furthermore, tenants were often obligated to return the areas cultivated with artificial pasture or, in other cases, with still fruit-bearing trees, receiving no payment for these "improvements." Whether contracts were renewed after they expired was a matter of negotiation between owners, tenants, and the state. No doubt, in land-scarce areas, greater state pressure was applied to maintain tenancies. However, owners with a combination of political power and legal property titles could resist these pressures.[77]

Legally, cessions of land had to be voluntary unless they originated from Law no. 758, which prohibited landowners from maintaining large tracts of unused land. Although only applicable to areas over 100 hectares and rarely necessary in the end, this legislation provided an effective threat in many cases. Documents reveal various instances of formal notice being given to owners under this law.[78] In general, however, private owners with substantial idle areas were first "persuaded" to contribute to the campaign. Some of these owners offered vast areas. For instance, Guillermo Hahn of Puerto Plata delivered 628 hectares in the section of Arroyo Llano; Ramón Martínez, 692 hectares in the commune of Cabrera; and the powerful landowner Oscar Valdez, 922 hectares near Higüey.[79]

In some cases, the juntas acted more unilaterally than official procedure dictated, even distributing land before it had been offered. It was only after 176 hectares belonging to the Amistad sugar company in Imbert, Puerto Plata, had already been handed out by the Bajabonico junta that the company announced that it would inform Carretero whether it was "feasible for this enterprise to offer several thousand tareas of montes to be distributed among small agriculturists." This letter appears to have been a diplomatic protest against the state's action, a move that the Amistad considered its own prerogative. In this case, the central state retreated and ordered the distributions temporarily suspended. On the other hand, individuals and corporations with less power and autonomy were unable to protest as effectively. When Antonio Núñez complained that two agriculturists, Gerónimo Gómez and Pedro Aquino, were farming his property, the Bayaguana junta simply informed him that the junta had already given them contracts and that it was obligated to ensure their rights. Núñez, however, was permitted to add his signature to the contracts as the landowner.[80]

Large landowners were not the only contributors to the land campaign. Outside the East, there were relatively few latifundistas. Correspondingly, private lands were often ceded by medium and even small landowners. In interviews conducted throughout the country, I encountered various individuals with fewer than six hectares of land who were forced by the alcalde pedáneo to permanently cede terrains, a phenomenon also evinced in official documents.[81]

Although strong pressure was often needed to make owners "offer" territory, it may have sometimes been profitable for them to do so, as their land would then be cleared and prepared by recipients without any cost to owners. One function of agrarian reforms in general is simply to oblige landowners to be more productive in order to avoid expropriation. In the Dominican Republic, private land distributions under Trujillo offered owners an especially innocuous and convenient version of this process. Although in practice even the smallest areas of idle land were subject to distribution, the expropriation remained only temporary. Inefficient private landowners forced to cede their idle terrain could reclaim their property soon after if they were ready to expand production, perhaps with new capital to hire laborers or to graze more cattle. The area had probably been monte before, but with a boost from tenants who had cleared the terrain it might now be used for pasture, for instance, or sold to someone else ready to utilize the land. On the other hand, recipients were not always easy to evict, and the state sometimes pressured owners to renew or continue indefinitely the free tenancies.[82] Furthermore, occupants posed a threat in that they might later be granted property rights to the area by the Land Court if the "owners" did not hold secure titles.

If tenants were evicted at the end of their contracts (or contract renewals), it was a not insignificant cost for them to have to return the area sown with pasture or, in some cases, perhaps still fruit-bearing perennial plants. Yet, this was less of a disincentive than sharecropping, which typically required one not only to leave the area cultivated at the end of the allotted period but also to pay the owner one-fifth to one-half of the crop every year except the last. Although sharecropping had never dominated Dominican agriculture, it became more common in the early twentieth century as increasing amounts of the nation's territory had been claimed, land was valorized, and owners became reluctant to permit squatters. The expanding demands for sharecropping were anathema to peasants accustomed to free land access in much of the country. Ramón Suárez, a self-described "young fan of agriculture" from Villa Rivas complained to Trujillo of the "outrages committed by the landlords against the peasants." "We will die of hunger," he wrote, if forced to deliver one-third of the rice crop to landowners. This letter was forwarded to Andrés Pastoriza, secretary of agriculture, who, in turn, sent it to Carretero with "the understanding that when you form the Agricultural Juntas in these Communes this problem will be resolved."[83]

Although similar to the regime's private land distributions, other traditional forms of tenancy were also more problematic for the peasantry than the contracts guaranteeing free access for at least four or five years. Prior to the spread of commercial agriculture and the scramble to consolidate property rights, putative landowners had frequently permitted tenants to clear a portion of land and harvest crops a couple of times before returning it to them sown with pasture. In other cases, owners simply "tolerated" squatters who cleared their lands. Often, however, upon seeing the soil bear fruit, owners quickly sought to evict occupants, generally without compensation for improvements, as no written agreement prevented ejection at any time. Jorge Guichardo Reyes of Pretiles, Valverde, complained to Trujillo that a few months before, ten peasants had been permitted by a local landowning family to clear an area of monte and cultivate it, but then after they had "sweated and put their heart into it" the owners told them to abandon their crops before they ever had the chance to harvest them. Although the state was unable to return the lands to peasants in this case, as there were no junta contracts and the owners presumably held clear titles, the regime did seek to ameliorate such practices, which were seen as discouraging peasant production. In this instance, the Department of Agriculture required that the owners, Melchor and Perucho González, pay the occupants for their improvements in the amount estimated by the state agricultural instructor.[84]

As tenancy had been insecure and sometimes limited to one or two years, there was little incentive or opportunity to grow perennial crops and to produce beyond subsistence needs. Furthermore, these periods were too short for trees such as bananas or cacao to bear even their first harvest, and other crops were not considered feasible given sharecropping terms. For example, peasants in Villa Mella had complained to Trujillo:

[We] would like to work but have no where to do so. . . . Where [the owners] do give us land . . . [it is] under the condition that we stay only a year and a half . . . which is not enough time for growing bananas. . . . And with rice . . . they only let us work if we give them half the crop . . . and we must also sell them part of the small bit of rice that we keep at prices set by the owners. . . . Since we wish to work, we are writing to you . . . with the hope that you will offer us your noble assistance.[85]

Thus, at its worst, temporary land "distribution" was a modus vivendi between the free land access that peasants wished to maintain and the sharecropping that owners sought to impose.

The existence of plentiful uncleared areas largely without property owners was a necessary prerequisite to the Trujillo regime's rural policies and land distributions. In the few places where unused and unowned terrains were scarce, as in the eastern sugar areas around Ramón Santana and La Romana, the government was compelled to buy land to mitigate the grievous problems produced by land monopolization. Notwithstanding the objections of Carretero and numerous other state officials, hundreds of families had been ejected in the 1930s by the U.S.-owned La Romana sugar company (assignee of the Vicini estate) from the once comunero site of Campiña, with the company reportedly paying many peasants twenty-five centavos per tarea for crops but no compensation for (collective) pasture or woods. To mollify dire conditions, Trujillo permanently distributed land, among other places, in nearby La Noria, which had belonged to the Vicini family's Compañía de Inversiones Inmobiliarias (Real Estate Investment Company). Others, such as Martín Maldonado, temporarily received adjacent lands, for example, in Magarín (a section in the town of Ramón Santana) owned by the Central Romana. Some fifteen years later, however, the company refused to continue lending out its land there (following two renewals of five-year contracts). Subsequently, the state bought almost 500 hectares in the area from the Coiscou family—lands the family had reportedly intended to sell to the Angelina sugar mill—and the area was permanently ceded to landless peasants. Maldonado received—and in 1994 still owned—two plots totaling 2.4 hectares in "de Silvain" (Ramón Santana).[86]

In an interview in 1994, Maldonado stated that "for the poor, Trujillo was the best there ever was." When asked then why Trujillo had permitted the eviction from Campiña, Maldonado articulated attitudes I found to be common among elderly peasants:

Trujillo did not want to do it, to the poor, to the *infeliz* [the humble]. . . . Some say bad things about Trujillo, but I do not agree. Trujillo gave us land, seeds, tools, and food and ten pesos on Saint Rafael's day. . . . Trujillo showed great respect for agriculture. What he wanted was production. He always said his "best friends are the men of work"; and those whom he disliked were the vagrants, the thieves, and the politicians. . . . Today people don't thank Trujillo. But Trujillo sent everyone to school . . . even though he didn't want people to deal with politics. In our school, he even got rid of a book on the history of past presidents. One couldn't turn against Trujillo. . . . The bad side of Trujillo was that if one person went against Trujillo, Trujillo might attack other members of the same family even though they had done nothing against Trujillo.

Maldonado's simultaneous appreciation and critique of the Trujillo regime echos the discourse of many elderly peasants in the Dominican Republic. No doubt, the land distribution campaign and agricultural assistance help explain peasant acceptance of Trujillo despite the regime's many negative aspects, which are also nonetheless vividly recalled. In addition to increased agricultural production the state anticipated greater political stability as a new class of sedentary, small landowners developed, tied to their property and chary of the type of revolutionary movements peasants had joined in the past. Furthermore, the regime's distribution policies, essentially a vast bureaucracy regulating land access, structured a society dependent on state "benevolence." It thereby strengthened the state's means of controlling behavior, both economic and political, through an elaborate system of rewards and punishments.

Conclusion

In earlier periods of Dominican history, such as the Haitian occupation (1822 to 1844), the state had similarly sought to draw peasants into commercial agriculture by distributing property and assisting production. Analogous peasant-state compromises had also been adumbrated by key intellectuals at the end of the nineteenth century.[87] But never before had the peasantry been willing, nor the state able (financially and administratively), to carry them out. In general, the peasantry had remained instead a dispersed class of largely autarkic producers who variously combined hunting, raising animals, and subsistence-oriented, slash-and-burn agriculture. Given ample access to the means of production and subsistence—land and animals—and minimal taxation, they

had been able to shun both proletarianization and large-scale integration into commercial markets.[88] Exceptions were made on a significant
scale only when market conditions were unusually attractive, such as
during the initial years of sugar expansion (the 1870s)—when wages
were high—and in the highly fertile Cibao region—where peasants
produced varying amounts of marketable tobacco, and later cacao and
some coffee, during the nineteenth century.

Yet, at the onset of the Trujillo regime, peasants saw themselves
being evicted from private lands while state and comunero lands were
being rapidly cordoned off with trochas and other property markers.
No longer were there ample lands for the traditional mode of existence
based on free ranging of livestock, hunting of wild animals, and slash-
and-burn cultivation. Even one's tiny *conuco* (agricultural plot) had become vulnerable to appropriation in the evolving land tenure and property system. Suddenly, state-protected access to land combined with
agricultural assistance (seeds, tools, pesticide, irrigation, roads, and so
on) made sedentary, intensive farming attractive to the peasantry for
the first time in Dominican history. And for the first time the state was
ready and able to provide some degree of protection and aid to peasant
producers.

The Trujillo regime's rural policies ameliorated the threats to the
peasantry implicit in the new private property laws, transition to
individualized ownership, and increasing land commercialization that
marked the previous few decades. The state greatly delayed the process of surveying, property division, and title determination; eliminated
escalating efforts to "symbolically" possess territory through surveys and
enclosures; and distributed to the peasantry land for cultivation and, in
most cases, for permanent usufruct and property rights. These actions
dovetailed with a development strategy that sought to extract a surplus
from the countryside without producing rural dislocation, instability,
and out-migration.[89] Most of the intellectual and policymaking elites in
the country believed that the best way to "modernize" was not to expropriate the peasantry and therein flood the labor markets and urban
zones, but to force the peasantry to "efficiently" cultivate the plethora
of idle and "underutilized" lands. In the early 1930s, most of these areas
had only problematic property claims to them based on trochas and
peso titles, and with the government's assistance they were eventually
awarded to the peasantry.

By offering peasants their own plot of land, the state helped an-chor a population accustomed to clearing new farms every few years in nearby montes as had formerly been possible. It thereby established the basis for peasants to obtain property rights via "prescription," which was awarded ipso facto following extensive occupation of a single plot, something impossible with shifting agriculture. Peasants considered "productive" were protected from eviction and could accumulate suffi-cient time so that when their land was surveyed and later adjudicated, it would be "prescribed" to them rather than divided up among the co-owners with "peso titles" who were not cultivating the land. In the end, peso titles meant very little. When property was definitively allocated in the Dominican Republic, it was carried out almost exclusively on the basis of prescription, and outside the sugar areas mostly on the basis of material possession rather than problematic enclosures and private surveys. Needless to say, the denouement might have been very differ-ent. Had Trujillo structured his political base upon a landed elite, then property claims based on peso titles, trochas, and private surveys would have prevailed over squatters' rights and land "distributions." In sum, Trujillo was not a dictator who favored a class of rural elites, but rather one who impeded the growth of a landed oligarchy.

There was a significant degree of coherence in the Trujillo regime's property and land reforms, which, however limited and problematic, were relatively favorable to the preservation of a semi-independent peas-antry, fostered an effective land to the tiller policy, and envisaged a peas-ant or small-farmer road to economic development. This conclusion, however, in no way denies that these policies were, in some instances, sharply contradicted by other measures that fostered latifundia. These included arbitrary appropriations by Trujillo and the political elite, as well as brutal evictions stemming from state policy occurring predomi-nantly in the later years of the regime. Most salient, the appropriation of peasant lands in the Monte Plata region to supply a rapidly expand-ing state sugar industry in the 1950s may have caused more hardship and certainly more proletarianization (given the decreased availability of land by that time) than even that produced by foreign sugar compa-nies in the 1880 to 1930 period. The anomalies in agrarian policy over time suggest the regime's multiple and shifting foundations, including the interests of the state itself, Trujillo and his inner circle, and vari-ous landowners and businessmen who were clients and associates of the regime. In addition, like many dictatorships, Trujillo's rule degenerated in the final years, becoming increasingly arbitrary, irrational, unpopular, and repressive. Yet however grim and important some clashes with the peasantry were, they did not represent the experience of most peasants over the course of the regime and should not be the sole focus of scholarly attention. The direction of public policy matters and should be closely treated even in the most corrupt, brutal, and theatrical of regimes, such as Trujillo's. Hence, this essay has sought to reveal the undisclosed and unexpected character of Trujillo's agrarian policies.

Prior to Trujillo's seizure of power, most of the intellectual elite had come to forcefully desire a peasant road to economic development that averted rural instability and the "ugliness" of "modernity" in small, late-developing nations, as had already been witnessed in the East: increasing unemployment, escalating rural-urban migration, large-scale foreign ownership, a vulnerable monocultural economy, and deepening economic, and thus political, dependence on other countries. The Trujillo regime sought to realize the improbable dream of establishing a viable, small-farmer, capitalist economy in the Dominican Republic that would provide political stability, economic diversification, and national self-sufficiency. Given both the strength of the state and the extant threats to peasants' control over their means of production, a long anticipated peasant-state compromise was finally possible. Trujillo maintained the peasants' traditional access to land in return for intensified peasant production and sustained political loyalty or acquiescence.

The economic and political success of this compromise during the Trujillo era helps explain the regime's thirty-one years of stable rule, despite Trujillo's well-documented brutality and corruption. Like most dictatorships, the Trujillo regime achieved hegemony and acquiescence not only through coercion but through the state's ability to carry out important policies appealing to key societal groups. Despite the profound changes being ushered in by capitalism and commercial agriculture, the peasantry maintained under Trujillo an unusual measure of economic security and continuity during the process of "modernization." At the same time, the country, in general, witnessed comparatively high levels of economic development and self-sufficiency that were sustained in part by an increasing agricultural surplus produced by the peasantry. This essay thus suggests both the limits of Trujillo's autonomous power and the degree to which the state was founded on the social as well as economic basis of a small, landholding peasantry.

Notes

I would like to thank John Coatsworth, Fernando Coronil, Emiliano Corral, Michael Ducey, Rosario Espinal, Friedrich Katz, Catherine LeGrand, Juan Linz, James Scott, Julie Skurski, and especially Raymundo González and Hannah Rosen, for input on this essay; Walter Cordero, Francisco Cueto, Jorge de la Cruz, Eddy Jáquez, Antonio Lluberes, Orlando Inoa, Domingo Mota, and, above all, Ciprián Soler, for research assistance; and the National Endowment for the Humanities, the Fulbright-Hays Program, and the Joint Committee on Latin American and Caribbean Studies of the Social Science Research Council and the American Council of Learned Societies with funds from the Andrew Mellon Foundation, for financial support.

1. Important exceptions are Pedro San Miguel, "The Dominican Peasantry and the Market Economy: The Peasants of the Cibao, 1880-1960" (Ph.D. dissertation, Columbia University, 1987), 304-305, and Rosario Espinal, *Autoritarismo y democracia en la política dominicana* (San José: CAPEL, 1987), 13-19, 52-77.

2. H. E. Chehabi and Juan J. Linz, "Sultanism: A Type of Non-Democratic Regime" (unpublished paper, 1995); Juan J. Linz, "Totalitarian and Authoritarian Regimes," in *Handbook of Political Science,* vol. 3, edited by Fred Greenstein and Nelson Polsby (Reading, Mass.: Addison-Wesley, 1975), 259-263.

3. For a similar perspective, see San Miguel, "The Dominican Peasantry," 48, 304-305; cf. Orlando Inoa, *Estado y campesinos al inicio de la era de Trujillo* (Santo Domingo: Librería La Trinitaria, 1994), 86-101.

4. Raymundo González, "Campesinos y sociedad colonial en el siglo dieciocho dominicano," Quinto Congreso Dominicano de Historia, Santo Domingo, October 24-27, 1991; Sidney Mintz, "The Question of Caribbean Peasantries: A Comment," *Caribbean Studies,* 1 (October 1961): 31-34.

5. See Richard Turits, "The Foundations of Despotism: Peasants, Property, and the Trujillo Regime in the Dominican Republic (1930-1961)" (Ph.D. dissertation, University of Chicago, 1997).

6. Executive order no. 404, February 16, 1920, *Gaceta Oficial,* no. 3094 (February 28, 1920). There are 15.9 tareas per hectare in the Dominican Republic.

7. Raymundo González, "Ideología del progreso y campesinado en el siglo diecinueve," *Ecos,* 1, no. 2 (1993).

8. Ibid. See also Michiel Baud, "Transformación capitalista y regionalización en la República Dominicana, 1875-1920," *Investigación y Ciencia,* 1, no. 1 (January-April 1986).

9. Nicolás Rizik, *Trujillo y la estadística* (Ciudad Trujillo: Editora Montalvo,

1945), 91–94; Pablo Mariñez, *Agroindustria, estado y clases sociales en la era de Trujillo (1935–1960)* (Santo Domingo: Fundación Cultural Dominicana, 1993), 50, 58, passim; Inoa, *Estado y campesinos,* 175, 180–208; San Miguel, "The Dominican Peasantry," 101–105, 296–298.

10. Interviews conducted from 1992 to 1994 in all provinces except Santiago, Valverde, Puerto Plata, and Samaná.

11. Terrenos comuneros were sites claimed jointly by numerous coowners without clearly defined rights.

12. Dominican Republic, Secretaría de Estado de lo Interior, Policía, Guerra y Marina, *Memoria, 1933* (Santo Domingo: n.p., 1934), 84–85.

13. H. F. Arthur Schoenfeld to the secretary of state, no. 1473, March 2, 1934, National Archives and Records Administration (hereafter cited as NARA), Washington, D.C., RG 59, 839.52/89, microfilm no. 1272 (role 32).

14. Memorandum of a conversation with Judge Robert Round, February 8, 1934, NARA, RG59, 839.52/89, M1272.

15. Schoenfeld to secretary of state, no. 1473, March 2, 1934, and enclosed circular from Tolentino, NARA, RG59, 839.52/89.

16. Inoa, *Estado y campesinos,* 66–70.

17. Trinidad to Trujillo, November 27, 1934, Archivo General de la Nación (hereafter cited as AGN), Secretaría de Estado de Agricultura (hereafter cited as SA), leg. 182, n.d.

18. Tolentino to secretary of the presidency, no. 5541, December 3, 1934, AGN, SA, leg. 182, n.d.

19. See, e.g., Pancho Retituyo et al. to Don Cocco, governor, La Vega, December 3, 1935, Sección del Supervisor de Juntas Agrícolas (hereafter cited as SSJA), AGN, SA, leg. 4, 1936. This analysis draws on James Scott, *Weapons of the Weak: Everyday Forms of Peasant Resistance* (New Haven, Conn.: Yale University Press, 1985), 309, 338–340. At the same time such appeals for "protection" reinscribed state authority and peasant dependency on the regime.

20. Carretero to Tolentino, January 28, 1935, AGN, SA, Sección del Supervisor de Juntas Agrícolas (hereafter SSJA), leg. 4, 1936.

21. Carretero to Tolentino, February 14, 1935, AGN, SA, SSJA, leg. 3, 1936; Carretero to Tolentino, February 5, 1935, AGN, SA, SSJA, leg. 3, 1936.

22. Paulino to Carretero, October 18, 1935, AGN, SA, SSJA, leg. 6, 1936; Enrique Curiel, report no. 454, April 18, 1934. AGN, SA, leg. 200, 1934.

23. Tolentino to Trujillo, no. 5144, November 8, 1934, AGN, SA, leg. 181, 1934.

24. "Campaña agrícola: socialización de la tierra, Ley No. 762," *Listín Diario* (Santo Domingo), January 3, 1935; memo to the Bajabonico junta, November 30, 1935, AGN, SA, SSJA, leg. 1a, 1936.

25. "Sobre el reparto de tierras," *Listín Diario,* May 27, 1935; "Habla el secrt.

pastoriza sobre la política agrícola e industrial que está desarollando El Generalísimo," ibid., July 15, 1935; Juez Alcalde, Tubano to secretary of agriculture, telegram, AGN, SA, leg. 6, 1936.

26. Michiel Baud, "The Origins of Capitalist Agriculture in the Dominican Republic," *Latin American Research Review,* 22, no. 2 (1987): 147–148; "El ejemplo de Cuba," *La Opinión,* July 6, 1927.

27. Arturo Mejía, "Campaña agrícola: socialización de la tierra. La tierra no se nos va," *Listín Diario,* January 9, 1935. Dominican proletarianization was not necessary for the sugar industry, because Haitian immigrants supplied most of the labor needed to cut cane. The horrific 1937 Haitian massacre ordered by Trujillo was directed not against Haitian sugar workers but rather small farmers in the frontier.

28. "El reparto de la tierra y el éxodo campesino," *Listín Diario,* June 26, 1935.

29. Víctor Garrido, secretary of transportation and public works, A. Rogers, advisory engineer to the executive power, and Tolentino to Trujillo, January 3, 1935, AGN, SA, leg. 207, 1935.

30. See "Párrafos de las memorias presentadas por D. Emiliano Tejera en su calidad de ministro de relaciones exteriores, al presidente de la República en los años 1906–1907 i 1908," *Clio,* no. 51 (1942): 15; Pedro Bonó, "Apuntes sobre las clases trabajadoras dominicanas," in *Papeles de Pedro F. Bonó,* 2d ed., edited by Emilio Rodríguez Demorizi (Barcelona: Gráficas M. Pareja, 1980), 225; and Francisco J. Peynado, "Deslinde, mensura y partición de terrenos," *Revista Jurídica,* no. 4 (1919): 3.

31. See Julie Franks, "The *Gavilleros* of the East: Social Banditry as Political Practice in the Dominican Sugar Region, 1900–1924," *Journal of Historical Sociology,* 8, no. 2 (June 1995): 165, and María González Canalda, "Gavilleros, 1904–1924," paper presented at the Quinto Congreso Dominicano de Historia, Santo Domingo, October 24–27, 1991.

32. "El reparto de las tierras," *La Opinión,* January 24, 1936.

33. "Sobre el reparto de tierras," *Listín Diario,* May 27, 1935.

34. Peynado, "Deslinde, mensura y partición de terrenos," 3.

35. "Discurso del Sr. Manuel M. Morillo, oficial mayor de la Secretaría de Agricultura en el mitín agrícola," *Listín Diario,* October 30, 1935.

36. See, e.g., Emilio Morel, "Intereses Azucareros," ibid., August 10 and 15, 1935. On rice, see Nemen Terc to Trujillo, January 29, 1931, and other documents in AGN, SA, leg. 111, 1935; and Rizik, *Trujillo y la estadística,* 113. Most rice was produced by the peasantry. Inoa, *Estado y campesinos,* 204.

37. Dominican Republic, Secretaría de Estado de Agricultura y Trabajo, *Memoria, 1935* (Ciudad Trujillo: n.p., 1936), 268–269, 275–276; Secretaría de Agricultura é Inmigración, *Memoria, 1926* (Santo Domingo: n.p., 1927), 7–9, 20–22; C. B. Curtis to secretary of state, no. 23, March 6, 1930, NARA, RG 59, 839.00/3356.

38. Garrido, Rogers, and Tolentino to Trujillo, January 3, 1935, AGN, SA, leg. 207, 1935.

39. Telegrams from Carretero to Trujillo, December 16, 1934, AGN, SA, leg. 182, n.d.; January 28, 1935, AGN, SA, SSJA, leg. 6, 1936; and n.d., October 16, 1935, January 29, 1935, and February 5, 1935, AGN, SA, SSJA, leg. 3, 1936.

40. Atwood to secretary of state, no. 3123, February 13, 1936, NARA, RG 59, 839.52/103, M1272; Dominican Republic, Junta Nacional de Alimentación y Agricultura, *Algunos aspectos sobre la situación agrícola y alimenticia de la República Dominicana, 1941–1945,* mimeograph, Ciudad Trujillo, 1946.

41. Rafael Trujillo Molina, *Evolución de la democracia en Santo Domingo,* 2d ed. (Ciudad Trujillo: Editora del Caribe, 1955), 38; rural producers were interpolated from Dominican Republic, *Cuarto censo nacional agropecuario, 1950* (Ciudad Trujillo: Dirección General de Estadística, Oficina Nacional del Censo, 1950), viii–ix and Dominican Republic, *Quinto censo nacional agropecuario, 1960* (Santo Domingo: Dirección General de Estadística y Censos, 1962), x. Unfortunately, the different categories of state, comunero, and private land were not disaggregated in these statistics. Distribution figures may also have been confused by double-counting recipients (those who received land more than once). On the other hand, some land was awarded to peasant occupants through state surveying and later title adjudication on the basis of "prescription," some of which, no doubt, was doubtless not included in the distribution figures.

42. Agricultural colonies offered property or permanent usufruct rights in communities supervised by the state. By my estimates the state distributed 2,864,773 tareas (189,174 hectares) of land to 20,396 "colonists" (a small number of whom were immigrants), some in the 1920s but mostly under Trujillo. See Turits, "The Foundations of Despotism."

43. There is no reason to believe that distributed lands were marginal ones. Distributed lands had been previously squatted on, collectively utilized, or idle for reasons described earlier: free-ranging livestock and wildlife, the only recent consolidation of private property forms, scarce factors of production, limited commercial agriculture, inadequate infrastructure, underpopulation, and so on. Nor is there reason to believe that distributed plots were generally too small for subsistence. The average plot size was 2.1 hectares (thirty-four tareas). Most elderly peasants I spoke with asserted that given the limited extent of "needs," commerce, and taxes, and given land fertility and minimal inputs, even ten tareas provided subsistence then, in contrast to today. Indeed, the regime's strict vagrancy laws had to force many peasants to cultivate even ten tareas. (See Turits, "The Foundations of Despotism"; cf. Inoa, *Estado y campesinos.*) Moreover, no evidence suggests that the land distribution campaign facilitated much semiproletarianization. In 1940, out of 218,060 landholders, only 1,922 were simultaneously farm workers (*jornaleros* and *peones*). Dominican Republic, Di-

visión General de Estado, *Censo agro-pecuario, 1940: Resumen nacional* (Ciudad Trujillo: Dirección General de Estadística Nacional, 1940), 1–2. Throughout the regime, agricultural wage labor remained consistently too low for this to have been a general phenomenon (see note 46).

44. In distinguishing between state, comunero, and private lands, I will argue that most lands never had to be returned by recipients. Moreover, had the reported 60,000 families who received land in 1935 and 1936 all been required to return their land a few years later, there would have been social chaos and much disillusionment that would still be recalled today. Yet, in the hundreds of hours of interviews I conducted in 1992 with elderly peasants, I was told of no such phenomenon. Nor was there any evidence of it in the press or the Department of Agriculture documents I reviewed from the 1940 to 1941 period, when most of the private lands were due to be returned.

45. Junta Nacional de Alimentación y Agricultura, *Algunos aspectos sobre la situación agrícola*, 2.

46. In 1950, only 4.5 percent of all rural producers were sharecroppers and 1.7 percent were renters, while 60.2 percent owned their own land, 13 percent were "free beneficiaries," 6.3 percent held the land by (state) grants, and 1.6 percent were colonists. Moreover, fewer than one-fourth of men over fourteen working in the countryside were engaged in paid labor (similar to 1940 and unexpectedly greater than in 1960). *Cuarto censo nacional*, vii–xiv, xvii; *Censo agro-pecuario, 1940*, 3; *Quinto censo nacional*, xii. Monetary taxes were not high on a still, largely autarkic peasantry. However, the annual cédula fee—one peso for most of the rural poor in the 1930s and 1940s (equivalent to three or four days of wage labor)—was hard for some to pay, precisely because of limited cash crops and proletarianization. Although rice was taxed significantly (one or two centavos a pound), prices were high (eight to sixteen centavos a pound in the 1940s), keeping independent peasant production, in general, relatively profitable, especially in irrigated areas, as was affirmed in the interviews I conducted and suggested by formidable increases in peasant cultivation. Decree no. 4703, November 8, 1947, *Gaceta Oficial*, no. 6709 (November 12, 1947); cf. Inoa, *Estado y campesinos*, 180–208).

47. Decree no. 4772, June 22, 1907, *Gaceta Oficial*, nos. 1800–1801 (June 29 and July 3, 1907).

48. Arts. 2219–2270, in *Código Civil de la República Dominicana*, edited by Fabio Rodríguez C. (Ciudad Trujillo: Editora Montalvo, 1950), 376–382.

49. By 1929, an estimated one-sixth of the country's area had been officially surveyed in order to demarcate landholdings (a process called *la mensura*), a large portion of that having been submitted to or completed saneamiento, the separate judicial process of determining property titles. The proceedings had been mostly limited to the eastern sugar areas. "El catastro nacional y un nuevo

impuesto," *La Opinión,* January 29, 1929. Sugar comprised 9 percent of the nation's cultivated land in 1940, most of it owned by a few U.S. corporations. *Censo agro-pecuario,* 4–5.

50. Law no. 670, April 19, 1934, *Gaceta Oficial,* no. 4672, April 21, 1934; law no. 766, October 16, 1934, ibid., no. 4727, October 20, 1934.

51. Rocha to Hostos, AGN, SA, SSJA, leg. 5, 1936; Jacinto Pérez to Hostos, no. 5, May 21, 1936 and Pérez to Carretero, no. 6, May 22, 1936, AGN, SA, SSJA, leg. 1a, 1936.

52. Tenares junta to juntas general supervisor, November 6, 1936, AGN, SA, SSJA, leg. 6, 1936.

53. AGN, SA, SSJA, leg. 2, exps. 15–23, 1936.

54. See, e.g., Neyba junta report, April 1, 1936, AGN, SA, SSJA, leg. 1a, 1936; Alcibíades Ogando, presidente Junta Protectora de la Agricultura, to Agrónomo Encargado del Servicio de Colonización, no. 44, December 31, 1940, AGN, SA, leg. 1, 1941.

55. The regime assisted this process by substantially reducing the necessary period for prescription, ultimately to a ten-year maximum. Law no. 585, October 24, 1941, *Gaceta Oficial,* no. 5661, October 28, 1941; law no. 5478, February 2, 1961, *Gaceta Oficial,* no. 8547, February 4, 1961. In the 1940s and 1950s, the state underwrote the surveying of most of the country to demarcate land occupations. Subsequently, after a series of long procedures, titles were gradually adjudicated. Probably most beneficiaries — as well as other occupants — of state and comunero lands were eligible for prescription.

56. Santiago Rodríguez to secretary of agriculture, November 30, 1936, AGN, SA, SSJA, leg. 5, 1936.

57. Carretero to Trujillo, February 14, 1935, AGN, SA, SSJA, leg. 3, 1936. Also see Miguel Rivera to Encargado de la Secretaría de Colonización, no. 12, January 18, 1951, AGN, SA, leg. 175, 1951.

58. Félix Tomás del Monte i Andujar to Carretero, March 13, 1935 and Carretero to Modesto Díaz, subsecretary of agriculture, no. 231, AGN, SA, SSJA, leg. 4, 1936; Carretero, n.d., AGN, SA, SSJA, leg. 4, 1936; Carretero to secretary of agriculture, no. 225, March 6, 1935, AGN, SA, SSJA, leg. 1, 1936.

59. Neyba junta report, February 15, 1936, AGN, SA, SSJA, leg. 1a, 1936.

60. Juan Herrera to Hostos, telegram no. 225, June 28, 1936, AGN, SA, SSJA, leg. 6, 1936; Higüey junta reports, February 15 and March 15, 1936, AGN, SA, SSJA, leg. 6, 1936; La Vega junta reports, February 29, 1936 and March 14, 1936, AGN, SA, SSJA, leg. 4, 1936; interview with Antonio Taveras, La Romana, Jima Abajo, November 1994.

61. Memorandum of December 22, 1934, AGN, SA, SSJA, leg. 4, 1936.

62. Tolentino to Pagán, May 22, 1934, and letter from Pagán, April 23, 1934, AGN, SA, SSJA, leg. 4, 1936, AGN; Agricultural Instructor Manuel Reyes

Mota to supervisor of the agricultural district of Trujillo in Monte Plata, June 6, 1940, and report of Pedro C. Renvill, special agricultural Instructor, AGN, SA, leg. 174, 1940.

63. La Vega junta report, February 29, 1936, AGN, SA, SSJA, leg. 4, 1936.

64. Law No. 961, May 23, 1928, *Gaceta Oficial,* no. 3979, June 9, 1928; interview, e.g., with Angel Luciano Novoa, Linor de los Santos, and various peasant recipients, Las Zanjas, San Juan de la Maguana, October 4, 1992. Formalized into law in 1907, *prestación del servicio* referred to a type of obligatory community labor dating back to the nineteenth century and devoted primarily to the building and maintenance of country roads. Peasant attitudes toward this onerous compulsory labor varied depending on the type of work required—whether it was seen as addressing a local need or not—and whether there was land compensation, as there was with most irrigation labor. See Turits, "The Foundations of Despotism."

65. Félix Olivares, "Fundación de las primeras colonias agrícolas" (unpublished manuscript, 1992).

66. Trujillo Molina, *Evolución de la democracia,* 37–38. These estimates may be high, as a probably small portion of owners paid in cash rather than land, as was permitted by the 1942 law mentioned in the text that follows. (However, the estimates may also be low, as some newly irrigated areas were state lands and thus could be entirely distributed.) Also, during 1952 state policy shifted to selling rather than distributing outright some irrigated lands when ceded areas were not part of a formal state colony.

67. See, e.g., memo no. 2121, September 5, 1931, AGN, SA, leg. 111, 1935, and law no. 124, November 10, 1942, *Gaceta Oficial,* no. 5826, November 17, 1942; cf. Olivares, "Fundación de las primeras colonias."

68. See AGN, SA, leg. 46, 1947.

69. Manuel Aguiles Comas, topographer for Colonization Services, to subsecretary of agriculture, December 19, 1936, and engineer José Fernández, chief of the National Irrigation Service, to secretary of agriculture, no. 154, March 3, 1937, AGN, SA, leg. 40, 1937.

70. Rodríguez to Hostos, no. 143, November 21, 1936, AGN, SA, SSJA, leg. 5, 1936.

71. Díaz to Bogaert, September 21, 1944, AGN, SA, leg. 10b, 1944; Bogaert to Díaz, no. 22885, September 30, 1944, AGN, SA, leg. 10b, 1944.

72. See, for example, César Gómez Portes to Manuel Salvador Gautier, secretary of agriculture, November 7, 1937; Gautier to Gómez, December 6, 1937, AGN, SA, leg. 40, 1937. However, territories smaller than a certain size were not ultimately appropriated, as one-fourth of an already tiny plot would serve no one.

73. See Turits, "The Foundations of Despotism." It would be hard to overdraw the regime's Caligulesque excesses and horrors. I do not question the truth

or extremity of these phenomena, but rather their centrality in the everyday life of most peasants.

74. Interviews with elderly peasants, La Vega province, 1992; Marlin Clausner, *Rural Santo Domingo: Settled, Unsettled, and Resettled* (Philadelphia: Temple University Press, 1973), 226–227.

75. Leonidas Grullón to secretary of the treasury and commerce, November 26, 1938, AGN, SA, leg. 326, 1938, AGN; Secretary of Agriculture Juan Román to secretary of the treasury and commerce, no. 9415, December 14, 1938, AGN, SA, leg. 326, 1938.

76. "Lo que ha hecho 'La Opinión' en dos años de intensa lucha por el prestigio, el engrandecimiento y el porvenir de la República," *La Opinión,* January 10, 1929.

77. Interviews with Juan Bautista Mercedes, El Regajo (Ramón Santana), December 18, 1992; Esperanza Salazar (a member of the Gaspar Hernández Junta Protectora under Trujillo), El Cruce de Naranjo, Nagua, November 1994; and Narciso Núñez, Mata Bonita (Nagua), November 1994.

78. *Gaceta Oficial,* no. 4725, October 13, 1934. See, e.g., Hostos to Carretero, no. 669, October 28, 1935, AGN, SA, SSJA, leg. 4, 1936.

79. J. Joaquín Cocco, governor, Puerto Plata, to Trujillo, no. 455, May 27, 1935, AGN, SA, SSJA, leg. 3, 1936; Francisco Alemany, president of the Cabrera Junta, to Hostos, n.d., AGN, SA, SSJA, leg. 5, 1936; Carretero, n.d., AGN, SA, SSJA, leg. 4, 1936.

80. Carretero to Cornelio Julián, November 30, 1935, and Julián to Carretero, November 30, 1935, AGN, SA, SSJA, leg. 1a, 1936; Rafael Saldaña, síndico and president of the Bayaguana Junta, to Juan Bautista Mejía, no. 24, December 4, 1936, AGN, SA, SSJA, leg. 1a, 1936.

81. Interview with Juan Bautista Mercedes, El Regajo (Ramón Santana), December 18, 1992; Angel Pérez, síndico of Guayubín, n.d., SA, SSJA, leg. 2, exps. 15–23, 1936.

82. See Turits, "The Foundations of Despotism."

83. Suárez to Trujillo, September 23, 1935, AGN, SA, SSJA, leg. 1, 1936; Pastoriza to Carretero, no. 4440, September 30, 1935, AGN, SA, SSJA, leg. 1, 1936.

84. Reyes to Trujillo, March 19, 1935, AGN, SA, leg. 207, 1935; Agustín Hernández to Modesto Díaz, May 12, 1935, AGN, SA, leg. 207, 1935.

85. Letter to Trujillo, Yagüaza, February 12, 1935, AGN, SA, SSJA, leg. 4, 1936. Carretero asked local authorities to find them land without these obligations. Carretero to síndico, Villa Mella, no. 86, February 18, 1935, AGN, SA, SSJA, leg. 4, 1936.

86. Turits, "The Foundations of Despotism." Reinaldo Roa, Ramón Santana Junta report, May 16, 1936, AGN, SA, SSJA, leg. 5, 1936; interview with Maldonado, de Silvain (Ramón Santana), November 1994.

87. See Frank Moya Pons, "The Land Question in Haiti and Santo Do-

mingo," in *Between Slavery and Free Labor: The Spanish-Speaking Caribbean in the Nineteenth Century,* edited by Manuel Moreno Fraginals, Frank Moya Pons, and Stanley Engerman (Baltimore: Johns Hopkins University Press, 1985), 186–198, 203–206. Cf. Michiel Baud, "Ideología y campesinado: el pensamiento de José Ramón López," *Estudios Sociales* 19, no. 64 (April–June 1986), and Raymundo González, "Bonó, un intelectual de los pobres," *Estudios Sociales* 18, no. 60 (April–June 1985).

88. In 1919, a graduated land tax was imposed by the U.S. military dictatorship (and abolished by Trujillo in 1935). Given most peasants' small plots (five to fifty tareas), their lack of titles, and low land values (around thirty-five centavos a tarea for unirrigated land in *most* areas by 1930s estimates), the .5 percent tax would generally have been almost insignificant even if applied (which is doubtful given the transaction costs): a maximum of ten centavos a year for the vast majority. For land prices, see José Fernández to secretary of agriculture, no. 704, AGN, SA, leg. 40, 1937.

89. Contrary to the received wisdom, the rural portion of the population fell only modestly between 1935 and 1960, from 82 to 70 percent, though in the 1950s the rate of decline increased significantly in the wake, inter alia, of sugar expansion. Mariñez, *Agroindustria,* 58.

LOWELL GUDMUNDSON AND FRANCISCO A. SCARANO

Conclusion

Imagining the Future of the Subaltern Past— Fragments of Race, Class, and Gender in Central America and the Hispanic Caribbean, 1850–1950

❋

The peoples of Central America and the Hispanic Caribbean faced daunting challenges in their attempts at nation-state formation during the nineteenth and early twentieth centuries. Not the least of these challenges was the systematic undermining of national sovereignty by other, more powerful states, particularly the United States. U.S. geopolitical interests appeared to require the proliferation of small, weak states at the same time that the United States endangered their very existence through overt and recurrent manipulation and intervention. Whether or not their viability as nation-states was compromised by arbitrary geographic or economic boundaries, foreign interventionism generated a hypernationalist resistance that served to further highlight that these states valued their sovereignty, despite its perception by outsiders as dubious and contested.

In most cases the dominant nationalist discourses invoked a moral and historical dualism as simplistic as it was effective: a demonized North American or imperialist "other" frustrating the national aspirations of a heroic, ever more homogeneous "people." Whether in the hands of the earliest generations of upper-class or creole political leaders, or in the more heated rhetoric of would-be reformists and revolutionaries of the middle classes, it was within this frame of reference that the laboring classes made their demands for incorporation and defined themselves as citizens with rights to defend and a historical identity to (re)claim.

This essentially elite-generated if deeply popular vision of a shared historical identity cast long shadows indeed. Working people and their intellectual leaders tended to employ to their own advantage official nationalist icons and values in the most varied ways as they struggled both to assert a collective identity and to demand inclusion within the official discourse. However, just as important as the fact of the often shared or borrowed terminology were the silences of laboring peoples' oppositional struggles and their subsequently forgotten or buried processes of class and ethnic "othering," or delegitimizing, within national life. It is to this extraordinary diversity of historical experiences, far too often buried beneath a homogenizing discourse of nationalist unity thereafter, that the present collection of essays effectively speaks.

Working peoples' experiences in the creation of nation-states and the broadening of the meaning of citizenship defy easy categorization, as the preceding essays demonstrate so clearly. That they did exert substantial influence, in the most diverse of contexts, can no longer be doubted, however. In thinking about just how that influence was brought to bear, above and beneath the not always tranquil waters of the so-called American Mediterranean in which these ships of state were forced to navigate, these essays reveal a surprising amount of factual divergence from popularly enshrined contemporary understandings of that same historical experience. They document great diversity of experience by time period and place within and among nations, and they offer a much more subtle understanding of how working people defined themselves in oppositional terms at different points in time and how those identities could both challenge and support official nationalist discourses with regard to issues of ethnicity, class, gender, or region.

Although not reducible to the three or four "dirty little secrets" of working peoples' struggles in the region, these essays explore a number of shared problems of considerable importance for historical revisionism. They highlight the various processes of ethnic othering so deeply embedded in the region's labor and national histories. They reveal the pervasive silencing of the gender issue and women's rights movements in the name of national and popular unity, often with a complex relationship to issues of ethnic identity as well. More generally, they offer multiple approaches to debunking the popular and pernicious myth of an "immaculate conception," wherein workers and peasants were either brought to political action for the first time by visionary national leaders or were kept entirely at arm's length by a dictatorial state committed only to their repression. In sum, they offer novel perspectives on the complex and inconclusive processes of struggle over the meaning of nationhood and citizenship so visible in the region in our own time.

Redefinitions of the appropriate standard of judgment for the nation's "race"—past, present, and future—figure prominently in many of these essays. Whether in Central America or the Hispanic Caribbean, there was a popular undercurrent of antiblack thinking, as unfortunate as inescapable, in newfound definitions of the national and the foreign. Whether expressed in virulent prejudice against West Indian and Haitian immigrant laborers in Cuba, or anti–West Indian ideology and actions in Honduras and Costa Rica, mixed-race or mestizo models of nationalist belonging were anything but race neutral.[1] Moreover, in Guatemala, Nicaragua, and Honduras, the choice of a mestizo or ladino future, however much based on a heroic Indian past, was unintelligible removed from the framework of both antiblack and anti-Indian policies in the present. That the United States and its corporate interests were often directly responsible for creating the labor markets that helped produce such outcomes has long been recognized. What is novel in these essays is the discovery of just how the popular movements' imagery and actions responded to these new situations in several nations.

Dominant racial ideologies proved malleable and dynamic in Central America and the Hispanic Caribbean. These qualities are evident in the way that elites conceived of, and valued, mestizaje. As in much of the rest of Latin America, in imagining their nations many Hispanic Caribbean writers and political leaders posited an intermediate racial grouping as the defining, albeit not always ideal, national type. Others rejected the ideal of mestizaje altogether and identified their country with a peculiar, ad hoc construction of whiteness. In every case, however, as Lomnitz-Adler has observed about mestizaje ideologies in general, the whitening of the population over time was deemed a desirable and achievable project—thus the inescapably racist character of the nation-building projects.[2]

Within this general racist impulse, elites' views of race mixture and of its significance to nation building were understandably diverse across the Hispanic Caribbean. On the ground, the "race question" appeared as stubborn as the national projects were themselves complex. Thus, for instance, dominant groups' conceptions of mestizaje—in two of its possible meanings: as intermarriage itself and its resultant creation of new phenotypes, and as a racial mythology of the nation[3]—varied across the Greater Antilles almost as much as it did between the two subregions covered in this book (Central America and the Hispanic Caribbean). The sources of this variation were understandably complex. They included the different mental images and standards by which dominant classes gauged their countries' racial and ethnic composition (Hoetink's "somatic norm image"),[4] the specific context and politics of slave emancipation,[5] the presence or absence of racially distinct immigrant workers and the timing of their arrival, and the nature and intensity of political and cultural relations with other countries, especially—in the Hispanic Caribbean—Haiti and the United States.[6] In the end, although all elites racialized the images of their nations in such a way as to negate their African heritage and exclude any claims on the nation based on this heritage, each set of beliefs and policies concerning the racialized nation was grounded in a unique conception of "whiteness" and "blackness." Furthermore, elites deployed the racialized conception of the nation for substantially different reasons and with diverse results.

The Cuban case presents the starkest contrast of all between the widespread negation of race prejudice in social and cultural practice as well as in political discourse, and an equally pervasive manipulation of racial images and fears for nation-building purposes. In a recent study of postemancipation Cuba, Aline Helg has brilliantly discussed how this contradiction played itself out as the country underwent a rapid succession of defining events: the abolition of slavery, a violent anticolonial struggle, the formation of an independent nation-state, massive economic change, and U.S. neocolonial intervention.[7] She rests her analysis on what she perceives to be a kind of Cuban exceptionalism, within Latin America, in the manner that race boundaries were drawn. This alleged exception is critical to understanding how certain ideas of whiteness and blackness came to influence nationalist ideologies and the nation-building process itself.

According to Helg, amidst Cuba's nineteenth-century sugar-and-slavery cycle, elite discourses of race in Cuba began to place all people of African descent, including light mulatos, in the unflattering category of *la raza de color*. As in the United States, but in a fashion unusual for an Ibero American society, people of intermediate phenotypes were lumped together into a "black" category. After independence in 1902, infused with this genotypic view of race, Cuban elites disparaged the social and cultural expressions of Afro Cubans and hoped for a day when, through European immigration and higher birthrates for whites, Cuba's population would be whitened. In the end, argues Helg, the Cuban elites' unusually bipolar conception of their nation's "race" helps explain the brutal repression that victimized Afro Cuban organizations and suffocated cultural expressions associated with blackness. This repression reached its zenith after the founding in 1907 of the Partido Independiente de Color (Independent Party of Color), which in 1912 was the target of a wave of official violence against black Cubans that claimed an estimated 5,000 lives.

Elites in the other Hispanic Caribbean countries generally followed the Cuban pattern of affirming the nation's present or eventual whiteness, while negating the social and political significance of race. Despite this similarity, however, the historical trajectories and contexts from which such official racism arose, and its ideological and rhetorical manifestations, were so distinct in each case as to merit more attention than they have hitherto been given.

In Puerto Rico, where marriage across racial lines had occurred more frequently than perhaps anywhere else in the Caribbean before 1900, and where, as a result, a large intermediate group existed, constructions of a "national race" proved similar to Cuba's, in that—paradoxically, perhaps, in this racially mixed setting—lo nacional became associated with unadulterated whiteness.[8] Equating nation and whiteness had much to do with the Puerto Rican elites' own social and racial insecurity. In the wake of the American takeover of 1898, these elites, burdened by a crushing infusion of U.S. capital and a metropolitan racism that questioned the racial purity and fitness of the locally dominant groups, alongside their manliness, affirmed the European ancestry of the common man—and, by implication, of themselves—by idealizing the image of the jíbaro peasant, the presumably white inhabitant of the interior highlands. Writers from Virgilio Dávila and Miguel Meléndez Muñoz in the 1900s and 1910s to Antonio Pedreira in the 1930s traced the jíbaros' ancestry to the earliest Spanish settlers and built up his image with an ancient, if rustic, nobility now weighed down by the pathologies of a miserable existence.[9] The jíbaro was a repository of patriarchal and Catholic virtues, who had now been turned into a pathetic shadow of himself by the exploitation of American colonial capitalism.[10]

Dominican elites similarly rejected their African roots and posited their essential whiteness, made concrete by a notion of *hispanidad* (Hispanicity), or essential communion with Spain and Catholicism. They traced this nexus with hispanidad to the time when Hispaniola was the first Spanish colony in the Americas and Santo Domingo the undisputed capital of the empire. Postulating a bold line of ethnic and racial difference vis-à-vis their Haitian neighbors and erstwhile occupiers, these elites fiercely rejected their African roots. To explain the prevalence of dark skin among the Dominican population, national thinkers embraced a precocious version of mestizaje that substituted Indians for Africans in the bioracial constitution of the Dominican people.[11] The image of Dominican folk that they came up with painted the people as descendants of Spaniards and Indians, with little African contribution. Accordingly, the dark skin common in the Dominican population was transformed into a trait inherited from Indian ancestors through the peaceful vector of miscegenation with Spaniards.[12] *Antihaitianismo* (anti-Haitianism) and this version of an immunizing, precocious, Indian Spaniard mestizaje as a tale of ethnic creation went hand in hand. Together they not only helped coalesce a sense of Dominican nationhood; they also affirmed the supposed racial difference that justified the brutal exploitation of Haitian braceros in Dominican cane fields and dictator Rafael L. Trujillo's massacre of an estimated 30,000 Haitians along the border in 1937.

The racialized images of the nation that in the Hispanic Caribbean infused nationalist projects from above need to be examined in greater depth and specificity than scholars have thus far attempted. We can no longer be satisfied with generalizations that take dominant discourses and national policies at face value. Although the scholarship has advanced beyond simplistic early generalizations about supposed cultural ("Iberian") prescriptions of race and the more tolerant racial climate presumably derived from them, at best we remain informed only about elite discourses of race and nation. For the Hispanic Caribbean as well as for Central America, we remain largely ignorant about how these notions were received, understood, and contested from below, and how they informed the struggles of workers, peasants, women, and other dispossessed or disenfranchised groups. One of the more pressing items on the agenda for future research would seem to be the significance of race to the politics of emerging worker activism. The essays in this collection boldly underscore how historical narratives constructed "from the bottom up" challenge and even unhinge those generalized from elite behavior and ideology. Clearly, it is necessary to undertake more detailed studies, both at the level of individual countries and in a regionally comparative way, of how ambiguous nation-building constructs such as "race," "mestizaje," and "whitening", or even the apparently simpler notions of "whiteness" and "blackness," were contested and modified by subaltern actors.

The task is difficult but achievable. It will involve not only new questions but also new source materials, or older ones treated in novel ways. One example of sources generally discounted by historians, but whose scrutiny may be fruitful for grasping the operation of racial ideologies among popular actors, are the vast stores of collective knowledge generally classified as "folklore," whose social wisdom historians often note but rarely exploit. Already some studies have begun this difficult task of reading folklore for its insight into fragmentary popular discourses. By carefully sifting through a wealth of *décimas* (sung verses), riddles, stories, and other popular expressions of "folklore" collected in Puerto Rico in the 1910s, and looking in them for clues of a popular social *mentalité*, Lillian Guerra has shown, for example, that it is possible to draw a vivid picture of popular attitudes and beliefs, including those that reflected understandings of gender and race.[13] Equally suggestive, though not based on the same kind of sources, is Lauren Derby's study of cross-border interactions along the Dominican-Haitian border. Her investigation brings into bold relief the inadequacy of certain commonplace concepts, like antihaitianismo, for an understanding of popular conceptions of "self" and "other" along the highly charged, but not always violent, Hispaniolan divide.[14]

Central American variations on the race and national identity question involved a greater reliance on Indian-white than on black-white imagery, but they proved no less complex, with politicians and intellectuals both ill at ease in the present and hopeful for the future. In their respective chapters on Nicaragua and Honduras, Gould and Euraque show that the exaltation of an imagined mestizo nation, as present and future standard of judgment, was both a choice of ethnic identity on the part of nationalist elites and a means of ignoring the continuing Indian or black presence in those societies. The means by which that presence was ignored varied significantly among national cases, but the process can be traced to purposeful actors and policies. In Nicaragua, Hispanic or mestizo nationalist thought tended to create, via historical exaltation most often but at times as a sort of "pity the underdog" reflex, a newly abstract Indian identity as a form of shared, pan-ethnic past. Thus, standards of judgment for ethnic Indianness created by the Hispanic intelligentsia reflected a distant historical practice rather than contemporary reality (language, dress, communal landholding, preliteracy, or illiteracy as a marker of a nature both "alien" and in a certain vague sense "timeless").

Identity thus became a category always in a state becoming or of moving into a shared future for mestizaje's proponents, and always extinguished or buried in the past for its victims. Perversely enough, mestizaje's proponents would work to create such a pan-ethnic Indian identity, but one forever consigned to an alternately heroic and tragic past shared with both groups' ever more distant Indian forbearers. This process of official mestizaje and its ideological baggage were visible everywhere in Central America, regardless of the ethnic makeup of the overall populations. These same mental acrobatics and manipulation of genuinely popular symbols are evident whether mestizaje's proponents reveled in their distant indigenous heritage (as in El Salvador, Honduras, and Nicaragua) or denied any and all racial "stain" after the infusion of the blood of the proverbial Indian princesses of the conquest era (as in Costa Rica).

Continuing work on what Sandino defined as his "Indo Hispanic" nationalism has revealed additional elements of official mestizaje's newly "custodial" relationship with contemporary Indian communities.[15] Although not so transparently motivated by economic advantage as the military zone commanders cum labor recruiters, many of the Hispanic regional defenders of Indian rights used their "Indian expert" credentials to make themselves indispensable to Indians and government officials alike. In the process they not infrequently came into possession of formerly communal lands, paradoxically as part of the same processes by which the indigenous were to be ideologically resurrected by a national authority committed to their extinction in both theory and practice.

This new research has opened up a whole new perspective on the Liberal era of Central American history. However, we are yet far from understanding many of the dynamics of the reorganization internal to the Indian communities themselves. Studies analogous to Joanne Rappaport's remarkable rendering of Colombian indigenous communities' understandings of their own history and its bases in property rights, ethnic identity, and what she refers to as their "paraliteracy," would add immeasurably to this newly rediscovered field of study: the history of Indian communities where commonsensical understandings had long ago written them off.[16] As has too often been the case in the past, most such studies have focused on highland Guatemala and its unmistakable Indianness. The brilliance of many such studies of distinctively Guatemalan processes cannot compensate fully for the fact that they are being done where, in comparative Central American and historiographic terms, they are least in need.

Official mestizaje ideology also developed its imagery in a distinctly gendered language. The "passive," or female, role characteristically was assigned to Indians, both past and present.[17] It was from the "Indian mother," after all, that the pan-ethnic Indian historical identity was presumed to have come. But this gendered and virulently sexist interpretation of the social order and ethnic identities also meant that contemporary Indian males were "feminized" in both old and new ways. Not only were they still denied their presumably "natural" active or dominant role, particularly vis à vis non-Indian males, but they were increasingly stereotyped as uniquely autocratic and irrational heads of families, a combination of incorrigible wife beaters and impenetrable illiterates. None of the preceding chapters reveals the highly explosive nature of face-to-face conflict, interethnic or not, so well as Alvarenga's work on rural El Salvador. The colorful language of Inés Perdido's challenge to the newly designated authorities clearly reveals the gendered nature of local honor codes and challenges to them, leading to instances of bloody conflict provoked by triumphant Liberalism's early, unfunded attempts at "neighborhood policing."

Gender may have been deeply embedded in popular nationalist language and ideology, but gender issues and women's rights rarely played comparably significant roles in popular movements. That is perhaps why many scholars who, under the mantle of a "new history," revisited during the 1970s and 1980s the formative processes of workers' movements in the Hispanic Caribbean, failed to identify gender inequities and women's sexual exploitation as salient concerns of unions and federations alike.[18] Eileen Findlay's chapter makes plain, however, that women's issues and an emphasis on sexuality and its relationship to social power were central to labor's agenda and vocabulary in the beginning. By the same token, women were not missing from the movement's intellectual corps and political leadership, as they would be later. Rather, as Findlay suggests, for the Puerto Rican case at least, women's issues were quite prominent on labor's earliest agenda as worker-intellectuals, some of them women themselves, launched a radical critique of social conditions at the turn of the twentieth century. In her view, both the issues themselves and the intellectuals who most often raised them were gradually subsumed and subordinated by other concerns and by the increasingly masculine agenda of the leaders. This silencing took place at the same time as the incipient labor movement underwent a pivotal transformation in philosophy and methods. However, we do not know how different forms of working-class consciousness and strategies may have been related to struggles over women's representation and the meaning of women's emancipation in the class struggle. As the silence fell over the woman question, the Puerto Rican organizations described by Findlay were undergoing a dramatic shift, from the anarchosyndicalism of the earliest associations of the 1880s and 1890s, to the trade unionism patiently nurtured after 1898 by Samuel Gompers's American Federation of Labor, whose support of the Free Federation of Laborers proved critical in Puerto Rican labor's ability to confront the daunting power of corporate plantations.[19] Were labor's waning interest in women's issues and the more reduced participation of women in leadership roles a sure sign of the shifting paradigm? Because the AFL was never able to fully tame the strike impulse of their colonial comrades, one wonders to what extent the AFL could alter the deeply held convictions of colonial workers and their leaders. The question is, of course, worth asking.

Findlay's contribution raises the fascinating additional issue of how a compact between labor organizations across the metropole/colony divide could have been lubricated by a common, if evolving, understanding of women's proper roles in the household, the workplace, and the union halls. The suggestion is provocative; indeed, it may hold a key for our understanding of gender as a critical element of colonial consensus in its multiple forms. Could a variety of colonial compacts have been similarly cemented? How can we better grasp the gendered assumptions of the colonial juggernaut? Findlay's work points fruitfully to the building of multiple lines of consensus across long distances, each one involving metropolitan and colonial actors. What was the significance of gender for the maintenance and reproduction of these ties?

Gender had always been a key dimension of all working-class politics and ideology, of course. This maxim is clearly applicable to the politics of cross-class alliances during the latter years of the Spanish colonial period, which in Cuba and Puerto Rico lasted until the United States' 1898 intervention in Cuba's Second War of Independence. During the 1890s, the politics of a still embryonic labor movement had been profoundly informed by notions of proper masculine and feminine roles and behavior. The same was true of the political blocs formed by workers in concert with elements from the middle sectors, to advance a liberal agenda. These alliances were often glued together by common understandings of gender roles and prescriptions. Worker politics and bourgeois politics intersected precisely on issues related to the control of women and their sexuality. Findlay's larger work, "Domination, Decency, and Desire: The Politics of Sexuality in Ponce, Puerto Rico, 1870–1920" from which her chapter in this book derives, shows just how powerfully the image of the sexually pure, respectable wife and mother functioned as the key metaphor of the patrician-plebeian alliance that undergirded Puerto Rico's liberal-autonomist politics as the Spanish period drew to a close. The liberal-autonomist concept of the Puerto Rican nation as a "great family" (*la gran familia puertorriqueña*) helped mobilize an alliance of artisans, other workers, and many members of the professional elites against the conservative bloc made up of high clergy, high officialdom, import-export merchants, and large sugar hacendados.[20] In Ponce, the key urban space in which liberal-autonomist politics functioned, this alliance of socially unequal men was cemented during an 1890s campaign against prostitution, which Findlay has interpreted primarily as the terrain upon which men who occupied rather different class positions forged common understandings.

If gender was usually silenced as an issue in nationalist thought, its language and imagery were almost invariably used both to judge decorous female behavior and to express male competition and conflict. One particularly good example of this is the way in which official mestizaje ideology everywhere erased the contemporary male Indian, in part by heroizing and feminizing his ancestors, in part by feminizing him in the present. In Central America, as we have seen, this was a major feature of official ideologies of mestizaje. However, whereas Indians were potentially heroes, if suitably removed to a remote historical past, Central American nationalist thought usually proved far less charitable in its rejection of any black present or future for the nation. Just as with the overt antiblack racism (thinly disguised as anti-immigrant senti-ment) in Cuba and the Dominican Republic, both the spasmodic race war in the mining camps of Costa Rica and the much more oblique re-jection of black groups in the Indian hero nationalism of Honduras in-volved casting blacks in the role of alien menace. Nationalist rejections of Jamaican and Haitian immigrant laborers were clearly part of a more general discourse that placed blacks in a quasi-probationary status in terms of cultural allegiance.[21] While Cuban nationalists may have been less overtly violent toward Haitians in their midst than their Domini-can counterparts, and the Hondurans less so than the Costa Ricans in terms of West Indians in the cases dealt with here, the discursive simi-larities are striking nonetheless.

In Costa Rica and Honduras, West Indian blacks were at times de-fined as the enemy by many early nationalists, both elite and popular. In one of the worst-case scenarios, this involved bloody uprisings in Costa Rica's few isolated mining camps. These episodes formed part of a much larger process of "conquest and taming" of nature and the jungle by European and North American traders, but one characteristically in-volving West Indian immigrant footsoldiers, successors to the "buffalo soldier" tradition of the U.S. plains as well. Indeed, the Costa Rican mayhem is eerily similar to that described in far more grotesque detail by Taussig in his treatment of the barbarian immigrant gunmen who policed the dialectic of civilization and wildness among rubber traders and collectors in the Colombian Putumayo at this time.[22] In instances when blacks were not demonized and persecuted, Central American nationalist imagery still routinely called into question the nationality, patriotism, and "suitability" of African American peoples, immigrant and native-born, even when they clearly constituted regional majorities, as was the case early on in both Costa Rican and Honduran Atlantic coasts.

However, Central America's ethnically distinctive black populations in Costa Rica, Honduras, and Guatemala also became entwined with a heroic nationalist tradition as the embodiment of "proletarian" and militant organized labor.[23] These shifting images became so complex that unraveling them even in any single context proves difficult. None-theless, both Euraque and Chomsky have shown in other studies how central ethnicity and region were to later nationalist movements, in par-ticular the roles of the Lebanese community of San Pedro Sula, Hon-duras, and the West Indians of Limón in Costa Rica.[24] Moreover, the same "heroic" ladino banana workers' union of Guatemala analyzed by Forster owed a great deal to the pioneering role of West Indians, in a context not fully understood yet today.[25]

In addition to our pressing need for studies from multiple angles on Guatemalan banana regions and their societies, in the cases of Honduras and Costa Rica we need to pursue the insights offered by these studies. In particular, we do not yet understand how interethnic conflict played itself out within and among the popular classes on the Honduran north coast, as distinct from the image of the coast and its peoples in intraelite conflict and reform so well developed by Euraque. More detailed historical research will be needed if we are to move beyond ideology and imagery and comprehend regional ethnic relations as lived by people at the time. In the same fashion, we have not fully come to grips with the shifting nature of popular movements in Costa Rica that could both demonize West Indians in the Guanacasteco mining camps and celebrate them in the banana plantations of the Atlantic. Although the repressive and management roles assigned to blacks in the mining camps and analyzed by Chomsky in great detail herein may appear to make any further "explanation" redundant, the larger point remains that Costa Rica's Hispanic working people could simultaneously attack and embrace West Indians in the worlds of imagery and action without fully reconciling the issues of ethnic conflict with their class and nationalist discourses.

The mining enterprises virtually collapsed after 1929 and banana production dropped dramatically throughout the next two decades, but the migrant plantation workforce never fully disbanded and would expand dramatically on both coasts after World War II. What we need now, then, is a study of how relations among West Indians, domestic Hispanics, Nicaraguan immigrants, and Talamanca Indians developed in the lowland and peripheral regions of Costa Rica during the key period of 1920 to 1950, when West Indians withdrew from most plantation field labor. Philippe Bourgois's study offers a general overview and a number of welcome insights, particularly regarding West Indian community transformation and the arrival of Talamanca Indian labor to the plantations along the Panamanian border, but a study focused on domestic Hispanic and Nicaraguan immigrant relations might yield great dividends.[26]

Hispanics were, after all, the backbone of the plantation labor force during this period, replacing the West Indians and building the Communist Party and its successor parties into national institutions. And regardless of shifts in the placement of black West Indians in reformist imagery since then, it is the Hispanic Nicaraguan "illegal immigrants" and the native Hispanic Costa Rican who have been kept apart politically, if not at each others' throats, by nearly all post-1948 popular nationalist discourse, despite their common laboring and general social situations in the same communities, with particularly disastrous consequences for organized labor. In a sense, the same management and elite strategies of division evident in the hiring of West Indian police for the mining districts, and in the ethnic segmenting of banana plantation labor somewhat later, replayed the "black versus white" divisions of popular protest with no less effective "Nicaraguan versus Costa Rican" and "Indian versus Hispanic" ploys. And, unfortunately, Costa Rican working people proved no less susceptible to these divisive ethnic claims, despite the "class first" discourse of their political and union leadership.

If the history of West Indian societies and the imagery spawned by their presence is murky for Costa Rica and Honduras, it is virtually unknown in Guatemala. Here Forster's descriptions of Guatemala's Pacific coast banana workers and their experiences in Tiquisate make a real contribution, despite the fact that ladino workers were always the majority there. Her representation of their dynamism, literacy, assertiveness, and boundless optimism about redeeming their nations' political life squares well with what we know about this most "heroic" of periods in Central American labor history. That they were not only defeated but massacred for such optimism is as sobering a thought as the eloquent words Forster has found to describe these unspeakable acts.

However, just as with the rest of Central America, we need to know far more about the period of 1920 to 1950 in Guatemala. Not only will we need to know how Atlantic coast operations of the United Fruit Company and its labor force may have differed from those in Tiquisate and those in Guatemala, Honduras, Costa Rica, and Panama, but we will need to come to grips with a union and leftist ideological leadership that was, in many ways, Pan Central American if not Pan-American. Much of the labor movement's leadership remains remarkably unappreciated and understudied, with the vast imbalance of coverage traceable to revolutionary hagiography surrounding individuals such as Sandino and Farabundo Martí, as well as to the focus on the momentary role of labor in broader political movements, such as the revolution of 1920 in Guatemala.[27] Within this framework the likelihood of the emergence of a broad-based social history of early labor has always been slim.

Nonetheless, examples abound suggesting how one might approach these issues, even from the vantage point of a leadership notorious for its ambulatory lifestyle and cosmopolitanism. The Costa Rican socialist Vicente Sáenz, long in self-exile in Mexico and engaged in print combat with U.S. foreign investment and the United Fruit Company for several decades after 1920, is a good example of the many interwar labor leaders whose work has been virtually ignored.[28] Likewise, the Guatemala-born, Mexico-raised, and California-educated labor leader Luisa Moreno remains virtually unknown in her native land, despite the fact that she rose to become the vice-president of the California CIO and cofounder of the Congress of Spanish-Speaking Peoples in the United States in the 1930s and 1940s.[29] Moreno was deported to Mexico early in the McCarthy era witch-hunts, but her life experiences are still reflective, perhaps in extreme form, of that of many Central American labor leaders of the 1920s to 1940s, who often worked as organizers in many different nations in the isthmus and beyond. More detailed and inventive research on labor leaders in the interwar years, as well as on the rank and file, may well offer a key to a more comprehensive understanding of labor's rich history, nowhere better reflected than in the inhabitants of banana zones such as Tiquisate, whom Forster has both recaptured and memorialized here.

Contrary to the assertions of many nationalist and most labor parties in the region, however, the idea of class unity around common and unchanging interests failed to account for the wide variety of changing circumstances faced by working people in Central America and the Hispanic Caribbean. Neither proletarians nor peasants, neither uniformly impoverished nor immobile, their varied ethnicity, nationality, and circumstance made them poor candidates indeed for singular nationalist or class messages as rallying cries. As so many of the essays in this volume demonstrate, people and conditions themselves could change even more readily than ideas in some contexts. And given this speed and depth of economic, social, and political change no moralizing retrospective nationalism claiming a working peoples' history free from the sins of misguided allegiance and action, or of internal complexity and division, can stand up to the light of fresh research.

Two particularly pervasive versions of what we called the immaculate conception view are most effectively challenged by these essays. The first is the idea of relatively constant and lamentable conditions of life for working people, in particular peasants and plantation laborers. Whether this finds expression in analyses of peasant marginalization from land ownership by export agriculture, or in critical views of plantation labor recruitment and conditions, popular oppression, and elite conspiracy, doom and gloom are the recurrent themes. Even without the evidence offered here, such a framework bears sufficiently suspicious resemblance to the patronizing attitude toward working peoples' ability to control their own lives so willingly expressed by their "betters." The guiding principles of the villains in the morality play being readopted in such a way warrants caution on the part of readers.

The second is the equally pernicious idea of popular passivity or isolation in relation to politics and the state prior to the mid twentieth century. Whether ignoring popular participation out of historiographical ignorance, or in the misguided attempt to hide or cleanse the sin of illicit association with a repressive state, the idea that working people, in particular peasants, did not share in the land privatization schemes that swept over the region since the late nineteenth century, or in the remarkably destructive conflicts often orchestrated by the state, stretched credulity well beyond the breaking point. Such views have born up far better under the weight of repetition than scholarly scrutiny.

Questions like these have no easy answers, in part because historians have not raised them quite this way before. That they are now doing so underscores the shift that the last twenty years have witnessed in our understanding of social power. In current views influenced by Antonio Gramsci and Michel Foucault, although power certainly devolves to those with money, state legitimacy, weapons, or social prestige, it can also emanate from the socially subordinate through seemingly commonplace acts of collaboration or resistance. Encounters between workers and capitalists at the point of production are full of just such everyday possibilities. Even under circumstances that appear sharply slanted in favor of the more powerful, and which portend little room for resistance, time and again workers seem to make the best of their ability to move about in search of better surroundings, to feign compliance when they might desire otherwise, to eke out subsistence alternatives from the most unlikely ecologies and economic spaces, and to undermine the symbols of propertied authority. These are the "everyday" struggles whose shape and effect are strikingly similar whether we are talking about peasants, industrial proletarians, or plantation workers.[30]

Inspired by just this sort of rendering of worker agency, Carr's essay in this collection underscores the ability of thousands of rural proletarians from the plantation zones of eastern Cuba to maneuver and negotiate with capitalists and their hired agents. He deems the workers of Oriente capable of buffering the demands placed upon them by some of the world's leading "corporate land-and-factory combines," in an area whose rapid development as a sugar zone after 1906 was intimately related to a deepening of American hegemony in Cuba.[31] His chapter suggests the need to reexamine, for eastern Cuba at least, the standard model of plantation economic and social organization, which, earlier in this century, became in the hands of economists and social scientists a powerful tool for the study of large portions of the tropical and subtropical world.[32] Although the concept of "plantation society" as it took shape in this literature never denied the workers' ability to change the basic circumstances of their lives, it clearly put more emphasis on capitalists' ability to control land and labor and on the organic connection that existed between such control and imperialist power.[33] The story of plantation areas was often told as one of capitalist dominance and imperialist hegemony. Few laid out this narrative better than Luis Muñoz Marín, who in his socialist youth remarked of his island nation that "[the] American flag found Puerto Rico penniless and content. It now flies over a prosperous factory worked by slaves who have lost their lands and may soon lose their guitars and their songs."[34]

In contrast to the utter helplessness evoked by Muñoz Marín's aphorism, Carr sees both native and immigrant workers in Oriente as engaged in a struggle they did not always lose. In carrying out this struggle, the *orientales* forced corporate management to adopt what Carr sees as "paternalism" in labor relations. In asserting this, he confirms what scholars of other sugar-dominated societies have noted about planter strategies of labor control, especially during the earlier stages of capitalist development: that when attempting to organize labor in an efficient and secure way, managers did not seem driven by a preordained plan or logic, but often appeared flexible and willing to experiment.[35] Such experimentation ranged in tactics from outright force and coercion to benevolent paternalism. Most plantation managers settled upon one or another combination of tactics for a short period of time; then, with a change in circumstances (in staple prices, labor supply, government policies, and so forth), they initiated a new search for the proper mix of rewards and punishments.[36]

Carr's view of worker agency in Oriente reflects this awareness of an experimentation pushed, in large measure, by the workers' resistance. That this was the way things worked in eastern Cuba should not be surprising, because the workers possessed more leverage there than in comparable settings. Wages in Oriente were among the highest in the sugarcane tropics. The space for maneuver opened up for workers by the practical existence of land for peasant farming—an option that many eastern freedmen seized eagerly—was another reason why, despite the arrival of thousands of contract workers, labor remained scarce and expensive. One wonders, however, whether some of what Carr describes as "negotiation and maneuver" is not also reflective of managers' wish to open up the space between themselves and workers, a space that, once created, was not only available for negotiating the labor compact from below, but also for the exercise of the managers' prerogative to distance themselves from worker needs and problems. The question seems especially relevant for eastern Cuba, given that, as Carr notes, the length of the harvest decreased significantly through the first three decades of the century. Laborers' mobility and independence could well have reflected their leverage and negotiating skills, but it may also have relieved managers from some social responsibilities they would rather not perform.

The essays by Lauria-Santiago, Charlip, and Turits offer perhaps the clearest examples of widespread "peasant" participation in landholding and patronage systems traceable to decidedly dictatorial regimes, the virtual embodiments of the "antipopular" in contemporary nationalist understandings of history. The Dominican case bears considerable resemblance to the very same "sultanic" regime being constructed in Somoza's Nicaragua, as well it should given the similarity in social background of both caudillos and their respective U.S.-trained national guards, the products of U.S. interventions shrewdly manipulated by local allies.[37]

In his chapter on the Dominican Republic, Turits pleads forcefully and convincingly for a reassessment of the negotiation and distribution of power between the state, rural landowners, and peasants during the first half of Rafael L. Trujillo's dictatorship. He carefully documents and explains Trujillo's policy of shaking up the country's landholding structure by withdrawing property rights from the largest claimants (or, at the very least, limiting these rights, some of which dated from the colonial period) and redistributing the surplus lands to squatters and other smallholders. At the start of the Trujillo era in 1930, many productive lands were still held in collective fashion, without proper surveying or registration. The government's modernizing program led to a significant redistribution of agrarian property, to the benefit of the peasant masses. Turits perceptively views this as Trujillo's rather successful attempt at developing a popular clientele, with whom he would later counterbalance the power of regional elites and of the country's remaining caudillos. On a more conceptual plane, his chapter proposes a view of the Trujillista state that complicates the common image of the all-powerful monolith often found in the literature. It allows for a more nuanced understanding of the negotiations and compromises with subaltern actors the regime needed to carry out before its terror machine could operate as efficiently as it infamously did. Thus, in Turits's able rendition, the Trujillato reveals its often hidden consensual dimension.

The challenge to students of Dominican history implicit in this account is twofold. First, there is a need to revisit rural politics during Trujillo's increasingly repressive regime to reveal how clientelist reforms, such as the land redistributions, coexisted with, and perhaps even legitimated, the practices of coercion and terror the dictator unleashed almost concurrently on his enemies, many of them peasants. How were these two approaches woven together? Did the combination of terror and negotiation lend the regime some of its well-known strength and durability, as some scholars have suggested?[38] Second, historians will want to account for Trujillo's rise to power in terms that better reflect the convergence of modernizing forces from within the island nation and from without. It is a well-known tenet of the historiography that U.S. occupation policies, such as the creation of the Guardia Nacional (National Guard), the pacification of the countryside, and the building of a national infrastructure, paved the way for Trujillo's brutal dictatorship. But what is not often seen is that Trujillo's policies toward the peasantry had deep roots in the modernizing ideologies of Dominican intellectuals and nation builders.[39] The dictator's attempts at rural modernization, such as those revealed in Turits's chapter, had as much to do with preexisting Dominican ideologies of nation and society as they did with the "structural" conditions for his ascendance that were laid down by U.S. occupying forces.

The regional studies by Lauria-Santiago and Charlip focus on the extraordinary complexity of processes and outcomes in land privatization, credit, and production for export in key areas of Salvadoran and Nicaraguan agriculture. In neither case is it possible any longer to seriously argue that coffee and Liberal reform dispossessed peasant majorities, readily converting them into estate laborers. In the two areas studied at least, the outcomes were, on the contrary, a testimony to broad-based peasant participation in the cash economy and a not inconsiderable ability to maneuver in the land and credit markets, such as they were at the time.

Although the economic resources controlled by these "peasants," and their resourcefulness in preserving and augmenting them, are clear in these two studies, we only begin to see how these communities related to national-level politics. Whereas Gould's Nicaraguan Indians, however absent as agents themselves, are the icons at the center of a new elite discourse, these rural people are almost entirely absent from capital-city concerns. Whereas Charlip's incessantly ambulatory mestizo peasants appeared to face few obstacles to land use and even ownership, at the same time Indian communities in other close-by regions were being dispossessed. Paradoxically, this activity was taking place within the same political space and discursive framework of nation-state formation. We will need to know much more about how Carazo's peasant cultivators related to the emerging national state if their extraordinary mobility is to be fully understood. Likewise, following up on the minimal visibility of women, as wives, daughters, and heads of household, in these lending and crop-lien documents will require additional sources and research strategies to offer us a better understanding of the peasant household economy in colonization zones such as Carazo.[40]

For future work on the politics of such newly discovered peasant cum family-farming communities Lauria-Santiago offers a particularly valuable insight when he notes that the most important long-term achievement of Liberal reform was not dispossession, and not even privatization itself, but the dissolving of previously communal and often ethnic identities and localist loyalties by means of the emerging national state. By stimulating individual or familial definitions of private interests in the land and commodity markets, and imposing national rather than municipal mediation of land titles, the state undermined the possibility of the old-style, nineteenth-century "monolithic" response of villages, Indian or ladino, in support of Conservatives or the Church or simply against distant authority. Far more than a particularly oligarchic or egalitarian outcome of land titling on the ground, it was this politically centralizing dynamic that proved of interest to Liberal statesmen after the 1880s.[41]

Popular and peasant political participation not only predated the rise of the "popular" leftist parties of the 1920s, but such participation occasionally took the form of support, voluntary or not, for what became exceedingly antipopular repressive policies and institutions. The two most glaring examples offered here are El Salvador and the Dominican Republic. In Alvarenga's novel, richly documented, and disturbing treatment of peasant recruitment into the rural police forces prior to the creation of the Salvadoran Guardia Nacional in the 1920s, we see just how deeply the roots of the "civil guard" reach in Central America, a tradition tied to death squad activity in many areas and a highly conflictive topic in Guatemala yet today. And given the scarcity of historiographical work on modern El Salvador, one is often led to comparisons more literary than historical. There is an unsettling resemblance of the paramilitary "Rodríguez brothers" to the infamous "William," informer and torturer of genuinely peasant extraction, of Manlio Argueta's classic *One Day of Life*.[42] Such an honest treatment of the tragedies of descent into civil war in the countryside, characteristic of Argueta in many of his novels, finds at least partial confirmation in Alvarenga's historical revelations. Although historical work on El Salvador has been slow to emerge, we should not underestimate the importance, and at times historical accuracy, of the genre-crossing work of Salvadoran writers such as Argueta, Claribel Alegría, and Roque Dalton.

As future work explores these new sources and perspectives on El Salvador's bloody twentieth-century history, we will need to pursue into later periods many of Alvarenga's questions. How did the collaborator framework relate to ethnic lines of division within and among villages in the *matanza* (massacre) of 1932? Were self-defined "Indian" communities more likely to resist collaboration en masse? At what price to themselves? If such a civil guard system was re-created in its entirety in Guatemala in the 1980s, then the question "How formal was this system in El Salvador after the creation of the National Guard and the expansion of armed forces authority?" has repercussions for insights into Guatemala's future. Did the civil guard system in El Salvador play any substantial direct role in the counterinsurgency of the 1970s, prior to the full-blown civil war after 1979?

If Alvarenga's implicit comparison is with El Salvador's civil war of the 1980s, then Forster's much more explicit focus is on the background to Guatemala's counterrevolutionary terror following 1954. Her work, on both coffee harvester groups in San Marcos and banana workers in Tiquisate, makes it clear that there was far more pressure from below for the land and labor reforms of 1944 to 1954 than most analysts have recognized. Even the most recent work by Jim Handy, which recognizes much more widespread peasant mobilization and "success" than had once been thought the case, would not be easily reconciled with Forster's picture of extraordinary militance and direct action, requiring the intervention of a regular army to maintain harvest labor discipline well before even the beginning of the official land reform in 1952.[43] Moreover, Forster's development of oral history sources represents a welcome departure from reliance on the both spotty and heavily distorted and even censored written records earlier scholars have been forced to rely on. In this regard, her work joins the select company of such scholars as Levenson-Estrada and Gould, whose pathbreaking studies of Central American contemporary history have made inventive use of oral testimony from surviving participants in the events being analyzed.[44]

Wage-earning harvesters in San Marcos appeared capable of organizing effectively in advance of formal legislative support for their demands, and this occurred despite both internal class and ethnic differences. They embraced an Indian ethnic identity rather than shunning it or falling prey to ethnic division. To the extent that Forster's representation proves accurate for other areas as well, then the widespread surprise—bordering on disbelief—on the part of both contemporary elite and subsequent scholarly opinion, at the "sudden" emergence and growth of the Comité de Unidad Campesina (Committee of Campesino Unity; cuc) in the late 1970s in Guatemala's western highlands, piedmont coffee zones, and south coast may be misplaced. In that case, we would only be witnessing a resurgence and transformation of structures of both resistance and organization experienced before by the parents and grandparents of the late 1970s militants. Even those analysts who accept the fact of widespread popularity of cuc's organizing in the late 1970s have seen it as having more of a basis in Acción Católica (Catholic Action) catechizing, literacy, and leadership training in indigenous society in the 1960s than as a revival of grassroots militancy parallel to that witnessed in the October Revolution period itself.[45]

Rescuing the history of popular organizations and struggles from the silence of the mass grave, thanks in large part to the use of oral testimony, is no small achievement. However, Forster's treatment of the militancy and organizational success of both laboring groups serves ultimately to highlight their most vicious repression by the counter-revolutionary victors in 1954. In the end, one must also face issues of accountability on the part of a leadership that could have brought its flock to the edge of such a cliff without any more effective means of self-defense, flight, or regrouping, especially as regards the banana workers, who appear to have suffered even more bloody repression in the aftermath of the 1954 coup. In a sense, the price of an analysis that so extols popular militancy is the lack of any accounting of how misguided optimism, manipulation, or revolutionary fervor ("triumphalism") may have contributed to this most disastrous of outcomes; an example of the latter kind of analysis is Levenson-Estrada's subtle analysis of how self-deception and miscalculation affected urban industrial workers and their struggles in the 1970s and 1980s in Guatemala. Building an analytical bridge between the parallel tasks of recovering the historical evidence of worker radicalism and assessing its political strategies and impact is surely as desperately needed today in Guatemala as it was in the past. Political openings and possibilities for the future will be no less contingent on understanding the past than were the impossibilities and self-defense needs of the era of counterrevolutionary repression following both 1954 and 1980.

Imagining a future for the subaltern past in Central America and the Hispanic Caribbean remains a formidable challenge. Nations, peoples, identities, and interests have often remained incipient, incomplete, and bitterly contested from within, while they are constrained, when not embattled, from without. In a present characterized by enormous transformations throughout the region, there exists all the more reason to insist on a careful analysis of subaltern visions and strategies for action in the past. The shape of the region's future will continue to depend not only on the visions of its dominant groups and leaders, but even more directly on the lives, hopes, and possibilities of its working peoples. Our understanding of this level of popular consciousness and agency is incomplete in the extreme. However, the research presented in these case studies points us in both novel and promising directions.

Notes

1. For comparative purposes see Richard Graham, ed., *The Idea of Race in Latin America, 1870–1940* (Austin: University of Texas Press, 1990), especially the chapters dealing with Cuba by Aline Helg and Mexico by Alan Knight.

2. For an understanding of whitening ideologies in such diverse contexts as Brazil, Venezuela, and Mexico, see Thomas E. Skidmore, *Black into White: Race and Nationality in Brazilian Thought* (New York: Oxford University Press, 1974); Winthrop R. Wright, *Café con Leche: Race, Class, and National Image in Venezuela* (Austin: University of Texas Press, 1990); and Claudio Lomnitz-Adler, *Exits from the Labyrinth: Culture and Ideology in the Mexican National Space* (Berkeley: University of California Press, 1992).

3. Carol A. Smith, "Myths, Intellectuals, and Race/Class/Gender Distinctions in the Formation of Latin American Nations," *Journal of Latin American Anthropology*, 2, no. 1 (Fall 1996): 150.

4. H. Hoetink, *Slavery and Race Relations in the Americas: Comparative Notes on Their Nature and Nexus* (New York: Harper & Row, 1973), 192–210, and by the same author, *The Two Variants in Caribbean Race Relations: A Contribution to the Sociology of Segmented Societies*, translated by Eva M. Hooykaas (London: Oxford University Press for the Institute of Race Relations, 1967).

5. For an incisive comparison of the processes and outcomes of emancipation in plantation areas of the New World, see Rebecca J. Scott, "Defining the Boundaries of Freedom in the World of Cane: Cuba, Brazil, and Louisiana after Emancipation," *American Historical Review*, 99, no. 1 (February 1994): 70–102.

6. Despite some scholars' assertion, following Tannenbaum, that Ibero American societies shared broadly similar conceptions of color and race, recent scholarship has shown that constructions of whiteness and blackness, and by implication, of the mixed categories, exhibited sharp variations even within regions whose component units experienced colonization and capitalist development in quite parallel ways. For the classic statement on the operation in early Latin America of a milder form of Iberian slavery leading to a greater tolerance of racial difference in contemporary Latin American nations, see Frank Tannenbaum, *Slave and Citizen: The Negro in the Americas* (New York: Alfred Knopf, 1946). In this same vein is Herbert S. Klein, *Slavery in the Americas: A Comparative Study of Virginia and Cuba* (Chicago: University of Chicago Press, 1967). On conceptions of whiteness and blackness in Latin America, see Peter Wade, *Blackness and Race Mixture: The Dynamics of Racial Identity in Colombia* (Baltimore: Johns Hopkins University Press, 1993).

7. Aline Helg, *Our Rightful Share: The Afro-Cuban Struggle for Equality, 1886–1912* (Chapel Hill: University of North Carolina Press, 1995). For a differ-

ent view of the 1912 massacre, see Louis A. Pérez Jr., "Politics, Peasants, and People of Color: The 1912 'Race War' in Cuba Reconsidered," *Hispanic American Historical Review*, 66 (August 1986): 509–539.

8. According to a recent study of the free people of color in Puerto Rico, this island may have been one of the most racially mixed of Iberian societies in the New World. It thus arrived at its nineteenth-century sugar-and-slavery cycle with as many as 40 percent of its population having mixed African, European, and Indian descent. Jay Kinsbruner, *Not of Pure Blood: The Free People of Color and Racial Prejudice in Nineteenth-Century Puerto Rico* (Durham, N.C.: Duke University Press, 1996). For a thoughtful discussion of the race questions in Puerto Rico, especially as it pertains to elite thought, see Arcadio Díaz Quiñones, "Tomás Blanco: la reinvención de la tradición," *Op. Cit., Boletín del Centro de Investigaciones Históricas*, no. 4 (1988–1989): 147–183, and his "Tomás Blanco: racismo, historia, esclavitud," in *El prejuicio racial en Puerto Rico*, by Tomás Blanco (Río Piedras: Ediciones Huracán, 1985), 15–91.

9. On the reification of the jíbaro, especially in fiction, see Enrique A. Laguerre and Esther M. Melón, comps., *El jíbaro de Puerto Rico: símbolo y figura* (Sharon, Conn.: Troutman, 1968). On the politics of elite identity formation around the jíbaro icon, see Francisco A. Scarano, "The Jíbaro Masquerade and the Subaltern Politics of Creole Identity Formation in Puerto Rico, 1745–1823," *American Historical Review*, 101, no. 5 (December 1996): 1398–1431.

10. For a perceptive treatment of these issues, see Lillian Guerra, "Understanding Self, Community, and Nation in Early Twentieth-Century Puerto Rico: An Exploration of Popular and Elite Perspectives" (M.A. thesis, University of Wisconsin, Madison, 1994).

11. For the significance of race in Dominican nation building, see H. Hoetink, *The Dominican People, 1850–1900: Notes for a Historical Sociology*, translated by Stephen K. Ault (Baltimore: Johns Hopkins University Press, 1982). See also Meindert Fennema and Troetje Loewenthal, "La construcción de raza y nación en la República Dominicana," *Anales del Caribe* (Cuba), 9 (1989): 191–227, and Pedro San Miguel, "Discurso racial e identidad nacional en la República Dominicana," *Op. Cit., Boletín del Centro de Investigaciones Históricas*, 7 (1993): 67–120.

12. The novelist Manuel de Jesús Galván had encouraged this belief in the Indian origins of the nation in his novel *Enriquillo* (1882), which told the story of an accommodating Indian who had rebelled against the Spaniards after a conquistador seduced his wife, Mencía. In Enriquillo's rebellion and the Crown's acknowledgment of its righteousness, Galván symbolized Dominican ethnicity. The novel, according to Doris Sommer, continues to give "consistent service as [a] popular handbook of national history." Doris Sommer, *Foundational Fictions: The National Romances of Latin America* (Berkeley and Los Angeles: University of California Press, 1991), 247.

13. See Guerra, "Understanding Self, Community, and Nation in Early Twentieth-Century Puerto Rico: An Exploration of Popular and Elite Perspectives."

14. Lauren Derby, "Haitians, Magic, and Money: *Raza* and Society in the Haitian-Dominican Border, 1900–1937," *Comparative Studies in Society and History*, 36, no. 3 (July 1994): 488–526.

15. Jeffrey L. Gould, *To Die in This Way: Nicaraguan Indians and the Myth of Mestizaje, 1880–1965* (Durham, N.C.: Duke University Press, 1998).

16. Joanne Rappaport, *The Politics of Memory: Native Historical Interpretation in the Colombian Andes* (Durham, N.C.: Duke University Press, 1998), and her *Cumbe Reborn: An Andean Ethnography of History* (Chicago: University of Chicago Press, 1994).

17. For an analysis of the options, and their limits, available to indigenous women in terms of gender and ethnic roles, see Carol A. Smith, "Race-Class-Gender Ideology in Guatemala: Modern and Anti-Modern Forms," *Comparative Studies in Society and History*, 37, no. 4 (1995): 723–749.

18. Angel G. Quintero Rivera, *Workers' Struggle in Puerto Rico* (New York: Monthly Review, 1976), and his "La proletarización del artesanado en Puerto Rico: cultura obrera y organización sindical," *Historias*, 23 (1990): 119–139. Significant exceptions began to appear the late 1980s, as historians of labor increasingly turned their attention to women. See, for example, María del Carmen Baerga Santini, "La articulación del trabajo asalariado y no asalariado: hacia una re-evaluación de la contribución femenina a la sociedad puertorriqueña (el caso de la industria de la aguja)," in *La mujer en Puerto Rico: ensayos de investigación,* edited by Yamila Azize Vargas (Río Piedras: Ediciones Huracán, 1987), 89–111; and Amílcar Tirado Avilés, "Notas sobre el desarrollo de la industria del tabaco en Puerto Rico y su impacto en la mujer puertorriqueña," *Boletín del Centro de Estudios Puertorriqueños 2,* no. 7 (Winter 1989–1990): 18–29.

19. Angel G. Quintero Rivera, "La clase obrera y el proceso político en Puerto Rico," *Revista de Ciencias Sociales,* 18, nos. 1–2 (1974): 147–198, and his "Socialista y tabaquero: la proletarización de los artesanos," *Sin Nombre,* 8, no. 4 (1978): 100–137.

20. Eileen J. Findlay, "Domination, Decency, and Desire: The Politics of Sexuality in Ponce, Puerto Rico, 1870–1920" (Ph.D. dissertation, University of Wisconsin, Madison, 1995); Astrid Cubano Iguina, *El hilo en el laberinto: claves de la lucha política en Puerto Rico (siglo XIX)* (Río Piedras: Ediciones Huracán, 1990). On the centrality of the gran familia concept to the autonomists, see Angel G. Quintero Rivera, *Patricios y plebeyos: burgueses, hacendados, artesanos y obreros. Las relaciones de clase en el Puerto Rico de cambio de siglo* (Río Piedras: Ediciones Huracán, 1988), and his "El desarrollo de las clases sociales y los conflictos políticos en Puerto Rico," in *Problemas de desigualdad social en Puerto Rico* (Río Piedras: Ediciones Librería Internacional, 1972).

21. Helg, *Our Rightful Share;* Aviva Chomsky, "Race, Class, and Resistance: Afro-Cubans and West Indian Migrants After 1912," paper presented at the Latin American Studies Association Meeting, Washington, D.C., September 1995, and her "West Indian Migrant Workers and National Identity in Cuba, 1910–1930," paper presented at the Latin American Labor History Conference, Duke University, April 1996.

22. Michael Taussig, *Shamanism, Colonialism, and the Wild Man: A Study in Terror and Healing* (Chicago: University of Chicago Press, 1987), 23, 37–38, 43–47.

23. Perhaps the classic literary identification with this heroic tradition was the novel *Mamita Yunai* by the Costa Rican Communist Party militant and intellectual Carlos Luis Fallas. There were many other works within this tradition throughout Central America.

24. For Honduras see Nancie L. González, *Dollar, Dove, and Eagle: One Hundred Years of Palestinian Migration to Honduras* (Ann Arbor: University of Michigan, 1992), and Darío Euraque, *Reinterpreting the Banana Republic: Region and State in Honduras, 1870–1972* (Chapel Hill: University of North Carolina Press, 1996). For Costa Rica see Aviva Chomsky, *West Indian Workers and the United Fruit Company in Costa Rica, 1870–1940* (Baton Rouge: Louisiana State University Press, 1996), and her "West Indian Workers in Costa Rican Radical and Nationalist Ideology, 1900–1950," *Americas: A Quarterly Review of Inter-American Cultural History,* 51, no. 1 (July 1994): 11–40.

25. The lack of work on this topic in Guatemala and, to a lesser extent, in Honduras, is made all the more evident by the fact that in Costa Rica there are recent book-length studies, in addition to the monograph by Chomsky: Philippe Bourgois, *Ethnicity at Work: Divided Labor on a Central American Banana Plantation* (Baltimore: Johns Hopkins University Press, 1989); Ronald Harpelle, "West Indians in Costa Rica: Racism, Class, and Ethnicity in the Transformation of a Community" (Ph.D. dissertation, University of Toronto, 1992); and Carmen Murillo Chaverri, *Identidades de hierro y humo: la construcción del ferrocarril al Atlántico, 1870–1890* (San José: Porvenir, 1995). An important study of the peoples of Nicaragua's Atlantic coast, although not of banana-producing regions, is Charles R. Hale's *Resistance and Contradiction: Miskitu Indians and the Nicaraguan State, 1894–1987* (Stanford, Calif.: Stanford University Press, 1994).

26. Bourgois, *Ethnicity at Work.*

27. Good examples of the linking of labor history to political conjuncture in this period can be found in the works by Carlos Figueroa Ibarra: "Contenido de clase y participación obrera en el movimiento antidictatorial de 1920," *Política y Sociedad,* 4 (1977), 5–51, and "Marxismo, sociedad y movimiento sindical en Guatemala, 1920–1931," *Anuario de Estudios Centroamericanos,* 16, no. 1 (1990), 57–86. For an important overview of this field and period, see Víctor Hugo

Acuña Ortega, "Clases subalternas y movimientos sociales en Centroamérica (1870–1930)," in *Historia general de Centroamérica,* vol. 4: *Las repúblicas agro-exportadoras,* edited by Victor Hugo Acuña Ortega (San José: FLACSO, 1994), 255–323.

28. The titles of three of his many polemical works give some idea of his singularity of purpose: *Norteamericanización de Centroamérica, Hispanoamérica contra el colonaje,* and *Rompiendo cadenas.* Symptomatic of this long-standing pattern itself, the Salvadoran Mario Flores Macal penned a commentary on the isthmian importance of and unwarranted disregard for Sáenz in his homeland of Costa Rica and on the author's long-term home in exile: "Ante el olvido de Vicente Sáenz," *Diario de Costa Rica,* June 8, 1973.

29. Basic biographical information on Moreno is provided by Mario T. García, *Mexican Americans: Leadership, Ideology, and Identity, 1930–1960* (New Haven, Conn.: Yale University Press, 1989). Moreno's unique contributions are honored, along with those of the Puerto Rican Arturo Schomburg, by Mount Holyoke's annual Schomburg-Moreno lecture, begun in 1995.

30. Its relevance to a wide array of social circumstances is one of the strengths of James C. Scott's understanding of "everyday forms of resistance," a concept he has developed in *Weapons of the Weak: Everyday Forms of Peasant Resistance* (New Haven, Conn.: Yale University Press, 1985) and *Domination and the Arts of Resistance: Hidden Transcripts* (New Haven, Conn.: Yale University Press, 1990).

31. On the expansion of sugar cultivation in eastern Cuba, see especially Oscar Zanetti Lecuona and Alejandro García Alvarez, *Caminos para el azúcar* (Havana: Editorial de Ciencias Sociales, 1987), and Louis A. Pérez Jr., *Cuba under the Platt Amendment, 1902–1934* (Pittsburgh: University of Pittsburgh Press, 1986).

32. For a sample of representative approaches, drawn from a variety of social science disciplines, see the proceedings from the Seminar on Plantation Systems of the New World, *Plantation Systems of the New World: Papers and Discussion Summaries* (Washington: Pan American Union, 1959). A comprehensive bibliographic orientation to the field is Edgar T. Thompson, *The Plantation: An International Bibliography* (Boston: G. K. Hall, 1983). The economic history of eastern Cuba during the first three decades of the twentieth century is succinctly treated in Robert Bruce Hoernel, "A Comparison of Sugar and Social Change in Puerto Rico and Oriente, Cuba: 1898–1959" (Ph.D. dissertation, Johns Hopkins University, 1977).

33. The classic discussion of the plantation as a type of social organization in which power is grossly concentrated is Eric R. Wolf and Sidney W. Mintz, "Haciendas and Plantations in Middle America and the Antilles," *Social and Economic Studies,* 6, no. 3 (1957): 380–412.

34. Cited in Bailey Diffie and Justine Diffie, *Porto Rico: A Broken Pledge* (New York: Vanguard, 1931), 33. Muñoz Marín went on to found the Popular Democratic Party in 1938 and to lead the populist effort of the 1940s through the 1960s to industrialize the island while claiming more autonomous power from its metropole, the United States.

35. For examples see Michael J. Gonzales, *Plantation Agriculture and Social Control in Northern Peru, 1875–1933* (Austin: University of Texas Press, 1985), and Teresita Martínez-Vergne, *Capitalism in Colonial Puerto Rico: Central San Vicente in the Late Nineteenth Century* (Gainesville: University Press of Florida, 1992).

36. Gonzales, *Plantation Agriculture.*

37. For the Nicaraguan case, see Jeffrey Gould, *To Lead As Equals: Rural Protest and Political Consciousness in Chinandega, Nicaragua, 1912–1979* (Chapel Hill: University of North Carolina Press, 1990), and Knut Walter, *The Regime of Anastasio Somoza, 1936–1956* (Chapel Hill: University of North Carolina Press, 1993).

38. Pedro L. San Miguel, "Un libro para romper el silencio: *Estado y campesinos al inicio de la era de Trujillo,* de Orlando Inoa," *Estudios Sociales* (Dominican Republic), 27, no. 98 (1994): 83–92.

39. For a discussion of changing views of the peasantry among Dominican intellectuals and politicians, see Michiel Baud, *Peasants and Tobacco in the Dominican Republic (1870–1930)* (Knoxville: University of Tennessee Press, 1995).

40. Elizabeth Dore has argued both that there was considerably more land grabbing in the coffee zones around Granada and that women heads of households may have participated in and benefited from the land privatization processes more often than Charlip's research suggests for Carazo. See Elizabeth Dore, "Patriarchy and Private Property in Nicaragua, 1860-1920," in *Patriarchy and Economic Development,* edited by Valentine M. Moghadam (Oxford, England: Clarendon, 1996), 56–79; her "Land Privatization and the Differentiation of the Peasantry in Nicaragua's Coffee Revolution, 1850-1920," *Journal of Historical Sociology,* 8, no. 3 (September 1995): 303–326; and her "Property, Households, and Public Regulation of Domestic Life: Diriomo, Nicaragua, 1840–1890," paper presented to the Third Central American Congress of History, San José, Costa Rica, July 1996.

41. For two recent studies that argue along these lines, see Greg Grandin, "The Strange Case of 'La Mancha Negra': Maya-State Relations in Nineteenth-Century Guatemala," *Hispanic American Historical Review* 77, no. 2 (May 1997): 211–243, and Aldo Lauria-Santiago, "Land, Community, and Revolt in Indian Izalco, El Salvador, 1850-1900" (unpublished manuscript, 1998).

42. Argueta, *One Day of Life* (New York: Vintage, 1983).

43. Jim Handy, *Revolution in the Countryside: Rural Conflict and Agrarian Reform in Guatemala, 1944–1954* (Chapel Hill: University of North Carolina Press, 1994).

44. Deborah Levenson-Estrada, *Trade Unionists against Terror: Guatemala City, 1954–1985* (Chapel Hill: University of North Carolina Press, 1994); Jeffrey Gould, *To Lead as Equals*.

45. For an important reinterpretation of the relationship between indigenous ethnicity and political mobilization in this period that focuses on the CUC to a large extent, see Greg Grandin, "To End with All These Evils: Ethnic Transformation and Community Mobilization in Guatemala's Western Highlands, 1954–1980," *Latin American Perspectives*, issue 93, vol. 24, no. 2 (March 1997): 7–34. The basic sources on the CUC are the works by Rigoberta Menchú, *I, Rigoberta Menchú: An Indian Woman in Guatemala*, edited and introduced by Elisabeth Burgos-Debray and translated by Ann Wright (London: Verso, 1984), and her *Trenzando el futuro* (Mexico City: GAKA, 1992); and José Manuel Fernández Fernández, *El Comité de Unidad Campesina: origen y desarrollo* (Guatemala City: CERCA, 1988). Central to any future work on the case of San Marcos will surely be the extraordinarily detailed studies of migration to this region after the late nineteenth century by Richard Adams. Early findings were presented at the Tercer Congreso Centroamericano de Historia in San José, Costa Rica, July 1996.

Selected Bibliography

Ackelsberg, Martha. *Free Women of Spain: Anarchism and the Struggle for the Emancipation of Women*. Bloomington: Indiana University Press, 1991.

Acuña Ortega, Victor Hugo. "Clases subalternas y movimientos sociales en Centroamérica (1870–1930)." In *Historia general de Centroamérica*. Vol. 4: *Las repúblicas agroexportadoras*, edited by Victor Hugo Acuña Ortega. San José: FLACSO, 1994.

Acuña Ortega, Victor Hugo, and Iván Molina Jiménez. *Historia económica y social de Costa Rica (1750–1950)*. San José: Editorial Porvenir, 1991.

Adams, Richard N. *Crucifixion by Power: Essays on Guatemalan National Social Structure, 1944–1966*. Austin: University of Texas Press, 1970.

———. "Ethnic Images and Strategies in 1944." In *Guatemalan Indians and the State*, edited by Carol A. Smith. Austin: University of Texas Press, 1990.

Albert, Bill. "The Labor Force on Peru's Sugar Plantations 1820–1930: A Survey." In *Crisis and Change in the International Sugar Economy, 1860–1914*, edited by Bill Albert and Adrian Graves. Norwich, England: ISC Press, 1984.

Alvarenga Patricia. *Cultura y ética de la violencia: El Salvador, 1880–1932*. San José: EDUCA, 1996.

Alvarez Estévez, Rolando. *Azúcar e inmigración, 1900–1940*. Havana: Editorial de Ciencias Sociales, 1988.

Anderson, Thomas. *Matanza: El Salvador's Communist Revolt of 1932*. Lincoln: University of Nebraska Press, 1971; rev. ed. Willamantic, Conn.: Curbstone, 1992.

Andrews, George Reid. *Blacks and Whites in São Paulo, Brazil, 1888–1988*. Madison: University of Wisconsin Press, 1991.

Araya Pochet, Carlos. "El enclave minero en Centroamérica, 1880–1945: un estudio de los casos de Honduras, Nicaragua y Costa Rica." *Revista de Ciencias Sociales*, 17–18 (1979): 13–59.

Argueta, Mario. *Historia de los sin historia*. Tegucigalpa: Editorial Guaymuras, 1992.

Ayala, César J. "Social and Economic Aspects of Sugar Production in Cuba, 1880–1930." *Latin American Research Review*, 30, no. 1 (1995): 95–124.

Azize, Yamila. *La mujer en la lucha*. Río Piedras: Editorial Cultural, 1985.

Baerga Santini, María del Carmen. "La articulación del trabajo asalariado y no asalariado: hacia una re-evaluación de la contribución femenina a la sociedad puertorriqueña (el caso de la industria de la aguja)." In *La mujer en Puerto*

Rico: ensayos de investigación, edited by Yamila Azize Varga. Río Piedras: Ediciones Huracán, 1987.

———, ed. *Género y trabajo: la industria de la aguja en Puerto Rico y el Caribe hispánico.* Río Piedras: Editorial de la Universidad de Puerto Rico, 1993.

Bakan, Abigail B. *Ideology and Class Conflict in Jamaica.* Montreal: McGill-Queen's University Press, 1990.

Baldrich, Juan José. *Sembraron la no siembra: los cosecheros de tabaco puertorriqueños frente a las corporaciones tabacaleras, 1920–1934.* Río Piedras: Ediciones Huracán, 1988.

Barahona, Amaru. "El gobierno de José Santos Zelaya y la fase inicial del proceso de acumulación originaria en Nicaragua." *Revista de Historia,* 1, no. 1 (January–June 1990): 83–96.

Barahona, Marvin A. *El silencio quedó atrás: testimonios de la huelga bananera de 1954.* Tegucigalpa: Editorial Guaymuras, 1994.

———. *La hegemonía de los Estados Unidos en Honduras (1907–1932).* Tegucigalpa, Honduras: Centro de Documentación de Honduras, 1989.

Barrancos, Dora. *Anarquismo, educación y costumbres en la Argentina de principios del siglo.* Buenos Aires: Editorial Contrapunto, 1990.

Baud, Michiel. "Ideología y campesinado: el pensamiento de José Ramón López." *Estudios Sociales,* 19, no. 64 (April–June 1986): 63–81.

———. "The Origins of Capitalist Agriculture in the Dominican Republic." *Latin American Research Review,* 22, no. 2 (1987): 134–153.

———. *Peasants and Tobacco in the Dominican Republic (1870–1930).* Knoxville: University of Tennessee Press, 1995.

———. "Transformación capitalista y regionalización en la República Dominicana, 1875–1920." *Investigación y Ciencia,* 1, no. 1 (January–April 1986): 17–45.

Bauer, Arnold. "Rural Workers in Spanish America: Problems of Peonage and Oppression." *Hispanic American Historical Review,* 59, no. 1 (1979): 34–63.

Baumeister, Eduardo. "Agrarian Reform." In *Revolution & Counterrevolution in Nicaragua,* edited by Thomas W. Walker. Boulder, Colo.: Westview, 1991.

Beckford, George L. *Persistent Poverty: Underdevelopment in Plantation Economies of the Third World.* New York: Oxford University Press, 1972.

Beckles, Hilary. "The Female Slave in Cuba during the first half of the Nineteenth Century." In *Engendering History: Caribbean Women in Historical Perspective,* edited by Verene Shepherd, Briget Brereton, and Barbara Bailey. New York: St. Martin's, 1985.

Bergad, Laird. *Coffee and the Growth of Agrarian Capitalism in Nineteenth-Century Puerto Rico.* Princeton, N.J.: Princeton University Press, 1983.

———. *Cuban Rural Society in the Nineteenth Century: The Social and Economic History of Monoculture in Matanzas.* Princeton, N.J.: Princeton University Press, 1990.

Bethell, Leslie, ed. *Central America since Independence*. Cambridge: Cambridge University Press, 1991.

Biderman, Jaime. *The Development of Capitalism in Nicaragua: Economic Growth, Class Relations and Uneven Development*. Stanford, Calif.: Stanford-Berkeley Joint Center for Latin American Studies, 1982.

Blanchard, Peter. *The Origins of the Peruvian Labor Movement*. Pittsburgh: University of Pittsburgh Press, 1982.

Booth, John A., and Thomas W. Walker. *Understanding Central America*. 2d ed. Boulder, Colo.: Westview, 1993; first published 1989.

Bourgois, Philippe. *Ethnicity at Work: Divided Labor on a Central American Banana Plantation*. Baltimore: Johns Hopkins University Press, 1989.

Brass, Tom, "The Latin American Enganche System: Some Revisionist Interpretations Revisited." *Slavery and Abolition*, 11, no. 1 (May 1990): 74–101.

Browning, David. *El Salvador: Landscape and Society*. Oxford, England: Clarendon, 1971.

Burns, E. Bradford. *Patriarch and Folk: The Emergence of Nicaragua, 1798–1858*. Cambridge: Harvard University Press, 1991.

Bushnell, David, and Neill Macaulay. *The Emergence of Latin America in the Nineteenth Century*. 2d ed. New York: Oxford University Press, 1994.

Calder, Bruce. *The Impact of Intervention: The Dominican Republic during the U.S. Occupation of 1916–1924*. Austin: University of Texas Press, 1984.

Cambranes, J. C. *Coffee and Peasants: The Origins of the Modern Plantation Economy in Guatemala*. Stockholm: Institute of Latin American Studies, 1985.

Cardoso, Ciro F. S. "The Formation of the Coffee Estate in Nineteenth-Century Costa Rica." In *Land and Labour in Latin America*, edited by Kenneth Duncan and Ian Routledge. Cambridge: Cambridge University Press, 1977.

———. "Historia económica del café en Centroamérica (siglo XIX)." *Estudios Sociales Centroamericanos*, 4, no. 10 (1975): 3–57.

Cardoso, Ciro F. S., and Héctor Pérez Brignoli. *Centroamérica y la economía occidental (1620–1930)*. San José: Editorial de la Universidad de Costa Rica, 1977.

Carmack, Robert M. *Rebels of Highland Guatemala: The Quiche-Mayas of Momostenango*. Norman: University of Oklahoma Press, 1995.

———. ed. *Harvest of Violence: The Maya Indians and the Guatemalan Crisis*. Norman: University of Oklahoma Press, 1988.

Carr, Barry. "Mill Occupations and Soviets: The Mobilisation of Sugar Workers in Cuba, 1917–1933." *Journal of Latin American Studies*, 28, no. 1 (1996): 129–158.

Casanova Fuertes, Rafael. "¿Héroes o bandidos? Los problemas de interpretación de los conflictos políticos y sociales entre 1845 y 1849 en Nicaragua." *Revista de Historia* (Managua), 2 (1992–1993): 13–26.

Cassá, Roberto. *Movimiento obrero y lucha socialista en la República Dominicana (desde los orígenes hasta 1960).* Santo Domingo: Taller, 1990.

Chakrabarty, Dipesh. *Rethinking Working Class History: Bengal 1890–1940.* Princeton, N.J.: Princeton University Press, 1989.

Charlip, Julie A. "Cultivating Coffee: Farmers, Land and Money in Nicaragua, 1877–1930." Ph.D. dissertation, University of California, Los Angeles, 1995.

Chomsky, Aviva. "West Indian Workers in Costa Rican Radical and Nationalist Ideology, 1900–1950." *Americas: A Quarterly Review of Inter-American Cultural History,* 51, no. 1 (July 1994): 11–40.

————. *West Indian Workers and the United Fruit Company in Costa Rica, 1870–1940.* Baton Rouge: Louisiana State University Press, 1996.

CIERA-MIDINRA. *Por eso defendemos la frontera: historia agraria de las Segovias Occidentales.* Managua: MIDINRA, 1984.

Clausner, Marlin. *Rural Santo Domingo: Settled, Unsettled, and Resettled.* Philadelphia: Temple University Press, 1973.

Coelho, Ruy Galvão de Andrade. *Los negros caribes de Honduras.* Tegucigalpa: Editorial Guaymuras, 1981.

Comaroff, Jean, and John Comaroff. *Of Revelation and Revolution: Christianity, Colonialism, and Consciousness in South Africa.* Chicago: University of Chicago Press, 1991.

Comaroff, John. "Of Totemism and Ethnicity." *Ethnos,* 52, nos. 3–4 (1987): 301–323.

Cooper, Patricia. *Once a Cigarmaker: Men, Women, and Work Culture in American Cigar Factories, 1900–1919.* Urbana: University of Illinois Press, 1987.

Cuadra, Pablo Antonio. *La aventura literaria del mestizaje.* San José: Libro Libre, 1988.

Cubano Iguina, Astrid. *El hilo en el laberinto: claves de la lucha política en Puerto Rico (siglo XIX).* Río Piedras: Ediciones Huracán, 1990.

Dávila Santiago, Rubén. *El derribo de las murallas: orígenes intelectuales del socialismo en Puerto Rico.* Río Piedras: Editorial Cultural, 1988.

del Cid, Rafael. "Populating a Green Desert: Population Policy and Development, Their Effect on Population Distribution. Honduras, 1860–1980." Ph.D. dissertation, University of Texas, 1988.

de la Cruz, Vladimir. *Las luchas sociales en Costa Rica.* San José: EDUCA, 1984.

Dembicz, Andrzej. *Plantaciones cañeras y poblamiento en Cuba.* Havana: Editorial de Ciencias Sociales, 1989.

Derby, Lauren. "Haitians, Magic, and Money: *Raza* and Society in the Haitian-Dominican Borderlands, 1900–1937." *Comparative Studies in Society and History,* 36, no. 3 (July 1994): 488–526.

Díaz Hernández, Luis Edgardo. *Castañer: una hacienda cafetalera en Puerto Rico.* Barcelona: Teorema, SA, 1982.

Díaz Quiñones, Arcadio. "Tomás Blanco: la reinvención de la tradición." *Op. Cit.*, *Boletín del Centro de Investigaciones Históricas*, no. 4 (1988–1989): 147–183.

Dore, Elizabeth. "Land Privatization and the Differentiation of the Peasantry in Nicaragua's Coffee Revolution 1850–1920." *Journal of Historical Sociology*, 8, no. 3 (September 1995): 303–326.

———. "Patriarchy and Private Property in Nicaragua, 1860–1920." In *Patriarchy and Economic Development: Women's Position at the End of the Twentieth Century*, edited by Valentine M. Moghadam. Oxford, England: Clarendon, 1996.

Dosal, Paul J. *Doing Business with the Dictators: A Political History of United Fruit in Guatemala, 1899–1944*. Wilmington, Del.: Scholarly Resources, 1993.

Duarte Hurtado, Martín. "La abolición de la esclavitud y las discusiones en torno a la repercusión de este hecho en la oferta de fuerza de trabajo." *Santiago*, no. 61 (March 1986): 133–154.

Dumoulin, John. *Azúcar y lucha de clases, 1917*. Havana: Editorial de Ciencias Sociales, 1980.

Dunkerley, James. *Power in the Isthmus: A Political History of Modern Central America*. London: Verso, 1988.

Echeverri-Gent, Elisavinda. "Forgotten Workers: British West Indians and the Early Days of the Banana Industry in Costa Rica and Honduras." *Journal of Latin American Studies*, 24 (1992): 275–308.

———. "Labor, Class and Political Representation: A Comparative Analysis of Honduras and Costa Rica." Ph.D. dissertation, University of Chicago, 1988.

Edelman, Marc. *The Logic of the Latifundio: The Large Estates of Northwestern Costa Rica since the Late Nineteenth Century*. Stanford, Calif.: Stanford University Press, 1992.

Espinal, Rosario. *Autoritarismo y democracia en la política dominicana*. San José: CAPEL, 1987.

Euraque, Darío A. *Estado, poder, nacionalidad y raza en la historia de Honduras: ensayos* (Tegucigalpa: Centro de Publicaciones, Obispado de Choluteca, 1996).

———. "Estructura económica, formación de capital industrial, relaciones familiares y poder político en San Pedro Sula, 1870s–1958." *Revista Polémica* (Costa Rica), 18 (September–December 1992): 31–50.

———. "Formación nacional, mestizaje y la inmigración árabe palestina a Honduras, 1880–1930." *Estudios Migratorios Latinoamericanos*, 9, no. 26 (April 1994): 47–66.

———. *Reinterpreting the Banana Republic: Region and State in Honduras, 1870–1972*. Chapel Hill: University of North Carolina Press, 1996.

———. "The Social, Economic and Political Aspects of the Carías Dictatorship in Honduras: The Historiography." *Latin American Research Review* 29, no. 1 (1994): 238–248.

Falla, Ricardo. *Masacres de la Selva, Ixcan, Guatemala (1975–1982)*. Guatemala City: Editorial Universitaria, 1992.

Fallas Monge, Carlos Luis. *El movimiento obrero en Costa Rica, 1830–1902*. San José: EUED, 1983.

Feijoo, María del Carmen. "Las trabajadoras porteñas a comienzos del siglo." In *Mundo urbano y cultura popular: estudios de historia social argentina*, edited by Diego Armus. Buenos Aires: Editorial Sudamérica, 1990.

Fennema, Meindert, and Troetje Loewenthal. "La construcción de raza y nación en la República Dominicana." *Anales del Caribe* (Cuba), 9 (1989): 191–227.

Fernández Fernández, José Manuel. *El Comité de Unidad Campesina: origen y desarrollo*. Guatemala City: CERCA, 1988.

Fernández Robaina, Tomás. *El negro en Cuba, 1902–1958: apuntes para la historia de la lucha contra la discriminación racial en la neocolonia*. Havana: Editorial de Ciencias Sociales, 1990.

Figueroa Ibarra, Carlos. "Contenido de clase y participación obrera en el movimiento antidictatorial de 1920." *Política y Sociedad*, 4 (1977): 5–51.

Findlay, Eileen J. "Domination, Decency, and Desire: The Politics of Sexuality in Ponce, Puerto Rico, 1870–1920," Ph.D. dissertation, University of Wisconsin, Madison, 1995.

Forbes, Jack. *Africans and Native Americans: The Language of Race and Evolution of Red-Black Peoples*. 2d ed. Urbana: University of Illinois Press, 1993.

Foucault, Michel. *Discipline and Punish: The Birth of the Prison*. New York: Vintage, 1979.

Franks, Julie. "The Gavilleros of the East: Social Banditry as Political Practice in the Dominican Sugar Region, 1900–1924." *Journal of Historical Sociology*, 8, no. 2 (June 1995): 158–181.

García, Gervasio Luis. *Historia crítica, historia sin coartadas: algunos problemas de la historia de Puerto Rico*. San Juan: Ediciones Huracán, 1985.

———. "La historia de los trabajadores en la sociedad pre-industrial: el caso de Puerto Rico (1870–1900)." *Op. Cit., Boletín del Centro de Investigaciones Históricas*, 1 (1985–1986): 17–28.

García, Gervasio Luis, and A. G. Quintero Rivera. *Desafío y solidaridad: breve historia del movimiento obrero puertorriqueño*. Río Piedras: Ediciones Huracán, 1982.

García Añoveros, Jesús. *La reforma agraria de Arbenz en Guatemala*. Madrid: Ediciones Cultura Hispánica, Instituto de Cooperación Iberoamericana, 1988.

Georges, Eugenia. *The Making of a Transnational Community: Migration,*

Development, and Cultural Change in the Dominican Republic. New York: Columbia University Press, 1990.

Gleijeses, Piero. *A Shattered Hope: The Guatemalan Revolution and the United States, 1944–1954.* Princeton, N.J.: Princeton University Press, 1991.

Gobat, Michel. "Granada's Conservative Revolutionaries: Anti-elite Violence and the Nicaraguan Civil War of 1912." Paper presented at the Third Central American Congress of History, San José, Costa Rica, July 15–18, 1996.

Gonzales, Michael J. *Plantation Agriculture and Social Control in Northern Peru, 1875–1933.* Austin: University of Texas Press, 1985.

González, Nancie L. Solien. *Sojourners of the Caribbean: Ethnogenesis and Ethno-history of the Garifuna.* Urbana: University of Illinois Press, 1988.

González, Raymundo. "Bonó, un intelectual de los pobres." *Estudios Sociales,* 18, no. 60 (April–June 1985): 65–77.

———. "Ideología del progreso y campesinado en el siglo diecinueve." *Ecos,* 1, no. 2 (1993): 25–43.

González Canalda, María. "Gavilleros, 1904–1924." Paper presented at the Quinto Congreso Dominicano de Historia, Santo Domingo, October 24–27, 1991.

González Casanova, Pablo, ed. *América Latina en los años treinta.* Mexico City: Siglo Veintiuno, 1970.

———. *América Latina: historia de medio siglo.* Mexico City: Siglo Veintiuno Editores, 1981.

———. *Historia política de los campesinos latinoamericanos.* Vol. 2. México: Siglo Veintiuno Editores and Instituto de Investigaciones Sociales de la UNAM, 1985.

González García, Lydia Milagros. *Una puntada en el tiempo: la industria de la aguja en Puerto Rico (1900–1929).* Río Piedras: CEREP, 1990.

Gould, Jeffrey. *To Die in This Way: Nicaraguan Indians and the Myth of Mestizaje, 1880–1965.* Durham, N.C.: Duke University Press, 1998.

———. "El trabajo forzoso y las comunidades indígenas nicaragüenses." In *El café en la historia centroamericana,* edited by Héctor Pérez-Brignoli and Mario Samper. San José: FLACSO, 1992.

———. "'La raza rebelde': las luchas de la comunidad indígena de Subtiava, Nicaragua (1900–1960)." *Revista de Historia* (Costa Rica), nos. 21–22 (1990): 69–117.

———. *To Lead as Equals: Rural Protest and Political Consciousness in Chinandega, Nicaragua, 1912–1979.* Chapel Hill: University of North Carolina Press, 1990.

———. "Y el buitre respondió, Aquí no hay indios: la política y la etnicidad en Nicaragua Occidental." In *Las etnias en Nicaragua,* edited by Marcos Membreño. Managua: Editorial de la Universidad Centroamericana, forthcoming.

Goyer, Doreen S., and Eliane Domschke. *The Handbook of National Popula-*

tion Censuses: Latin America and the Caribbean, North America, and Oceania.
Westport, Conn.: Greenwood, 1983.

Graham, Richard, ed. *The Idea of Race in Latin America, 1870–1940.* Austin:
University of Texas Press, 1990.

Grandin, Greg. "To End with All These Evils: Ethnic Transformation and
Community Mobilization in Guatemala's Western Highlands, 1954–1980."
Latin American Perspectives, issue 93, vol. 24, no. 2 (March 1997): 7–34.

———. "The Strange Case of 'La Mancha Negra': Maya-State Relations in
Nineteenth-Century Guatemala." *Hispanic American Historical Review,* 77,
no. 2 (May 1997): 211–243.

Grieb, Kenneth. *Guatemalan Caudillo: The Regime of Jorge Ubico in Guatemala,
1931–1944.* Athens: Ohio University Press, 1979.

Griffith, W. J. "The Historiography of Central America since 1830." *Hispanic
American Historical Review,* 40, no. 4 (November 1960): 548–569.

Gudmundson, Lowell. *Costa Rica before Coffee: Society and Economy on the Eve
of the Export Boom.* Baton Rouge: Louisiana State University Press, 1986.

———. "Las luchas agrarias del Guanacaste, 1900–1935." *Estudios Sociales
Centroamericanos,* 11, no. 32 (May–August 1982): 75–95.

———. "Lord and Peasant in the Making of Modern Central America." In
*Agrarian Structure and Political Power: Landlord and Peasant in the Making
of Latin America,* edited by Evelyne Huber and Frank Safford. Pittsburgh:
University of Pittsburgh Press, 1995.

———. "Peasant, Farmer, Proletarian: Class Formation in a Smallholder Coffee Economy, 1850–1950." *Hispanic American Historical Review,* 69 (May
1989): 221–258.

———. "Peasant Movements and the Transition to Agrarian Capitalism: Freeholding versus Hacienda Peasantries and Agrarian Reform in Guanacaste,
Costa Rica, 1880–1935." *Peasant Studies,* 10, no. 3 (Spring 1983): 145–162.

Gudmundson, Lowell, and Héctor Lindo-Fuentes. *Central America, 1821–1871:
Liberalism before Liberal Reform.* Tuscaloosa: University of Alabama Press,
1995.

Guerra, Lillian. "Understanding Self, Community, and Nation in Early Twentieth-Century Puerto Rico: An Exploration of Popular and Elite Perspectives." M.A. thesis, University of Wisconsin, Madison, 1994.

Guerra y Sánchez, Ramiro. *Sugar and Society in the Caribbean,* translated by
Marjory M. Urquidi. New Haven, Conn.: Yale University Press, 1964.

Guerrero C., Julián N., and Lola Soriano de Guerrero. *Caciques heróicos de
Centroamérica, rebelión indígena de Matagalpa en 1881 y expulsión de los jesuitas.*
Masaya, Nicaragua: Sold by Librería Loaisiga, 1982.

Guevara Berger, Marcos, and Rubén Chacón Castro. *Territorios indios en Costa
Rica: orígenes, situación actual y perspectivas.* San José: García Hermanos, SA,
1992.

Guidos Vejar, Rafael. *El ascenso del militarismo en El Salvador.* San Salvador: UCA Editores, 1980.

Hale, Charles R. *Resistance and Contradiction: Miskitu Indians and the Nicaraguan State, 1894–1987.* Stanford, Calif.: Stanford University Press, 1994.

Hall, Carolyn. *El café y el desarrollo histórico-geográfico de Costa Rica.* San José: Editorial Costa Rica and Universidad Nacional, 1976.

Handy, Jim. *Revolution in the Countryside: Rural Conflict and Agrarian Reform in Guatemala, 1944–1954.* Chapel Hill: University of North Carolina Press, 1994.

———. "'A Sea of Indians': Ethnic Conflict and the Guatemalan Revolution." *Americas: A Quarterly Review of Inter-American Cultural History,* 46, no. 2 (October 1989): 189–204.

Harpelle, Ronald. "West Indians in Costa Rica: Racism, Class, and Ethnicity in the Transformation of a Community," Ph.D. dissertation, University of Toronto, 1992.

Helg, Aline. *Our Rightful Share: The Afro-Cuban Struggle for Equality, 1886–1912.* Chapel Hill: University of North Carolina Press, 1995.

Helly, Denise. *Idéologie et ethnicité: les chinois macao à Cuba: 1847–1886.* Montreal: Les Presses de l'Université de Montréal, 1979.

Herrera, Tomás. *Guatemala: Revolución de octubre.* San José: Editorial Universitaria Centroamericana, 1996.

Hoernel, Robert Bruce. "A Comparison of Sugar and Social Change in Puerto Rico and Oriente, Cuba: 1898–1959." Ph.D. dissertation, Johns Hopkins University, 1977.

———. "Sugar and Social Change in Oriente, Cuba 1898–1946." *Journal of Latin American Studies,* 8 (November 1976), 220–230.

Hoetink, H. *The Dominican People, 1850–1900: Notes for a Historical Sociology,* trans. Stephen K. Ault. Baltimore: Johns Hopkins University Press, 1982.

———. *Slavery and Race Relations in the Americas: Comparative Notes on Their Nature and Nexus.* New York: Harper & Row, 1973.

———. *The Two Variants in Caribbean Race Relations: A Contribution to the Sociology of Segmented Societies,* translated by Eva M. Hooykaas. London: Oxford University Press for the Institute of Race Relations, 1967.

Ibarra, Carlos Figueroa. "Marxismo, sociedad y movimiento sindical en Guatemala, 1920–1931." *Anuario de Estudios Centroamericanos,* 16, no. 1 (1990): 57–86.

Ibarra, Jorge. *Cuba, 1898–1921: partidos políticos y clases sociales.* Havana: Editorial de Ciencias Sociales, 1992.

———. *Cuba, 1898–1958: estructura y procesos sociales.* Havana: Editorial de Ciencias Sociales, 1995.

Inoa, Orlando. *Estado y campesinos al inicio de la era de Trujillo.* Santo Domingo: Librería La Trinitaria, 1994.

James, Joel, José Millet, and Alexis Alarcón. *El vodú en Cuba*. Santo Domingo: Ediciones CEDEE/Casa del Caribe, 1992.

Kaimowitz, David. "Agrarian Structure in Nicaragua and Its Implications for Policies towards the Rural Poor." Ph.D. dissertation, University of Wisconsin, Madison, 1987.

Kinsbruner, Jay. *Not of Pure Blood: The Free People of Color and Racial Prejudice in Nineteenth-Century Puerto Rico*. Durham, N.C.: Duke University Press, 1996.

Klein, Herbert. *African Slavery in Latin America and the Caribbean*. New York: Oxford University Press, 1986.

————. *Slavery in the Americas: A Comparative Study of Virginia and Cuba*. Chicago: University of Chicago Press, 1967.

Knight, Alan. "Debt Bondage in Latin America." In *Slavery and Other Forms of Unfree Labour*. History Workshop Series, edited by Leonie J. Archer. London and New York: Routledge, 1988.

Knight, Franklin. *Slave Society in Cuba during the Nineteenth Century*. Madison: Wisconsin University Press, 1970.

Kruks, Sonia, Rayna Rapp, and Marilyn B. Young, eds. *Promissory Notes: Women in the Transition to Socialism*. New York: Monthly Review, 1989.

Lauria-Perricelli, Antonio. "A Study in Historical and Critical Anthropology: The Making of the People of Puerto Rico." Ph.D. dissertation, New School for Social Research, 1989.

Lauria-Santiago, Aldo. "An Agrarian Republic: Production, Politics, and the Peasantry in El Salvador, 1740–1920." Ph.D. dissertation, University of Chicago, 1992.

————. "Land, Community, and Revolt in Indian Izalco, El Salvador, 1850–1900." Unpublished manuscript, 1998.

————. "Los indígenas de Cojutepeque, la política faccional y el estado nacional en El Salvador, 1830–1890." In *Identidades nacionales y estado moderno en centroamérica*, comp. Arturo Taracena Arriola and Jean Piel. San José: Editorial de la Universidad de Costa Rica, 1995.

LeGrand, Catherine C. "Campesinos y asalariados en la zona bananera de Santa Marta, 1900–1935." *Anuario Colombiano de la Historia Social y de la Cultura*, 11 (1983): 235–250.

————. "Informal Resistance on a Dominican Sugar Plantation." *Hispanic American Historical Review*, 75, no. 4 (November 1995): 555–596.

Levenson-Estrada, Deborah. *Trade Unionists against Terror: Guatemala City, 1954–1985*. Chapel Hill: University of North Carolina Press, 1994.

Lindo Fuentes, Héctor. *Weak Foundations: The Economy of El Salvador in the Nineteenth Century*. Berkeley: University of California Press, 1990.

Linz, Juan J. "Totalitarian and Authoritarian Regimes." In *Handbook of Politi-*

cal Science, 3, edited by Fred Greenstein and Nelson Polsby. Reading, Mass.: Addison-Wesley, 1975.

Little, Todd. "Guatemala en el período liberal: patria chica, patria grande, reflexiones sobre el estado y la comunidad en transición." In *Identidades nacionales y el estado moderno en Centroamérica,* compiled by Arturo Taracena Arriola and Jean Piel. San José: Editorial de la Universidad de Costa Rica, 1995.

Lomnitz-Adler, Claudio. *Exits from the Labyrinth: Culture and Ideology in the Mexican National Space.* Berkeley: University of California Press, 1992.

López Larrave, Mario. *Breve historia del movimiento sindical guatemalteco.* Guatemala City: Editorial Universitaria, 1976.

Lovell, W. George. *Conquest and Survival in Colonial Guatemala: A Historical Geography of the Cuchumatán Highlands, 1500–1821.* Montreal: McGill-Queen's University Press, 1995.

Luzón, José Luis. *Economía, población y territorio en Cuba (1899–1983).* Madrid: Ediciones Cultura Hispánica del Instituto de Cooperación Iberoamericana, 1987.

MacCameron, Robert. *Bananas, Labor, and Politics in Honduras, 1954–1963.* Syracuse, N.Y.: Maxwell School of Citizenship and Public Affairs, 1983.

Macleod, Murdo J. *Spanish Central America: A Socioeconomic History, 1520–1720.* Berkeley and Los Angeles: University of California Press, 1973.

Mariñez, Pablo A. *Agroindustria, estado y clases sociales en la era de Trujillo (1935–1960).* Santo Domingo: Fundación Cultural Dominicana, 1993.

———. *Resistencia campesina, imperialismo y reforma agraria en República Dominicana (1899–1978).* Santo Domingo: Ediciones CEPAE, 1984.

Martínez-Alier, Verena. *Marriage, Class and Colour in Nineteenth-Century Cuba: A Study of Racial Attitudes and Sexual Values in a Slave Society.* Ann Arbor: University of Michigan Press, 1974, 2d ed. 1989.

Martínez Peláez, Severo. *La patria del criollo: ensayo de interpretación de la realidad colonial guatemalteca.* San José: EDUCA, 1973; 10th ed. Ciudad Universitaria Rodrigo Facio, Costa Rica: EDUCA, 1985.

Martínez-Vergne, Teresita. *Capitalism in Colonial Puerto Rico: Central San Vicente in the Late Nineteenth Century.* Gainesville: University Press of Florida, 1992.

McCreery, David. "Coffee and Class: The Structure of Development in Liberal Guatemala." *Hispanic American Historical Review,* 56 (1976): 438–460.

———. "Debt Servitude in Rural Guatemala, 1876-1936." *Hispanic American Historical Review,* 63, no. 4 (1983): 735–759.

———. "Land, Labor and Violence in Highland Guatemala: San Juan Ixcoy (Huehetenango), 1893–1945." *Americas,* 45 (October 1988): 237–249.

———. *Rural Guatemala, 1760–1940.* Stanford, Calif.: Stanford University Press, 1994.

———. "'This Life of Misery and Shame': Female Prostitution in Guatemala City, 1880–1920." *Journal of Latin American Studies*, 18 (1988): 333–353.

Menchú, Rigoberta. *I, Rigoberta Menchú: An Indian Woman in Guatemala*, edited and introduced by Elisabeth Burgos-Debray and translated by Ann Wright. London: Verso, 1984.

Menjívar, Rafael. *Acumulación originaria y desarrollo del capitalismo en El Salvador*. San José: EDUCA, 1980; 2d ed. 1995.

———. *Formación y lucha del proletariado industrial salvadoreño*. San José: EDUCA, 1979.

Mintz, Sidney W. "The Culture-History of a Puerto Rican Sugar-Cane Plantation, 1876–1949." *Hispanic American Historical Review*, 33, no. 2 (1953): 224–251.

———. "The Folk-Urban Continuum and the Rural Proletarian Community." *American Journal of Sociology*, 59, no. 2 (1953): 136–143.

———. "The Question of Caribbean Peasantries: A Comment." *Caribbean Studies*, 1 (October 1961): 31–34.

———. "The Role of Forced Labour in Nineteenth-Century Puerto Rico." *Caribbean Historical Review*, 2 (1951): 134–141.

———. *Worker in the Cane: A Puerto Rican Life History*. New Haven, Conn.: Yale University Press, 1960.

Molina Jiménez, Iván, and Steven Palmer, eds. *Héroes al gusto y libros de moda: sociedad y cambio cultural en Costa Rica (1750–1900)*. San José: Editorial Porvenir and Plumsock Mesoamerican Studies, 1992.

———. *El paso del cometa: estado, política social y culturas populares en Costa Rica (1800/1950)*. San José: Editorial Porvenir and Plumsock Mesoamerican Studies, 1994.

Montejo, Esteban. *The Autobiography of a Runaway Slave*. London: Bodley Head, 1968.

Moreno Fraginals, Manuel. "Migraciones asiáticas a Cuba: 1849–1959." In *La historia como arma y otros estudios sobre esclavos, ingenios y plantaciones*. Barcelona: Editorial Crítica, 1983.

———. "Plantations in the Caribbean: Cuba, Puerto Rico, and the Dominican Republic in the late Nineteenth Century." In *Between Slavery and Free Labor: The Spanish-Speaking Caribbean in the Nineteenth Century*, edited by Manuel Moreno Fraginals, Frank Moya Pons, and Stanley L. Engerman. Baltimore: Johns Hopkins University Press, 1985.

———. *The Sugar Mill: The Socioeconomic Complex of Sugar in Cuba, 1760–1860*, translated by Cedric Belfrage. New York: Monthly Review, 1976.

Moya Pons, Frank. "The Land Question in Haiti and Santo Domingo." In *Between Slavery and Free Labor: The Spanish-Speaking Caribbean in the Nineteenth Century*, edited by Manuel Moreno Fraginals, Frank Moya Pons, and Stanley Engerman. Baltimore: Johns Hopkins University Press, 1985.

Murillo Chaverri, Carmen. *Identidades de hierro y humo: la construcción del ferro-carril al Atlántico, 1870-1890*. San José: Editorial Porvenir, 1995.

Negrón Portilla, Mariano. *Cuadrillas anexionistas y revueltas campesinas en Puerto Rico, 1898-1899*. San Juan: Centro de Investigaciones Sociales, 1987.

Okihiro, Gary Y. *Cane Fires: The Anti-Japanese Movement in Hawaii, 1865-1945*. Philadelphia: Temple University Press, 1991.

Oliva Medina, Mario. *Artesanos y obreros costaricenses, 1880-1914*. San José: Editorial Costa Rica, 1985.

Ortega Arancibia, Francisco. *Cuarenta años de historia de Nicaragua, 1838-1878*. Managua: Banco de América, 1975.

Palmer, Steven Paul. "A Liberal Discipline: Inventing Nations in Guatemala and Costa Rica, 1870-1900." Ph.D. dissertation, Columbia University, 1990.

Pérez, Louis A., Jr. *Cuba under the Platt Amendment, 1902-1934*. Pittsburgh: University of Pittsburgh Press, 1986.

———. "Insurrection, Intervention, and the Transformation of Land Tenure Systems in Cuba, 1895-1902." *Hispanic American Historical Review*, 65, no. 2 (1985): 245-254.

———. *Lords of the Mountain: Social Banditry and Peasant Protest in Cuba, 1878-1918*. Pittsburgh: University of Pittsburgh Press, 1989.

———. "Politics, Peasants, and People of Color: The 1912 'Race War' in Cuba Reconsidered." *Hispanic American Historical Review*, 66 (August 1986): 509-539.

Pérez Brignoli, Héctor. "Indians, Communists, and Peasants: The 1932 Rebellion in El Salvador." In *Coffee, Society, and Power in Latin America*, edited by William Roseberry, Lowell Gudmundson, and Mario Samper Kutschbach. Baltimore: Johns Hopkins University Press, 1995.

Pérez de la Riva, Francisco. "La habitación rural en Cuba." *Revista de Arqueo-logía y Etnología* 7, nos. 15-16 (January-December 1952): 294-392.

Pérez de la Riva, Juan. "Cuba y la migración antillana 1900-1931." In *La re-pública neocolonial: anuario de estudios cubanos*. Vol. 2. Havana: Editorial de Ciencias Sociales, 1979.

Petrusewicz, Marta. "Wage-Earners but Not Proletarians: Wage Labor and Social Relations in the Nineteenth Century Calabrian Latifondo." *Review* (Fernand Braudel Center), 10, no. 3 (Winter 1987): 471-503.

Picó, Fernando. *Amargo café*. Rio Piedras: Ediciones Huracán, 1981.

———. *1898: la guerra despúes de la guerra*. Río Piedras: Ediciones Huracán, 1987.

———. *Libertad y servidumbre en el Puerto Rico del siglo xix*. San Juan: Ediciones Huracán, 1983.

———. *Los gallos peleados*. Río Piedras: Ediciones Huracán, 1983.

Piedra, José. "Literary Whiteness and the Afro-Hispanic Difference." In *The*

Bounds of Race: Perspectives on Hegemony and Resistance, edited by Dominick LaCapra. Ithaca: Cornell University Press, 1991.

Piel, Jean. *Sajcabaja: muerte y resurrección de un pueblo de Guatemala, 1500–1970.* Mexico City: Centro de Estudios Mexicanos y Centroamericanos and Guatemala City: Seminario de Integración Social, 1989.

Pinto Soria, Julio César. *Raíces históricas del estado en Centroamérica.* Guatemala: Editorial Universitaria de Guatemala, 1983.

Pollitt, Brian. "The Cuban Sugar Economy and the Great Depression." *Bulletin of Latin American Research,* 3, no. 2 (1984): 3–28.

Portilla, Juan. *Jesús Menéndez y su tiempo.* Havana: Editorial de Ciencias Sociales, 1987.

Posas, Mario. *Luchas del movimiento obrero hondureño.* San José: Editorial Universitaria, 1981.

Quintero Rivera, Angel G. *Conflictos de clase y política en Puerto Rico.* 5th ed. Río Piedras: Ediciones Huracán, 1986.

———. "El desarrollo de las clases sociales y los conflictos políticos en Puerto Rico." In *Problemas de desigualdad social en Puerto Rico.* Río Piedras: Ediciones Librería Internacional, 1972. Also in Angel G. Quintero Rivera, *Conflictos de clase y política en Puerto Rico.* 5th ed. Río Piedras: Ediciones Huracán, 1986.

———. "La clase obrera y el proceso político en Puerto Rico." *Revista de Ciencias Sociales,* 18, nos. 1–2 (1974): 147–198.

———. "La proletarización del artesanado en Puerto Rico: cultura obrera y organización sindical." *Historias,* 23 (1990): 119–139.

———. *Patricios y plebeyos: burgueses, hacendados, artesanos y obreros. Las relaciones de clase en el Puerto Rico de cambio de siglo.* Río Piedras: Ediciones Huracán, 1988.

———. "Socialista y tabaquero: la proletarización de los artesanos." *Sin Nombre,* 8, no. 4 (1978): 100–137.

———. *Workers' Struggle in Puerto Rico.* New York: Monthly Review Press, 1976.

Ramos, Julio, ed. *Amor y anarquía: los escritos de Luisa Capetillo.* Río Piedras: Ediciones Huracán, 1992.

Ramos Mattei, Andrés. *La hacienda azucarera: su crecimiento y crisis en Puerto Rico (siglo xix).* San Juan: CEREP, 1981.

Rappaport, Joanne. *Cumbe Reborn: An Andean Ethnography of History.* Chicago: University of Chicago Press, 1994.

———. *The Politics of Memory: Native Historical Interpretation in the Colombian Andes.* Cambridge: Cambridge University Press, 1990.

Rivera, Marcia. "Incorporación de las mujeres al mercado de trabajo en el desarrollo del capitalismo (esbozo para un análisis)." In *La mujer en la sociedad puertorriqueña,* edited by Edna Acosta Belén. Río Piedras: Ediciones Huracán, 1980.

Rodney, Walter. "Plantation Society in Guyana." *Review,* 4, no. 4 (Spring 1981): 643–666.

Roseberry, William. "Beyond the Agrarian Question in Latin America." In *Confronting Historical Paradigms: Peasants, Labor, and the World System in Africa and Latin America,* by Frederick Cooper, Florencia E. Mallon, Steve J. Stern, Allen F. Isaacman, and William Roseberry. Madison: University of Wisconsin Press, 1993.

———. *Coffee and Capitalism in the Venezuelan Andes.* Austin: University of Texas Press, 1983.

———. "*La falta de brazos:* Land and Labor in the Coffee Economies of Nineteenth-Century Latin America." *Theory and Society,* 20 (1991): 351–382.

Roseberry, William, Lowell Gudmundson, and Mario Samper Kutschbach, eds. *Coffee, Society, and Power in Latin America.* Baltimore: Johns Hopkins University Press, 1995.

Samper, Mario. *Generations of Settlers: Rural Household and Markets on the Costa Rican Frontier, 1850–1935.* Boulder, Colo.: Westview, 1990.

San Miguel, Pedro Luis. "Discurso racial e identidad nacional en la República Dominicana." *Op. Cit., Boletín del Centro de Investigaciones Históricas,* 7 (1993): 67–120.

———. "The Dominican Peasantry and the Market Economy: The Peasants of the Cibao, 1880–1960." Ph.D. dissertation, Columbia University, 1987.

———. *El mundo que creó el azúcar: las haciendas en Vega Baja, 1800–1873.* San Juan: Ediciones Huracán, 1989.

Santamaría, Daniel J. *Azúcar y sociedad en el noroeste argentino.* Buenos Aires: Ediciones del IDES, 1986.

Santiago-Valles, Kelvin A. *"Subject People" and Colonial Discourses: Economic Transformation and Social Disorder in Puerto Rico, 1898–1947.* Albany: SUNY Press, 1994.

Scarano, Francisco A. "The Jíbaro Masquerade and the Subaltern Politics of Creole Identity Formation in Puerto Rico, 1745–1823." *American Historical Review,* 101, no. 5 (December 1996): 1398–1431.

———. *Puerto Rico: cinco siglos de historia.* San Juan: McGraw-Hill, 1993.

———. *Sugar and Slavery: The Plantation Economy of Ponce, 1800–1850.* Madison: University of Wisconsin Press, 1984.

———, ed. *Inmigración y clases sociales en el Puerto Rico del siglo xix.* Río Piedras: Ediciones Huracán, 1982.

Schnakenbourg, Christian. "From Sugar Estate to Central Factory: The Industrial Revolution in the Caribbean (1840–1905)." In *Crisis and Change in the International Sugar Economy 1860–1914,* edited by Bill Albert and Adrian Graves. Norwich, England: ISC Press, 1984.

Schroeder, Michael J. " 'To Defend Our Nation's Honor': Toward a Social and Cultural History of the Sandino Rebellion in Nicaragua, 1927–1934." Ph.D. dissertation, University of Michigan, 1993.

———. "Horse Thieves to Rebels to Dogs: Political Gang Violence and the State in the Western Segovias, Nicaragua, in the Time of Sandino, 1926–1934." *Journal of Latin American Studies*, 28, no. 2 (May 1996): 383–434.

———. "The Sandino Rebellion Revisited: Civil War, Imperialism, Popular Nationalism, and State Formation Muddied up Together in the Segovias of Nicaragua, 1926–1934." In *Close Encounters of Empire: Writing the Cultural History of U.S.–Latin American Relations*, edited by Catherine C. LeGrand, Gilbert M. Joseph, and Ricardo D. Salvatore. Durham, N.C.: Duke University Press, 1998.

Schwartz, Rosalie. *Lawless Liberators: Political Banditry and Cuban Independence*. Durham, N.C.: Duke University Press, 1989.

Scott, James. *Domination and the Arts of Resistance: Hidden Transcripts*. New Haven, Conn.: Yale University Press, 1990.

———. *Weapons of the Weak: Everyday Forms of Peasant Resistance*. New Haven, Conn.: Yale University Press, 1985.

Scott, Joan. *Gender and the Politics of History*. New York: Columbia University Press, 1988.

Scott, Rebecca J. "Class Relations in Sugar and Political Mobilization in Cuba 1868–1899." *Cuban Studies*, 15, no. 1 (Winter 1985): 15–28.

———. "Defining the Boundaries of Freedom in the World of Cane: Cuba, Brazil, and Louisiana after Emancipation." *American Historical Review*, 99, no. 1 (February 1994): 70–102.

———. *Slave Emancipation in Cuba: The Transition to Free Labor, 1860–1899*. Princeton, N.J.: Princeton University Press, 1985.

———. "The Transformation of Sugar Production in Cuba after Emancipation, 1880–1900: Planters, Colonos and Former Slaves." In *Crisis and Change in the International Sugar Economy 1860–1914*, edited by Bill Albert and Adrian Graves. Norwich, England: ISC Press, 1984.

Seligson, Mitchell. *Peasants of Costa Rica and the Development of Agrarian Capitalism*. Madison: University of Wisconsin Press, 1980.

Seminar on Plantation Systems of the New World. *Plantation Systems of the New World: Papers and Discussion Summaries*. Washington: Pan American Union, 1959.

Shepherd, Verene, Bridget Brereton, and Barbara Bailey. *Engendering History: Caribbean Women in Historical Perspective*. New York: St. Martin's, 1995.

Skidmore, Thomas E. *Black into White: Race and Nationality in Brazilian Thought*. New York: Oxford University Press, 1974.

Smith, Carol A. "Ideologías de la historia social." *Mesoamérica*, 14 (1987): 355–366.

————. "Myths, Intellectuals, and Race/Class/Gender Distinctions in the Formation of Latin American Nations." *Journal of Latin American Anthropology*, 2, no. 1 (Fall 1996): 148–169.

————. "Race-Class-Gender Ideology in Guatemala: Modern and Anti-Modern Forms." *Comparative Studies in Society and History*, 37, no. 4 (1995): 723–749.

————, ed. *Guatemalan Indians and the State: 1540–1988*. Austin: University of Texas Press, 1990.

Smith, Carol, and Jefferson Boyer. "Central America since 1979, Part I." *Annual Review of Anthropology*, 16 (1987): 197–221.

Smith, Carol, Jefferson Boyer, and Martin Diskin. "Central America since 1979, Part II." *Annual Review of Anthropology*, 17 (1988): 331–364.

Sommer, Doris. *Foundational Fictions: The National Romances of Latin America*. Berkeley and Los Angeles: University of California Press, 1991.

Steward, Julian, Robert A. Manners, Eric R. Wolf, Elena Padilla Seda, Sidney W. Mintz, and Raymond L. Scheele. *The People of Puerto Rico: A Study in Social Anthropology*. Urbana: University of Illinois Press, 1956.

Stoner, K. Lynn. *From the House to the Streets: The Cuban Women's Movement for Legal Reform, 1898–1940*. Durham, N.C.: Duke University Press, 1991.

Taller de Formación Política. *¡Huelga en la caña!* Rio Piedras: Ediciones Huracán, 1982.

Tannenbaum, Frank. *Slave and Citizen: The Negro in the Americas*. New York: Alfred Knopf, 1946.

Taracena Arriola, Arturo. "Contribución al estudio del vocablo 'ladino' en Guatemala (S. XVI-XIX)." In *Historia y antropología: ensayos en honor de J. Daniel Contreras*, compiled by Jorge Luján Muñoz. Guatemala: Facultad de Humanidades, USAC, 1982.

Taussig, Michael. *Shamanism, Colonialism, and the Wild Man: A Study in Terror and Healing*. Chicago: University of Chicago Press, 1987.

Teplitz, Benjamin. "Political Foundations of Modernization in Nicaragua: The Administration of José Santos Zelaya, 1893–1909." Ph.D. dissertation, Howard University, 1974.

Thome, Joseph R., and David Kaimowitz. "Agrarian Reform." In *Nicaragua: The First Five Years*, edited by Thomas W. Walker. New York: Praeger, 1985.

Thompson, Edgar T. *The Plantation: An International Bibliography*. Boston: G. K. Hall, 1983.

Tirado Avilés, Amílcar. "Notas sobre el desarrollo de la industria del tabaco en Puerto Rico y su impacto en la mujer puertorriqueña." *Boletín del Centro de Estudios Puertorriqueños*, 2, no. 7 (Winter 1989–1990): 18–29.

Tomich, Dale W. *Slavery in the Circuit of Sugar: Martinique and the World Economy, 1830–1848*. Baltimore: Johns Hopkins University Press, 1990.

Torres Rivas, Edelberto. *History and Society in Central America,* translated by Douglass Sullivan-González. Austin: University of Texas Press, 1993.

———. *Interpretación del desarrollo social centroamericano.* San José: EDUCA, 1971.

———, general coordinator. *Historia general de Centroamérica.* 6 vols. Madrid: Sociedad Estatal Quinto Centenario; San José: FLACSO, 1993.

Trouillot, Michel-Rolph. *Haiti: State against Nation: The Origins and Legacy of Duvalierism.* New York: Monthly Review Press, 1990.

Turits, Richard. "The Foundations of Despotism: Peasants, Property, and the Trujillo Regime in the Dominican Republic (1930-1961)." Ph.D. dissertation, University of Chicago, 1997.

Urtecho, José Coronel. *Reflexiones sobre la historia de Nicaragua.* 2 vols. León, Nicaragua: Instituto Histórico Centroamericano, 1962.

Vargas, Oscar-René. "Acumulación, mercado interno y el desarrollo del capitalismo en Nicaragua: 1893-1909." Unpublished manuscript, n.d.

———. *La revolución que inició el progreso: Nicaragua, 1893-1909.* Managua: Ecotextura, 1991.

Vega Suñol, José. "La colonización norteamericana en el territorio nororiental de Cuba: 1898-1933." *Anales del Caribe,* 10 (1990): 211-234.

Viotti da Costa, Emilia. *The Brazilian Empire: Myths and Histories.* Chicago: University of Chicago Press, 1985.

Von Houwold, G. *Los alemanes en Nicaragua.* Managua: Banco de América, 1975.

Wade, Peter. *Blackness and Race Mixture: The Dynamics of Racial Identity in Colombia.* Baltimore: Johns Hopkins University Press, 1993.

Walter, Knut. *The Regime of Anastasio Somoza, 1936-1956.* Chapel Hill: University of North Carolina Press, 1993.

Wasserstrom, Robert. "Revolution in Guatemala: Peasants and Politics under the Arbenz Government." *Comparative Studies in Society and History,* 17, no. 4 (1975): 443-478.

Wheelock, Jaime. *Imperialismo y dictadura.* Managua: Editorial Nueva Nicaragua, 1985.

———. *Raíces indígenas de las luchas anticolonialistas.* Managua: Editorial Nueva Nicaragua, 1981.

Williams, Brackette F. *Stains on My Name, War in My Veins: Guyana and the Politics of Cultural Struggle.* Durham, N.C.: Duke University Press, 1991.

Williams, Robert G. *Export Agriculture and the Crisis in Central America.* Chapel Hill: University of North Carolina Press, 1986.

———. *States and Social Evolution: Coffee and the Rise of National Governments in Central America.* Chapel Hill: University of North Carolina Press, 1994.

Wolf, Eric R. "Specific Aspects of Plantation Systems in the New World:

Community Sub-cultures and Social Classes." In *Plantation Systems in the New World*, edited by Angel Palerm and Vera Rubin. Social Science Monograph no. 7. Washington: Pan American Union, 1959.

———. "Types of Latin American Peasantries." *American Anthropologist*, 57 (1953): 452–471.

Wolf, Eric R. and Sidney W. Mintz. "Haciendas and Plantations in Middle America and the Antilles." *Social and Economic Studies*, 6, no. 3 (1957): 380–412.

Wolfe, Joel. "Anarchist Ideology, Worker Practice: The 1917 General Strike and the Formation of São Paulo's Working Class." *Hispanic American Historical Review*, 71, no. 4 (1991): 809–846.

———. *Working Women, Working Men: São Paulo and the Rise of Brazil's Industrial Working Class, 1900–1935*. Durham, N.C.: Duke University Press, 1993.

Wolfe, Justin. "Becoming Mestizo: Ethnicity, Culture and Nation in Nicaragua, 1850–1900." Paper presented at the Third Central American Congress of History, San José, Costa Rica, July 15–18, 1996.

———. "La Riqueza de un País: Land and Community in the Creation of the Nicaraguan Nation-State, 1850–1900." Paper presented at Southwest Council of Latin American Studies, Austin, Texas, February 20–22, 1997.

———. "Rising from the Ashes: The Formation of the Nicaraguan Nation-State, 1850–1900." Ph.D. dissertation, University of California, Los Angeles, 1997.

Woodward, Ralph Lee, Jr. "The Historiography of Modern Central America since 1960." *Hispanic American Historical Review*, 67, no. 3 (August 1987): 461–496.

———. "Liberalism, Conservatism, and the Response of the Peasants of La Montaña to the Government of Guatemala, 1821–1850." *Plantation Society in the Americas*, 1 (1979): 109–129.

Wright, Winthrop R. *Café con Leche: Race, Class, and National Image in Venezuela*. Austin: University of Texas Press, 1990.

Zanetti, Oscar, and Alejandro García. *United Fruit Company: un caso del dominio imperialista en Cuba*. Havana: Editorial de Ciencias Sociales, 1976.

Index

Page references followed by "t" refer to information in tables, while page references followed by "n." or "nŋ." refer to information in notes.

Contributors

PATRICIA ALVARENGA completed her Ph.D. at the University of Wisconsin, Madison. She teaches history at the Universidad Nacional de Costa Rica and is a researcher at the Instituto de Investigaciones Históricas of the University of Costa Rica. Her research has ranged from studies of colonial Costa Rican history to a book-length study of repression and politics in El Salvador: *Cultura y ética de la violencia: El Salvador, 1880–1932.*

BARRY CARR teaches Latin American history at La Trobe University in Melbourne, Australia. He received his undergraduate and doctoral degrees from Oxford University. He has researched and written on labor and agrarian history in twentieth-century Mexico and Cuba and on the history of the Latin American Left. His books include *El movimiento obrero y la política en México 1910–1929; Marxism and Communism in Twentieth-Century Mexico* and (with Steve Ellner) *The Latin American Left: From the Fall of Allende to Perestroika.* He is currently researching the history of work and workers in the Cuban sugar industry from 1910 to 1935 and the development of cross-border worker and union networks in Mexico, the United States and Canada from 1900 to 1997.

JULIE A. CHARLIP received her Ph.D. from the University of California, Los Angeles. She teaches Latin American history at Whitman College. Her research focuses on the social, economic, and political impact of the expansion of coffee production, and such related areas as land tenure and peasants, in Nicaragua during the nineteenth century.

AVIVA CHOMSKY is an associate professor of history at Salem State College in Massachusetts. She has also worked as an assistant professor at Bates College in Maine. She received her Ph.D. in history at the University of California, Berkeley, and is the author of *West Indian Workers and the United Fruit Company in Costa Rica, 1870–1940.* Her current research explores social and cultural aspects of U.S. involvement in Cuba and Haiti in the early twentieth century.

DARÍO A. EURAQUE is originally from Honduras and received his Ph.D. in Latin American history from the University of Wisconsin, Madison, in 1990. He is now an associate professor of history at Trinity College, Hartford. Euraque's main area of research is late nineteenth- and twentieth-century Honduras in a comparative context. He has published articles on modern Honduran history in journals in the United States, Honduras, and throughout Latin America and the Caribbean. He is the author of *Reinterpreting the Banana*

Republic: Region and State in Honduras, 1870–1972 and of *Estado, poder, nacionalidad y raza en la historia de Honduras: ensayos.*

EILEEN J. FINDLAY is an assistant professor of Latin American history at American University in Washington, D.C. She is currently revising a manuscript on sexuality and politics in turn-of-the-century Puerto Rico, forthcoming from Duke University Press.

CINDY FORSTER teaches history at Scripps College in Los Angeles County. She does research on Guatemalan labor history.

JEFFREY L. GOULD is an associate professor of history at Indiana University and director of the Latin American Studies program there. He is the author of *To Lead as Equals: Rural Protest and Political Consciousness in Chinandega, Nicaragua, 1912–1979* and *To Die in This Way: Nicaraguan Indians and the Myth of Mestizaje Mestiza, 1880–1965* (Duke University Press, 1998). He has published extensively on the history of Nicaragua's class and ethnic relations since the 1880s.

LOWELL GUDMUNDSON, professor and chair of Latin American Studies at Mount Holyoke College, taught in the Costa Rican University system for seven years during the 1970s and 1980s. His books include *Costa Rica before Coffee* and (with Hector Lindo-Fuentes) *Central America, 1821–1871*, and he was a coeditor of *Coffee, Society and Power in Latin America*. He is currently working on agrarian and social history projects in both Guatemala and Costa Rica.

ALDO LAURIA-SANTIAGO is originally from Puerto Rico. He is currently an assistant professor of history at College of the Holy Cross in Massachusetts. He also worked as an assistant professor at the New School for Social Research in New York City. He completed his Ph.D. at the University of Chicago in 1992. His research focuses on the agrarian history of El Salvador during the nineteenth and early twentieth centuries. He is now completing a book manuscript on the history of the Salvadoran peasantry during the nineteenth century.

FRANCISCO A. SCARANO teaches Caribbean and Latin American History at the University of Wisconsin, Madison. He is the author of *Sugar and Slavery in Puerto Rico: The Plantation Economy of Ponce, 1800–1850* and *Puerto Rico: cinco siglos de historia*, among other works.

RICHARD L. TURITS is an assistant professor of history at Princeton University. He received his Ph.D. from the University of Chicago in 1997. He has published articles on the Dominican Republic and Cuba and is currently completing a book-length manuscript on peasant-state relations under the Trujillo regime as well as a research project on the 1937 Haitian massacre in the Dominican Republic.

Library of Congress Cataloging-in-Publication Data

Identity and struggle at the margins of the nation state : the laboring peoples
of Central America and the Hispanic Caribbean / edited by Aviva Chomsky,
Aldo Lauria-Santiago.

p.   cm.

Includes bibliographical references and index.

ISBN 0-8223-2202-1 (cloth : alk. paper). — ISBN 0-8223-2218-8 (pbk. : alk.
paper)

1. Working class—Central America—History.   2. Working class—Caribbean
Area—History.   3. Peasantry—Central America—History.   4. Peasantry—
Caribbean Area—History.   I. Lauria-Santiago, Aldo.   II. Chomsky, Aviva.

HD8123.A7   1998

305.5'62'09728—dc21   97-44374